President *of the* Other America

EDWARD R. SCHMITT

President *of the* Other America

ROBERT KENNEDY AND THE
POLITICS OF POVERTY

UNIVERSITY OF MASSACHUSETTS PRESS

AMHERST AND BOSTON

Copyright © 2010 by
University of Massachusetts Press
All rights reserved
Printed in the United States of America
LC 2009044280
ISBN 978-1-55849-730-6

Designed by Richard Hendel
Set in Chaparral with Aller display type by
the Westchester Book Group
Printed and bound by Thomson-Shore, Inc.

Library of Congress Cataloging-in-Publication Data
Schmitt, Edward R., 1970–
President of the other America : Robert Kennedy and the
politics of poverty / Edward R. Schmitt.
p. cm.
Includes bibliographical references and index.
ISBN 978-1-55849-730-6 (cloth : alk. paper)
1. Kennedy, Robert F., 1925–1968.
2. Poverty—United States—History—20th century.
3. United States—Social conditions—1960–1980.
4. United States—Social policy—20th century.
5. Presidents—United States—Election—1968.
6. United States—Politics and government—1969–1974.
I. Title.
E840.8.K4.S335 2009
973.924—dc22

2009044280

British Library Cataloguing in Publication data are available.

CONTENTS

Illustrations follow page 128.

ACKNOWLEDGMENTS

I wish to extend my thanks to many people for their generous and varied help throughout the stages of this project.

In what now seems a time long ago, this book had its genesis in a conversation after a graduate seminar course on American nationalism at Marquette University. My instructor, Robert Hay, had mentioned something about Bobby Kennedy, and I approached him after class asking hopefully, but guardedly, "Do you think there is anything more to be written about him?" Without blinking he offered in his Tennessee drawl, "About compelling historical figures there is *always* more that can be said." The project took flight from there, and I will always be grateful for his confidence and for our conversations that propelled me through the early stages of this project. I hope I have said something more and something useful in these pages.

Other history professors at Marquette were wonderful scholarly models and provided very helpful commentary on my early work, especially Athan Theoharis, Steven Avella, Thomas Jablonsky, and James Marten.

A number of writers gave generously of their time to comment on portions of the book. Historians Robert Bauman, Robert Weise, John Milton Cooper, Kenneth O'Reilly, Carl Brauer, Jon Teaford, and Steven Lawson, along with journalist Victor Navasky, offered sage advice, and this work is much the better for their having read and responded to my drafts.

I am particularly indebted to three historians—John Buenker, James Hilty, and Thomas Jackson—who plowed through the entire manuscript and offered thorough and always insightful reflections.

This book would not have been possible without the help of the outstanding staff at the John F. Kennedy Presidential Library and Museum. Stephen Plotkin, curator of ert F. Kennedy Papers, was an unfailingly accessible, informative, atient recipient of my many queries, and Laurie Austin was an indis- sable help as I sought to acquire audio recordings and photographs. It is ard to a picture a reading room with a better view or a cafeteria with better clam chowder, and the people and the facilities made the Kennedy Library a wonderful place to work.

Oral histories proved to be among the most valuable sources for this book. When at one point during his lengthy 1964 interviews with RFK the journalist Anthony Lewis asked him to respond "for the historians," I thought, "Hey, that's me!"—and the gap between present and past vanished. It was one of innumerable times my sense of wonder regarding the power of primary sources to bring the past to life was renewed. I am grateful to the staffs of the Kennedy and Lyndon B. Johnson Presidential Libraries for their assistance in lending the many useful oral history transcripts recorded there. Oral historians from both libraries did yeoman work recording the reflections of hundreds of Kennedy and Johnson associates, and their efforts stretching over two decades will continue to provide fertile soil for historians. I would particularly like to recognize the labors of Larry J. Hackman and Roberta Greene of the Kennedy Library, and Michael Gillette and Stephen Goodell of the Johnson Library.

Jean Stein's edited, published collection of interviews about RFK is an outstanding source in its own right, but when I learned she had preserved the many full interview transcripts and she generously granted me access to them, I knew I was in business. Many of the reflections shared by her interviewees proved essential to the story and to my interpretations here, and for her work and her generosity I am most grateful.

I wish to thank many people at the University of Wisconsin–Parkside. My students were always encouraging, and those in my Poverty in American History course helped shape and clarify my thinking in ways they likely never realized. My colleagues were a terrific help, particularly Tricia Steele, our interlibrary loan officer, whom I kept busy with waves of requests and a steady stream of overdue notices; our former provost Rebecca Martin for substantial research grant support; Professor Gail Gonzalez for her translations of Spanish-language newspapers; Dean Donald Cress; and my fellow historians Nat Godley, Jeff Alexander, David Bruce, and Sandy Moats for yes, their professional counsel, but more importantly for their friendship. I especially want to thank Laura Gellott, our department chair, for the many ways she has supported my growth as a teacher and a scholar. I feel very fortunate to have a home at Parkside.

It is hard to imagine having a better experience with a publisher than I have had with the University of Massachusetts Press. Senior editor Clark Dougan embraced this project from the outset and put it through an absolutely first-rate review process. Managing editor Carol Betsch has been a pleasure to work with, and Amanda Heller provided superb copyediting. To everyone at the press I am most grateful.

I want to thank my friends (too many to mention here) for sustaining me down this long road. To Brian Walter, Bob Kaye, Jeff Gunderson, Steve Zingsheim, Baskara Wardaya, Daryl Webb, Julie Leonard, Carol and Gerry Mross, Janet Popelier, Sarah Fadness (who ordered the first copy of this book online even before I wrote these acknowledgments!), and Christopher Miller—thank you!

My deepest gratitude goes to my family. Thank you, Carrie, for your limitless enthusiasm for your big brother's work. For Dan and Elaine McKinney and my sisters-in-law Linda, Laura, and Lisa McKinney (and their families), my heartfelt thanks. To my mom and dad, Mary and Bob Schmitt—thank you for dreaming big dreams for me. For my wife Luann—you have been with me each step of the way and without you my hopes for this book, and for so many other things, would never have been realized. A mere thank you here would be the weakest line between these covers, but attempting to say more seems equally futile. All my love and gratitude to you.

Finally, for my children, Trey, Laine, and Mariel: I know you're unaware what you at times sacrificed for this project and how much you vitalized it (and me) in countless ways, small (I don't think I'll ever tire of hearing, "My daddy is an author!") and large. It is to you this book is dedicated. May you inherit a world more nearly approaching the one which Robert Kennedy envisioned, and may you find your own ways to help build the true community that so many still need.

President *of the* Other America

INTRODUCTION

Robert Kennedy's abbreviated 1968 presidential run has assumed mythical proportions in the American memory. His campaign has been romanticized in part because of its tragic end, but also because of the foreign and domestic crises that made politics in that year seem a matter of life and death. While most media coverage initially focused on Kennedy's opposition to the Vietnam War as the catalyst for his candidacy, *Washington Post* reporter Richard Harwood began to note Kennedy's near "obsession" with discussing another issue on the stump: poverty. "Kennedy dwells on the tragedy of the poor," the journalist observed, describing his speeches as a "catalogue of pain."[1] Recalling that months earlier the New York senator had dismissed his opponent Eugene McCarthy's antiwar candidacy as single-themed, Harwood pronounced it one of the great ironies of the primary contest that it was Kennedy who seemed to be emerging as the one-issue candidate. His cause was the escalation of Lyndon Johnson's declared war—against poverty at home.

The makeup of his audiences seemed to matter little, as Kennedy repeated the same antipoverty themes before college students in Kansas and Indiana, loggers and semiskilled female production workers in Oregon, farmers and suburban consumers in Nebraska, and business groups across the country.[2] The responses of predominantly white audiences ranged from starstruck cheering, to resistance to his assertions that poverty remained an urgent problem, to apathy. When an aide asked if Kennedy was sure he wanted to discuss the topic of hunger in America before another potentially unconcerned college audience, the candidate muttered, "If they don't care, the hell with them."[3]

In contrast, racial minority groups at the margins of the nation's economic, social, and political life had developed a unique devotion to Kennedy by the spring of 1968. César Chávez described the sentiments of Mexican American farm workers: "It's that line that you very seldom cross—I've never seen a politician cross that line and I don't think that I'll ever live to see another. . . . It was like respect, admiration, love, idolized. God, I can't explain it."[4] Congress of Racial Equality (CORE) leader Sonny Carson recalled: "There was a strangeness that caused blacks to love him. He was this younger brother full of pain."[5] According to Native American author and activist Vine Deloria Jr., Kennedy "became as great a hero as the famous Indian war chiefs precisely because of his ruthlessness. Indians saw him as a warrior, the white Crazy Horse."[6]

For many observers, Robert Kennedy's political journey in the 1960s was a curious one. His political persona early in the decade was popularly characterized by the supposed ruthlessness referred to by Deloria. Kennedy was seen—by whites and racial minorities alike—as the steely political operative for his brother, and he was identified with the illiberal goals of cracking down on domestic subversives and labor unions. Kennedy's later emergence as what Arthur Schlesinger Jr. called "the tribune of the underclass" thus required an explanation, and two interpretations have endured.[7] Critics saw his new political persona as the culmination of an opportunistic liberal shift designed to outflank President Johnson to the left.[8] Conversely, Kennedy's admirers viewed his empathy for the nation's racial and economic outsiders as evidence of personal growth set in motion by the assassination of President John F. Kennedy, the event that one former Justice Department official believed connected him "to the world's pain."[9] Both of these narratives—emphasizing either Robert Kennedy's political calculation or his wounded transformation—offer historical insights. But the evolution of his relationship with the political issue of poverty and, more powerfully, with poor Americans themselves is eminently richer and more complex.

Perhaps not surprisingly, Kennedy himself dismissed the idea of any radical transformation. "People are making too much of my so-called conversion to liberalism," he said in 1966. "Liberals had an emotional thing about me," he contended, "maybe because of [Joseph] McCarthy, maybe because of my Roman Catholicism, maybe because of my fights with [Hubert] Humphrey and [Adlai] Stevenson. I'm not that different now. I know more now and I stay up late at night more often thinking about these problems. But I was never all that ruthless, as the liberals said."[10]

In examining his work on issues related to poverty and race, I contend that while Kennedy indeed changed over time, it was less a dramatic transformation than a steady political evolution, a process that began earlier than has been understood. Utilizing a broad range of primary sources, including congressional hearings, manuscript collections in the John F. Kennedy Library in Boston and elsewhere, well over one hundred oral history interviews, and perhaps most distinctively the publications of racially and economically excluded groups, this book reveals Kennedy's centrality to the national debate on poverty from the reemergence of the issue in the early 1960s, to the genesis of a large-scale federal antipoverty initiative, to the urban crisis following the Watts riot, to the fight over the poverty program's survival, to his presidential campaign. Kennedy consistently focused public attention on the issue throughout the 1960s, and his policy proposals, while limited and flawed, were also substantive and creative.

Although Vietnam and the civil rights movement have dominated both popular memory and the historical scholarship of the 1960s, the problem of poverty in the United States spanned that tempestuous decade with nearly the same prominence. A cursory look at any newspaper between the years 1964 and 1969—in both urban and rural America—demonstrates how pervasive and contentious the debate over the issue was.

Defining poverty can be a confounding endeavor, but it is important to establish the framework within which I consider the issue here. Teams of social scientists and government officials labored mightily to reach consensus on the nature of the problem in the postwar era. In large measure because it rendered the tortuous matter subject to quantification, poverty was officially defined by the U.S. government in the early 1960s as the absence of basic material necessities required to sustain a decent life. Serious observers nevertheless understood that poverty was more complicated than anything that might be submerged beneath an official "poverty line."[11] Poverty is always somewhat relative, shaped by social, economic, and historical contexts. Those considered poor in wealthier contemporary societies have comparatively greater access to food, clothing, and shelter than those in less developed nations, or even perhaps in the advanced nations of the past. In the early eighteenth century an indentured servant named William Moraley captured the contextual nature of poverty when he observed that colonial America was "the best poor man's country." Moraley's observation did not, however, signify his celebration of poverty in America. His insight did not relieve his pain.[12]

Social and intellectual historians have long identified *exceptionalism* as a central theme in U.S. history—the idea that the nation was special and even "chosen" to be a global exemplar.[13] Given this exalted and enduring self-identity, a national focus on the problem of poverty has emerged only episodically, driven either by mass deprivation endemic to downward swings in the national economy, or by startling exposés of suffering as incongruous with general American good fortune.

As Jacob Riis had seventy years earlier, Michael Harrington sought to shock Americans into the recognition of poverty in their midst with his 1962 book *The Other America: Poverty in the United States*. Setting aside critical analysis of Harrington's methodology and prescriptions, one finds it hard to overestimate the influence of his framing of the poverty problem in the 1960s. Harrington contended that 40 to 50 million citizens were living in a hidden and disconnected America at a time when the nation's problem-solving capacities seemed limitless, in the midst of what Thomas Hine has called the nation's "greatest shopping spree," which brought material prosperity to masses of American working people.[14] The poor were "internal exiles," wrote Harrington, who charged that "as long as America is less than its potential, the nation as a whole is impoverished[,] . . . [and] as long as there is the other America, we are, all of us, poorer because of it."[15]

Harrington catalogued the groups who made up this lost world, from the place-bound aged, to Appalachian whites secluded in their beautiful but remote region, to racial minorities in suffocating inner cities. He acknowledged that America's poor had largely escaped the extreme material deprivation of other nations; yet while the "other Americans" were "the first poor minority poor in history," they were nevertheless "maimed in body and spirit" and "victimized by mental suffering to a degree unknown in Suburbia." Beyond all this, their social and economic exclusion was accompanied and sustained by political isolation. The "other Americans" of the 1960s, unlike poor urban immigrants of earlier generations, were "the first poor whom the politicians could leave alone."[16] At least until Harrington's book appeared. Despite the relative nature of poverty, he insisted that the problem could not morally be allowed to stand.

The Other America was read by many in the midst of the dramatic events of the civil rights movement, and some discussion of the interrelationship between civil rights and poverty is in order, as the two are inextricably linked. The question of race is central to the problem of poverty in America. While Harrington found that poverty transcended race, the color line dictated economic access in American life in these years. The civil rights movements of African Americans and other racial minorities would be deeply concerned with the problem of poverty.

Our popular and too often even our academic reference point for "civil rights" remains the southern phase of the movement and its focus on the desegregation of schools and other public accommodations. In actuality the civil rights movement was a long, national, broad-based push to gain first-class citizenship for African Americans in the form of equal access to all aspects of society, from education, to public accommodations, to housing, to economic and political power.[17] Recent studies have demonstrated that there was no common progression in the drive for access across regions of the nation. In the South the focus of the movement generally evolved from social and political issues to an emphasis on economic opportunity, but even here these emphases were often concurrent. In northern and western cities, where the inequities were sometimes less dramatically obvious than in the Jim Crow South, taking the form of de facto segregation, African American civil rights leaders had focused primarily on economic integration all along.[18] For the purposes of this book I conceptualize poverty broadly, focusing on economic access, but I also take into account the efforts of racial minorities to gain full access to all aspects of American life.

Similarly, I utilize the term "other America" more expansively than did Michael Harrington. Whereas Harrington investigated the dispirited and defeated poor who were left with little recourse to improve their conditions, I use "other America" here as a collective description of racial minority groups and poor whites who had been excluded historically and structurally from the full promise of American society. As a result, my focus on Robert Kennedy's mass appeal to these groups—surveying responses from the poorest and most politically disengaged to movement leaders—at times reveals significant internal social and political divisions.

If the 1960s would unfold in many ways as a period of great division, *The Other America* was a call for community. Harrington's socialist political identity was widely known, but his book was not a call for class warfare (he was in fact highly critical of communism), which would have been an implausible popular appeal at the height of broad cold war American consensus. The book was instead a call to embrace the outcasts within and make the nation whole. Many other prominent and disparate voices in the 1960s, including Jane Jacobs, Lewis Mumford, and Martin Luther King Jr., would bemoan the decline of community in the United States, with each developing distinctive and constructive visions to remedy the ills of modern American life.

There were of course as many or more voices attributing the social difficulties of the decade to an absence of freedom. The quest for individual or group freedom and the desire for community are not necessarily mutually exclusive, however. These broad categories are interdependent and are in fact opposite sides of the same coin.[19] Nevertheless, the subtle shift in the language of movement leaders from a quest for *integration* to the waging of a *freedom struggle*—around the time that direct action protests were revealing clearly that there were forces of social oppression from which blacks needed liberation—suggests the difference between a desire to be part of the larger whole and one's own agency to choose what elements of that whole one wishes to access.[20] For most African Americans, the semantics meant little. They still wanted a better job or a nicer home (if they had either in the first place); ultimately they sought first- rather than second-class citizenship.[21]

The sometimes negligible differences in the objectives of calls for either freedom or community would have greater significance, however, in the realm of politics and policy choices. For example, the historian Gareth Davies has contended that the eventual antipoverty course chosen by many liberals in the 1960s—to protect the poor with guaranteed entitlements—was an overzealous governmental project that abandoned the traditional liberal individualistic emphasis on freedom.[22] This, according to Davies, set social policy on the flawed course that engendered an equally problematic conservative counterreaction. One need not agree with Davies's assessment to see, however, that a difference in political vision favoring either community or freedom can have significant policy implications.

I contend that Robert Kennedy was guided by a distinctive communitarian conception of government—one influenced by a number of factors, a vision not wholly without a role for individualism, and an approach at variance with the new liberal course Davies deplored.[23] Kennedy's search for community was central to most—though not all—of the domestic issues he engaged. His application of the notion of community was elastic, at times fuzzy, and often perhaps naïve. Kennedy would be drawn to the issue of poverty as a threat to all levels of community in the United States, and his policy proposals would reflect a consistent vision of the interrelationship between the individual, the local "grassroots" community, and the national community.

In recent years commentators have tagged as "populist" any political attempt to raise the issue of poverty. As the historian Michael Kazin has demonstrated, populism has taken a number of forms since the days of farmers' revolts, but it has always revolved around a clash with various types of elites.[24] Robert Francis Kennedy was manifestly an elite figure in American life—politically, socially, and economically. His evolving, sometimes groping approach to poverty was not populist, however, but communitarian. He sought the commitment of the powerful to and their cooperation with the powerless in an attempt to strengthen local communities and link them to the central government in a new form of federalism.

Kennedy's interest in poverty was not merely a quixotic "profile in courage." It was from the first intertwined with the exigencies of electoral politics. "Lots of the Robert Kennedy cult," aide Fred Dutton later reflected, "tends to idealize him as a much more idealistic, even naïve person. He was not that. He was a power operator."[25] Whether in his brother's presidential campaign, his activities in the Justice Department, or his Senate career, Kennedy was closely attuned to the political implications of his antipoverty activities.

Nevertheless, time and again his sense of moral outrage would lead him to extend his commitment beyond what many of his seasoned advisers thought wise. He would seek the presidency sooner than many of those same political aides counseled, and he did so in a year that proved as consequential for American attitudes toward poverty as any in the postwar era. As other historians have contended, the presidential election of 1968 turned less on the war in Vietnam than on domestic matters, particularly the problems of urban violence and racial discord which were closely linked to the broader problem of poverty.[26] Ultimately the law-and-order, anti–Great Society message trumpeted by both the victorious Richard Nixon and rival George Wallace carried the day in the general election; but until his death Robert Kennedy occupied a unique position in the electoral debate. By 1968 he had emerged as the last viable advocate for a broader war against poverty. In his absence the rhetoric of Nixon and Wallace laid the groundwork for a new thirty years' war targeting welfare dependency and federal social spending.

The United States has declared unconditional war on poverty only once in its history. Lyndon Johnson's call for an assault on the entrenched poverty at the margins of American society was issued at the peak of U.S. power in the cold war and at the height of the idealism and hubris of that epoch. Johnson's ambition, sense of timing, and political skill made the most sweeping antipoverty legislation in three decades a reality without the overwhelming groundswell of popular support that had buoyed the New Deal. Johnson expended his political capital on the initiative—the centerpiece of his Great Society—and took the heat for its failures. By his final year in office, however, Lyndon Johnson was not the political leader many poor Americans regarded as their champion.

As Robert Kennedy awaited election returns from the California Democratic primary, he sat for what would be his final interviews with network reporters. Sander Vanocur of NBC asked the candidate about Eugene McCarthy's success among higher-income voters. "The great divisions in the country at the present moment," Kennedy said in measured tones, "are between those who are less affluent—our black citizens, Mexican Americans, and those who are poor whites—and the rest of the United States. They feel that they have been disenfranchised or that they have no association or identification with the United States government or with our society." The candidate then offered a historical interpretation of the new threat to the social order and discussed the importance of a national sense of community. "The division isn't between, for instance, the AFL-CIO and business as it was during the 1930s," Kennedy said.

> It's not between the North and the South as it was in the fifties or the early 1960s. It's between those who are less well off and those who are more affluent. I think that I have an association with those who are less well off where perhaps we can accomplish something, bringing the country back together, and that we can start to put into effect—all of us working together—some programs that will have some meaning. That's why I think these elections are promising. If that grows, if that division continues as . . . it has over the period of the last two or three years, we're going to have nothing but chaos and havoc here in the United States. And I think that if we can have that identification with those who, at the present time, feel that they've been left out of our society, I think it's very important.[27]

While this book is an examination of an important political issue and the historically significant strategic steps and policy prescriptions that a major political figure offered, it is in large part an account of what Kennedy deliberatively and dispassionately referred to as that "association." It was a unique political alliance which generated passion and hope rare in American history, and though cut short before the full actualization of its promise, the story of Robert Kennedy and his efforts to assist the "other Americans" is essential to an understanding of the politics of poverty in the pivotal decade of the 1960s.

1

FROM THE NEW DEAL
TO THE NEW FRONTIER
POSTWAR PROSPERITY,
POVERTY, AND THE
KENNEDYS

Poverty was a central issue in American politics through-out much of Robert Kennedy's youth. His childhood was, however, famously insulated from the suffering that millions of Americans endured in the Great Depression. His wealthy and politically powerful family was on display for ordinary Americans when Franklin Roosevelt appointed his father, Joseph P. Kennedy, the first Irish American U.S. ambassador to Great Britain in 1937. Readers of popular magazines such as *Reader's Digest* and *Ladies' Home Journal* learned of the "Nine Kennedys and How They Grew" and the "Nine Young U.S. Ambassadors."[1] The story of the family patriarch, the second-generation Boston Irish immigrant who became a millionaire and raised his children to move in the elite strata of American life, soon became part of the nation's folklore.

While Joseph Kennedy wanted his young charges to succeed above all else, he also instilled a large measure of noblesse oblige. Writing to eight-year-old son Teddy in 1940, Kennedy described the scene after the German Luftwaffe attacked London: "It is really terrible to think about . . . all those poor women and children and home-less people down in the East end of London all seeing their places destroyed. I hope when you grow up you will dedicate your life to trying to work out plans to make people happy instead of making them miserable, as war does today." He wrote to fourteen-year-old Robert that same fall: "I do hope you will put in a good effort this year. It is boys of your age who are going to find themselves in a very changed world and the only way you can hold up your end is to prepare your mind so that you will be able to accept each situation as it comes along."[2] In an oral history interview in the 1960s Robert Kennedy insisted that as a child he was constantly reminded of his social responsibility, that "there were a lot of people that were less fortunate, and a lot of people that were hungry."[3] His experience of such suffering, however, was only peripheral, confined to fleeting images glimpsed through the window of a train or car.[4]

While his own challenges could not be compared to those at the margins of American social and economic life, family members and school friends later suggested that the young Kennedy knew something of what it meant to feel excluded. As the seventh of nine children in a family with a clear line of descent, he was a natural at none of the endeavors his family valued, from athletics to academics to social hobnobbing. His brother John called him "Black Robert" because of his prudishness and his often morose disposition, and his siblings celebrated his dashing older brothers, Joseph Jr. and John, leaving him an afterthought. "Nothing came easy for him," one of his sisters reflected. "Perhaps that gave him sympathy later in life for those who were less fortunate. He, in some peculiar way, understood their soul."[5]

His father shuffled the middling student through a number of different schools, finally transferring him from a Catholic prep school to Milton Academy, an elite, predominantly Protestant feeder school for Harvard. Robert was the most religious of the Kennedy brothers, and his devout Catholicism marked him there as an outsider.[6] One of Kennedy's few friends at Milton suggested that the socially awkward young man "must have felt like an immigrant."[7] Another, David Hackett, was a star athlete at Milton, but he too never felt entirely comfortable there because of his working-class background. "We were both," Hackett later reflected, "in a way, misfits."[8] Kennedy and Hackett would remain close socially and, eventually, politically. "Things were not easy for him," Hackett concluded, "so I think he just had a natural connection to the underdog."[9]

Kennedy was also left out of the glory his family and his generation drew from the World War II experience. His older brothers raced to demonstrate their valor overseas, driven to embody the family codes of achievement and social responsibility. Eventually John became a war hero for his Pacific rescue of a PT boat shipmate, and Joseph died in a bombing run over Germany. Near the end of the war, eager to follow in the footsteps of his brothers, young Robert failed to qualify as a naval aviator and was relegated to mundane postwar ship duty.

If Kennedy grew up at the tail end of (and having made minimal contributions to) the "greatest generation," which survived the Great Depression at home and conquered tyranny overseas, he came of age politically in a far different America. The postwar years were characterized by an unprecedented international struggle with the Soviet Union and unsurpassed domestic prosperity. In all of these developments the federal government was playing a dramatically increased role. In part because of the perceived successes of the New Deal and Washington's management of the war effort, and in part because of the growing size and complexity of problems in the modern world, Americans were turning with greater confidence and frequency to government to provide solutions. Recognizing this early on, Joseph Kennedy pushed his sons toward public service, convinced that elective office would be the most consequential of postwar vocations. John Kennedy was elected to Congress in 1946, but Robert, ill-suited for the glad-handing of politics, would again follow his brother's path to a less enthralling destination. After graduating from law school, Robert Kennedy received his introduction to government service as a staff member on the second Hoover Commission. Former president Herbert Hoover was attempting to streamline the rapidly expanding executive branch of the federal government, and while Kennedy appreciated the direct contact with the Great Engineer, he found the assignment soporific.[10]

With the end of World War II, many Americans feared the return of the depression conditions which had doomed Hoover's presidency. The postwar economy instead produced one of the most impressive periods of growth in U.S. history. As the nation's aggregate economy grew, the number of American families living in poverty declined. According to one study, the percentage of poor families shrank from 48 in 1935 to 27 in 1950. The numbers dwindled further by 1960, when only 21 percent of families were living in poverty.[11]

Not surprisingly in this age of increasing economic abundance, poverty received considerably less attention on the national political level than before the war. President Harry Truman attempted to revive the activist domestic agenda of the New Deal, but with little success. He did secure passage of the Housing Act of 1949, which authorized funding for over 800,000 new units of low-income public housing and provided $1 billion for slum clearance in "blighted" urban areas. The Second Great Migration of southern blacks to overcrowded northern cities was a major catalyst for the legislation, but the construction of affordable new units lagged, and urban renewal generally resulted in the destruction of poor neighborhoods and subsequent removal of residents to other ghetto areas. Rather than improving conditions for the urban poor, it exacted a heavy psychological and economic toll.[12] Unemployment rates among urban blacks were more than double those of whites by 1963.[13]

A few lawmakers focused on poverty in the prosperous postwar years precisely because they perceived it to be a troubling anomaly. Senator John Sparkman of Alabama conducted long-running hearings on employment problems and their impact on families beginning in the late 1940s, with particular attention to the persistence of poverty "in the midst of plenty."[14] A decade later Illinois Democrat Paul Douglas convened similar Senate hearings examining the emerging issue of "depressed areas" such as southern Illinois and the coal mining regions of Appalachia, which came to be seen as nettlesome "pockets of poverty" in a nation awash in economic opportunity.

After his election to the Senate in 1952, John Kennedy also seized upon the issue, emphasizing the human costs of the slumping textile industry in New England.[15] Kennedy and Minnesota senator Hubert Humphrey cosponsored a limited measure to deal with regional and localized poverty. Douglas expanded the Humphrey-Kennedy proposal and introduced depressed areas legislation that later passed in both houses of Congress, only to meet a veto from President Dwight Eisenhower in 1958 and again two years later.[16]

While antipoverty legislative accomplishments in the 1950s were minimal, other developments of that era would have a longer-term significance for social welfare policy. Although Eisenhower wanted to restrict federal spending on a number of fronts (including the military), he did not attempt to roll back New Deal social programs significantly, and he basically accepted the expanded federal role in the area of social welfare. The real growth industry in relation to poverty in the postwar era was social science, which resulted in a number of new perspectives that challenged entrenched thinking and remained influential for decades to come.[17]

Until the twentieth century, poverty was seen almost solely as the problem of the individual and viewed through a moral lens. From the days of the Puritans, who believed that laziness and destitution among the able-bodied were marks of being beyond the salvific grace of God, Americans have tended to divide the needy into the "worthy" or "deserving" poor—those too infirm, aged, or otherwise burdened to provide for themselves—and the "unworthy" or "undeserving" poor. This duality also had its origins in the Elizabethan Poor Law, which the first English colonists used as their model when they arrived in North America. The material scarcity of the colonial frontier reinforced the necessity to prioritize and categorize community needs.[18] Until well into the nineteenth century, this individualized, moralistic approach to poverty consigned care for the poor to localities and to the benevolence of churches and other private charities. As this *individualist* perspective endured into the mid-twentieth century, it took two forms. Individual moral or character flaws probably remained the prevailing popular understanding of the cause of poverty, but the new casework approach of social work, emphasizing problems in an individual's social and psychological adjustment to his or her environment, introduced a less moralistic modern variant.[19]

Environmental theories of poverty—which focused on social or economic causes and remedies—had their roots in the Progressive Era and became more influential after World War II. The *conservative functionalist* perspective emphasized that economic inequality was inevitable and contended that a society remained stable because varying levels of social status and economic rewards kept it in a state of balance. The conservative functionalists did not believe that class differences in America were pronounced, or that poverty as it existed should be of major concern.[20]

The *liberal* perspective, advocated by social scientists such as those on the National Resources Planning Board and the social workers and bureaucrats who administered federal social welfare programs, assumed the need for a permanent welfare system on the basis of their firsthand experience of the intractability of the problem and the operational challenges in running programs. Proponents of this pragmatic liberal approach focused successfully in the 1950s on incremental improvements to the welfare system.[21]

The *Keynesian aggregationist* approach relied on economic growth as the most important element in reducing poverty. Best summarized later in John Kennedy's phrase "a rising tide lifts all boats" (economist and Kennedy adviser Robert Lampman was among the most optimistic of the aggregationists), the Keynesian belief was that government intervention in and management of the economy were essential to speeding overall growth. The aggregationists did not see poverty as a relative condition, as they believed that a larger economic pie meant more for everyone.

In contrast the *structuralists* contended that overall economic growth left many behind. They saw persistent social and economic blockages—such as racism, a crippled regional economy, and job skills deficits—which prevented impoverished local communities or segments of the population from advancing. Structuralists contended that society had to confront such entrenched problems more proactively and aggressively. They proposed measures to address racial integration, regional development, poor wages, and unemployment, and they urged the redistribution of income through social welfare spending and progressive taxation. Prominent postwar structuralists included economist John Kenneth Galbraith and sociologist Gunnar Myrdal, whose book *An American Dilemma* examined the unique impediment of race in American society and the consequent rise of an enduring "underclass" of black Americans.

Finally, adherents of the emerging *culture of poverty* theory, first advanced by sociologist Oscar Lewis, ascribed the problem to inescapable cultural traps. The poor were conditioned by their poverty to adopt attitudes and behaviors that the larger society deemed counterproductive, limiting their ability to take advantage of social and economic opportunities. Poverty was not just an absence of resources; it produced people who, through no fault of their own, were different.

These analytical categories were not always mutually exclusive. Michael Harrington leveled a structuralist critique at the American market economy while also becoming the most influential proponent of the culture of poverty theory, asserting that the new poor he studied were marked not only by material deprivation but also by debilitating feelings of fatalism and helplessness. Unlike poor turn-of-the-century immigrants depicted by Jacob Riis, who were "the adventurous seeking a new life and land," the "other Americans" of the early 1960s were "the failures . . . those driven from the land and bewildered in the city[,] . . . old people suddenly confronted with the torments of loneliness and poverty, and minorities facing a wall of prejudice."[22]

Harrington's arguments did not reach a wide audience until the early 1960s, however, and any focus on poverty, much less any rigorous scholarly analysis, was basically absent from the popular consciousness of mainstream white America in the 1950s. While we now understand more of the tumult beneath the surface of that decade, including cold war anxieties and the beginnings of social rebellions, the face of the 1950s was characterized by conformity, optimism, and a burgeoning consumer culture. Suburban living became a national ideal and an attainable dream for increasing numbers of white working-class Americans. Thomas Hine coined the term "populuxe" to describe this unique historical period when mass prosperity met the mass production of affordable consumer items. Ranging from push-button gadgetry to tail-finned automobiles of all colors, the commercial abundance of the 1950s prompted aspirations to one's "own little Versailles along a cul-du-sac."[23] The thoroughgoing triumph of this new mentality permeated even the cold war confrontation with the Soviet Union when Richard Nixon proclaimed in his famed "kitchen debate" with Nikita Khrushchev that American superiority was manifest in the new technologies of washing machines and color television sets.

Television was both an end of and a means to this new consumer Valhalla. Advertising and primetime programming—featuring model white middle-class families—were essential to the fashioning of these new American dreams. Television was deployed less effectively as a window into the nation's problems in the 1950s. TV news was slow to develop, confined to fifteen-minute broadcasts until 1963, but a significant exception was coverage of several sensational congressional hearings that aimed to investigate threats that lay beneath the Madison Avenue portrait of American life. His roles in two of these televised exposés first brought Robert Kennedy to public attention and shaped the enduring image many Americans held of the young Boston attorney.

In 1953 a family friendship with Wisconsin Republican Joseph McCarthy afforded Kennedy the opportunity to join the staff of his high-powered Senate subcommittee. By that time McCarthy's scattershot charges of communist influence in the federal government had riveted the nation's attention for three years. Kennedy's principal task was probing the intricate and—in contrast with McCarthy's other inquiries—somewhat pedestrian issue of Western trade with the communist government of China. Although he sparred behind the scenes with McCarthy's right-hand man Roy Cohn, resigned from the committee, and later claimed to be repulsed by McCarthy's recklessness, Kennedy was nevertheless forever tainted in the eyes of some liberals horrified by the earthquake McCarthy's tactics had triggered in the nation's public square. Nevertheless, Kennedy made no apologies for his anticommunism. "I thought," he later said, "there was a serious internal security threat to the United States; I felt at that time that Joe McCarthy was the only one doing anything about it."[24] After leaving the McCarthy committee, Kennedy remained transfixed by the dangers of communism and visited the Soviet Union with Supreme Court Justice William O. Douglas in 1955. Upon his return he went on a speaking tour to share his observations from the belly of the beast. "We are dealing with a government," he told journalists, "to whom God, the family or the individual means nothing."[25]

Kennedy parlayed his work on the McCarthy committee into the lead role in another congressional investigation, this time examining corruption in labor unions. It was a risky political endeavor for a northern Democrat to probe organized labor, one of the key pillars of the Roosevelt coalition. It was all the more perilous as John Kennedy was carefully positioning himself for a presidential run, and Robert Kennedy took the job only after a rare clash with his father.[26] The televised McClellan committee hearings put both Kennedys in the national spotlight, with Robert as the aggressive interrogator of Jimmy Hoffa and other leaders of the Teamsters Union. His work on the McCarthy and McClellan committees forged Robert Kennedy's reputation as a crusading "tough guy," willing to go after and consort with unsavory figures in American life. While critics charged that his pursuit of Hoffa amounted to a personal vendetta, Kennedy framed the broader problem of corruption in organized labor as a moral issue, calling Hoffa's operation of the union a "conspiracy of evil." In *The Enemy Within*, his published account of the hearings, Kennedy charged that among the most damaging effects of Hoffa's iron-fisted rule was its incapacitating impact on laborers: "People . . . ask why the rank and file put up with gangsters and corruption. . . . [T]he terrible truth of the matter is that the rank and file are powerless."[27] According to the liberal columnist Murray Kempton, Kennedy "looked at the labor racketeers as upon men who had betrayed a priesthood" and "became, for the occasion, a Catholic radical."[28]

If Robert Kennedy was in any way radical in the 1950s, his extremism lay in the energy and conviction he brought to his pursuit of both communism and corruption. Kennedy's Catholicism was otherwise quite representative of the American church in this period. Spurred by both official teachings (including the 1937 papal encyclical *Divini Redemptoris*, which urged resistance to "atheistic communism") and popular devotion (Catholics embraced the message of a 1917 Marian apparition at Fatima urging them to pray the rosary for the conversion of Russia), anticommunism became the most important political issue for many American Catholics in the 1950s and marked the final stage in their full assimilation into American society.[29] Their anticommunism was perceived to be so reliable that J. Edgar Hoover, director of the Federal Bureau of Investigation, developed a preference for recruiting graduates of Catholic universities as FBI agents.[30] While Kennedy clearly stood to gain socially and politically by embracing the issue—as did all of his coreligionists—his aversion to communism was by all accounts both moral and personal.

Kempton's real insight was that Kennedy's Catholicism shaped his political worldview. A number of studies have suggested that American Catholics have a relatively greater inclination than members of other faiths to adopt communitarian political perspectives, that is, to assess issues on the basis of potential threats or benefits to community, with particular attention to the most vulnerable.[31] The American political spectrum has been strongly influenced by the individualistic perspective that has been reinforced by a wide variety of powerful cultural, social, and economic impulses, including laissez-faire economic liberalism, nineteenth-century romanticism, and an evangelical Christian emphasis on the salvation of the individual. Political scientist William Lee Miller has written, "America's Protestantism has entered into the common creed . . . as an unchallenged set of assumptions that are not argued, but taken for granted as self-evident." Miller contended that American politics were suffused with "an anti-authoritarian, anti-traditional, anti-corporate strand."[32] The Catholic communitarian view, which is far from absolute and is influenced on the individual level by a wide variety of factors, has historically produced what appear to be inconsistent clusters of political perspectives. From the New Deal onward, American Catholics tended to support liberal calls for an activist federal government on a range of economic issues but more conservative positions on cultural issues or matters such as crime and other threats to social order.[33]

Kennedy identified a communitarian nexus between communism and corruption, the two "enemies within" that dominated his concerns in the 1950s. He saw each as threatening various levels of community from the local to the national. Kennedy charged, for instance, that the activities of Teamster leaders Dave Beck and Jimmy Hoffa and the crooked businessmen with whom they dealt represented a rising tide of "corruption, dishonesty, and softness" at home that was undermining the international struggle with the Soviet Union.[34] While he would certainly change in other ways, and at times other concerns—particularly his brother's political self-interest—would temper or surmount the moralistic tendencies in his political judgment, Kennedy would nevertheless continue to filter his political decision making through this moralistic, communitarian prism in the years ahead.[35]

Kennedy did not extend his moral fervor toward the other major issue that most clearly threatened all levels of community in the 1950s. When editors of *U.S. News & World Report* asked Kennedy about his 1955 trip to the Soviet Union and inquired about Russian perspectives on America, he said that the most common question he encountered was "about the Negroes and whether they were mistreated and discriminated against, segregated and lynched."[36] The firestorm over the Mississippi murder of an African American teenager named Emmett Till broke out while Kennedy was in the communist nation, and the young lawyer demonstrated an amazing insensitivity to the problem, along with a tone deafness for international cold war politics. Rather than warning Americans about the way the nation's racial injustices appeared overseas and how this could serve Soviet propaganda interests, Kennedy suggested only that the Harlem Globetrotters basketball team might make a goodwill tour of Russia.[37] While other progressive Catholics, including his brother-in-law Sargent Shriver, were deeply concerned about the racial challenges the nation was facing at the time, Kennedy later admitted, "I wasn't lying awake nights thinking about the Negro in this country."[38]

Not nearly enough white political leaders were, and race remained a multifarious barrier to full participation in American life. Racial minorities were struggling in the midst of what John Kenneth Galbraith labeled "the affluent society," with over half the nation's nonwhite population living in poverty in 1960.[39] The investigation Kennedy and his staff conducted during the McClellan hearings at least tangentially exposed him to the problem. In the spring of 1958 he noted that "sub-standard sweetheart contracts with crooked labor union leaders" were yielding only "starvation wages to uneducated Puerto Rican and Negro workers," and he later told a reporter that "his stomach turned" at the low wages paid to some laborers.[40] It would require presidential politics, however, to force the Kennedys to engage the questions of race and poverty in greater depth.

After his star turn at the 1956 Democratic convention elevated John Kennedy to the status of presidential contender, the Massachusetts senator initially directed most of his attention toward building bridges to southern Democrats. He staked out moderate positions on civil rights, avoiding a progressive stance on the desegregation of southern schools and siding with southern leaders on key votes as the Civil Rights Act of 1957 moved through the Senate. It worked. In Mississippi, the state most deeply anchored in the Jim Crow system, Governor J. P. Coleman called Kennedy "temperate" and "no hell raiser," and the Massachusetts Democrat also gained the trust of James Eastland and John Stennis, the state's two segregationist senators.[41]

Not surprisingly, African Americans sizing up the likely presidential candidate were displeased. The *Chicago Defender*, the nation's preeminent African American daily newspaper, editorialized that Kennedy "will not only compromise on school segregation, but also on the poll tax, voting rights, filibuster, lynching, and all other aspects of violated civil rights." In the midst of the fight over the 1957 civil rights legislation, the paper charged that Kennedy would "damage the party's cause and impair its chances for victory. We don't mind the donkey as a traditional emblem of the Democratic party, but a jackass is out of the question."[42] Robert Kennedy, publicly emerging as his brother's confidant and strategist, also appeared in a less than favorable light in the black press. The *Defender* reported the unfounded rumor that the younger Kennedy "painstakingly dug up all the old statutes in reference to civil rights and gave them to the southerners [in Congress] to use as ammunition to gut the bill of its most potent parts." In his syndicated newspaper column National Urban League executive director Lester Granger urged Kennedy to drop the "safe" investigation of labor rackets in exchange for the more urgent "anti–civil rights racket."[43] And if it weren't already painfully obvious to ordinary African Americans that the Kennedys lived in an entirely different socioeconomic orbit, a curious reminder appeared just weeks before John Kennedy announced his presidential candidacy. The *Defender* ran a photo of a black man feeding a sea lion intended as a Christmas present for Robert Kennedy's children in 1959. It had escaped from the family swimming pool while they were on vacation in Jamaica.[44]

Even as John Kennedy courted key southern leaders, with the civil rights movement rapidly building momentum and moral urgency, the Kennedys realized that they could not ultimately win as latter-day doughfaces. John Kennedy had never been anathema to the black community; he had in fact tried to maintain connections through regular appearances before black professional groups and fraternal societies, speaking before African American audiences about the problems of all poor and working-class urban constituencies.[45] Nevertheless, such conventional attention seemed inadequate to an increasing number of civil rights leaders as battle lines were being drawn in the showdown over Jim Crow in the South. Kennedy was fortunate that his most important primary election contests with liberal Minnesota senator Hubert Humphrey—who had been popular with African Americans since his advocacy of a strong civil rights plank at the 1948 Democratic convention—took place in Wisconsin and West Virginia, states with small black populations.[46]

The pivotal West Virginia primary turned instead on the campaign's response to the conditions faced by poor whites.[47] As his brother's campaign manager, Robert Kennedy was initially opposed to running in the overwhelmingly Protestant Mountain State, as he feared that anti-Catholic sentiments could prove too great an obstacle.[48] Once John Kennedy decided to challenge Humphrey, however, he employed cutting-edge political techniques, sending pollster Louis Harris out to learn more about West Virginians' concerns about his candidacy. Harris found that aside from his Catholicism, voters worried that "as a man of wealth, he would have little care for the woes of the poor."[49] Blending the new with an older form of political intelligence gathering, both the candidate and the campaign manager heard similar admonitions in extensive parleys with local Democratic leaders. Armed with such understanding, Robert Kennedy set out to convince West Virginia voters that in spite of his religion, his brother was a Democrat in the Roosevelt mold, even enlisting Franklin Roosevelt Jr. to stump for the Massachusetts senator. The battle plan in the Mountain State, Robert Kennedy told subordinates, was to focus on "food, family, and flag."[50]

West Virginia and other coal mining states had been badly hurt by the rise of mechanized mining in the 1950s.[51] "This place hits the unprepared outsider between the eyes," said columnist Joseph Alsop of one mining town in the coalfields. "You wind down a deep-pocked road into a cramped, pit-like hollow in the hills," he wrote, describing "the hundred or so decrepit-looking houses; the tipples of the two mines; the bare minimum of shabby schools and board-built churches; and the company store and office, all bleak, graceless, and scurfy with coal dust."[52]

As John Kennedy surveyed such scenes, he lambasted the White House for inattention to the economic hardships there, referring to the boarded-up windows as "Eisenhower curtains." Kennedy insisted that he was no neophyte on the issue, trumpeting his attempt to pass legislation to aid depressed areas; but the candidate had never witnessed the kind of grinding poverty he found in the coal towns and hollows of West Virginia.[53] Journalist Theodore White recounted how the candidate "could scarcely bring himself to believe that human beings were forced to eat and live on these cans of dry relief rations, which he fingered like artifacts of another civilization." The senator muttered privately to an aide, "Just imagine kids who never drink milk."[54]

The verbose and passionate Humphrey, whose modest background appeared to render him the more naturally sympathetic figure for West Virginians, proclaimed his understanding of their struggles and railed against Kennedy. In the closing days of the campaign, perhaps sensing the race slipping away from him, the usually good-natured Humphrey grew shrill, complaining that unlike his opponent, he couldn't "afford to run through with a checkbook and a little black bag." The Massachusetts senator, Humphrey charged, was a "spoiled candidate and he and that young, emotional, juvenile Bobby are spending with wild abandon."[55] Conversely, Kennedy focused on the problems of his audience, conveying, in White's words, "shock at the suffering he saw . . . with the emotion of original discovery."[56]

The Kennedys—the entire family blanketed the state—practiced a visceral, tactile brand of politics, eagerly rubbing shoulders with the local residents, descending into the coal mines (on one occasion the candidate narrowly missed being electrocuted by a high-voltage line), and bridging—if only momentarily—the obvious social and economic gap with Appalachian residents. One miner asked about rumors that Kennedy had never worked a day in his life. "Well I guess there is some truth to that," the amused candidate replied. "Well you haven't missed a goddamn thing," the miner cracked. Kennedy basically lived in West Virginia for a month, and with the advantage of the resources Humphrey condemned—including a nearly limitless budget and a campaign plane—he was almost certainly seen personally by many more prospective voters than the Minnesota senator. This enabled Kennedy to engage more effectively the oral political culture of the mountains, which emphasized retail politics and gave downcast local residents the sense that an influential outsider really wanted to learn about their problems.[57]

The conventional wisdom at the time, reasserted in several later studies, credited John Kennedy's substantial 61 to 39 percent victory to massive infusions of Kennedy money, and well-founded allegations of vote buying were rampant. This, along with the campaign manager's apparent decision to use a member of the revered Roosevelt family to raise Humphrey's lack of World War II military service (Humphrey had a legitimate medical deferment), reinforced Robert Kennedy's image as a hard-nosed political operator. Those machinations notwithstanding, oral history interviews with a range of state officials and Kennedy supporters attributed the outcome to the Massachusetts senator's ability to convince voters of his concern and commitment to help.[58]

Robert Kennedy was also stunned by what he saw in West Virginia. "Technically," campaign aide and Kennedy friend William Walton later said, "this was the first time that he had ever moved through the houses of the poor and examined the ways that they lived."[59] Throughout the rest of his political career, until he saw firsthand the distended bellies and Third World diseases among residents of the Mississippi Delta in 1967, Kennedy would refer to what he had seen in the hollows of West Virginia as the worst poverty in the nation.[60] David Hackett contended that Kennedy viewed the conditions as "very simply . . . unfair" and believed that "something had to be done about it."[61] Beyond his outrage, the campaign manager recognized the political rewards of appealing to constituencies left out of "populuxe" America. As he left the state for the last time before the fall election, he told Charleston Gazette reporter Thomas Stafford: "We love West Virginia and what it has done for us. If we win . . . we won't forget you."[62]

After John Kennedy survived the challenge from Humphrey, he groped for a way to perform the high-wire act of attracting black votes while maintaining southern white support. In the very different electoral dynamics of the fall, the Kennedy campaign saw African American votes as a key to victory. African Americans had voted reliably Democratic since Roosevelt's New Deal, but the segregationist brushfire set by the Dixiecrats in 1948, the weak civil rights planks in the Democratic platforms of 1952 and 1956, and the moderate civil rights record of the Eisenhower administration led Democratic strategists to fear significant defections in 1960. John Kennedy asked his brother-in-law Sargent Shriver, who had accrued political cachet with African American leaders because of his interracial work in Chicago, to set up a civil rights arm of the campaign. For assistance, Shriver recruited Harris Wofford, a young Notre Dame law professor, counsel to the U.S. Commission on Civil Rights, and friend of Martin Luther King Jr. The campaign manager sought Wofford's tutelage, confiding: "We're in trouble with Negroes. We really don't know much about this whole thing. . . . I haven't known many Negroes in my life. . . . Tell us where we are and go to it."[63]

The strategy the campaign arrived at balanced idealism and pragmatism. The civil rights section orchestrated a successful effort to register thousands of new African American voters, and Wofford and Shriver crafted a very progressive civil rights message for the platform committee. Both were astonished when Robert Kennedy, confident that sufficient southern white support was in hand, backed the plank "unequivocally."[64] While John Kennedy was privately less sanguine about the plank, his public support for it paid immediate dividends. The *Washington Afro-American* praised the document as "a victory for human rights" and editorialized that Kennedy "beat down the opposition of the Dixiecrats, Senate Majority Leader Lyndon Johnson, old professionals like Adlai Stevenson, Humphrey, [Senator Stuart] Symington and Truman and did it expertly and overwhelmingly. Unquestionably he is the leader of his party. . . . The liberals were pushing Nixon. Kennedy was leading the liberals from the beginning."[65]

Shriver, in most ways more liberal and idealistic than the candidate (who jokingly dubbed him the family's "house communist"), nevertheless recognized that the day of the "old professionals" and backroom tactics had not yet completely passed. "Civil rights was not the primary appeal when you went to get the black or other minority votes," Shriver later confessed of the period. "I'm sorry to say that a lot of it was based on just distributing money at election time or just having very good contact with leaders of the black community."[66] Drawing upon his Chicago ties, Shriver asked former *Chicago Defender* editor Louis Martin to advise the campaign on African American outreach. Martin urged several practical steps, including a rapprochement with African American newspapers. He urged the Kennedys and the Democratic National Committee to settle significant advertising debts to the black media dating from the 1956 presidential campaign, and he strongly encouraged (and later oversaw) a major advertising campaign in the fall.[67] Martin also cautioned the Kennedys against continuing to ignore the two biggest urban power brokers in African American politics, congressmen William Dawson of Chicago and Adam Clayton Powell Jr. of New York City, whom Martin knew could still deliver votes en masse.

Robert Kennedy was reluctant to deal with either, insisting that the Harlem Democrat "always extracts a price, a monetary price, for his support. He always bids one party off against another."[68] That had in fact been the case, as Powell even cozied up to the Eisenhower administration in the 1950s in the hope of getting a better hearing from both parties at the national level. The Kennedys had not been shy in using money to generate votes, but ongoing questions about Powell's loyalty plagued the campaign manager. Concerned that polls showed Nixon with a slight edge among African American voters, Robert Kennedy chastised the campaign's civil rights section in September, in what Martin called a "mocking and acid" manner.[69] Martin was angered by the reprimand and came back at the younger Kennedy, questioning his commitment to gaining African American support. "You're talking about what we haven't done," Martin said, telling Kennedy: "You haven't done what you're supposed to do. You haven't linked up with the guys who have been in this party for twenty years. You don't know the officers. You don't know anybody." After the meeting ended, the young campaign manager asked to meet further with Martin and quickly came to value his political acumen.[70]

After he was persuaded to cultivate ties with Powell and Dawson, John Kennedy began following the lead of Martin, Wofford, and others in the civil rights section on other matters. In his opening statement of his first televised debate with Richard Nixon, the Democratic candidate cited bleak statistics Wofford had uncovered on the constricted economic and educational opportunities facing minority children. The prominence of the statement was noted by African American newspapers and by Roy Wilkins, head of the National Association for the Advancement of Colored People

(NAACP), who found it deeply moving.[71] Kennedy also began making campaign stops in the black communities of northern cities, most prominently the South Side of Chicago and Harlem.

In Louis Martin's eyes, the turning point in the push for African American support was a nominally (and paradoxically) nonpartisan civil rights conference assembled by the Democratic Party in New York City in early October to generate proposals for the next administration. The National Conference on Constitutional Rights—planners deliberately avoided the term "civil rights" at vice presidential nominee Lyndon Johnson's behest to try to minimize antagonizing southern Democrats—was an attempt to build ties to the civil rights leadership, which remained skeptical of the Democratic nominee.[72] Both of the Kennedys also made time during the conference, which was not focused exclusively on African American concerns, to meet privately with Native American and Mexican American leaders, attention that each group would find heartening.[73]

While organizing such a gathering likely helped Kennedy's standing with civil rights leaders, the Nixon campaign's response maximized its impact. Stumping in New York during the conference, Nixon's running mate, Henry Cabot Lodge Jr., promised a black cabinet official in a Republican administration, and many black leaders saw it as a shamelessly telegraphed counterpunch. Worse still, Nixon, who was increasingly courting white southern voters, disavowed Lodge's comments and forced a retraction. Immediately following the conference Adam Clayton Powell emerged arm-in-arm with John and Jacqueline Kennedy and formally endorsed the candidate before a Harlem crowd of eight thousand. Martin considered it a powerful symbolic moment:

> Here was the elite of the land, in the middle of the ghetto, vowing their concern and friendship for those born and living in exile from the main body of American society. Here too promises were being made that this exile, with its overtones and undertones of humiliation and debasement, would come to an end if the Prince and Princess got into the White House. The magic wand was in the hands of the little people, and on the first Tuesday in November they could put a piece of paper in a box and change the course of history.[74]

Not all African American observers were similarly enchanted. *New York Amsterdam News* editor James Hicks suggested that Kennedy looked good on race only in comparison to his rival, because the Massachusetts senator "at least admitted he did wrong" when he "'chickened' out to Senator Eastland on the civil rights bill," while the Republicans were so misguided that Lodge had made the campaign's short-lived pledge to name a black cabinet officer while speaking in Spanish Harlem.[75] The newspaper even afforded more coverage to prodigal tennis champion Althea Gibson's return to Harlem than to Powell's blessing of the Democratic nominee.

The Kennedy campaign, more attuned to the importance of popular culture than was Nixon, actively sought the endorsements of black entertainers and athletes, and it succeeded in garnering more high-profile support. The most prominent holdout was Jackie Robinson, who was not simply the most revered athlete in the black community but the very symbol of both the promise and the challenges of integration in the postwar era. Robinson was now also an unflinching newspaper columnist, and he doubted John Kennedy's sincerity and commitment to civil rights, predicting before the Wisconsin primary that if nominated, Kennedy "would get less Negro votes than any Democrat ever."[76] Robinson continued to castigate the nominee through the summer, and in late August, Robert Kennedy tried to blunt the force of his critiques by charging on a popular New York radio program that the Hall of Famer and his coffee company employer were antilabor. Robinson called the accusation "gutter tactics" and would remain critical of the Kennedys in years ahead, but by October even the Brooklyn great conceded that Kennedy was gaining the edge among black voters.[77]

As the very tight fall campaign headed into the home stretch, a growing number of commentators were proclaiming that the black vote might be decisive.[78] While evidence suggests that there was significant movement toward Kennedy before the last week of the campaign, popular and scholarly understanding has focused on one high-profile incident in late October as the game changer.[79] Among the civil rights organizations still weighing the relative merits of a Kennedy versus a Nixon presidency, the Southern Christian Leadership Conference (SCLC), headed by Martin Luther King Jr., was most influential. Increasingly the mainstream press looked to King as the voice of the entire civil rights movement, and when the SCLC scheduled a special board meeting for mid-October, both candidates considered attending. When Kennedy indicated that he would appear, three southern Democratic governors insisted that their states would end up in the Nixon column. Kennedy nevertheless planned to attend until it became clear that the organization would endorse neither man. Again calculating the risk to his southern support, Kennedy eventually backed out; the meeting was subsequently called off, and King went home to Atlanta.

Kennedy's decision inadvertently led to another chance to gain a hearing in the black community. Back in Atlanta, King joined student sit-in protests at a prominent department store and was arrested for trespassing. He was subsequently released and then jailed again for a parole violation stemming from trumped-up traffic charges the previous spring. Kennedy's advisers weighed issuing a statement. Concerned that the Democratic mayor of Atlanta had already suggested (inaccurately) that the candidate had played a role in King's first departure from jail, the candidate consented to the recommendation of Martin and Wofford that he simply telephone King's wife, Coretta, to offer his support. When Robert Kennedy learned of the call, he erupted, fearing that Wofford and Martin's advice had lost the South and the election. After some consideration, however, he decided himself to call the judge who had jailed King, in part because of his own outrage—he privately muttered, "You can't deny bail on a misdemeanor"—but also because the situation presented a political problem. Warned by the Georgia Democratic Party secretary that King's release could cost the Democrats his state, Robert Kennedy retorted, "If he isn't released, it might cost us Massachusetts."[80] After departing the state prison in Reidsville, King thanked John Kennedy and later commended him for his "courage . . . to do this, especially in Georgia."[81]

It was not technically an endorsement, but the events in Georgia, capped by King's statements, triggered an avalanche. King's father, formerly a Nixon supporter and a prominent Baptist minister in his own right, praised Kennedy's virtue and declared, "I've got all my votes and I've got a suitcase and I'm going to take them up there and dump them in his lap."[82] King's closest friend and SCLC lieutenant Ralph Abernathy, who had also been leaning toward Nixon, said that he was "beginning a campaign right now for Kennedy, because of the concern in this case." Asserted Abernathy, "He has won my vote and, I believe, the vote of every colored person in America."[83] The prominent African American social psychologist Kenneth Clark also switched to Kennedy, as did the previously skeptical James Hicks of the *New York Amsterdam News*, who told readers, "I left my friends and went AWOL from the Democratic Party in 1956 when Eisenhower persuaded me to go over the hill with him—but I'm rejoining my company on November 8—simply because the last four years have been the most dissatisfied four years of my life." For Hicks, Nixon's silence regarding King was the last straw, and while he wasn't "so dumb as to believe that Jack Kennedy was sitting up nights losing any sleep over Rev. King being in jail," the phone call was "a real human gesture" on the part of a

Democratic nominee who—unlike Nixon—at least had enough interest in the black vote to speak up.[84]

The Kennedy campaign did not leave the matter there, however, instead flooding northern African American communities with 2 million pamphlets titled "The Case of Martin Luther King." Louis Martin and the cadre of African American leaders who had joined the civil rights section of the campaign also sought to publicize Kennedy's role by contacting black newspaper editors across the country, including Hicks, who acknowledged as much in his column but contended, "It was a damn good story . . . whether it came from his advisors or not."[85]

The publicity blitz was effective. One letter writer told editors of the *Chicago Defender* that Kennedy's intervention had not simply "put an ease to the most troubled mind of the Negro" regarding his commitment to civil rights but even inspired among African Americans thoughts of having the candidate's name "inserted in some of their most famous ballads and spirituals."[86] On a less poetic but more politically consequential plane, black voters in the end sided overwhelmingly with Kennedy. The Massachusetts senator won nearly three quarters of the African American vote nationwide and recovered Democratic Party losses from the 1956 election. Given the very narrow margin of the popular vote totals, most analysts, including Thruston Morton, chairman of the Republican National Committee, contended that the margin and turnout among black voters had been essential to Kennedy's victory.[87]

Nearly all analysts identified the King intervention as pivotal, but Kennedy's greater overall willingness to confront the civil rights issue, beginning with the Democratic civil rights plank, was also critical. African American observers noted Nixon's persistent silence on the issue and his transparent attempts to lure white southern votes. A general frustration with the administration's civil rights inactivity also contributed to Kennedy's success with black voters. On election night at the Baby Grand in Harlem, comedian Nipsey Russell joked: "Eisenhower is my shepherd and already I am in want. He leadeth me beside the jimcrow busses of Alabama . . ."[88]

The religious faith of the Democratic candidate was also a factor in the African American vote, but the impact was less clear. Some news reports uncovered trepidation among African Americans, the vast majority of whom were Protestant, about the influence of Kennedy's Catholicism. It was a sentiment openly voiced by Martin Luther King Sr. before his full-throated endorsement of Kennedy.[89] Overall there is little evidence of significant anti-Catholicism among African American voters. To the contrary, some sources suggest that African Americans viewed Kennedy more sympathetically because of his religion and the discrimination American Catholics had historically faced, sometimes at the hands of the same tormentors. The *Washington Afro-American* editorialized: "Catholics constitute one of the largest minority groups in our country. If a member of the Catholic minority cannot be president simply because of his religion, what hope is there for equal rights and a square deal for smaller minority groups?" The editors endorsed Kennedy and asserted that his victory would mean "we shall have elected to the nation's highest office one who has felt the lash and sting of prejudice and can sympathize with others who suffer under its handicaps."[90]

Kennedy's Catholicism proved an even greater source of identification for two other racial minority groups the Democratic campaign targeted. While the African American civil rights movement was building new momentum in 1960, Mexican Americans were also struggling economically and socially at the dawn of the new decade, while receiving far less attention. About one third of all Mexican American families were living below the federal poverty line of $3,000 per year in 1960, and they faced unemployment rates twice those of whites.[91] In the late 1950s Mexican Americans in the southwestern United States formed their first regional and national political organizations. The Mexican American Political Association (MAPA) was founded in California, the Political Association of Spanish-Speaking Organizations (PASO) was formed in Texas, and the American Coordinating Council on Political Education (ACCPE) emerged in Arizona.

In Los Angeles a young organizer named César Chávez met with then prospective Democratic candidate John Kennedy in 1959 to discuss the work on registering Mexican American voters in East Los Angeles already under way. Chávez, who had been trained by legendary Chicago organizer Saul Alinsky, explained the plight of poor farm workers to the Massachusetts senator and made the case for a door-to-door grassroots effort across California. Chávez requested a continuing free hand in registration efforts, and Kennedy concurred. After Kennedy declared his candidacy, the campaign assigned staffer Carlos McCormick to promote interest in the formation of "Viva Kennedy" clubs in states with large Mexican American populations.[92] Albert Peña Jr., a Texas Democrat who would later play leading roles in both PASO and MAPA, agreed to help develop the Viva Kennedy effort as long as Mexican American leaders could work directly with the Kennedys and bypass the state party officials, who Peña said "always sell us down the river."[93] Robert Kennedy agreed, and the continued combination of grassroots organizing, the Viva Kennedy groups, and direct attention from both Kennedys helped generate overwhelming Mexican American support.[94] Nationwide, 85 percent of Mexican American voters pulled the lever for Kennedy; historian Ignacio García has contended that since the states with the largest Latino populations were among the most important on the electoral map, and those decided in Kennedy's favor went to him by the narrowest of margins (particularly Texas and Illinois), the Viva Kennedy effort was pivotal.[95] Robert Kennedy realized as much, and while such a historically slim margin allowed him the liberty of plausibly telling many groups they had made the difference, the campaign manager insisted to a Mexican journalist that it was "the votes of Mexican Americans and other Latin Americans in the United States" that put his brother in the White House.[96]

Kennedy's Catholicism was undoubtedly part of his appeal to Latino voters, the vast majority of whom shared his faith.[97] As César Chávez later said, "Every time that he got put down for being a Catholic this made points with the Mexicans."[98] Kennedy also ran up large majorities among predominantly Catholic Puerto Rican voters. Under the aegis of "The Puerto Rican New Deal Democratic Union," one Kennedy poster proclaimed that "a mammoth nationwide religious attack" was being waged against the Democratic nominee, and insisted that if religious division continued, "only the communists will win and all America will lose."[99]

The Puerto Rican presence in the U.S. electorate had grown exponentially through the postwar era, most prominently in New York City. Puerto Rican voter turnout had historically been low, but community leaders in New York mounted a 1960 registration drive seeking to double the number of voters to nearly one quarter of a million.[100] Robert Kennedy campaigned for his brother in Spanish Harlem in late August, promoting the possibility of Puerto Rican and Mexican American ambassadors to Latin American nations; promising a boost for the minimum wage, housing, and educational opportunities; and apologizing for his fumbling attempts to speak Spanish.[101] Puerto Ricans threw three quarters of their support to Adlai Stevenson in 1956, but Republicans mounted their first serious effort for the Puerto Rican vote in 1960, including a platform plank supporting Puerto Rican statehood.[102] John Kennedy would nevertheless run up a percentage slightly better than Stevenson's, but with more than twice the turnout, and the Puerto Rican vote helped Kennedy win New York comfortably.[103]

Kennedy's Catholicism was even part of the campaign's pitch to Native Americans. National Congress of American Indians (NCAI) official Frank

George campaigned for Kennedy in western states, contending that the Massachusetts senator would be sensitive to Native American needs because Irish Catholics had also faced discrimination.[104] It is unclear to what extent the message resonated, but the Kennedys followed a similar template with Native Americans as with other racial minority groups, including direct appeals to leaders, new voter registration drives, and the message that Kennedy, far better than Nixon, understood their excluded status in American life. No group faced greater economic challenges than Native Americans, and Kennedy courted Native voters by pledging that he was "intent on doing something about the conditions of poverty and disease which afflict so many."[105] He wrote to Oliver LaFarge, president of the Association on American Indian Affairs, promising a government that "discharges its moral obligation to our First Americans" by enacting programmatic help for "their health, education, and economic well-being."[106]

Racial minorities turned to John Kennedy in 1960 for a range of reasons, but as important as any other was their economic distress. Even in the booming economy of the 1950s racial minorities had shared little of the bounty, but an economic recession in 1960 was leaving them feeling the squeeze even more acutely.[107] "It costs more to live all the time," one Puerto Rican Kennedy supporter told a *New York Times* reporter. Said another, "Nixon talks about highways; Kennedy talks for more food, more jobs, more salary."[108] An African American pharmacist from Chicago's South Side said, "All of a sudden more and more people I see are for Kennedy . . . because they feel as if the Democrats will put employment back where it was before."[109] The *Wall Street Journal* interviewed hundreds of African Americans in northern cities and concluded that "only the upper-income, better educated minority is primarily concerned with civil rights," finding most blacks skeptical that either party would do much about that issue.[110] Lester Granger concurred, asserting, "Wise or misguided, the Negro vote was a bread-and-butter vote; it really declared to both candidates and their parties, 'We don't believe either of you is really sincere about civil rights and therefore we'll take ham-on-rye.'"[111]

Examining the issue from very different perspectives, both the business-oriented *Wall Street Journal* and the *Chicago Defender* concluded that African Americans, "like other underprivileged groups, tend to vote Democratic for economic reasons. This has been so ever since the FDR era."[112] The significance of Kennedy's wide margins of victory among racial minorities, however, was that there had been significant erosion of support in key components of the old New Deal coalition—particularly among racial minorities and working-class whites—and Kennedy was able to turn back the tide. Native Americans had voted as a bloc for Franklin Roosevelt and his "Indian New Deal," but they had no clearly defined allegiance to either major party in 1960, and while their turnout had historically been low, their vote totals had grown in the 1950s and shifted toward Eisenhower.

Not surprisingly, then, Kennedy deliberately ran as the heir to Franklin Roosevelt. The campaign bought newspaper advertisements in distressed areas such as West Virginia and urban African American communities declaring that Kennedy would be "A Leader Like Roosevelt," and regularly employing Rooseveltian rhetoric about the dangers of a government "frozen in the ice of its own indifference" to make the case for an activist presidency. Kennedy also ran a full-page advertisement in the New York Times in September proclaiming, "The great program started by Franklin D. Roosevelt in 1933 will be reborn with Johnson and Kennedy in 1961."[113]

In addition to racial minorities, the other key component of the New Deal coalition that had seen defections to Eisenhower was organized labor. But the recession and the growing sense that the Republican administration had done little for working-class Americans led organized labor to make what the New York Times called "the most intensive political drive in its history." The Times surveyed industrial centers across the country and uncovered deep-seated concern about unemployment. "Old Ike hasn't done me any good," a Pittsburgh machinist claimed. "My father is out of work in the coal mines; my two brothers are out of work in the steel mills and it looks like automation is going to knock me out of a job. We need a man with new ideas, and Kennedy's the man." In spite of Joseph Kennedy's fears that his sons' roles on the McClellan committee might hurt John Kennedy's 1960 presidential run, the candidate gained nearly the complete backing of organized labor. According to the New York Times, the nation's largest union, the AFL-CIO, "turned [its] offices into campaign headquarters for the Kennedy-Johnson ticket." The lone exception, not surprisingly, was the Teamsters Union, as Jimmy Hoffa declared that workers "would be better off" with Richard Nixon, who knew "what it means to be poor and to have to earn a living."[114]

In spite of his success among key components of the New Deal coalition, Kennedy as the new Roosevelt was an uneasy fit for some, particularly white liberals. The Kennedy patriarch was a lightning rod for those on the left, as Joseph Kennedy's high-profile departure from the Roosevelt administration over his opposition to U.S. involvement in World War II, and his rejection of expansive New Deal federal activism, rendered him a reactionary figure. The Kennedy family's association with Joseph McCarthy, along with John Kennedy's less than vigorous record on civil rights, also left real doubts in the mind of white liberals—including Eleanor Roosevelt herself—about the young senator's worthiness to assume the Roosevelt mantle. Over time and with a direct appeal on Kennedy's part, the former first lady modified her views somewhat and endorsed the nominee after the convention, telling fellow liberal Arthur Schlesinger Jr. that no one since her husband had "had the same vital relationship with crowds."[115]

There were of course many significant differences between Roosevelt's depression-era campaigns and the 1960 race, but despite the most obvious difference—economic deprivation as a mainstream condition as opposed to a marginal one—Kennedy made poverty an important issue in the fall campaign. The West Virginia primary had fixed a national spotlight on the existence of poverty, and Kennedy did not leave the problem in the Mountain State, pointing to it as a key domestic example of the Eisenhower administration's drift and the need to "get the country moving again."[116] Over the summer he stepped up his legislative activities in the Senate, cosponsoring an amendment to a health care bill for elderly Americans that would not require them to establish their destitution, saving them "the humiliation of a pauper's oath." He also called for raising the minimum wage and stated, "We can no longer tolerate growing patches of poverty and injustice in America—substandard wages, unemployment, city slums . . . and the sad plight of migratory workers." At a twenty-fifth anniversary commemoration of the Social Security Act in August, Kennedy called for a new "war on poverty."[117]

In September the Democratic candidate declared that the next president "must assert leadership on three fronts" in his first ninety days in office. The first was action on national defense, the second was a foreign aid program in concert with the United Nations to assist in regional development and contain the lure of communism, and the third was "an all-out attack on poverty" with the goal of wiping it out. Kennedy placed the issue in the context of the cold war struggle as well, as evidence "to prove to a watching world that we are the wave of the future."[118] The *Washington Post* editorialized that while the call for increased defense capabilities might have been expected, "the most significant part of the address was Mr. Kennedy's willingness to look critically at the remaining hard problems of poverty in this affluent society," which the *Post* called "a reproach to the national conscience."[119]

At stop after stop on the campaign trail, local political leaders asked the candidate to discuss job losses and area redevelopment legislation, to the point where Kennedy remarked to an aide, "Isn't there any place in the country that is not a depressed area?"[120] According to one study the Democratic candidate raised the issue of area redevelopment over sixty times, and the issue continued to provide a clear line of attack on what he called "Republican indifference and neglect."[121] During the first televised debate, Kennedy recounted the story of children saving some of their school lunches to bring home to parents inadequately nourished by the Agriculture Department's surplus commodities program, and on another occasion Kennedy and Nixon sparred over the issue of hunger in America.[122] When Kennedy charged that 17 million people went to bed hungry on a nightly basis, Nixon dismissed the accuracy of the claim and called it "grist for the Communist propaganda mill."[123]

In the end, the recession and Kennedy's emphasis on economic issues played a vital role in his very narrow Election Day triumph. The coincidence of his West Virginia experience and the national economic slowdown was pivotal. Aside from its effectiveness as a political issue, the candidate remained troubled by what he had seen, telling aide Richard Goodwin in the middle of the campaign: "You can't imagine how those people live down there. I was better off in the war than they are in those coal mines. It's not right. I'm going to do something about it. If we make it."[124]

After the election Kennedy did take immediate steps on the issue, convening a group of government, business, and labor leaders to provide recommendations for action to deal with chronic unemployment in stagnant regional economies within sixty days. Paul Douglas of Illinois, an economist and author of the most recent depressed areas legislation, chaired the committee, which was subdivided into seven separate areas of inquiry, with one subcommittee looking specifically at the problems of West Virginia. On the recommendation of Douglas's group, Kennedy's first executive order, issued the day after the inauguration, called for an expansion of the nation's surplus commodities program, to distribute "to all needy families a greater variety and quantity of food out of our agricultural abundance."[125]

Most mainstream journalistic accounts focused on other storylines, and historical interpretations of the 1960 campaign have minimized the significance of domestic issues aside from civil rights, but the issue of poverty was central to the outcome of the presidential election, as poor Appalachian whites and economically oppressed racial minorities provided the margins Kennedy needed for victory. For the broad majority of Americans still enjoying the abundance of the postwar economic boom, the issue was brought home in a striking way on Thanksgiving Day, as legendary newsman Edward R. Murrow presented a haunting network television documentary on the plight of migrant farm workers, titled *Harvest of Shame*. Middle-class viewers were shocked. Even before the issue became a matter of wider public discussion, Americans who shared the lot of those in the report had already found grounds for optimism about the incoming administration.[126]

Robert Kennedy's role in that administration remained indeterminate for weeks after the election. In an attempt to hear multiple perspectives, John Kennedy would forgo the selection of a White House chief of staff, a gatekeeper post that Eisenhower had used to great effect. It was commonly understood, however, that access to Robert Kennedy was as good as access to the president. Among those who sought out the president's brother in the weeks before Inauguration Day was the octogenarian John L. Lewis, hoping to persuade the new administration to move boldly to shore up the coal economy of Appalachia. After spending half of his life as president of the United Mine Workers of America, Lewis had stepped down months earlier. The labor reporter Victor Riesel highlighted the significance of the event. "Two eras met for a few hours," Riesel wrote, noting that Lewis's first encounter with a new Democratic administration had taken place twenty-seven years earlier at the dawn of the New Deal.[127]

Robert Kennedy initially resisted his brother's insistence that he serve as attorney general in the new administration. Historically the post was a plum awarded to the president's campaign manager, and to a certain extent Joseph Kennedy saw it as a reward for Robert Kennedy's devotion.[128] But the president-elect also wanted his brother in the position so he might remain his closest confidant while wielding real power. Robert Kennedy harbored well-founded fears about charges of nepotism and inexperience, and he worried about negative reaction from civil libertarians and union leaders who found his past activities unacceptable. His appointment in late December 1960 did provoke a strong reaction, but he was nevertheless confirmed without difficulty.

Robert Kennedy's other concern about heading the Justice Department was its orientation in the eye of the largest unresolved storm of the Eisenhower years: civil rights. A United Press International story on New Year's Eve 1960 suggested that given the Democratic platform and the Kennedys' "expected fight for Negro rights," some concerned Democrats believed that "Bobby's part in future civil rights cases might turn the South against him and the incoming president." One stated flatly, "Mark my words, the name Kennedy is going to become anathema in the South."[129]

Others were invigorated by the coming challenge. Chief among these, predictably, were those in the campaign's civil rights section. Even though Louis Martin joked that the new president was going to have a hard time getting Congress "to pass a Mother's Day resolution" (along with Kennedy's narrow margin, the Democrats actually lost twenty House seats and one Senate seat), he was eager to contribute to the first administration that seemed likely to make major strides on civil rights in his lifetime. Martin had confessed occasional doubts about Robert Kennedy, but when the campaign manager woke him in the dead of a late October night to inform him of his intercession in the King case, the stunned publisher bestowed on the young Irishman a new title: "honorary brother."[130] Kennedy enjoyed the appellation; but over the next three years, competing fraternal obligations—old and new—would pull him in different directions. The tug-of-war and the bruising clashes ahead would forge for him a new popular reputation and a new national role.

2

AT THE FULCRUM OF THE MOVEMENT

DECIDING TIME

America at the dawn of the rumbling upheaval of the 1960s, many observers have noted, looked no different from the seemingly conformist, carefree country of the 1950s. Cultural styles, social mores, even the parameters of the mainstream political spectrum—what has been called the postwar liberal consensus—remained static upon John Kennedy's ascent to the White House.[1] Increasingly, however, a central element of the divide that would rend the fabric of the nation was becoming manifest. The United States was on the verge of something approaching a second civil war, and strange, sporadic new kinds of skirmishes were multiplying, erupting on such mundane battlefields as cafeterias, public beaches, and Greyhound buses.[2] Nonviolent offensives were led by young African Americans, and their efforts met with stiff resistance and sometimes bloody reprisals. The civil rights movement entered a new phase in the first years of the decade, as these protesters wrested command on the front lines of the struggle away from established organizations. In the eyes of these emerging grassroots leaders, it was deciding time. At mass meetings the Freedom Singers of the Student Nonviolent Coordinating Committee (SNCC) resuscitated the labor anthem of Kentuckian Florence Reece, soulfully importuning, "Which Side Are You on Boy, Which Side Are You On?"

The sit-in movement seized the nation's attention in an electrifying (and to some frightening) new way in 1960, and it would send a youthful charge through the rest of the decade, exemplified by the attachment of the suffix "-in" to countless forms of protest that followed.[3] Even more important than this tactical innovation was the larger social momentum of the African American civil rights movement, which would serve as the leading edge of other freedom struggles. Marginalized groups in American society—particularly other racial minorities that had been laboring mightily for decades to gain their own leverage—looked on with great interest and sought to create, in the wake of African American successes, a broader "rights revolution."[4]

Upon reluctantly accepting the post of attorney general, Robert Kennedy stepped into the pivotal space where the burgeoning civil rights movement would have its primary interaction with the federal government, as it pressed for—among many other goals—integration of public accommodations in the South and a hastening of the enforcement of school desegregation ordered by the Supreme Court's *Brown v. Board of Education* decision seven years earlier. Movement leaders recognized that the Court decision (and its reaffirmation one year later) basically brought one branch of the federal government over to their side. To achieve its political objectives fully, however, the movement needed the other two. Given the considerable entrenched power of segregationist southern Democrats and their strident pledge of massive resistance to the *Brown* decision, civil rights strategists recognized that securing legislation from Congress would be a tall order. Their hopes thus turned to the presidency. Enforcement of the order lay in the power of the executive, as did a key role in supporting the legislation that would be necessary to desegregate public accommodations in the South. Perhaps most important, the modern presidency had become a "bully pulpit" beyond anything Theodore Roosevelt likely imagined. From the New Deal onward, the American people increasingly looked to the White House for social, cultural, and even moral direction.

Through the mid-1950s the moderation and color-blind rhetoric of Dwight Eisenhower as the standard-bearer of the party of Lincoln, to at least a growing number of African Americans, seemed a plausible alternative to the posture of the Democratic Party, which had countenanced so many signatories to the segregationist Southern Manifesto.[5] Nevertheless, in spite of his decision to use federal power in the integration of Little Rock Central High School and his support for the Civil Rights Act of 1957, Eisenhower's gradualist approach and his extreme reluctance either to condemn racial violence or to intervene in the South in any way soon exasperated both movement leaders and blacks in general, who came to see his presidency as more of an obstacle than an aid.[6] "President Eisenhower was a fine general and a good, decent man," Roy Wilkins said, "but if he had fought World War II the way he fought for civil rights, we would all be speaking German today."[7] The *Washington Afro-American* editorialized in 1960 that Eisenhower had "allowed too many golden opportunities to escape him during the past eight years," leaving African Americans "to depend upon the Supreme Court to secure and preserve our liberties." Eisenhower's successor, the *Afro* insisted, "must be no middle of the roader."[8] After decades of heartache and struggle, there seemed to have been real progress and validation with the *Brown* ruling, and marking time no longer seemed an option. You were with the movement or against it. It was deciding time.

The Kennedys had waded into the politics of civil rights warily, seeking to preserve the tenuous intraparty balance Robert Kennedy had spelled out to the Georgia Democratic Party secretary before calling the presiding judge in the King case. Given the dynamics of the fall campaign, they were able to pull off the high-wire act, winning Georgia by an even larger margin than Kennedy's home state of Massachusetts. As was the case with other minority groups, the election's outcome and the attention paid to their concerns heartened African Americans, and this was reflected in optimistic forecasts in black publications. The *Chicago Defender* predicted that Kennedy would be a "great president," and the popular monthly magazine *Ebony* proclaimed that "a vast majority" of African Americans expected "the most encouraging period for racial progress in U.S. history."[9] Reporter Edward Peeks of the *Washington Afro-American* was convinced that Kennedy's campaign demonstrated he could "handle Dixie," calling his intervention for King "a first rate political action" which showed "there are ways to make reluctant Southern Democrats join the march ahead for human dignity and a better country. . . . More of the same should follow from action by the president-elect and his administration."[10] In spite of these euphoric hopes for a new consensus, on the issue of civil rights there would soon no longer be a center in the Democratic Party that could hold. It would again be deciding time.

Robert Kennedy appeared to have little relevant transferable experience for his new and monumental task as the operational arm of the White House on civil rights. The *California Eagle* was leery of the appointment, given the younger Kennedy's nonexistent civil rights record and his only apparent qualification for the office: his tenure as counsel for "bitter-end segregationist" John McClellan's committee. But the paper held out hope that the new attorney general would "tackle the civil rights problems with the vigor for which he has been so widely acclaimed."[11] Through the 1960 campaign Robert Kennedy had certainly developed political sensitivities to the complex national contours of the struggle, and it is fair to say that at the outset his primary goal was to contain the explosive issue politically, with the hope of sustaining the electoral balance the campaign had struck so successfully in the fall. But as the new attorney general prepared to take office, it was clear that African American grassroots leaders were not interested in bolstering the administration by opting for renewed incrementalism after the dynamic sit-in movement of the previous year. The incoming administration was joining a battle already in progress, and even though the Kennedys had garnered sufficiently greater sympathy from the majority of African Americans than had Richard Nixon and the Republican Party for the purpose of pulling a lever in the voting booth, movement leaders at all levels retained the initiative in their fight for equal opportunity.

Much excellent scholarship has been produced assessing the Kennedys' actions, motives, tactics, and vision on civil rights, the single most important domestic matter with which the administration was confronted.[12] Political historians have skillfully analyzed White House and Justice Department decision making and the reactions of major civil rights leaders. The focus here is instead on how African Americans more broadly viewed the Kennedys, with particular attention to the attorney general, through this critical period. The views of both the commanders and the nonviolent foot soldiers of the civil rights battles in the South sometimes varied significantly from the views of those at a distance, so it is important to consider African American perspectives during this critical period through a wider-angle lens.[13] In the longer term of Robert Kennedy's career, particularly as he sought African American votes outside the South and moved to address the economic aspect of the fight for equality, those popular perspectives are essential to understanding his historical significance on the mass political level.

Even more broadly, Robert Kennedy's highly visible role in directing federal efforts on civil rights in the South during the early 1960s was critical to his emergence as a champion of racial minorities and the poor in the later phases of the growing movement for equal opportunity in American life. His attorney generalship came during the key moment when that larger social revolution was reaching a tipping point. In a fascinating early 1962 editorial titled "All the Natives Are Restless," *Ebony* magazine contended: "The Negro is not the only native dissatisfied with his lot. All over the world political, ethnic [and] religious minorities are demanding more cake from the table, less crumbs from the floor. . . . All of the natives not accepted into American life are dissatisfied with anything short of full integration, so they are moving off the reservations, away from their islands and out of the ghettos."[14] Because this emerging rights revolution was inspired and informed by the black freedom struggle, Robert Kennedy's relationship with the civil rights movement would be pivotal in shaping his political image for the rest of his career. In part because he gained a large measure of credibility with African Americans, Kennedy developed unique political cachet with other excluded groups struggling to emulate their successes.

Definitively assessing popular opinion is always challenging for historians. While opinion polls were emerging in modern form during the 1950s and 1960s, relatively less polling data was gathered from African American and other minority communities. Aside from such polls, the most incisive instruments for gauging widely held perspectives are African American publications, particularly newspapers. These were the primary communications organs of African American communities, and while they were published in cities, the immediacy of migrations from the rural South kept them closely tied to events there.[15] Northern and western cities would also serve as Robert Kennedy's eventual political base, and the evolving attitudes of urban African Americans during this period are critical to understanding his later popularity. Although newspapers have their limits as indicators of public opinion and must be used with care—publishers, editors, and reporters are always subject to relationships, influence, and alliances—a survey of African American newspapers reveals remarkably consistent perspectives. In spite of the fact that the Kennedy White House was as media savvy as any in American history— Louis Martin was continuing to court black editors, and Robert Kennedy cultivated relationships with the African American press—African American newspapers were independent enough to fervidly praise and yet harshly criticize the administration.[16] The attorney general would be subjected to unremitting, unvarnished assessment, and his treatment by the African American press would both reflect and help shape his compelling political relationship with African Americans in the trial by fire of this crucial period.

Louis Lautier was one of the most respected African American journalists in the United States in the early 1960s. He had been reporting from the nation's capital since the late 1940s, was the first African American to be named to the National Press Club in 1956, and published a column syndicated in many black newspapers. A lifelong Republican, Lautier offered measured criticism of John Kennedy during the presidential campaign, and he remained skeptical as the new administration prepared to take office. Commenting on the attorney general designate's confirmation hearings, Lautier wrote that Robert Kennedy "was very cautious and dexterous" in answering the few civil rights questions he received, and "was not reassuring that he would be a crusader." Lautier nevertheless remained hopeful that Kennedy's past zeal in chasing "organized crime, corruption, and racketeering . . . will be transferred to the field of civil rights."[17]

Lautier's critical analysis incisively pinpointed the Kennedy approach to civil rights in the administration's opening months. The Kennedy blueprint, Lautier wrote, was to "reward colored Democrats with good political appointments, upgrade colored personnel in the classified civil service, make special efforts to recruit colored personnel for civil service jobs, hit racial segregation and discrimination wherever it can be hit by executive action, enforce federal court orders in school desegregation cases, and more against deprivation of voting rights."[18] The strategy had been crafted by Harris Wofford with an eye to John Kennedy's razor-thin margin of victory; as Wofford later contended, "the approach was designed to build the precarious coalition between northern Democrats and moderate southern Democrats that Kennedy needed to get programs through Congress and to be re-elected."[19] Emphasizing litigation along with both executive and administrative efforts to integrate fields within the president's direct purview was a course designed to generate important but relatively low-risk achievements while eschewing legislative proposals or other forms of intervention that would more directly threaten the entire system of southern segregation.

At the same time, Robert Kennedy decided to send a clear signal to white southerners about where the administration stood on civil rights while inviting them to reconsider the issue in a larger frame. He delivered his first formal address as attorney general on Law Day at the recently desegregated University of Georgia. Kennedy broke the tension by expressing appreciation for his brother's margin of victory in the state and joking: "The last attorney general who came down into the South . . . hid in a plane in South Carolina. That wasn't very successful . . . so I'm trying the other approach." He presented the administration's perspective on civil rights as a matter of law enforcement, noting the southern reverence for duty and law, and depersonalizing the issue by stating that he agreed with the *Brown* decision, but "my belief does not matter. It is now the law." Kennedy also attempted to link civil rights to the cold war consensus, even proclaiming that the eventual graduation of recently admitted students Charlayne Hunter and Hamilton Holmes would, by affirming the American promise for peoples of color in emerging nations, "aid and assist the fight against communist political infiltration, and even guerrilla warfare." Ultimately, however, the attorney general's message was clear and divisive. "You may ask, will we enforce the civil rights statutes?" the attorney general said. "The answer is yes, we will."[20]

The speech was yet another attempt to sustain the implausible Massachusetts-Georgia axis that the administration hoped to expand, and for a brief moment it seemed to work. Anthony Lewis of the *New York Times* reported that 1,600 law students and alumni "sat in silence through remarks about Negro rights. But at the end there was enthusiastic applause that lasted thirty seconds."[21] Northern African American observers commended Kennedy even more wholeheartedly. The *New York Amsterdam News* reported that the attorney general had used "firm language in a voice that was even firmer as he spoke," and noted that a group of prominent Harlem lawyers had sent him a congratulatory telegram, one of hundreds Louis Martin said had been pouring in to the Democratic National Committee.[22] NAACP leaders also hailed the address for its "sweep and emphasis."[23]

Other African American leaders endeavoring to effect integration in the South outside the more conservative and conventional means of litigation were also pleased with the administration's tone. The Reverend Fred Shuttlesworth of Birmingham, Alabama—the most racially volatile city in the South—was a longtime advocate of direct action protest and an important leader in Martin Luther King Jr.'s Southern Christian Leadership Conference. In the spring of 1961 Shuttlesworth wrote that "segregationists find no hint of compromise" in the new administration, and declared that John Kennedy "has, it seems, committed his administration to the business of at least moving ahead." Nevertheless, Shuttlesworth cautioned newspaper readers, "this is not to praise Kennedy too highly. . . . [I]t may be too much to expect Kennedy to be a cure all and do all. The basic job is ours to do." Shuttlesworth was no doubt mindful of plans under way to conduct interracial protests on buses traveling through the heart of the South when he wrote: "We shall see what we shall see. . . . [O]ur prayers and hopes ride with this administration."[24]

Already working their way south from the nation's capital as the attorney general spoke in Georgia, the Freedom Rides would prove the first major test of the Kennedys' willingness to intervene more directly in the South. The protests were designed by CORE to create political pressure by exposing segregation in bus terminals throughout the Jim Crow region. The rides were the last thing the Kennedys wanted as they sought to preserve hard-won trust in the South. An angry John Kennedy told Harris Wofford: "Stop them! Get your friends off those buses."[25] Robert Kennedy's response demonstrated the ad hoc crisis management approach that would be repeated and honed over the next three years as civil rights movement leaders sought to maintain the momentum of the sit-ins and press their advantage through further direct action protests. His handling of the Freedom Rides would also prove the political antipode of his Georgia speech, diminishing the attorney general in the eyes of many white southerners and African Americans alike. For one of the two constituencies, the damage would prove far more irreparable.

As incensed white mobs mercilessly pummeled the Freedom Riders, firebombed a bus, and threatened to overrun a church where African American supporters had massed, Kennedy reflexively decided that intervention was his only option. With local law enforcement missing in action, he attempted to find a kind of middle path by using U.S. marshals rather than federal troops to protect the protesters, but he pledged his full assistance in extricating the riders trapped in Birmingham. The attorney general upbraided a Greyhound representative for the bus company's inability or unwillingness to provide a driver to move the protesters out of the state, and sent a personal emissary, John Seigenthaler, to negotiate their departure. The situation soon became dramatically more unstable, as Seigenthaler was knocked unconscious by a pipe-wielding segregationist, and more civil rights protesters rallied to the cause—as had occurred during the sit-in movement a year earlier—and boarded southbound buses.

After intense lobbying efforts with Alabama governor John Patterson and Mississippi senator James Eastland, Robert Kennedy was able to shield the first group of riders from further violent attacks, but subsequent developments yielded a bitter political harvest. A transcript of his discussion with the Greyhound representative was circulated widely and seemed to implicate the administration, in the eyes of white southerners, as co-conspirators in the Freedom Rides. "That was damaging," Kennedy later said. "I never recovered from it."[26] But when the besieged attorney general called for a "cooling-off period" and a moratorium on further rides, urging "all persons in Alabama and elsewhere to use restraint and weigh their actions carefully" in light of both the threat of violence and the perception of the events overseas as President Kennedy prepared to meet with Nikita Khrushchev in Vienna, African Americans were even more outraged.[27]

Black newspapers uniformly blasted the attorney general. A *Washington Afro-American* political cartoon depicted Kennedy whispering, "Cool off, man! Cool off!" in the ear of a black Freedom Rider being kicked into submission by a cigar-chomping white southerner. The paper called the attorney general's request "disappointing advice," and after praising Kennedy for sending in federal marshals, said he was like "a man who kicks over the pail after milking the cow."[28] The drama of events and the passion over their significance invited multiple metaphors. James Hicks of the *New York Amsterdam News* compared Kennedy's request to asking one's wife for a temporary divorce in order to cavort with prostitutes. Calling it "the most insulting proposition which a high government official has ever made to a group of freedom-loving Americans," Hicks charged Kennedy with suggesting that African Americans "momentarily violate and desert all the sanctity of their citizenship and enter into an illicit, unholy, un-American relationship with a minority of cutthroats and disrespectful thugs who are prostituting the accident of birth as white Americans." He concluded that the Freedom Rides "MUST and WILL go on even if they ride Robert Kennedy into oblivion."[29] Louis Lautier criticized the attorney general for failing to "see the struggle in its true perspective," contending that "the fight of colored people for first-class citizenship is more than something which can have an injurious effect upon the talks of President Kennedy. . . . [T]he very survival of the United States may depend upon the outcome of this fight."[30]

Ordinary African Americans were upset as well. The *Pittsburgh Courier* queried city residents about Kennedy's statement, and while some found it reasonable—local entertainer "Shorts" Davis said, "It would be a good idea to go along with the Attorney General, I think, because his brother, President Kennedy, seems to be on our side"—more respondents agreed with security officer George Christian, who said: "I figure like this—if they cool off now, they will never get started again."[31] A New York City mother named Cora Walker was disgusted by the entire situation, and shared a deeply personal story with readers of the *Amsterdam News*. Unable to explain to her sons *Life* magazine's "gruesome pictures" of bloodied Freedom Riders, she wrote, "When the boys began to fire questions at me, such as 'Where were the police? Do they have telephones down there? Weren't there any police on duty that day?' I was speechless." Magnifying her frustration, the incident was closely followed by a news report of the attorney general's prediction on Voice of America that blacks were making swift progress, potentially culminating in an African American president forty years hence. In light of events in Alabama, she called the proclamation "sheer mockery" and insisted: "We can no longer stand on the sidelines and mumble to ourselves. We must yell from the rooftops."[32]

The Freedom Rides marked a generational awakening for others. In a powerful column James Hicks acknowledged that young people had taken the lead in the civil rights movement and made the case that it was deciding time for their elders:

> Our kids started out fighting the Eastlands and the Pattersons in Mississippi and Alabama. They were the bad guys and we, as parents, said "Hooray!" and the "good" white guys egged us on. But now the fight has led to the door of John F. and Robert Kennedy and they are the "good" white people. And now that the fight is at the door of Good Guy Robert Kennedy he has snapped his finger to you and me and said: "Okay— that's enough now! If you keep on fighting you will embarrass ME!" And when he said that both you and I at first reacted like we have reacted for 40 years—we stopped short like trained animals—because we simply have been brainwashed to react to "good" white people like Pavlov's dog. But our kids just kept on fighting like Hell, because to them Robert Kennedy was simply another white man who pulls on his pants one leg at a time like everyone else. . . .
>
> So what happens? Our children are sitting in a Mississippi jail still fighting, by starving themselves inside the jail, and Bob Kennedy is standing on the steps of the White House demanding that we use our paternal love to persuade or force our children to give up the fight so that he and his brother won't be embarrassed. And you—where are you . . . ? I'll tell you where you are—you are walking around like a schizophrenic patsy—trying to make up your mind whether to crush your child in a Mississippi jail and make Robert Kennedy happy—or crush him to your bosom and let Robert Kennedy and all the rest of the Kennedys stew in the juice the good white people and the bad white people both brewed. You've got to make a choice. I've made mine. I'm "rewashing" my brain. I'm sticking with my kids—and letting the chips fall where they may!"[33]

The Freedom Rides thus spurred the first serious reevaluation of the Kennedys on the part of African Americans. It exposed Robert Kennedy's template for federalism on civil rights, which gave maximum latitude to local and state officials. To many civil rights leaders and other observers such as Hicks, the Kennedy approach smacked of more delay and gradualism. Journalist Victor Navasky later noted that the attorney general applied this model of federalism inconsistently, contending that when Robert Kennedy "wanted to do something specific he had no hesitation," but that the default position of the Justice Department was to deny that "it had legal power to do what one or another civil rights organization demanded, only to confound the civil rights community some months later by doing it."[34] Conversely, on an issue in which presidential prerogative was not subject to the constraints of this model of federalism—an executive order regarding federal housing on which John Kennedy had promised swift action during the campaign—the White House stalled. For a growing number of frustrated observers within the movement, administration priorities seemed to be guided by a sliding scale of political calculations.

While the attorney general respected the courage of the young people James Hicks so admired, he viewed their activities primarily as a grave political threat. The Kennedys, only a year removed from their tutorials under Harris Wofford and Louis Martin, did not yet fully recognize the magnitude of the tectonic social shift that was taking shape in the United States. Even as it began to give way in the spring of 1961, both the attorney general and the president were attempting to keep one foot on either side of the racial fault line, which bisected their own base of political power. Both men were inclined to attribute the volcanic eruption in the South to the civil rights protesters rather than to segregationist southern whites, and they were eager to praise any signs of southern moderation. Over time their mistrust of the young activists manifested itself in various ways. The attorney general made time to attend the conferences of African American fraternities and professional organizations throughout 1961, but a conspicuous scheduling conflict prevented his accepting an invitation to speak at the SNCC convention the following spring. On one occasion an angry John Kennedy charged that SNCC leaders had "an investment in violence" and privately called them "sons of bitches."[35]

The feeling was mutual during the heated events in the summer months of 1961. CORE and SNCC leaders took umbrage at the administration's inability to recognize the essential nature of the problem, and at what some believed to be the cheap backroom political tactics the attorney general employed to defuse it. When Robert Kennedy invited representatives of the two organizations to his Justice Department office, he offered draft exemptions to young civil rights activists who would turn their efforts toward voter registration and away from direct action protest. For CORE leader James Farmer—jailed with Freedom Riders in Mississippi at the time—this was beyond the pale. According to Farmer's post mortem, which circulated among movement leaders, the attorney general asked: "'Why don't you guys cut out all that shit, Freedom Riding and sitting-in shit, and concentrate on voter education.' Says, 'If you do that I'll get you a tax exemption.' That cold-blooded." The confab between the youthful attorney general and the young leaders of CORE and SNCC grew so tense that in the telling of some observers, fisticuffs nearly ensued.[36]

The administration was indeed deliberately trying to channel the zeal of movement leaders into what appeared to be the less confrontational field of voter registration. The tax exemption Farmer referred to was actually directed toward the creation of a new nonpartisan organization launched by the administration, called the Voter Education Project (VEP). The umbrella organization was an attempt to bring the three civil rights organizations geared toward direct action protest—SCLC, CORE, and SNCC—into a partnership with the NAACP and the National Urban League, with the administration promising resources (through alliances with private foundations) and, many civil rights leaders presumed, protection.[37] The president and the attorney general undoubtedly desired the multiple political benefits that could accrue both to the White House and to other liberals with increased African American numbers on the voting rolls, but the strategy wasn't entirely a reaction to the Freedom Rides. The Kennedys, in the words of Victor Navasky, "focused on the franchise as the open-sesame to all other rights," and the Justice Department had already been working on voting rights cases by the spring of 1961.[38] While some saw it as an attempt to buy them off, other civil rights leaders, including Martin Luther King Jr., recognized the potential of the project and supported it. SNCC itself joined in August 1961, as leaders such as Robert Moses understood that whatever the administration's motives, the resources the VEP might provide could help them continue the essential work of building grassroots political power.[39]

The attorney general's private reaction to African American criticism in the spring and summer of 1961 is not entirely clear, but his public actions were responsive. In addition to Justice Department efforts to cobble together the VEP, Kennedy delivered a measure of justice to the Freedom Riders through legal channels, announcing in September that the entire bus-burning mob had been apprehended. More significantly, after Kennedy heeded Martin Luther King's novel suggestion that he petition the Interstate Commerce Commission, the agency announced its ruling in late September that all terminals and interstate buses were to be integrated.[40]

In spite of their extreme dismay over his attempt to quell the direct action initiatives of the Freedom Riders in the heat of the struggle, African American commentators reassessed the attorney general in the wake of his subsequent activity. The *Washington Afro-American* editorialized in the fall of 1961 that Kennedy had been "virtually drummed out of the ranks of those we considered our friends. But, he promised that he would take action, and he did. In so doing, he kept faith with 18,000,000 American colored people."[41] Jackie Robinson, who had sparred with Robert Kennedy a year earlier, wrote that he was "deeply impressed with the younger Kennedy's obvious dedication to the elimination of discrimination . . . and, more important, with his courage in backing up that dedication with action." The baseball legend called the attorney general "Our Big Stick," and even suggested that the "cooling-off" statement had been imposed on him by the president, since "he didn't even offer it with the conviction which is so characteristic of him."[42]

Robinson noted the beginnings of what was a subtle but deliberate decoupling of the president and the attorney general on civil rights, with Robert Kennedy recognizing that it might be politically helpful to serve as the shock absorber for his brother on the issue.[43] The good cop/bad cop routine had the desired result, as southern whites soon focused their hostility on the younger Kennedy. The virulently racist public safety commissioner of Birmingham, Bull Connor, publicly derided the attorney general as "that little ol' Bobby Sox"; Alabama segregationist George Wallace called him a "sapling Caesar"; and other administration foes referred to him as "Raoul," a reference to Fidel Castro's younger brother.[44] In 1962 a member of the New Orleans White Citizens' Council sought retribution through reverse Freedom Rides, offering southern blacks a free one-way bus ticket to northern destinations, including Hyannis Port, Massachusetts, site of the Kennedy compound. When the attorney general condemned the stunt as "a disgrace" and "deplorable," the project's initiator said, "I don't know why Bobby Kennedy was so upset," noting that Kennedy had been "busy in Washington last year directing freedom rides through southern states."[45]

Conversely, given the ultimate success of the Freedom Rides and apparent progress in the field of voter registration, by the end of 1961 the attorney general was being recognized by African American commentators as the administration's "good cop." Wyatt Tee Walker of the SCLC named him "the American of the year" for giving "clear evidence that his department means business." The *New York Amsterdam News* congratulated him "for the relentless way he is using the power of his office to bring about fair play. . . . [W]e can almost say that oppressed minorities have found a new secret weapon to aid them in their fight." *Ebony* ran a glowing account of the attorney general's reception in Ivory Coast—publisher John H. Johnson was invited along for the trip—calling him "Mr. Civil Rights" and asserting that his "general acceptance stemming from officialdom down to the masses" proved that "as long as the U.S. continues to make gains clearing barriers of discrimination, its reputation in underdeveloped countries will not easily be changed by Russian propaganda. Because of his record in human relations, Attorney General Robert F. Kennedy appears to be one of the best ambassadors of good will the U.S. can send overseas."[46] At the same time, Chuck Stone, a brilliant young *Washington Afro-American* columnist unafraid to criticize the administration, defended the president against growing charges of temporizing, asserting that "with all of the historical, built-in limitations of the presidency as an office with shallow pretenses of honest-to-goodness executive powers, President Kennedy is doing a remarkably outstanding job."[47]

Thus by early 1962, despite a bruising first year in office, the administration's civil rights strategies were established and the Kennedys were widely regarded by African Americans as allies. Because of the hopes raised in their first year in office, African Americans continued to expect support from the White House. In the spring of 1962 the Southern Regional Council (SRC), an interracial civil rights organization, issued a one-year evaluation of the administration's record and concluded: "The executive branch has placed its power in support of civil rights. That power is immense." The council offered the balanced assessment that the White House and the Justice Department had "built momentum for civil rights into the structure and the policies of government," but nevertheless criticized the administration for failing to engage the next target toward which movement leaders were pressing: legislation to desegregate public accommodations.[48]

By the spring of 1962 a chorus of influential journalists added their voices to the critical portion of the SRC report. In his *Afro* column Chuck Stone questioned how badly the president wanted action on civil rights, and shortly before his death Louis Lautier charged that President Kennedy had "reneged on the sweeping promises of the Democratic platform and his own campaign pledges."[49] Lautier particularly criticized John Kennedy for the absence of legislative proposals, an as yet unfulfilled pledge for an executive order to desegregate federally aided housing, and a failure to enunciate the moral imperative of civil rights. The *California Eagle* of Loren Miller, who had successfully argued the *Barrows v. Jackson* Supreme Court case against restrictive racial covenants in housing a decade earlier, provided regular reminders that the administration had yet to fulfill the housing pledge Kennedy made during the 1960 campaign.[50]

Robert Kennedy also faced growing concerns among African Americans that racial violence in the South was again spiraling out of control, as well as questions about his willingness to use federal power to protect both African American residents and civil rights workers. Mississippi became the locus of much of this violence, in part because of local pushback against voter registration efforts stimulated by the VEP initiative. As voter registration efforts there and elsewhere accelerated, leaders on the ground grew frustrated with the lack of federal protection and implored the attorney general to fulfill the expectations raised at the launching of the project.[51] In the fall of 1961 NAACP field secretary Medgar Evers asked the attorney general and the president to come to Mississippi and investigate firsthand the "evil of segregation" and "make your pronouncements for what is right and wrong."[52] Over time, as the Justice Department continued to maintain that the federal government had to respect the jurisdiction of local law enforcement, the bitterness of civil rights workers grew. Suspending his entertainment career to work on registration efforts in Greenwood, Mississippi, comedian Dick Gregory charged that "if Bobby Kennedy or any of his family came down here painted black, they wouldn't send troops but missiles."[53]

The inability or unwillingness of Kennedy's Justice Department to press more aggressively for protection of voter registration workers created "a sense of betrayal," according to white civil rights leader Harold Fleming. The betrayal was rooted in the hopes the administration had engendered. "The climate was created not by the Kennedys with an intention to deceive, but by the ethos of the moment. The feeling was," Fleming later reflected, "after Ike, at least we'll have an activist Administration. We were all unsophisticated about power. We thought it was there to be used." Resistance to the extension of federal power, along with the physical violence from which they were left unprotected, inflicted other wounds on those struggling to improve conditions in the Deep South. "Not protecting the kids was more than a cold-blooded, calculated reckoning," according to Fleming. "It was bruising and deeply emotional. To have the FBI looking out of the courthouse windows while you were being chased down the street by brick throwers deeply offends the sensibilities. So people wept and cursed Robert Kennedy and Burke Marshall [head of the Justice

Department's Civil Rights Division] more than the FBI, whom they never had any confidence in to begin with."[54]

The disappointment was not limited to civil rights workers, and it had generational consequences that lasted beyond the Kennedy administration. A couple of years later Marian Wright, a young African American Yale Law School graduate working for the NAACP in Mississippi, read a story written by a nine-year-old girl in a Freedom School there. It was about a black girl named "Cinderlilly" who desperately wanted to go to the annual downtown ball attended by all the whites in town. Her mother tried to discourage her so her hopes would not be crushed, but the girl insisted she had invitations in the form of the Fourteenth Amendment and the Civil Rights Act of 1964. When the mother asked who would take her, Cinderlilly said, "Prince Charming, Bobby Kennedy, is going to take me. . . . I'm sure he's going to show up." The night of the ball, in Wright's telling, "Prince Charming called and said he couldn't come!" The deflated little girl found the resolve to go anyway, with her "invitations" in her pockets. After she got there and the door was finally opened, everyone simply laughed at her as she stood there crying. When Wright told then Senator Robert Kennedy the story a few years later, he was speechless.[55]

African American newspapers did not, for the most part, lambaste the attorney general for the difficulties facing civil rights workers on the ground in the South; the *Chicago Defender* instead recognized the attorney general for his leadership on other voting issues, including legislation to end literacy tests and poll taxes.[56] By the fall of 1962, however, the *Defender* contended that the pace of registration in the South was not markedly better than during the Eisenhower years. "Our leaders obviously were impressed by these assurances that they could quickly build up formidable power at the polls with government assistance," the *Defender* regretfully reported. "They agreed to concentrate their efforts on voter registration. The militant tactics that had caused anxieties in the White House were assigned secondary importance. With an important fall election upon us, the high hopes held out by the Administration have lost much of their glitter."[57]

Even as the program was initially proving less successful than expected at its stated task, the Kennedys' hopes that the VEP might guide the movement away from direct action protest were also dashed. Akin to coronary bypass surgery that increases blood flow through all the arteries rather than just through the alternative routing, the movement redoubled its efforts in all fields from late 1961 through 1963. The first major direct action campaign since the Freedom Rides emerged out of the voter registration efforts of SNCC workers in Albany, Georgia. Local law enforcement leaders proved adept at avoiding open mass confrontation—though violence and intimidation remained central to local white resistance—and the campaign there, which strove for desegregation on many fronts, did not lead to immediate breakthroughs. But the Albany movement and the failure of the Kennedy administration to provide protection there suggested to civil rights leaders that they would have to increase the pressure for political action, particularly for legislation to desegregate public accommodations. "This administration has reached out more creatively than its predecessors to blaze some new trails," said Martin Luther King, but he contended that its activity was "aggressively driving toward the limited goal of token integration."[58]

The most highly visible example of this symbolic integration occurred in the fall of 1962, when twenty-nine-year-old James Meredith, empowered by a federal court order, sought to become the first African American to attend the University of Mississippi. When Governor Ross Barnett vowed to bar Meredith's entry, the Kennedy Justice Department deployed all of its resources to facilitate his enrollment. A donnybrook ensued, as a seething mob massed on the campus and then began to riot. U.S. marshals and federal troops were both required to disperse the crowd, and in the melee two people were killed and 160 were injured. It was exactly the type of confrontation the administration had hoped to avoid. Once Meredith's registration was secured, the attorney general sought to recast the significance of the event, calling the incident an example of "a democratic nation putting its house in order." Meredith "brought to a head and lent his name to another chapter in the mightiest struggle of our time," said Kennedy, comparing his "faith and courage" to that of the nation's astronauts, and even improbably suggested that events in Oxford mirrored the recently defused Cuban Missile Crisis, calling each a clash between believers in "freedom and human dignity" and advocates for "the supremacy of the state."[59] (Medgar Evers also juxtaposed the two events, calling for a "quarantine" of Mississippi in the form of an economic boycott like the one against Cuba.)[60] Kennedy's reaction marked another stage in his evolution on the black freedom struggle. Rather than using cold war rhetoric to decelerate the civil rights movement, he recognized the early critique of Louis Lautier and others when he publicly declared that in the international fight for freedom, "what we do at home, in the final analysis, is just as important."[61]

In the aftermath of Oxford, African American leaders throughout the nation praised the attorney general's unmistakable application of federal power.[62] The *Chicago Defender* assessed overall civil rights progress in 1962 and declared that southern blacks were "moving on a broad front . . . to gain full stature. It is a campaign on political, economic, and cultural levels." The *Defender* pronounced the gap between African Americans and whites "narrower today than it has ever been before," reiterating, "We count on strong support from the government." A year after the *New York Amsterdam News* called Robert Kennedy the "secret weapon" of African Americans, the *Defender* asserted that his Justice Department "makes no secret of its determination to stand behind the Negro drive to get the right to vote everywhere."[63]

Two years into his tenure as attorney general, African Americans had experienced and expressed a wide range of emotions and opinions toward Robert Kennedy, who was the face of the administration on civil rights. As the battle over Jim Crow became a multi-front war, the attorney general became progressively aware of the impossibility of remaining an honest broker between southern Democrats and African Americans. His public statements emphasized that the status quo was unsustainable. Kennedy acknowledged both the danger and the hypocrisy of the racial situation in the United States, including de facto segregation in the North, calling it a "time bomb" and a potential "disaster," on one occasion asserting, "Our country means nothing if we treat a portion of our people as inferiors."[64]

Robert Kennedy's understanding of the full toll of racism and segregation had not yet reached maturity by early 1963, but at the beginning of the final year of his brother's presidency, most African Americans remained convinced—in spite of serious disappointments—that both the attorney general and the president were firmly on their side, and were increasingly treating blacks as full political partners. On the centennial of the Emancipation Proclamation, Louis Martin suggested another symbolic gesture, inviting hundreds of African American leaders to a White House party—what would be the largest single gathering of African Americans there in history—for Lincoln's birthday. Aside from the political gamesmanship of appropriating the occasion from the Republicans, Martin hoped it would send the message that "if the president and first lady could entertain black guests in their home, who were the whites who felt blacks were socially unacceptable in *their* homes?"[65] While some black writers minimized the event as still another example of tokenism, the *Washington Afro-American*—the newspaper with the most proximate read on the social impact of the White House gala—editorialized that "a White House reception doesn't make us more equal. But it does set a precedent. It does break a barrier and it did give many, many people a feeling of what the Rev. Martin Luther King Jr. has called 'somebodyness.' And it is this feeling of 'somebodyness' which President Kennedy, like President Lincoln, has done much to develop."[66] The degree of comfort both John and Robert Kennedy felt with African Americans on a social level reinforced this new sense of dignity that black publications lauded.[67] Polling data suggested that nationwide, people increasingly saw the administration as being on the side of African Americans, with rising numbers of respondents concerned that the White House was moving too fast on integration—up from 32 percent in May 1962 to 42 percent in October 1962.[68]

By early 1963, however, growing numbers of civil rights leaders were expressing concern that the administration was not moving fast enough. Martin Luther King warned President Kennedy that the frustratingly slow pace of progress was pushing African Americans closer to desperate measures. While on the surface the events at Ole Miss and the White House reception appeared to have little in common, both principally served as symbols of episodic progress rather than systemic challenges to segregation. But, as the historian Carl Brauer has written, "symbolic gains made less of an impression on civil rights advocates in late 1962 than they had at the start of the administration." Brauer called the period the "winter of discontent" in the civil rights movement.[69] After a number of black leaders met with the president early in the year to discuss administration policies toward Africa, about which many of them were encouraged, one expressed anger over civil rights inertia at home, muttering: "We've gotten the best snow job in history. We've lost two years because we admired him."[70] In Brauer's words, the "thrill was gone," and Chuck Stone asserted that political recriminations would likely accompany Kennedy's delay, with African American voters "by no means convinced . . . that their heart belongs increasingly to a Democratic daddy."[71]

While Kennedy finally issued an executive order prohibiting discrimination in federally funded housing in November 1962, the measure was very limited in scope and it left most African American commentators underwhelmed.[72] The two major unresolved issues on which civil rights leaders wanted speedy action were public accommodations legislation and a clear moral statement on the part of the president. Behind the scenes at the White House, Louis Martin was a lonely voice urging John Kennedy that now was the time to act on both matters.[73] Soon the pressure and leadership of the civil rights movement would finally create a political environment in which the administration felt compelled to move.

In the spring of 1963 Martin Luther King Jr., Fred Shuttlesworth, and the SCLC finalized plans for a direct action campaign in Birmingham, Alabama.

The demonstrations targeted the desegregation of public accommodations and the creation of increased economic opportunities for African Americans. This would prove to be what Harris Wofford called the "historic crossroad" in the politics of civil rights.[74] Planner Wyatt Tee Walker dubbed the campaign "Project C" for "confrontation," seeking to expose the brutality of Bull Connor and make the depth of southern racism more strikingly apparent. The Justice Department attempted to preempt such a potentially violent showdown in what SCLC official Andrew Young later called an "almost para-governmental" way.[75] The attorney general quietly utilized such unlikely envoys as diplomat Averell Harriman to call and urge business leaders with a stake in a stable Birmingham to maintain a moderate position.[76] Robert Kennedy also traveled to Alabama once the demonstrations began to visit recently elected governor George Wallace, who had pledged to uphold "segregation now, segregation tomorrow, segregation forever." Greeted by white picketers waving signs reading "No Kennedy Congo Here" and "Mississippi Murderer," the attorney general shook hands with African American employees in the capitol while walking to the governor's office. Discussions about reducing the tensions in Birmingham left Kennedy convinced that Wallace was immovable.[77]

Mediation also failed to defuse the situation, in large part because that was the last thing SCLC wanted. More than any previous incident in the civil rights movement, the events in Birmingham created vivid images of a force of oppression in American society. Television news footage of fire hoses, attack dogs, and the jailing of children provided powerful evidence of a racist South that many whites in other regions of the country had never imagined.[78]

Some northern political leaders—including the entire city council of Cleveland—called upon the administration to act, contending that the First, Fourteenth, and Fifteenth amendments each provided just cause for intervention.[79] African American commentators criticized the administration for mishandling the situation. The *Chicago Defender* alleged that the Justice Department's failure to come down harder on Mississippi governor Ross Barnett during and after the Meredith case encouraged resistance by Alabama leaders, and the *New York Amsterdam News* called it "a pity that the federal government is compelled to move," asking: "Why must Negroes always wait? And wait?" Nonplussed editors charged that after his visit with Wallace the attorney general should have realized "that compromising and 'dealing' with the unreconstructed South is to no avail." The *Washington Afro-American* ran a political cartoon featuring an

African American schoolgirl labeled "US" tugging on the leg of a giant President Kennedy while pointing to a rough-looking white man labeled "Alabama racists" as she tells the president, "But you're bigger than he is."[80]

The resultant political pressure created by the national attention to the violence in Birmingham did lead to progress. The administration did not intervene to protect demonstrators, but Burke Marshall of the Civil Rights Division had been on the ground in Birmingham, quietly (though King did announce at a mass meeting that "some of the big fish" from the Justice Department were in town) helping to mediate negotiations between the SCLC and municipal leaders, with the two sides finally reaching a tenuous agreement to desegregate public accommodations in the city.[81]

African American newspapers were displeased with the attorney general when word leaked of another behind-the-scenes encounter attended by both Marshall and Kennedy. The attorney general arranged a meeting with author James Baldwin, who had written powerfully about the suffocating nature of northern urban racism in his best-selling book *The Fire Next Time*.[82] Kennedy asked if the author would assemble a group willing to discuss ideas about government action on the problems of northern cities, as the attorney general began focusing on de facto segregation and unemployment there.[83] Baldwin contacted several friends for a gathering that turned out to be what the social psychologist Kenneth Clark would later call "*the* most dramatic experience I ever had."[84]

Rather than discussing federal urban policy, Kennedy and Marshall were subjected to an emotional three-hour verbal barrage. Baldwin had assembled a varied group. The authorities on urban problems who were present—Kenneth Clark and Edwin Berry of the Urban League—were a distinct minority. Instead Baldwin's friends from the artistic community, including singers Harry Belafonte and Lena Horne, comedian Bill Cosby, and playwright Lorraine Hansberry, predominated. Clarence Jones, the sole attorney in the New York office of the SCLC, was also present.[85]

The most powerful voice in the discussion, however, belonged to Jerome Smith, a CORE field worker and Freedom Rider who had been badly beaten while working in the South and was in New York for medical care. From the outset he boldly and bluntly issued a series of warnings about the rapidly decreasing capacity of African Americans to remain nonviolent. He told Kennedy and Marshall that he was nauseated at the thought of having to explain to them the frustration of life as a black man in America, and threatened, "When I pull the trigger, kiss it good-by."[86] At one point Baldwin prompted Smith by asking if he would ever fight to defend the United States. "Never! Never! Never!" the young man asserted, leaving

Kennedy incredulous. "You shouldn't be worried about the Communists," Smith insisted. "The real dangers in America are inside."[87]

For a time Kennedy tried to defend administration initiatives, and even protested that his Irish family had known racism, but he eventually relented and simply withstood the assault. He felt betrayed by the meeting, calling the situation he had been put in "impossible" and the dialogue "on both sides . . . an emotional matter."[88] He was angered by Belafonte and Jones, who later told him that although many of his assertions were correct, they had refrained from defending him during the meeting for fear of losing their standing in the black community. A number of those present felt that the experience had little or no effect on Kennedy, and Kenneth Clark even feared that the breach had widened.[89]

African American journalists were troubled by accounts of the meeting, perhaps because they had been convinced that Kennedy was a knowledgeable ally who now appeared less sympathetic. They were most clearly stunned that the attorney general—who truly had hoped to meet with urban experts—had appeared to turn not to the rightful leaders of African American communities (including newspaper publishers and editors) but to entertainers. The *New York Amsterdam News* reported that "Harlemites were chuckling up their sleeves at what they considered the ineptitude of Bobby Kennedy in the fiasco he and author James Baldwin staged with some Negro 'leaders' last week. The question Harlem raised was, 'Who do they lead?'"[90] The *Pittsburgh Courier* declared that the meeting "accomplished nothing" since those present "were not truly representative of American Negroes," and the *Washington Afro-American* editorialized that the attorney general, "a man for whom we hold infinite affection and respect," was "simply kidding himself" by not meeting with the real power structure of the African American community.[91]

Two other journalists viewed the event somewhat differently, probing social divides in the African American community and in the freedom struggle itself. The *Afro*'s Ralph Matthews noted a class division, an "economic chasm between the people who faced the dogs and the sepia celebrities," which left "the pampered darlings of the literary and artistic field . . . further removed from the black masses than the Kennedys themselves," insisting that Baldwin was "as well known among colored working people as Genghis Khan." Matthews did not question the attorney general's judgment in attending the meeting, suggesting that historically "revolutions generally receive their guidance from the intellectuals." In this instance, however, Matthews and *Amsterdam News* editor James Hicks agreed that "it is the *brawn* of the *masses* rather than the *brains* of the *classes* which is moving things ahead." Hicks intimated that his principal concern was whether the African American's "brawn is truly represented when [the intellectuals and other elites] begin slicing up the civil rights pie, or whether his brains once more sell him down the river."[92]

Despite all the anger and regret it generated, the Baldwin meeting did make an impact on Kennedy. While he continued to dismiss the encounter, the impromptu jeremiad of Jerome Smith—the "brawn" of the meeting—deepened his understanding of the plight of many African Americans.[93] Within a few days after the experience, press secretary Ed Guthman recalled Kennedy saying of the CORE worker, "I guess if I were in his shoes, if I had gone through what he's gone through, I might feel differently about this country."[94] Five years later, having engaged in several similar gatherings, Kennedy explained their value to astronaut John Glenn on the way to a community meeting in Oakland, California: "This may not be a pleasant experience. These people have got a lot of hostility and lots of reasons for it. When they get somebody like me, they're going to take it out on me. . . . But no matter how insulting a few of them may be, they're trying to communicate what's inside them."[95]

African American newspapers were willing to reassess the Kennedys as well once tempers cooled. "The president has not," the *Washington Afro-American* noted, "been spared editorial lashings from the colored press and leaders in the colored community." In an attempt to offer perspective, the newspaper claimed that John Kennedy had done "20 times as much as former President Eisenhower in the field of civil rights." The *Afro* insisted that even though some aspects of his presidency had been deeply disappointing, it had ultimately been catalytic. "Because President Kennedy's actions have given new hope to colored Americans," the editors contended, "he has, in effect, touched off a series of demonstrations all over the country, started by colored Americans secure in the knowledge that their government was on their side. . . . [W]e must never forget that for the first time in many, many years, colored Americans have a true and sincere friend in the White House."[96]

That political consanguinity would deepen shortly after the Birmingham campaign, as events there finally led John Kennedy to address the two most urgent requests of civil rights leaders. The University of Alabama was the last major southern state university yet to be desegregated in 1963, and when a federal district court ordered its integration in May, the Kennedy administration sought to practice what it had learned from the turbulence at Oxford. Once George Wallace promised to stand in the schoolhouse door if necessary to block the entry of two African American students, another collision appeared imminent. Intricate planning and coordination by the Justice Department and National Guard troops facilitated the enrollment of two students without violent incident on June 11. In the aftermath of the Birmingham demonstrations, the president decided that he could no longer delay sending Congress legislation to desegregate public accommodations, and the successful conclusion of another confrontation in Alabama afforded the opportunity to address the issue. Robert Kennedy proposed that the president make a civil rights speech in support of his legislation that evening. Accordingly John Kennedy addressed the nation on television, calling civil rights "a moral issue . . . as old as the scriptures and as clear as the American Constitution."[97] Hours later, Medgar Evers was shot in the back and killed upon returning to his home in Mississippi. Thus ended perhaps the most dramatic day yet in the history of the civil rights movement.

Kennedy's willingness finally to put his political capital on the line impressed civil rights leaders, journalists, and the general African American population alike. Martin Luther King called Kennedy's address "eloquent" and "profound."[98] The formerly critical Jackie Robinson wrote, "I can honestly say that Mr. Kennedy has done everything I hoped he would do."[99] The *New York Amsterdam News* called the administration's efforts "a profile of courage" and asserted that "the president has laid the solution to the problem squarely at the feet of the Congress. . . . [T]he executive arm of government has done its part."[100] A July 1963 Louis Harris poll billed as "the most comprehensive survey ever taken of American Negro attitudes" more broadly affirmed African American goodwill. Nine of ten people surveyed believed Kennedy had done a good job, and he was rated as more popular than Franklin Roosevelt. The data suggested that the attorney general was just as popular as the president with African Americans in general, and even more popular with black leaders. The poll also found that African Americans had more faith in the federal government than in any single white group.[101]

In spite of this broad African American support, some of the leaders planning a massive demonstration in the nation's capital in the summer of 1963 were concerned that the March on Washington for Jobs and Freedom was being co-opted. What was originally conceived as a militant direct action protest against continuing inequities in American life, particularly economic injustice, was becoming a broad-based feel-good rally for interracial harmony and President Kennedy's civil rights bill, which was making little headway in Congress. The administration feared that massive (and potentially unruly) protests would be politically counterproductive, so Robert Kennedy assigned Justice Department official John Douglas, son of Illinois senator Paul Douglas, to work closely with demonstration planners Bayard Rustin and A. Philip Randolph to ensure a placid and orderly event.[102] While SNCC's John Lewis wanted to press the administration to go further—his prepared but undelivered remarks included a dismissal of the civil rights bill as "too little and too late," and a jab at the attorney general that in the fight for employment there would be no "cooling-off period"—the event was remembered for Martin Luther King's impassioned plea for a color-blind society and the peaceful gathering of over 200,000 people.[103]

The president responded to the march with an insistence that civil rights efforts be expedited "in all sectors of our national activity" and the assurance that "the gains of 1963 will never be reversed."[104] That optimism would be short-lived. A mere two weeks after the March on Washington, a bomb tore through the Sixteenth Street Baptist Church in Birmingham. Two adults and four young African American girls attending Sunday school were killed, while twenty-three others were wounded. The *Washington Afro-American* exposed the knife blade of emotion, with headlines reading "At Funerals for Birmingham Six—Dam Breaks—Men, Women Cry in Pain" and "Leaders Warn 'Our Folk Can't Take Much More.'" One *Afro* columnist urged the president: "Gov. Wallace will not stop [the violence]. It's doubtful that he can stop it now. So it's up to you. . . . Make your move now!"[105] An African American veterans' group insisted in a telegram to the attorney general that the bombing was nothing short of "organized crime" and "organized murder."[106] King and other leaders met with the president in the White House and requested the protection of federal troops. Undeterred by the public outcry, the attorney general announced that he saw no legal grounds for either troops or U.S. marshals, and President Kennedy again deferred to local law enforcement, sending instead two personal representatives as mediators. One of the two was the retired Army football coach, Colonel Earl "Red" Blaik, prompting Dick Gregory to crack: "We asked for the soldiers and he sent us the coach. . . . He must have thought we were up against the Redskins."[107]

The heat was back on the White House, as the horrific loss of innocent children again raised the stakes in the battle over civil rights. According to a new Gallup poll, taken in mid-September, 50 percent of respondents believed that the administration was "pushing integration too fast," up another ten points from the previous fall, and John Kennedy's disapproval rating reached the highest point of his presidency.[108] Neither popular sympathy following the church bombing nor the earlier goodwill generated by the March on Washington was sufficient to loosen the congressional bottleneck on the administration's civil rights bill. The *Washington Afro-American*, concerned that the administration was not fighting hard enough, asked, "Will the president grow soft when it comes time to slug it out with Congress?"[109]

At the same time both the *Pittsburgh Courier* and the *Chicago Defender* attributed Kennedy's sagging popularity to the cumulative effect of his civil rights initiatives. The *Defender* called the president "cautious" but insisted that he had nevertheless "kept pace with the sweep of events"; it fixed the blame for the stalled civil rights bill instead on Congress, which, it said, "slows him down" and "is using all the legislative machinery at its command to impede and delay."[110] The *Courier* suggested that the administration had developed the reputation for civil rights "militance" among some northern whites, and the *Defender* noted a "newly-formed political brigade which is bent on discrediting the president and his legislative program."[111]

There was evidence to support the charge. Republicans sought to exploit anger toward the attorney general among Italian Americans in South Philadelphia, where there had been racial strife. At a time when many Italian Americans were embarrassed by the televised spectacle of the hearings on organized crime featuring Mafia informant Joseph Valachi, they saw the administration siding with African Americans to such an extent that Republicans predicted several formerly Democratic wards were now "in the bag" for the GOP.[112] Months later a group called the Staten Island Committee for the Preservation of the American Republic distributed the telephone number for a recording attacking Robert Kennedy and his relationship with the civil rights movement.[113]

In an effort to get movement on the bill and also moderate the administration's image, the attorney general proposed eliminating Title III of the bill, thus removing the augmentation of Justice Department power to sue to protect an individual's constitutional rights. Despite (or perhaps because of) the fact that African Americans had come to see Robert Kennedy as their chief ally in the White House, he faced withering criticism in the final weeks of the administration. Civil rights leaders roundly condemned his shift as a politically expedient sellout. The *Chicago Defender* skewered the attorney general's insistence that he wanted "a bill, not an issue," as a "lame reason" for urging a weaker civil rights law. The *Pittsburgh Courier* called the modified bill "sabotage in the grand manner" and editorialized, "Bobby Kennedy Chickens Out."[114]

The attorney general had at times been a lightning rod for either side of the civil rights divide, and he regularly contemplated leaving his post to alleviate political pressure on his brother.[115] A poll in the vital state of Texas in the fall of 1963 indicated that John Kennedy's overall approval rating had dropped by ten points (and his disapproval rating jumped fifteen) since May. The poll also surveyed opinions about Texas Democratic governor John Connally, Vice President Lyndon Johnson, and Attorney General Kennedy, with only Connally—who announced his opposition to federal mandates on integration—gaining in stature. Robert Kennedy finished nearly twenty points lower than the president in the poll, with only 32 percent favorability and 51 percent of respondents disapproving of his performance.[116]

At his thirty-eighth birthday party in his Justice Department office on November 20, Kennedy delivered what sounded to some guests like an extemporaneous valedictory, joking that he had already assured his brother's reelection with the popularity of his civil rights interventions in the South.[117] The president's mind was also on the 1964 election and the South as he prepared to leave for Texas to mend a party rift and boost his political standing there.

Because so many African Americans were intimately acquainted with suffering and multiple forms of violence in their daily existence, because they deeply and personally understood the historic American tendency toward retribution against black political, economic, and social aspiration dating to Reconstruction and earlier, many instinctively ascribed the president's assassination to his support for their cause. A banner headline on the front page of the *California Eagle* blared, "NEGROES DOUBT OFFICIAL STORY OF ASSASSINATION: Believe Murder Linked to Civil Rights."[118] A letter to the editor of the *Washington Afro-American* pronounced that President Kennedy had been "killed by the same people who killed four little girls in Birmingham."[119] An *Afro* columnist wrote:

> The colored people were touched heavily. They perhaps understood what happened before any white man because they alone had managed (in spite of the continuing threat to safety and survival) to rise above chaos in the past. They have had to create a benefactor who they thought would do the job that they will finally have to do themselves. Blood had flowed under a Texas sun, and silently some Afro-Americans wondered if that trickle of blood from one man's body

had a raging river behind it, to fill every gulley and valley with a crimson line. A wind had blown away a deliverer and some collapsed and wept openly in the streets in the deepest despair born from great dependency.[120]

The shock and emotion surrounding John Kennedy's assassination in the midst of the political battle over the most significant civil rights legislation since Reconstruction bound ordinary African Americans to the Kennedy legacy in a way that would have been impossible in the normal course of events. That bond was publicly sanctified when Lyndon Johnson made the civil rights bill a memorial to the slain president. The mantle of shared suffering descended on the president's wife and brother. The *Washington Afro-American* compared Jacqueline Kennedy's "majesty" to that of Medgar Evers's widow, Myrlie, and to "the mothers of the Birmingham children."[121] In December the *Chicago Defender* published a photo of the attorney general at a Christmas party for low-income children with the caption, "Good to See Our Man Smile Again."[122] One private relationship most poignantly embodied this public sense of shared loss, as Robert Kennedy and Charles Evers, who took over his brother Medgar's leadership role in the Mississippi NAACP, became close friends.[123]

Such popular commiseration and sense of common purpose developed because most African Americans became convinced that John and Robert Kennedy were allies who were joined to them in a full political relationship, with all that that entailed, including brutally honest criticism and, finally, the expenditure of significant political capital. The alliance produced hope, doubts, scars, and ultimately trust. Even as civil rights leaders periodically grew frustrated to the point of exasperation and condemnation with the pace and quality of federal intervention, the overwhelming majority of African Americans believed that the Kennedys, and particularly the attorney general, were on their side.

Of course not all black leaders hailed the Kennedy presidency, and those on the front lines of the struggle to integrate the South frequently chafed at the limits which the administration imposed on itself with regard to intervention. As they all too frequently experienced the executive branch as a brake on their activities in the freedom struggle, civil rights leaders powerfully and rightly criticized both the White House and the Justice Department.

Revisionist historical assessments of the Kennedy administration's record on civil rights have emphasized this angle of vision and rendered critical verdicts, with Nick Bryant adjudging John Kennedy a "bystander" whose temporizing did more damage than merely slowing progress on integration. The Kennedys, according to this interpretation, were more interested in maintaining or expanding their political power than they were in applying it to a fundamentally just cause. Such revisionist studies have also emphasized the distance between myth—the popular adulation and public memory of Kennedy's leadership on civil rights—and the reality that in the wake of the assassination the martyred president received a disproportionate amount of credit for the progress on civil rights.

Decades earlier, in the first major scholarly study of the administration's significance to the civil rights struggle, Carl Brauer painted quite a different portrait, contending that John Kennedy displayed genuine and courageous leadership despite considerable political constraints. He described the abbreviated Kennedy presidency as a "vigorous and far-reaching effort to eliminate racial discrimination" which denoted the beginning of a "second Reconstruction." In Brauer's rendering, the Kennedy years thus marked the first major attempt by the federal government to finish the work left undone during the long, dark descent into the Jim Crow segregation of the South.

Each of these interpretations has substantial merit, but for the purpose of assessing the longer-term significance of the Kennedy years on the mass political level, with particular consideration for the social eruption still on the horizon in the 1960s, another nineteenth-century analogy seems more fitting. Of all the pivotal years in the sectional crisis immediately preceding the Civil War, historian Kenneth Stampp has contended that 1857 witnessed "the political point of no return."[124] The two most important developments of that year were the symbolic commitments by two of the three branches of the federal government to southern, pro-slavery interests. Early in the spring the Supreme Court handed down its ruling in the case of *Dred Scott v. Sandford*, strongly vindicating and supporting the South on the question of expanding slavery. In December, President James Buchanan, a Pennsylvania Democrat who had received most of his support from the South, staked his presidency on the same side when he threw his support behind the illegitimate, pro-slavery Lecompton constitution in "bleeding" Kansas. Historians have nearly universally condemned Buchanan's decision. It emboldened pro-slavery leaders and tore the Democratic Party—the only truly national political coalition remaining—in two. Buchanan's support for Lecompton ultimately upended the nation's fragile political equilibrium, and with two thirds of the federal government now supporting the South, the nation moved closer to an irreparable rupture.[125]

All historical analogies are ultimately flawed, but carefully employed they can be tools that render important insights. With regard to the politics of civil rights in the postwar era, the Kennedy years were, symbolically, Lecompton in reverse. Looking back with greater historical distance at the social and cultural war that the 1960s became, with continuing ripple effects and alliances that would reach decades into the future, we can see that the Kennedy administration marked the tipping point in the long black freedom struggle. African Americans had eagerly hoped to realize the promise of the Supreme Court's ruling in the *Brown* decision, but the noncommittal Eisenhower presidency and the southern influence in Congress kept political progress limited. The Kennedy campaign rhetoric and symbolic executive actions early on convinced most civil rights leaders that the executive branch was now on their side, and activists were emboldened to continue pressing their offensives, generally confident that they had friends in the highest places. *Ebony* journalist Simeon Booker summed it up well when he later reflected that John Kennedy "came at a time when everything was beginning to go downhill, and he gave [African Americans] a shot in the arm."[126]

Over time, civil rights leaders sparred with the administration, hoped for more progress, and at times felt deeply betrayed. SNCC leader Ivanhoe Donaldson was a signatory to a lawsuit the organization attempted to bring against the Justice Department in 1963 to force it to protect civil rights workers and, more broadly, all African Americans in the South. Donaldson reflected later that while John Kennedy "never really accomplished much . . . in a pragmatic sense[,] . . . he set a fantastic atmosphere in this country . . . that things would be done, things would be changed."[127]

The overwhelming majority of ordinary African Americans appear to have consistently seen the Kennedys as having adopted their cause. Roy Wilkins related the story of a critical speech he delivered before a black audience in North Carolina: "I went after Kennedy, hook, line and sinker. I said he hadn't done anything, and I blasted away. And they all sat on their hands. . . . Then I mentioned some little thing he did and the place went up in smoke with everybody cheering."[128] Newspaper coverage and editorial comment generally reflected and perhaps stimulated these favorable perceptions on the part of African Americans, and while limited in volume, available public opinion polling data also suggest the overwhelming popularity of the Kennedy administration with black Americans.

All of this is not to contend that revisionist scholars are incorrect in challenging John Kennedy's leadership on civil rights, for on that point they are essentially correct. The civil rights movement fundamentally drove the action and forced the issue on desegregation. But while the Kennedys generally failed to lead, they did something not entirely less historically significant. Though on occasion the administration operated as a major restraint on the movement, and initially it sought to be a neutral arbiter between North and South on racial questions, over time it most often served as a responsive facilitator, sometimes moving much more slowly than movement leaders wanted, but always clearly on the side of eventual progress. In the big picture, the mixed political motives, the strategic missteps, and the deliberate procrastination of the Kennedys are in some ways less historically significant than the way they were broadly perceived. In the course of the national schism over civil rights, which increasingly left little middle ground and had the centrifugal effect of forcing public figures to choose sides, the administration's stance produced the synergistic encouragement needed for the movement to keep moving.

The figure at the pivot point, the fulcrum where the civil rights movement met and began to turn the federal government, was Robert Kennedy. While he clearly evolved in significant ways on the issue as attorney general, within the first year of the administration African American journalists had already noted his distinctive importance in the struggle for civil rights. In late 1961 the *New York Amsterdam News* editorialized that Kennedy's Justice Department had "come to be looked upon by minorities in much the same way as the minorities looked on the Supreme Court—as a bulwark against bigotry and a refuge and haven for mistreated freedom-loving Americans."[129] In spite of disappointments and frustrations in the intervening years, in the weeks after Dallas, wondering aloud about Robert Kennedy's future, the *Chicago Defender* wrote, "We shudder at the prospect of trying to get passage of the civil rights bill now before the United States Congress without Robert F. Kennedy functioning as the attorney general," insisting that in "many of the great civil rights decisions" he had "provided the major leadership."[130] Kennedy would stay on for another eight months, but the political relationship he had developed with African Americans during this crucial period would remain central to his political interests and fortunes for the remainder of his public career. His role during this vital moment in American social history would also carry great weight with other racial minority groups, as both the rights revolution and Kennedy's career moved in new directions.

3

POVERTY

AND JUSTICE

DEFINING A

FEDERAL ROLE

Developments in the multifaceted struggle for civil rights would play an important role in deepening Robert Kennedy's awareness of poverty in America. The attorney general would encounter the problem in a number of significant ways, however, some of which were more clearly linked to the traditional jurisdiction of the Justice Department than others. Because of his relationship to the president, unique not only among attorneys general but also among modern presidential advisers generally—with perhaps only Harry Hopkins and Karl Rove holding similar levels of influence—Robert Kennedy ranged far afield from the conventional domain of Justice Department chief, playing a key role in foreign policy debates and serving as both the president's top political strategist and administration ombudsman.[1] It was not an issue with which the president's brother was widely identified at this stage in his career, but poverty assumed a steadily increasing importance in many of his activities. Kennedy's experiences as attorney general would be pivotal to both his preliminary diagnosis of the problem and his nascent commitment to the issue. His interest and his initiatives at the Justice Department elevated the prominence of poverty in the administration's policy debates, with consequences that would extend beyond his brother's presidency.

At his first press conference as United States attorney general in April 1961, Kennedy made several announcements. The first outlined an expected push for new anti-racketeering legislation, which was a natural extension of his high-profile work on the McClellan committee. The second unveiled a committee of prominent lawyers he had assembled to study the question of fairness for poor defendants in the federal justice system. The final announcement was the appointment of an assistant to guide the department's response to juvenile delinquency. While his organized crime drive received nearly all of the media attention, the other two announcements were signals of the direction in which Kennedy's political concerns would move, as the initiatives proved to be important pathways in the attorney general's engagement with the issue of poverty.[2]

Kennedy's sister Eunice first worked on the emerging problem of juvenile delinquency in the Truman Justice Department, and just before the inauguration she urged her brothers to take up the issue.[3] Countless academic studies and angst-ridden popular media explorations of juvenile delinquency had appeared in the 1950s. Like poverty in this period of affluence, delinquency stood out as a mysteriously vexing problem in the midst of perceived social stability, conformity, and optimism. Over time the two issues would become more closely associated, and the new attorney general would play a key role in the linkage.

Kennedy had an interest in young people, and delinquency was a criminal as well as a social issue, so he asked longtime friend David Hackett to begin shaping a Justice Department effort. Hackett had no expertise in youth problems, but he had proved to be a trusted operative in managing the presidential campaign's "boiler room" (which oversaw correspondence and monitored convention delegates). His selection was perhaps not coincidental, given the fact that his friendship with Kennedy had its origins in shared feelings of teenage alienation at Milton Academy.[4] Despite the nation's collective hand-wringing about the problem, the Eisenhower administration had paid it scant attention. Hackett estimated that there was a sum total of ten people, scattered between the Labor, Justice, and Health, Education and Welfare (HEW) departments, working on youth-related programs, and he learned of stalled attempts by a national coalition of activists to obtain funding for juvenile delinquency programs.[5] In May 1961 President Kennedy signed an executive order creating the President's Committee on Juvenile Delinquency (PCJD), a cabinet-level body comprising the secretary of labor, the secretary of HEW, and the attorney general, who served as chairman. Hackett would direct daily operations of the committee, which was given presidential authority to coordinate the anti-delinquency efforts of all three departments.

Hackett surrounded himself with leading thinkers on the problem of juvenile delinquency and undertook a crash course on the subject. He began soliciting ideas for elements of a bill to coordinate the existing meager and diffuse federal efforts and to obtain resources for federally funded demonstration projects. The leading academic in the early stages was Lloyd Ohlin, a Columbia professor trained at the influential University of Chicago department of sociology. Ohlin argued in his 1960 book *Delinquency and Opportunity*, coauthored with Richard Cloward, that the slum environment was more responsible for delinquency than individual social or moral inadequacy. Ohlin and Cloward's theory thus traced delinquent behavior to blocked social and economic opportunities.

The Ohlin-Cloward perspective, along with that of Chicago School sociologist Leonard S. Cottrell Jr., who was later placed in charge of reviewing demonstration projects for the committee, shared the structuralist view of causation based on social and economic systemic flaws. Still, opportunity theory differed in emphasis from the structuralist conceptions of John Kenneth Galbraith and others, which focused on broader problems at the national level. Whereas the conditions of localities were bound up in larger social and economic currents, Ohlin and Cloward instead concentrated on the effects of blocked local opportunities and the emergence of delinquent subcultures at the community level.[6] This community focus would ultimately mesh well with Robert Kennedy's political sensibilities.

The attorney general's involvement with the theoretical evolution of the PCJD and with Hackett's activities was nevertheless sporadic, usually limited to support for his old friend's direct requests. In March 1961 Hackett appealed to Kennedy's eagerness to view matters firsthand by setting up meetings with several groups of teenage gang members in New York City. "We were very green in understanding the problems," Hackett reflected later, adding: "We had a tendency to think of young people as like when we were young and sort of looked upon the solutions of their problems as like the solutions to our own. So, the conversations at the beginning were, perhaps[,] naïve in talking to them."[7]

Given Kennedy and Hackett's prep school background, the gap between their experience and that of "young toughs" (as they were frequently called) was considerable. Because of that divide, Kennedy was eager to learn about life on the streets. Aaron Schmais, a young legal assistant for the New York City Youth Board, took the attorney general on a forty-block tour through East Harlem to meet with gang members from the Puerto Rican Viceroys and the Italian Red Wings. After some initial silence and suspicion, Kennedy was able to break the ice. He had to be dissuaded from playing stickball by those leading his tour, and he defused the hostility of the Red Wings, who complained that he was always picking on Italians by joking with them and questioning them intently. Kennedy had been hardened to tales of violence by his years on the Rackets Committee, but he was left dumbstruck at the pride one youth took in recounting how he and five other gang members had pummeled a boy for occupying a park bench within their turf. He told them as one of four brothers he could understand scrapping, if it were a fair fight. One of the youths responded that they "just like to get into it."[8] The gang members in turn were amazed at Kennedy's naïveté regarding the availability of narcotics. "Give me some money," one told him, "and I'll be back in five minutes."[9] Kennedy asked what the government might do to help. The most common responses had to do with opportunities for work and places for recreation. The attorney general returned to Washington uncertain of a remedy but impressed with local efforts by dedicated youth workers to redirect the teens. "Maybe they're the best answer," Kennedy told his press secretary, Edwin Guthman.[10] Kennedy also made an impression. "Clearly," Schmais recalled, "the gang members and, I should add, the gang workers were taken with his ability to reach out and establish meaningful contact."[11]

Kennedy took a particular interest in the delinquency problem in Washington, D.C., and sought to make a visible impact there. In as stark a contrast as could be conceived, the District's poorest neighborhood—the Second Precinct—encircled the seat of the nation's political power in the Capitol.[12] The attorney general began regularly visiting schools in the area—the facilities of which were crumbling—and sent Justice Department official E. Barrett Prettyman Jr. to ask local police what could be done. As in Harlem, the absence of recreational facilities was cited as a major problem. Kennedy and Prettyman surveyed area playgrounds and swimming pools and were appalled at how many were in complete disrepair.[13] The attorney general even recruited celebrity inspectors to go along and focus attention on the problem, including legendary newsman Edward R. Murrow and actor Cary Grant, who shook his head in dismay at the condition of the junior high school that locals called "Shameful Shaw."[14]

City leaders had been pressing for the renovation of the pool at Dunbar High School, which had been closed for nearly a decade, but it took the political heft of the attorney general and his aide to get action. Kennedy phoned local religious leaders, and Prettyman secured $30,000 in donations from Protestant, Jewish, and Catholic groups in less than two weeks.[15] The attorney general told a press gathering that delinquency had resulted because young people were hanging out on street corners rather than swimming or working as lifeguards. The D.C. superintendent proclaimed him the most popular man at the school.[16] The enterprise strengthened Kennedy's faith that local resources and coordination could be mustered, in Prettyman's words, "for the right kind of project with the right kind of leadership."[17]

Despite foot-dragging by some District officials, Kennedy also pushed for the construction of a new playground utilizing excess military equipment on the site of a city lot that police were using to store wrecked automobiles.[18] With hopes that it would provide recreation for ten thousand children, it was no small-scale enterprise. Kennedy summoned millionaire businessman and D.C. transit system owner O. Roy Chalk to raise funds expected to exceed $100,000. Costs were eventually twice that amount, and the plans grew to include two decommissioned military jets, a tank, a tugboat, a nineteenth-century locomotive, a soap box derby track, an ice skating pond, and a pole vaulting pit. One gasping reporter aptly described it as "a cross between Disneyland and an alfresco Smithsonian."[19] The playground proved wildly popular, with local children making over 1 million visits in its first year of operation. The opening attracted national attention, and Congressman Edward Roybal of Los Angeles soon made arrangements to meet with Kennedy, hoping to reproduce its success in his predominantly Mexican American district.[20]

As Kennedy struggled to understand the genesis of juvenile delinquency, he viscerally rejected one of the most prevalent explanations, that of emotional and psychological maladjustment due to family and other environmental factors. The diagnosis so permeated popular awareness that it was parodied in the musical West Side Story, where one gang member mocks the idea that teen troublemakers "don't need a judge," just "an analyst's care!"[21]

Kennedy hosted informal academic discussions for the Washington elite at his northern Virginia home—known around the capital as the "Hickory Hill seminars"—and on one occasion invited respected psychoanalyst Lawrence Kubie to discuss the topic of "Urban Problems and Poverty Children." Kennedy insistently objected to Kubie's individualized, therapeutic approach to the problems of ghetto youth. "That's the biggest bunch of bullshit I've ever heard," Kennedy said. "You're trying to tell us that people can't help being what they are."[22] Lydia Katzenbach, herself a trained psychoanalyst and the wife of Assistant Attorney General Nicholas Katzenbach, saw Kennedy as "unconversant with any of the social sciences" and believed that the attorney general "had no understanding at that time for Kubie's frame of reference." Katzenbach concluded that "Kubie was interested in the one, and Bobby was interested in the many. There was so much to be done for so many that Bobby was outraged."[23]

And yet as Kennedy struggled to comprehend the plight of juvenile delinquents, through his personal experiences in New York City and Washington, D.C., along with some tutoring from Lloyd Ohlin on the potential impact of impoverished surroundings, he moved closer to an environmental understanding of the problem. A moment of epiphany came during a car ride to Capitol Hill with the Columbia professor. "Oh, I see," the attorney general confided. "If I had grown up in these circumstances, this could have happened to me."[24] Kennedy proceeded to share his insight with the House Subcommittee on Education and Labor during the question-and-answer period following his testimony on the anti-delinquency legislation the administration was proposing. "I think some of us who were more fortunate," the attorney general cautioned, "might also have been juvenile delinquents if we were brought up in different environments."[25]

Along with the causative emphasis Ohlin and others in Hackett's group were placing on local socioeconomic structural problems (particularly in urban slums, although the committee also looked into rural delinquency), the other important sentiment emerging in the PCJD was a grave mistrust of the capacity of federal dollars to solve problems at the local level.[26] Kennedy and Hackett took more tours of impoverished urban areas, including East Los Angeles and Watts. The discouraging conditions and ineffective local bureaucracies they observed led them to conclude, as Hackett put it, "you could spend thirty million dollars in one city and not have any impact whatsoever."[27]

In addition to his concerns about local inertia, the visits confirmed Kennedy's preexisting suspicions about the limits of federal efficiency in the post–New Deal era. While he believed strongly in an activist federal government, Kennedy had also been influenced by the postwar conservatism of his father. A former New Dealer, Joseph Kennedy proclaimed after World War II that "the state means to most untrained minds some vast, nebulous institution which will somehow or other assume all the burdens of life and support the individual who lacks the ambition or energy to support himself."[28]

Kennedy had also been exposed to federal bureaucratic inefficiency during his brief tenure on the second Hoover Commission, and while the young attorney hadn't viewed the experience as formative, Kennedy's initial approach to a federal role on poverty bore striking similarities to the model that Hoover developed as secretary of commerce in the 1920s. Historian

Ellis Hawley has described Hoover's efforts to craft an "associative state" wherein business associations and other private institutions could address social and economic problems, with the federal government playing the role of facilitator and coordinator.[29] Historian Bruce Lohof described how that vision played out most successfully during the relief effort for the Mississippi flood of 1927, as Hoover sought to "create an administrative machine which would gather the potential energies of disparate agencies, coordinate those energies and place them at the disposal of local leadership, which, imbued with a spirit of community, would unleash their potential." For Hoover, the federal role was not "to replace or stifle individual effort or community enterprise; rather, it would vitalize these activities by coordinating and rationalizing the resources upon which they draw. *Bureaucracy* and *individual*, then, were not adversaries, but parts of a larger scheme joined in easy reciprocity."[30]

Hoover's associative vision was an attempt to integrate progressive demands for a growing sphere of public responsibility with the long-standing and still prevalent American traditions of voluntary and private charitable obligation for social welfare. It was a cooperative, corporatist view of government's relationship with the economy, rather than the classic free market liberalism of the nineteenth century. Hoover's conception of the public sphere had limits, however. He wanted to avoid the welfare statism of European countries, and, as became apparent once the Great Depression dragged on, he had a moral aversion to direct federal aid to either local governments or individuals. This earned the former international hero the scorn of millions as the unemployed struggled through the depression, and it left the progressive elements of his vision buried for historians to recover many decades later.[31]

Insofar as the attorney general and his advisers saw the New Deal as an outmoded, centralized, top-down model of federalism, Robert Kennedy's initial conception of the federal role in fighting poverty was thus, in important ways, more similar to that of Herbert Hoover than that of Franklin Roosevelt. In the very different economic and political context of the early 1960s (and Roosevelt had, of course, considered his earliest flurries of federal activism only emergency measures), Kennedy was convinced that locally initiated efforts were the best way to deal with the problem of poverty. But he had no antipathy toward the host of federal programs already in place—believing these needed coordination rather than elimination—and he saw federal assistance as an incentive to spur action. Kennedy basically embraced a post–New Deal form of progressivism, which he described during a television interview with NBC correspondent

Martin Agronsky: "We can't go to Des Moines, Iowa, and say this is how you answer the problem. That's going to be up to the local government, the local authorities, the voluntary organizations. But we can say we can stimulate that . . . so that they have an overall plan to deal with the problem."[32]

Kennedy's interest in and evolving approach to poverty also coincided with contemporary developments in the Catholic Church. In May 1961 Pope John XXIII promulgated the landmark social encyclical *Mater et Magistra*. The document continued the development of the body of official Catholic social teaching begun seventy years earlier, emphasizing, among other principles, that globally the "enormous wealth, the unbridled luxury, of the privileged few stands in violent, offensive contrast to the utter poverty of the vast majority."[33] Catholic approaches to poverty and social reform have been distinctive in American life. The primacy that the church has placed on the issue, its tendency to avoid categorizing the poor as either worthy or unworthy, and its perspective on poverty as a test of the charity of the believer (as much as or more than a test of virtue for the poor) are themes that have often been overlooked by historians.[34] Given his religiosity, these also offer an important backdrop to Kennedy's activity.

For much of U.S. history the majority of Catholic leaders, in a tenuous social position owing to deep reservoirs of American anti-Catholic sentiment, had not been in the forefront of broad social and economic reform efforts. At the same time, according to historians Elizabeth McKeown and Dorothy Brown, the focus on charity for the individual became "a primary emblem of Catholic identity in American culture and the chief means by which the church established a public voice."[35] Official Catholic social teaching, which emerged in the late nineteenth century, allowed American Catholics to think more broadly about the challenges that industrialization had brought to Western societies such as their own. Papal encyclicals beginning with *Rerum Novarum* (1891) sought to protect the welfare of individuals from the abuses—including economic deprivation—of either a collectivist, socialist state or a capitalist market, with its unrestricted individualism.

Catholic social teaching conceived of society as an organic or corporate whole rather than an agglomeration of free individuals (in the classic liberal ideal so important to American political and economic thought) or warring classes (as in Marxism), and it thus emphasized the common good while urging social and economic cooperation. Catholic social teaching also sought to preserve control for what it considered intermediate and often more local sources of assistance, urging their protection from larger concentrations of political or economic power through the principle of subsidiarity—the notion that "greater and higher associations" should not subsume the work that "lesser and subordinate organizations can do."[36]

In recognition of the new social and economic challenges of the postwar world, John XXIII introduced in *Mater et Magistra* the principle of socialization, which held that, while the intermediate and localized emphasis on subsidiarity remained the preferred path, the complexity of the new, postindustrial world required the state to play some role in tending to the needy. Some progressive American Catholic leaders—most significantly the Reverend John A. Ryan—had contended decades earlier that the national government had a role to play in securing economic justice.[37] But *Mater et Magistra* clearly established something of a sliding scale and a creative tension in determining whether the most appropriate response to the social and economic problems of individuals should emanate from the local, the intermediate, or the national level.[38]

It is difficult to gauge Robert Kennedy's familiarity with these official social teachings of his church. He would undoubtedly have been aware of the 1961 encyclical, which generated some controversy among a coterie of conservative American Catholics (most notably Kennedy nemesis William F. Buckley Jr.), who disdained its openness to government intervention in social welfare.[39] It is unclear if he ever read the earlier texts, but as a religious youngster he would likely have heard discussions about the encyclicals from those conversant with this major theme in twentieth-century Catholicism, perhaps from his mother, from one of the many clergymen close to the family, or from instructors at Portsmouth Priory, the Catholic prep school he attended before arriving at Milton. Catholic social teaching was in the air that progressive American Catholics breathed in these years, and even if the doctrines did not consciously or directly shape Robert Kennedy's political perspectives, sociologists have suggested that a "religious imagination" rooted in the regular practice and rituals of one's faith can unconsciously influence an individual's worldview.[40]

Whether or not they were expressly influential, these Catholic ideals—concern for poverty, an emphasis on community and the common good, a preference for local initiative with a corresponding recognition that in the postwar world "greater and higher" associations in the form of government may need to take action—paralleled Kennedy's emerging vision of a federal social welfare role that could best overcome the inefficiencies of bureaucracies both in Washington and in local governments.

The federal action Kennedy proposed with regard to juvenile delinquency became law in September 1961 as Congress—with a full court press from the White House (including the congressional testimony of the attorney general and three other cabinet heads)—passed the Juvenile Delinquency and Youth Offenses Control Act. The legislation encouraged cities to compete for $30 million of federal money, which would finance sixteen demonstration projects. The hope was that the competition would "stimulate" inventive plans tailored to local situations. The grant applications were to be judged on two chief criteria. Reflecting the PCJD diagnosis of juvenile delinquency as arising from a lack of opportunity—opportunity theorist Lloyd Ohlin in fact helped draft significant portions of the bill—the first criterion was the confrontation of delinquency in a "comprehensive" way (that is, through programs covering a variety of needs, such as employment, education, and recreation). The second was the capacity to coordinate activity at the local level, to avoid a confusion of agencies and groups working at cross-purposes, and to "mobilize within a city all of the resources available to attack [the problem] across the board."[41] In addition to providing financial resources, the federal government would serve as a clearinghouse supplying communities with information on the types of local plans and programs that had been successful around the country.[42] Modest in scope, the legislation had been conceived according to progressive principles of utilization of expertise, an orderly and scientific approach to change, attention to environmental causation, and "good government" rationalization of resources, and in the Chicago School tradition of focusing on local communities.[43]

Hackett and his group convened informally on a regular basis to discuss ongoing plans and projects, beneath the notice of most officials in the Justice Department. According to participant Sanford Kravitz, Hackett infused the group with "an impending air of crisis" that kept members in constant search of new ideas and additional resources. With Kennedy's encouragement, the interagency committee's members strategized about "infiltrating" their own bureaucratic departments with their ideas and redirecting funds from other programs into the delinquency effort. Among those aware of their activities, they became known as "the guerrillas."[44]

Hackett's running symposium on delinquency was a characteristic Kennedy operation—deploying intellectuals to provide concrete ideas for political action.[45] Despite the impressive intellectual arsenal that Hackett had assembled, however, the committee produced no magic bullets. The planning proposals submitted by the cities also proved disappointing, offering only traditional solutions.[46] Nevertheless, the consensus in the

PCJD still held that better coordination of both federal and local activities would create more efficient use of federal money and manpower. Amidst his other activities, Robert Kennedy maintained a keen interest in the committee's work, but he remained somewhat detached from specifics of the discussions and emerging ideas of the group. Hackett was often nervous whenever the attorney general announced a grant recipient, uncertain about Kennedy's grasp of the concepts and details, though he ultimately found Kennedy to be "current [with] or ahead of" the thinking of the committee.[47]

Another appointee surprised by Kennedy's thorough awareness of his activities was University of Chicago law professor Francis Allen, who had been named chairman of the Attorney General's Committee on Poverty and the Administration of Federal Criminal Justice in 1961. Kennedy had created the committee to focus on the problem of inadequate legal representation for poor defendants and the need for a bail system that did not disproportionately punish the indigent. Upon hearing of the committee, Herbert Sturz, director of the Vera Foundation, a new bail reform advocacy institute, contacted David Hackett and told him about his work. Hackett passed the information on to the attorney general, who was interested. Kennedy encouraged Sturz to keep working with other bail reform groups and was told there weren't any.[48] Allen soon thereafter asked the Vera Foundation to conduct a study of bail practices in one New York district.

The results of the study indicated that among defendants released on their own recognizance rather than being forced to post bail, default rates (the failure to show up for trial) were nearly the same as among those released on bail bonds. The study also found that jailing defendants unable to post bail was an ineffective use of federal dollars. Kennedy was most troubled by the unfairness of dramatically different legal processes for the poor. When the committee presented its findings regarding the large number of defendants unable to meet bail or hire an attorney, he smiled and cryptically suggested, "I can solve that problem."[49] The "solution" was a letter to U.S. attorneys announcing that release on one's own recognizance was now the department's policy unless compelling reasons existed for holding a defendant. Kennedy also asked federal prosecuting attorneys to account for the procedures they used regarding bail.[50] Allen believed that the burden was thus shifted back onto prosecutors to justify pretrial incarceration, and that Kennedy's pressure "immediately, overnight reformed the practice."[51] In the next year, federal releases nationwide tripled with no significant change in default rates.

The Vera Foundation's Manhattan Bail Project also revealed much higher conviction rates for those unable to secure their freedom while awaiting trial. The study gained national attention, and Kennedy, Sturz, and Hackett, along with others in the Justice Department, strategized about how to continue to build momentum for reform. They agreed that a national conference to share information on the misuse of bail was the next step, and Kennedy suggested the appropriation of juvenile delinquency money rather than wading through the red tape of a congressional request for funding.[52]

In the spring of 1964 the Justice Department and the Vera Foundation cosponsored a national conference on bail reform that drew more than four hundred officials from across the nation, including attorneys, judges, prison officials, and bondsmen. Proclaiming that "our present attitudes toward bail are not only cruel" but also "illogical," Kennedy asked attendees to "see to it that America does not unjustly punish the man who is already serving a life sentence of poverty."[53] The effect was a dramatic increase in the number of experiments nationwide with release on the defendant's own recognizance. Their success helped provide the motive force behind the Federal Bail Reform Act of 1966, the first major change to the bail system in U.S. history.[54] The law made release on recognizance the default approach, allowed for case-by-case assessments of defendants, and quickly led to the reform of bail laws in more than a dozen states.[55]

The other significant offshoot of the committee on poverty and the justice system coincided with a Supreme Court decision handed down in March 1963. In *Gideon v. Wainwright* the Court determined that Clarence Earl Gideon, a poor white Floridian, had been wrongly convicted of theft because he had not had access to a competent defense. The issue was another the Allen committee had explored, and its report included a proposed draft of legislation to provide for such defense. The Kennedy administration submitted the bill, and the attorney general spoke on a number of occasions in support of it. He testified before Congress that "it is one thing if you are talking about an automobile, talking about a house, or talking about a meal. But when you are talking about the fundamental question of justice in the United States, the fact that if you are wealthy you have one system of justice for you, and if you are poor you have a different one, goes to the very core and heart of our society."[56] The bill eventually became the Criminal Justice Act of 1964 (as it was signed into law by Lyndon Johnson in August of that year), which provided public funding for poor defendants to gain access to an adequate defense, along with other services.

In contrast with the inexactitude of proposed causes and solutions for juvenile delinquency, the imbalance in the legal system lent itself to concrete, if incremental, steps. It was also an issue that Robert Kennedy saw in clear moral terms, rooted in a "basic sense of human justice."[57] While the social and economic concerns of the civil rights movement created the climate that made possible such a reform directed toward those at society's margins, and even though it was directly correlative with racial prejudice, criminal justice reform did not at this point generate vocal advocacy from racial minority groups.[58] Perhaps because Clarence Gideon, a white southerner, became the symbol of the cause, or more likely because civil rights groups were simply putting their energies into other fields at that point, criminal justice reform proved less politically charged than other issues Kennedy took on. He joked with segregationist North Carolina senator Sam Ervin during hearings for the 1964 bill that he appreciated "all of us being on the same side of this matter."[59]

The attorney general never lost sight of the political implications of any of his activities, but he paid acute attention to constituencies that had been instrumental in his brother's 1960 victory. Kennedy overrode PCJD review panel recommendations against what were seen as inadequate grant proposals from Chicago and Kanawha County, West Virginia, because of the importance of those localities to the president's winning coalition.[60] In early 1962 the attorney general also asked Louis Martin, now working as the number two man at the Democratic National Committee, to keep tabs on electoral districts nationwide with at least 10 percent non-white constituencies, as he planned to focus attention on them.[61]

Attention to this political base remained in order because over time, leaders of each group experienced some level of disappointment with the administration. While the Viva Kennedy clubs begun in 1960 were a watershed in the development of Mexican Americans as a national political force, and President Kennedy continued to enjoy broad support in Texas, key Latino leaders in Los Angeles were starting to chastise the administration for its failure to appoint Mexican American officials.[62] Tensions also surfaced as some Mexican American leaders began complaining that African American interests were receiving much greater attention from the administration, leading Robert Kennedy to prevail upon the California Democratic Party to get much more actively involved in Latino neighborhoods.[63]

Native Americans were also disenchanted by aspects of the administration's Indian policy. The most troubling issue for many was the president's reversal on a campaign pledge to stop construction of the Kinzua

Dam, which would abrogate a 1794 treaty protecting Seneca Indian land. The dam project, to provide flood relief and water reserves for western Pennsylvania, had been in the works since the mid-1930s, and after a congressional debate in the late 1950s, ground had been broken in October 1960. In part because of a political debt to Pennsylvania governor David Lawrence, Kennedy backed down on his pledge, and hundreds of Seneca families in Pennsylvania and New York were relocated to make way for the project.[64] Despite government promises to attend to the needs of the Seneca through the transition, one Indian publication justifiably pronounced that "nothing can really recompense the Senecas for the loss of homeland involved."[65]

Robert Kennedy had responsibility over two other matters of great concern to Native Americans. The Lands Division of the Justice Department oversaw the Indian Claims Commission, which was established after World War II to adjudicate the compensatory territorial claims of Native peoples. Kennedy departed from the course set by the Eisenhower Justice Department to urge more rapid settlement of claims, increasing the number of panels processing the disputes, and successfully pressing for the creation of a loan fund for tribes to secure adequate legal counsel to argue their cases. Nonetheless, as Ramsey Clark, head of the Lands Division, reflected: "The law had put the government in the unhappy posture of being [Native Americans'] antagonist in litigation. I thought this was theoretically, absolutely wrong, but our obligation as lawyers was to defend these cases. We initiated a settlement policy, and [Robert Kennedy] favored it. . . . I thought the thing to do was settle [the claims] and get them out of there."[66]

The process of settling claims was tedious, however, in view of the difficulty of agreeing on land values, the profiteering of some self-interested lawyers for Native American claims who benefited from endless negotiations, and a Congress resistant to any settlement payments. In an ill-advised March 1962 *Life* magazine article on the topic, Kennedy tried to focus public attention on the process. Drafted by Clark and others in the Lands Division, the article explained how hard the government was working to "right the wrongs which *may have* been done in the early days of our history, when the white man took this country from the Indian by force, by overpowering numbers or by unconscionably cheap treaty purpose."[67] The most noticeable features of the piece were anecdotes exposing the absurdity of putting compensatory values on land deals from two to three centuries earlier, and cartoons depicting Native Americans holding "invoices" for items ranging from "One 1882 Tepee" to "One Whole State of

California."[68] The article evoked an avalanche of protests, with one Indian newspaper editorializing that Kennedy belittled Native Americans "at the same time he and his brother, the President, were out telling the world that they were champions of oppressed minorities, who were living in squalor, ignorance, economic deprivation and want."[69] Reacting to the scorching responses, an angry Kennedy told Clark: "Thanks a lot. My God, is that the best we can do?"[70]

The attorney general took steps to mend fences. He personally assured Walter Wetzel, president of the National Congress of American Indians, that his intention had been to generate popular pressure for the faster settlement of claims. In an open letter to the organization Kennedy apologized for the cartoons and insisted that he never saw them until after publication. Furthermore, in June 1962 he convened a Washington meeting with NCAI officials and again promised rapid action on land claims. While many Native Americans got their day in court before the Indian Claims Commission, they rarely received satisfactory settlements.[71]

On an even more urgent matter, Kennedy pledged to investigate charges of police brutality against Indians in South Dakota, telling NCAI leaders, "Advise the Indian people to inform me of any violations of their civil rights." Kennedy sought personally to reassure Robert Burnette, the chairman of the Rosebud Sioux in South Dakota, and was "visibly angered" when Burnette told him of abuses by law enforcement officials in the state.[72] Ultimately, however, the Justice Department was cautious in bringing civil rights cases unless it could be assured of victory, which was rare, and the attorney general appealed to the same federal model he employed in the South, telling a Sioux leader that his influence was limited as long as the state was conducting its inquiries.[73]

At the same time, Native Americans and the other groups and regions at the nation's economic margins—to which John Kennedy had appealed during his presidential campaign—remained mired in poverty. The administration did move quickly to act on the recommendations of Paul Douglas's committee assembled after the election, placing particular emphasis on the problem of unemployment, which was more widespread at the beginning of Kennedy's term than it had been in two decades.[74] Historian James Patterson has insightfully called the administration's measures on poverty "conservative applications of partially structuralist diagnoses."[75] Kennedy's limited, hybrid approach was rooted in the widely held conviction that despite the recent downturn, jobs and economic resources were potentially accessible, if structural obstacles in the form of place (depressed local economies), race (discrimination), or skills deficits could be surmounted. The first significant legislation Kennedy signed (in May 1961) was Douglas's resubmitted depressed areas bill, designed to address the structural problem of regional or localized poverty. The Area Redevelopment Act (ARA), which provided $300 million for local business loans, upgrades to public facilities, and other measures, constituted a significant boost in federal help for Native Americans, extending nearly five times the economic assistance as that allocated by the Bureau of Indian Affairs.[76] In 1962 Kennedy signed the Manpower Development and Training Act (MDTA), which addressed the development of marketable skills. The MDTA proved a much longer-lasting program than the ARA, training more than 2 million citizens over the next decade. Both were ultimately minimal initiatives, however, with inadequate funding spread too thin to come anywhere close to Kennedy's campaign suggestion of wiping out poverty.[77]

The next administration initiative directly geared toward poverty was similarly circumscribed, but it would prove instrumental to Robert Kennedy's growing understanding of both the nature of poverty in the United States and his evolving vision of how to confront it. As Michael Harrington's book *The Other America* raised the visibility of poverty after its publication in 1962, Eunice Kennedy Shriver again approached the president with an idea. Since the Peace Corps had quickly been viewed as an administration success, and there was clearly a need at home, Shriver— Robert Kennedy once cracked that his brother used to tell him, "Let's give Eunice whatever she wants so I can get her off the phone and get on with the business of government"—recommended a domestic version.[78] The president asked the attorney general to take on the project, and Robert Kennedy rapidly assembled a task force. By November 1962 his group had produced a favorable initial report, endorsing a National Service Corps to provide the manpower needed to assist the 32 million "largely dependent Americans" (a figure somewhat lower than Harrington's estimates) who were "living at a lower level [of subsistence] than America is capable of providing for its citizens."[79] Among the groups studied were American Indians, migrant workers, impoverished residents of the Appalachian region, and the mentally ill. Initial public reaction was positive; 62 percent of respondents to a Gallup poll thought that a domestic version of the Peace Corps was a good idea.[80]

The development of the presidential initiative followed a familiar pattern. The attorney general asked David Hackett to head the program, and their proposal centered on the coordination of contributions from executive branch departments. As in the development of the juvenile delinquency committee, Kennedy went to observe the problem firsthand, which, in the words of one of the PCJD guerrillas, "got him in touch with a lot of the issues about the poor and the Indians and God knows what else."[81] While it is hard to document with certainty the number of trips Kennedy made to poor areas of the country as attorney general, Hackett contended that it was "a good many."[82] The two men visited Appalachia, Mexican American barrios, and Native American reservations. Some were planned trips in conjunction with Kennedy's role as committee chairman, but others were impromptu visits to blighted urban neighborhoods when he was in town on other business. During one political trip to Chicago, Kennedy asked FBI agents to drive him through slum areas; the special agent in charge noted that the attorney general "appeared to indicate dissatisfaction with youth development here."[83] In Hackett's estimation Robert Kennedy "had a better vantage point to work on [poverty] than his brother. He'd come much closer to it . . . maybe go into Harlem, which his brother couldn't, and talk to . . . all the Negro leaders and the Mexican-American leaders."[84]

An early 1963 task force meeting brought community leaders from around the country to Kennedy's Justice Department office. The official who planned the gathering and took a leading role in shaping the proposed National Service Corps was Richard Boone, a former captain of the juvenile division of the Chicago Police Department, who had emerged as a key member of the PCJD. Boone (who kept a photo of the legendary Chicago strategist and organizer Saul Alinsky over his desk) was also a product of the University of Chicago sociology department, and believed that social change would come only if those at society's margins demanded it. The meeting orchestrated by Boone proved consequential, as it suggested a potential new relationship between the federal government and leaders at the grassroots level. At one point during the discussion a tribal leader complained about Bureau of Indian Affairs abuses and stated that any initiative undertaken by a domestic Peace Corps to help Indians would have to be planned *with* them, not *for* them. He then challenged the attorney general: "And what are you going to do about it?" Amused and impressed by the leader's boldness, Kennedy responded, "Don't just look at me, look at them," referring to the others present, including Labor Secretary Willard Wirtz and HEW chief Anthony Celebrezze.[85]

While only a handful of community leaders nationwide could ever be afforded such an immediate hearing by the highest ranking of federal officials, the meeting hinted at a distinctive new model of federalism with regard to poverty that Kennedy would come to idealize throughout the rest of his career. Bureaucratic ossification and the inertia of existing local power structures were stifling opportunity for true grassroots leadership; the federal government needed to coordinate its own activities to help directly those leaders most representative of the poor. The federal government would, however, have to share power with the poor for progress to be made, or else top-down welfarism—what Kennedy and his allies identified as the legacy of the New Deal—would only strengthen local reactionary forces. Instead the grassroots poor in communities could gain access to power in the form of federal recognition and resources, and their bottom-up pressure would make local structures more representative and responsive.

Kennedy tried to imbue the program with an adventuring élan similar to that of the Peace Corps by choosing retired naval captain William Anderson (who skippered the first nuclear submarine to pass beneath the polar ice cap) as the formal head of the proposed program. As in the PCJD formula, the National Service Corps bill was modest in scale (only five thousand volunteers would be enlisted), designed as a pilot project, and intended to spark grassroots efforts. Instead of federal funding serving as the stimulant, volunteers themselves would be the catalysts for increased antipoverty activity in a community. Corps volunteers would be sent into localities only on request, and, as in the PCJD approach, the use of resources (the volunteers) would be determined by local residents themselves.

Kennedy pushed hard for the bill, meeting with local and congressional leaders and testifying for the legislation in late May 1963.[86] His statement detailed a litany of national ills resulting from "deprivation," including the strikingly abbreviated forty-two-year life expectancy of Native Americans and graphic stories of poverty among migrant workers and the mentally ill. Kennedy emphasized the theme of national community, declaring that "every sixth citizen in the United States needs our help; there are five of us who should help him," and appealed, in the same vein as William James's essay "The Moral Equivalent of War," to the sacrifice and service so readily summoned by Americans in times of combat.[87] He concluded with rhetoric that foreshadowed themes he would later emphasize as a senator and a presidential candidate. "We can have," Kennedy said, "the Polaris submarine and [astronauts] Gordon Cooper and John Glenn, but if we also continue to have large numbers of Indians who have lived for decades as second-class citizens, if we have migrant workers whose problems are being ignored[,] . . . then no matter how many orbits our astronauts make around the globe, no matter how the gross national product grows, we will leave other peoples unimpressed."[88]

Despite its limited scale and traditional emphasis on voluntarism and local control, the National Service Corps proved divisive and faced tough sledding in Congress for several reasons. While the liberal *New York Times* and the *Washington Post* endorsed the program, the conservative *Chicago Tribune* called it "a kind of refined baby-sitting operation" and an "unnecessary extension of the flabby doctrines of the 'welfare state.'"[89] Two Republican congressmen, H. R. Gross of Iowa and Samuel Devine of Ohio, challenged the bill from the outset, alleging that funds for the task force had been inappropriately reprogrammed from executive departments for political purposes.[90] Among those in Congress not unalterably opposed to the bill, some questioned the commitment of the president.[91]

The attorney general took the lead in promoting the program through the tumultuous spring and summer of 1963. Behind the scenes he pushed for media coverage, established a "citizens committee" (headed by *Fortune* magazine publisher Malcolm Forbes) to support its passage, and even procured a plane (which columnist Drew Pearson reported had last been used to remove the final prisoners from Alcatraz "and smelled like it") to fly potential congressional Republican supporters to witness the poverty on the nation's largest Native American reservation in Pine Ridge, South Dakota.[92] Ultimately the biggest impediments were the logjam of Kennedy's other legislation (the *New York Times* tabulated twenty major bills) and the show-stopping events in the civil rights movement during the summer of 1963.[93] The bill passed narrowly in the Senate but remained stuck in committee for the rest of the year.

Even as his advisers informed him that the program had "virtually no chance of passage" in the House, the attorney general continued to champion the legislation and to discuss the issue of poverty through the fall of 1963, with particular attention to Native Americans.[94] The domestic Peace Corps initiative alerted Robert Kennedy to the real depth of suffering among American Indians, and it was important to his emerging relationship with them. Robert Burnette of the NCAI strongly endorsed the proposal early on, promising "100 per cent support from all the tribes in our organization," and Kennedy received an invitation at to speak at the organization's September convention in North Dakota.[95] "What do you think?" Kennedy scrawled before forwarding the letter to Ramsey Clark. "It's a hell of a long way to go, but I like Indians."[96]

Upon his arrival in Bismarck, Burnette arranged for Kennedy to meet with victims of abuse at the hands of police from towns near reservations, including a young girl whose vision was impaired by a tear gas attack and a man whose face was scarred after he was run down by a deputy's car.[97] In his address at the NCAI convention the attorney general called poverty an "evil force," thereby categorizing it as a moral issue even more pointedly than the president had done with civil rights. He condemned conditions among Indians as "nothing less than a national disgrace," and again echoed the language of his brother's civil rights address in asserting that while the Indian "may be technically free," he was in reality "the victim of social and economic oppressions that hold him in bondage."[98] His speech was received warmly. Kennedy was adopted into the nearly one hundred tribes that made up the congress and was given the Indian name "Brave Heart."[99]

Robert Kennedy's experiences in planning for both the National Service Corps and the PCJD deepened his concern for and affirmed his own emerging structural understanding of poverty. He was continually shocked by the concentrated poverty he observed in the nation's inner cities, and he publicly forecast rioting unless serious efforts were made to improve conditions. As a result, one of the many bills the administration sent to Congress in 1963 was a jobs program for young people. The youth employment bill called for the creation of a Youth Conservation Corps (modeled on Roosevelt's Civilian Conservation Corps) and a Hometown Youth Corps. In February the attorney general told members of Congress he was convinced that young people "would much rather work than loaf or fight," and warned the Senate subcommittee deliberating on the bill that the nation was "racing the clock against disaster. . . . [W]e must give the members of this new lost generation some real hope in order to prevent a shattering explosion of social problems in the years to come."[100]

Soon thereafter Louis Martin went on a political information–gathering tour of northern cities and concluded that unemployment and the poor visibility of administration efforts to attack it were beginning to create major political problems. As he put it, "Some of our own political leaders seem to have a very vague conception of the nature of the economic thrust of the Kennedy Administration."[101]

The Kennedys' political headaches would intensify later that spring. The Birmingham campaign was a major catalyst for African American protests in northern and western cities that commentators soon began referring to as "the Negro Revolt." A CORE leader in Los Angeles reported that the organization "had a stack of membership applications at least six inches high" and that "Birmingham has done the recruiting for us." According to another CORE official, Birmingham "brought a drastic revision in our thinking. . . . [Y]ou can nibble at the surface for a thousand years and not get anywhere."[102] Organized demonstrations against segregation in housing and education took place in Englewood, New Jersey; Cambridge, Maryland; and Los Angeles. In Philadelphia, CORE and the NAACP launched campaigns against the exclusion of black laborers from municipal construction projects. "For the Negro," said NAACP national labor secretary Herbert Hill, "the arena of combat has shifted from courtrooms of America to fields of direct mass action."[103]

Ebony journalist Lerone Bennett Jr. probed the implications of what he called the "Freedom Now mood," writing, "The open protests in the South and the deep and awesome stillness in the ghettos of the north are portents of a volcanic threat that will not be denied." As a result, "for perhaps the first time in its history, America has a thoroughly restive minority population." Because they were hemmed in within the poorest neighborhoods in urban America, Bennett observed, those on the wrong side of the color line were "strategically placed to cause social chaos."[104]

Even though Robert Kennedy had seen for himself the stifling conditions faced by the urban poor and warned of their potential costs, neither he nor the president could grasp how rapidly African Americans' patience was dwindling. "They're awful tough to deal with now. . . . [T]hey're all mad," the attorney general said of the black community before a gathering of the president's closest advisers.[105] The attorney general had something of a taste for gallows humor, but in this deadly serious situation Kennedy turned to comedian and civil rights activist Dick Gregory for insight. Gregory, who was sometimes referred to as the "black Mort Sahl"—both were prominent among a new generation of edgy, topical comedians—had befriended Robert Kennedy the previous fall when the attorney general asked him to try to persuade a wavering James Meredith to stay enrolled at Ole Miss.[106] Gregory had been involved in protests in both the North and the South (including Birmingham), and he was well positioned to describe the sentiments of movement activists across the country. Gregory had in fact suggested that Kennedy meet with James Baldwin, and in their private discussions the comedian affirmed for the attorney general that the next civil rights battleground would be the cities of the North.[107]

The protests across the nation also forced the administration to propose relatively broader civil rights legislation. While a public accommodations bill had been discussed for some months, John Kennedy acknowledged in his civil rights address that African Americans were not yet free from economic oppression. The desegregation of public accommodations and schools was central to the legislation, but White House officials debated provisions to deal with structural unemployment based on race.

The most visible step the administration had thus far taken on employment for African Americans was the creation of the President's Committee on Equal Employment Opportunity (PCEEO). Chaired by Vice President Lyndon Johnson, it was an expanded version of a committee on government contracts that had been established in the Eisenhower years. While limited and underfunded, it did provide some recourse for victims of discrimination in hiring, and it shifted the burden of proof away from individual complainants to employers.[108] Another committee task was the compilation of statistics on minority hiring among businesses receiving government contracts. The numbers that surfaced in the spring of 1963 were appalling, and in the wake of events in Birmingham and elsewhere, including his meeting with James Baldwin, an angry Robert Kennedy fixed the blame on Lyndon Johnson. "I was so worked up about the Negroes getting jobs," he told an oral history interviewer later, admitting that he also feared the embarrassment the issue would cause his brother in the coming reelection campaign.[109] Kennedy put the vice president in the hot seat over the committee's performance during a meeting that further widened the rift between the two men.[110]

For the attorney general, employment had become the key to any real progress on civil rights.[111] Nevertheless, he was unwilling to advocate the steps that civil rights leaders and other liberals deemed most likely to produce swift results, namely, a permanent Fair Employment Practices Commission (FEPC) or a public works bill to create jobs more rapidly and directly.[112] John Kennedy was not opposed in principle to a public works bill, but he feared that combining it with the civil rights legislation would eliminate the votes of southerners who would otherwise support such a measure.[113] Nicholas Katzenbach asserted that the White House "was guided throughout by seeking the maximum we thought possible on the theory that success was vital." With regard to a permanent FEPC, "no one," Katzenbach reflected, "thought it had a chance of passage."[114] The White House did insert two measures that Robert Kennedy told congressmen "bear on the problem of poverty"—Title VI, outlawing discrimination in local and state programs supported with federal dollars, and Title VII, making the PCEEO a permanent body and expanding its access to funding.[115] Though he had failed to push for the most progressive employment measures, Kennedy's testimony before the House Judiciary Committee suggested his recognition of the interrelationship between civil rights and poverty, along with the reasons for the "Negro Revolt."[116] Not only had the demonstrations shown, Kennedy said, "that an ever-increasing number of our Negro citizens will no longer accept an inferior status," but also "they have drawn sharp attention to the handicaps which so many . . . experience simply because they are not white—or because years of unjust deprivation have left them in poverty and without the means or hope of improving their condition."[117]

Over time, the issues and efforts that had introduced Robert Kennedy to problem of poverty—civil rights, juvenile delinquency, the work of the Allen committee, the National Service Corps—worked together to increase the sense of urgency, and each element reinforced the findings and strategic approaches of the others. This became clearest in the final months of the administration as the president gave new priority to an attack on poverty, influenced by events, by political strategy—and by an essay.

There is no clear evidence that either John or Robert Kennedy ever read the book that framed the issue of poverty for the 1960s. Each, however, came to *The Other America* in his own way. Robert Kennedy was investigating what Michael Harrington had seen up close through his own intermittent and unsystematic "field research" for the planning of both the PCJD and the National Service Corps. John Kennedy, while he had been stunned by what he witnessed in West Virginia, had been detached from direct contact with the problem for three years by the time he sat down to read Dwight Macdonald's review essay about Harrington's book.[118] Harrington's findings moved the president to begin asking new questions about the nature and magnitude of poverty in early 1963.

John Kennedy had made clear campaign promises on the issue in 1960, but his chief economic concern during his first two years in office was a potential crisis in the international balance of payments for the United States.[119] Although the usual Keynesian remedy for a weak economy had been increased government spending, no popular mandate existed for significant new federal outlays—as evidenced by the reaction of conservative Republicans to even the lean National Service Corps proposal—and Secretary of the Treasury C. Douglas Dillon warned the president about the economic risks of new programmatic spending.[120] Walter Heller, the chairman of the Council of Economic Advisers, instead pressed for a tax reduction to effect the desired Keynesian deficits and spur growth. Kennedy assented, and the administration began its tax cut push in the summer of 1962.

At the same time that the national discussion of *The Other America* was spreading and John Kennedy's concern about the magnitude of the poverty problem was growing, reports filtering into the White House suggested the political advisability of a wider antipoverty drive. A television documentary on poverty hosted by newsman Howard K. Smith generated hundreds of sympathetic letters to the White House, which staff aides characterized as either hopes for "a mood of sympathy for the poor (like Eleanor Roosevelt)" or "vigorous demands for action (like FDR)."[121] Around the same time Louis Martin, after surveying attitudes in northern cities in the spring of 1963, informed the attorney general that many labor leaders and other party regulars, given their New Deal understanding of government management of the economy, were restless and confused about the president's tax cut proposal. "The philosophy of giving tax breaks to big business to stimulate the economy," Martin wrote, "seems to run counter to their general economic views."[122] Finally, Heller keenly noted criticism directed at the president by two prominent moderate New York Republicans—prospective presidential candidate Nelson Rockefeller and Senator Kenneth Keating. At a June 1963 event to kick off his reelection campaign for the following year, Keating urged his party to present its own antipoverty drive, leading Heller to advise the president to head off Keating and potentially like-minded Republicans at the pass.[123]

As a result of these factors, along with the new urgency of the economic demands arising from the black freedom struggle, Kennedy agreed that a political counterweight to the tax cut, in the form of a broader program for those at the lower end of the economic ladder, was in order. Throughout the fall of 1963 Heller solicited ideas within the executive branch departments for interagency antipoverty measures through a task force given the politically innocuous-sounding title "Widening Participation in Prosperity."[124]

The planning work of the National Service Corps task force and the PCJD would ultimately prove instrumental to the shape the amorphous new antipoverty drive would take. The PCJD had begun to reassess its strategic approach in 1963 as a result of three factors: increasing congressional pressure for greater thrift (led by Democratic congresswoman Edith Green of Oregon), disappointment in the creativity of the planning phase, and the high-profile failure of local coordination in the first federally funded project in Cleveland. The new avenue the PCJD began to traverse was the inclusion of a more prominent role for impoverished urban residents themselves in shaping and directing federal efforts.[125]

The new approach was itself the product of a number of forces. It was a response to rising demands in black communities, particularly Harlem, for participation in the decision-making process. The strategic shift was also encouraged by the predisposition of key figures in the PCJD such as Richard Boone and Paul Ylvisaker, who were both veterans of Ford Foundation

Gray Areas projects that included the poor in program development and operation. As historian Alice O'Connor has demonstrated, the juvenile delinquency committee became the port of entry for a stream of "poverty knowledge" crafted by social scientists and subsidized by private foundations throughout the postwar era, and the Gray Areas project that attempted to revive deteriorating urban areas was the most influential.[126] Finally, the lesson that Richard Boone and Robert Kennedy took from the National Service Corps task force—that programs should be shaped "with not for" the poor—seemed to suggest a new approach.[127]

The new strategy of participation by the poor was thus combined with the earlier emphasis on coordination to form a new mechanism for attacking the localized structural and environmental causes of juvenile delinquency that came to be known as "community action." Coordination and participation, though designed to go hand in hand to increase the efficiency of the delivery of government services, were also distinct concepts that could at times work at cross-purposes. In 1963, however, the tension between the two had yet to emerge, and the notion of participation struck a deeply responsive chord in the attorney general, who had famously been raised to embrace the value of participation in civic life. It also squared with Kennedy's faith in voter participation as the key to social change.[128] In time, however, Kennedy's ideal of federalism built on participation by the poor would be sorely tested by the realities of state and local power.

Emboldened by the work of Heller, David Hackett summarized for Robert Kennedy the lessons to be drawn from both the PCJD and the National Service Corps experiences. In a November 6 memo Hackett concluded that fighting poverty had been the actual PCJD objective all along: "Because of the intimate relationship between poverty and crime, our comprehensive programs of delinquency prevention and control have inevitably led to attempts to deal with poverty and its effects. The Juvenile Delinquency program has emphasized access to opportunity for youth as a way of combatting poverty; thus, the Juvenile Delinquency program has, in fact, concentrated its resources on attacks on poverty in selected cities."[129]

What Hackett proposed for a federal antipoverty program was the PCJD formula writ large. He noted that the experiences of both the PCJD and the National Service Corps study group demonstrated that local and federal coordination was paramount to success, and his recommendations outlined what could be done with existing resources. Hackett called for study committees, made up of those both in and outside the federal government, to reconceptualize the problem of poverty, assess existing programs on all levels, and recommend creative new legislation. Such task forces would continue to study "key areas of poverty throughout the United States."[130]

The coordination component of the Kennedy-Hackett plan found important allies at the highest levels. Labor Department official and occasional Hackett "guerrilla" Daniel Patrick Moynihan observed that the Bureau of the Budget (which he referred to as the "superego of the federal establishment") found the possibility of coordinated local services "intoxicating" because increased local energy, order, and efficiency could maximize each tax dollar spent.[131] Walter Heller and the Council of Economic Advisers were also attracted to the concept.[132]

The ultimate aim of Hackett's recommendations was not an all-out programmatic assault on poverty but additional demonstration projects, subject to continued assessment.[133] If much of the coming War on Poverty would emerge with a massive, sprawling battle plan, in early November 1963 David Hackett and Robert Kennedy were more cautious, determined to wage the limited guerrilla warfare learned in the juvenile delinquency committee.[134]

In October 1963 President Kennedy, moved to action by *New York Times* reporter Homer Bigart's stories of distressed eastern Kentuckians suffering devastating floods in that region, directed Undersecretary of Commerce Franklin Roosevelt Jr. to offer federal help.[135] Driven by fears of a "grim winter" without significant assistance, Richard Boone urged a "crash program" for the mountain crisis that ultimately proved something of a trial run for the models of federal assistance developed in both the National Service Corps and the PCJD.[136] Boone proposed the creation of the Appalachian Volunteers (AV) to put young people to work in shoring up homes in the region for winter, and informed Roosevelt that any programs to help in the region "should involve the residents as participants in rendering as well as receiving aid. Kentuckians will respond enthusiastically to an aid program which is administered in cooperation with the residents and, wherever possible, is based on self-help principles."[137]

Events in Appalachia and the findings of Heller's ad hoc committee would be an important subject in President Kennedy's last full cabinet meeting on October 29. A week later, as word of the president's antipoverty musings circulated inside the Beltway, diplomat George Kennan broke from his foreign policy presentation at another Hickory Hill seminar to quote the biblical injunction "the poor shall be with you always," suggesting that any such effort was futile. Heller leaped to the defense of his emerging plans, as did the attorney general.[138]

On November 19, before leaving on a trip for Japan, Heller went to see the president, concerned that momentum for a poverty program was waning.[139] "Yes, Walter, I am definitely going to have something in the line of an attack on poverty," Kennedy told Heller. "I don't know what yet. But yes, keep your boys at work, and come back to me in a couple of weeks."[140] Three days later David Hackett and others in the PCJD planned to call the attorney general into a meeting with the Washington, D.C., school superintendent, who was not cooperating with the local delinquency agency receiving federal funding in the nation's capital.[141] From that day on, however, the influence of both the juvenile delinquency committee and the attorney general would never be the same.

4

TROUBLES

AND TRIALS

FROM DALLAS

TO WATTS

For his remaining nine months at the Justice Department and through most of his first year in the Senate, Robert Kennedy was in search of direction. He had built his life around his brother's presidency, and his death left him rudderless and downcast. Through a period beginning and ending with two of the most stunning bursts of violence in the second half of the twentieth century—the assassination in Dallas and the Watts uprising of August 1965—Robert Kennedy was mired in a dark night of both his personal and his political soul. He considered a number of options, including leaving public life. Once he decided to stay in politics, Kennedy floated trial balloons about serving in any of several prominent posts, including the vice presidency and the ambassadorship to South Vietnam. One constant through this period of uncertainty was his involvement with the issue of poverty. Its growing prominence would ultimately lead him to a new role in American political life.

Associates have offered conflicting accounts of Kennedy's political engagement in the weeks and months after his brother's assassination. "It was as though someone had turned off his switch," David Hackett later said.[1] While Hackett felt that the attorney general was still able to work effectively through his staff, administrative assistant John Seigenthaler believed that Kennedy was in a constant state of emotional and even physical pain.[2] To friends and other observers he seemed lost in his own world, unresponsive at worst and monosyllabic at best. On one occasion Daniel Patrick Moynihan and Kennedy brother-in-law Sargent Shriver visited the attorney general; Moynihan later recalled that "at a certain point, Shriver stopped talking, and Kennedy said *nothing*. He had just forgotten that we were there. We both just got up and left."[3]

Children provided brief diversions from his grief. He hosted a Christmas party for students from poor Washington neighborhoods, hauling forty tons of crushed ice into the Justice Department courtyard for sleigh rides, and enlisting the Smothers Brothers and the Washington Redskins for entertainment.[4] In the middle of the fun, a young boy ran up to him and said, "Your brother is dead," silencing the room. As the child began to cry Kennedy picked him up and said, "Don't worry, I have another."[5] A group of black and Puerto Rican teenagers from Harlem came to the Capitol to petition House leaders for the passage of the Youth Conservation Corps and made the attorney general an honorary member of their "Young Adult Action Group," sponsored by the prominent anti-delinquency agency Mobilization for Youth. He congratulated them on their good citizenship and declared, "We're all in this fight together."[6]

The strained relationship between the attorney general and the new president diminished Robert Kennedy's status in the administration more than that of any other Kennedy appointee. The effects were felt by many of the "guerrillas" in the PCJD, who quickly sensed that Robert Kennedy's power—and their base in the administration—had "vanished overnight."[7] One member later reflected, "We had to get our licks in and do what we could today because we didn't know what tomorrow would be like."[8] Kennedy shared their frustration and privately told Arthur Schlesinger of the depth of his distrust for Johnson, warning the historian-adviser that once Johnson was elected on his own in November, the Kennedy holdovers would "all be dead." Whether he spoke out of self-pity, genuine concern, or likely some admixture of both, Kennedy suggested forming a shadow government, telling Schlesinger: "We must all stay in close touch and not let them pick us off one by one. I haven't the answer . . . but I am sure the fundamental principle now is collective action. . . . My brother barely had a chance to get started—and there is so much now to be done—for the Negroes and the unemployed and the school kids and everyone else who is not getting a decent break in our society. This is what counts. The new fellow doesn't get this. He knows all about politics and nothing about human beings."[9]

Kennedy's bunker mentality is perhaps understandable given the emotionally charged context and the previous tensions between the men.

Nevertheless, the new president did try to reach out to the attorney general in the weeks after Dallas, but Kennedy proved unable to overcome past animosities.[10] Their continuing rivalry created serious complications for both men, for the Democratic Party, and for the nation's assault on poverty in the coming years.

After the death of John Kennedy, Jacqueline Kennedy had his notes from the final cabinet meeting framed for her brother-in-law. The president had written and circled the word "poverty" six times.[11] The amount and depth of discussion between John and Robert Kennedy on the issue of poverty is uncertain, but it is clear that the attorney general believed his brother wanted to address the problem in the 1964 election year. The likely magnitude of such an effort is, however, debatable. In an oral history interview recorded that spring—one week after he testified in support of Lyndon Johnson's $1 billion poverty bill—the attorney general suggested that his brother had realized a satisfactory push would cost "several billions of dollars each year." Kennedy also claimed that the White House was awaiting passage of the tax cut bill before seeking outlays for such a major assault. Kennedy's assertion must be viewed with a large measure of skepticism, however, as his hours of recorded reflections serve as an extension of his efforts both to protect and to glorify John Kennedy, often at the expense of Lyndon Johnson. While John Kennedy may have recognized that a program on a very large scale was necessary, Robert Kennedy's own actions in the weeks after the assassination belied such a diagnosis, and others in key positions in the administration were uncertain that the president had had such grand designs.[12]

Whatever the scale of such an antipoverty initiative, Walter Heller shared the understanding that John Kennedy had wanted to move on the issue in 1964. He visited Lyndon Johnson for an economic briefing the day after the assassination. Early in their discussion Heller recounted his last conversation with the slain president. He briefed Johnson on the "Widening Participation in Prosperity" initiative and asked the new president about his inclinations. "Push ahead full-tilt," Johnson responded. "That's my kind of program. I'll find money for it one way or another. If I have to, I'll take money away from [other] things to get money for people." As the economist was leaving, Johnson insisted that he was "no budget slasher" and that Heller's friends should know that his record was that of a Roosevelt New Dealer. "To tell the truth," Johnson confided, "John F. Kennedy was a little too conservative to suit my taste."[13] It was the beginning of a reintroduction of Lyndon Johnson that would surprise and hearten many liberals in the difficult weeks after the assassination.[14]

While Kennedy did little in the Justice Department until after the holidays, he made it clear in a December meeting with top White House officials, including chief domestic adviser Theodore Sorensen, that he would like to head the emerging antipoverty effort.[15] Following the meeting Kennedy summarized his further thoughts in a memo to Sorensen, emphasizing two lessons from the juvenile delinquency committee experience. "Particular attention should be paid to how the poor view their situations," the attorney general noted, "and the ways in which they believe they can contribute to a solution of their problems." Kennedy also urged that the planners of the program "concentrate on developing strategies of self-help—not because we believe that self-help is the answer to poverty, but because we consider it a vital ingredient too often ignored in government programs."[16]

At first glance the inclusion of the principle of self-help seems a departure from the strategies that Kennedy had been embracing. He undoubtedly assumed that individual effort had to be part of any antipoverty initiative, but his rhetoric had consistently emphasized the need to help individuals and localities in ways they were unable to do for themselves. Given its overall context within the memo and the ideas and attitudes of both the PCJD and the National Service Corps task force, Kennedy's use of the expression "self-help" was closer in meaning to political involvement and empowerment than its more common connotation of bootstraps individualism. Richard Boone, perhaps aided by his no-nonsense demeanor and law enforcement credentials, had been craftily and effectively deploying the conservative-sounding term to explain the value of potential National Service Corps and Appalachian Volunteer programs in helping communities solve their own problems, and those meanings seem to have been Kennedy's.[17]

The other admonition the attorney general stressed to Sorensen was to "avoid becoming entangled in the federal government's system of vested interests." He called for an "administrative structure which clearly assigns responsibility" as a way of avoiding the problem, and his prescription was for the cabinet-level post recommended by Hackett—and presumably manned by Kennedy himself—to oversee coordination of the various interdepartmental programs involved in the antipoverty attack.[18]

Robert Kennedy did not view the nascent strategies developed in the PCJD and National Service Corps task force as final answers to the problem of poverty. His emphases on coordination and participation were changes of process that would yield further ideas and plans as they evolved.[19] Accordingly, the attorney general favored a continued examination of the problem, "a hard new look at poverty" by "competent and imaginative people drawn from within and outside the government." As in Hackett's November 6 memo, Kennedy called for a "study-action program."[20] The attorney general did not believe a nationwide large-scale effort was yet in order.

Kennedy's approach was at variance with the New Deal orientation Johnson pledged to Walter Heller, so Hackett, wary of an expansive, top-down strategy, sent a memo to the president under Kennedy's name in January, delineating PCJD ideas and concluding that "the anti-poverty program could actually retard the solution of these problems, unless we use the basic approach outlined."[21] If Kennedy, Hackett, and many of the PCJD and National Service Corps "guerrillas" were resistant to a massive, federally directed attack, the increasingly influential Richard Boone viewed President Johnson's enthusiasm differently. "Look," Boone told Lloyd Ohlin, chair of the PCJD, "let's take advantage of the opportunity we've got now. Let's get the money out there."[22] Despite his initial reservations, Kennedy would ultimately come around to Boone's way of thinking.

In the months after his ascent to the Oval Office, Lyndon Johnson was bound to the Kennedy legacy. "Let us continue," Johnson reverently intoned in his first speech as president, but he longed to forge his own path. The new president saw the poverty program as his chance to become the Franklin Roosevelt of the second half of the twentieth century, but Robert Kennedy's interest posed a threat to exclusive popular identification of Johnson as poverty warrior in chief.[23] It was thus highly unlikely that the new president ever seriously considered appointing Kennedy to head the War on Poverty. Johnson instead trained his persuasive energies on the reluctant Sargent Shriver, Kennedy's brother-in-law and the director of the Peace Corps. Johnson told Shriver that in spite of pressure to choose the attorney general or another administration official, he wanted to make it clear that Shriver was "Mr. Poverty, at home and abroad."[24] The new president's selection of Shriver was a political masterstroke. He thereby inoculated himself against charges that he was moving away from the intentions of John Kennedy while making the initiative his own (the *New York Times* would later describe it as "the first major legislative program to come exclusively from his administration"); and Shriver would prove an energetic and effective advocate for the War on Poverty.[25]

In spite of public perceptions, Shriver and Robert Kennedy were not close, and Shriver's selection effectively shut Kennedy out of any leading role.[26] After Shriver and his task force began deliberating how to wage war against poverty, he went to see Kennedy at the Justice Department with

Adam Yarmolinsky, his chief assistant during the planning period, and Peace Corps official Frank Mankiewicz. The attorney general, still struggling through the most difficult period of his adult life, asked only whether the emerging program was "what President Kennedy would have wanted." Granted this assurance—which was ambiguous at best given the fact that the president's thinking about poverty had been largely driven by the work of the attorney general and Walter Heller—Robert Kennedy stayed out of any direct planning for the War on Poverty.[27]

The omnibus poverty bill did absorb most of the Kennedy administration legislation still lodged in congressional committees. The program Johnson and Shriver found most appealing, the Job Corps, sprang from the provisions of the Youth Employment Opportunities bill. It was rooted in the same assessment of structural poverty as stemming from an absence of skills, and in addition to his role overseeing the many other moving parts of the War on Poverty, it was the one program Shriver wanted to direct personally. Robert Kennedy did intercede for two specific measures left over from the previous year that the task force viewed with skepticism. One was a revived National Service Corps and the other was community action.[28]

The Shriver task force debated the desirability of another domestic Peace Corps proposal, the program not only having stalled in Congress months earlier but also, in the assessment of Adam Yarmolinsky, having left a "bad odor" among conservative Republicans, who not only had concerns about duplication of services but also feared that it would be used for political purposes.[29] The national political calculus had shifted, however, and initiatives identified with the late president now met with greater popular sympathy. The attorney general pushed both publicly and privately for the program to go forward. In the estimation of Stephen Pollak, who had been the attorney for the National Service Corps task force a year earlier, the domestic Peace Corps would not have been realized without Kennedy's insistence.[30] Despite the fact that a domestic Peace Corps was considered a Kennedy item, ultimately, Pollak concluded, "it needed a champion to overcome this legislative tactical reluctance."[31] Although it was not the most important program in the War on Poverty, the domestic Peace Corps, renamed Volunteers in Service to America (VISTA), was enduring.

The second and more significant addition to the War on Poverty for which Robert Kennedy intervened was community action. While the attorney general did not participate directly in the task force, Richard Boone, who was assigned as the Justice Department representative, promoted community action tenaciously, later telling an interviewer that he "became a Mau Mau on the issue of [community] participation."[32] As task force deliberations unfolded, Adam Yarmolinsky told Boone, "You've brought that idea up several times." In Yarmolinsky's account, Boone replied: "'Yes, I have. How many more times do I have to bring it up before it gets into the program?' and I said, 'Oh, two or three.' He did, and it did."[33] Community action became the basis for Title II of the Economic Opportunity Act and the most important byproduct of the juvenile delinquency and National Service Corps experiences.

As it hatched and moved beyond the nest of the PCJD, however, the idea of community action proved to be a kind of gnosis, yielding different interpretations and often confusion. Norbert Schlei, who was sent from the Justice Department to help in the drafting of Title II, summed up its essential ambiguity: "It was a concept that had various ideas associated with it. But any two people you talked to about what a community action program was and what was important about it would grab hold of a different part of the elephant."[34] Significant aspects of the concept were left unexplored by the Shriver task force. Yarmolinsky offered the startling revelation a decade after its inception that he had never seen the Kennedy-Hackett plan for the implementation of community action.[35]

In a 1967 study Gordon J. Davis and Amanda Hawes discussed the emergence of four models of community action. The first was the "Bureau of the Budget Concept," which was "concerned with the *efficient* coordination of all programs directed at the elimination of poverty." The second they called the "Alinsky Concept," which "focused upon remedying the powerlessness of the poor by creating organizations controlled by the poor directed at disrupting the political and social status quo." The third understanding of community action was the "Peace Corps Concept," which attempted to "alleviate the pathology of poverty areas by increase of services and communication." Finally, the "Task Force Concept" emphasized political effectiveness—a program that would pass Congress and lead to "more jobs for the poor, participation by the poor in program administration, and recreation of local political machines."[36]

While these categories are helpful, they do not reveal the extent to which the models overlapped. In an essay discussing "community competence," a theory he developed "in a very concrete and practical manner" out of the PCJD experience, sociologist Leonard Cottrell described the need for both coordination and participation. "Competence" referred to the ability of a community to organize and coordinate itself to resolve some of its own damaged opportunity structures and to form a plan that might serve as the basis for outside help. Coordination was essential because of "the extensiveness and complexity" of the problems in an impoverished community, and widespread participation was necessary not just so residents would feel empowered but because "while technical experts might draw up excellent logical plans, no plan entailing the shifts in perceptions, perspectives, attitudes and practices this type of program required of practically all segments of the community could ever be implemented without the intensive participation of those segments in the process."[37]

Complicating matters further, important members of the PCJD emphasized different aspects of community action. Boone clearly promoted the politically empowering participation model.[38] Hackett was from the first compelled by the potentials for efficiency and coordination presented by community action. Robert Kennedy's understanding of community action in the spring of 1964 was, characteristically, distinctly nontheoretical and was instead based on a series of principles that to him seemed self-evident: any attack on poverty had to be comprehensive and address the multiple causations; the federal government should lead by "stimulating" and supporting localities; program development should be done *with* and not *for* the poor; and both federal and local efforts should be coordinated.

The particulars of Robert Kennedy's intervention on behalf of community action are unclear. Hackett has contended that Kennedy, through a series of confrontations with Shriver, "forced Title II to be a part of" the legislation.[39] Shriver was doubtful about the prospects for local coordination, as he had witnessed bitter local infighting in his experience with the Chicago Board of Education, and he was also unconvinced of its political appeal.[40] The guidelines President Johnson gave Shriver's task force went a long way toward facilitating the inclusion of the program. Johnson rejected both new welfare payments and spending programs requiring new taxes, and he directed the task force to complete its work in just six weeks.[41] "The only thing he gave me was community action," Shriver recalled.[42] Even so, Johnson knew little about community action and was initially skeptical. Nevertheless, it was far less expensive than a massive jobs program, and the Kennedy administration had left no detailed blueprint for action. The emerging PCJD model seemed the closest thing to an original, comprehensive approach to battling poverty as was practicable in early 1964. Johnson's time constraints, moreover, precluded a full exploration of the potential ramifications of community action, exemplifying Henry Kissinger's later observation that political leaders "are constantly locked in an endless battle in which the urgent constantly gains on the important. The public life of every political figure is a continual struggle to rescue an element of choice from the pressure of circumstance."[43]

Although he may have had reservations about the scale of the War on Poverty and its failure to adhere more closely to the PCJD template, under the pressure of circumstance Robert Kennedy chose action. As Yarmolinsky later observed, "The way to begin was to begin, and that was a typical Kennedy as well as Johnson approach."[44] Robert Kennedy testified before the House of Representatives on April 7 in support of Title II. His testimony emphasized that poverty was an urgent national problem. When conservative Republican David Martin of Nebraska contended that antipoverty initiatives should be driven solely by private efforts and individual will, Kennedy retorted, "Have you ever talked to the coal miners of West Virginia and told them what they needed was individual initiative?" When Martin insisted that localities should handle the problem of poverty on their own, Kennedy asserted that many communities were unable to do so. "They are citizens of West Virginia, of Kentucky, of Alaska, and they are also citizens of the United States. This is fundamental," Kennedy charged. "Those of us who are better off, who do not have that problem, have a responsibility to our fellow citizens who do."[45]

Kennedy cited the model of leadership by federal stimulation developed in the PCJD and extolled the principle of participation by the poor as he made the administration's case for community action. In explaining the rationale for participation, Kennedy uttered the phrase that would become the most controversial credo in the War on Poverty:

> The component programs of a community action program are important. But it is just as important that . . . they be built together. The institutions which affect the poor—education, welfare, recreation, business, labor—are huge, complex structures, operating far outside their control. They plan programs for the poor, not with them. Part of the sense of helplessness and futility comes from the feeling of powerlessness to affect the operation of these organizations. The community action programs must basically change these organizations by building into the program real representation for the poor. This bill calls for *maximum feasible participation* of the residents. This means the involvement of the poor in planning and implementing programs; giving them a real voice in their institutions.[46]

Surprisingly in hindsight, the attorney general was not questioned about the meaning or potential pitfalls of "maximum feasible participation." Democrat Roman Pucinski of Illinois, a product of Chicago mayor

Richard Daley's machine, did express concern that the federal government would "deal directly with organizations in local communities, bypassing local governments." This was, of course, one of the elements of community action that Kennedy and many in the PCJD found most appealing. While it was perilous for a Democrat to circumvent the urban political organizations that were major pillars of the party—particularly Daley's—Kennedy did not attempt to assuage Pucinski's fears, cautioning that additional provisions might sink the bill in Congress.[47]

Finally, Kennedy responded to questions about the costs of the program as a challenge to the national will. "I have confidence in the system," Kennedy said, "and I think the idea that we might have to go on for ten or twenty years or spend large sums of money should not deter us from taking the first step."[48] He told Oregon congresswoman Edith Green, "We talk about communism and how terrible it is, but this is something where you can really take a step in order to improve the situation in the United States for people who are less fortunate."[49] No statement better exemplifies Kennedy's emerging political priorities.

The attorney general had not resumed public appearances until the spring of 1964, and when he did, his focus most often turned to civil rights and poverty (as the Civil Rights Act, the Economic Opportunity Act, and the Criminal Justice Act were all moving through Congress). In an emotional St. Patrick's Day speech before the Friendly Sons of St. Patrick in Scranton, Pennsylvania, Kennedy appealed to the traditional Irish quest for freedom in asking listeners to recognize that "there are cities in America today that are torn with strife over whether a Negro should be allowed to drive a garbage truck" and that "walls of silent conspiracy" blocked the progress of African Americans.[50] In late April he paid a somber visit to the federally funded juvenile delinquency project in Charleston, West Virginia, and examined the impoverished black "triangle district" in the city and nearby poor white hollows. As in East Harlem three years earlier, a local youth worker shepherded the attorney general, this time through the cabins and shacks of Dry and Wet Branch. An out-of-work miner hugged him and told him: "We loved your brother. That sure was a dirty trick they did."[51] Kennedy met an abandoned mother of six whose four-year-old daughter suffered from cerebral palsy. He gathered the little girl into his lap, spoke gently with her, and placed his tie clasp on her dress. After hearing about the staggering unemployment and the absence of schooling for children in the area (school buses couldn't navigate the heavily rutted mountain roads), Kennedy mused aloud: "If we can't break into this cycle, we've had it. It will never end."[52]

Kennedy later shared his concern with graduates at Marquette University. "One can find," he said, "a bitter, hopeless America as easily as the confident America of polyethylene wrapping, new cars and camping trips in the summer." Discussing Michael Harrington's rendering of the poor as invisible Americans, the attorney general proposed that "the phrase can be reversible. . . . [F]or the unemployed city laborer or the uneducated Appalachian teenager or the ailing, elderly widower, it is the comfortable American who is invisible."[53]

As Kennedy gropingly edged back into public life in the spring of 1964, he held out an improbable hope that Lyndon Johnson would ask him to join the ticket for the fall campaign. As that appeared increasingly less likely, he considered overtures from New York Democratic leaders to run against Republican senator Kenneth Keating in the fall. After vacillating for most of the summer, and despite the moderate Keating's popularity and strength on Kennedy's bread and butter issues—he had even scored an honorable mention on *Ebony*'s list of "most trusted whites"—Kennedy decided to run.

The summer of 1964 was a turning point in many ways, what one author has called "the last innocent year" in postwar U.S. history.[54] The Tonkin Gulf incident would set the United States on the path to a land war in Southeast Asia, and inner city violence that summer heralded a period of the most significant urban social unrest since the Zoot Suit and Detroit riots during World War II. On July 16 a black teenager was shot and killed in the Bedford-Stuyvesant section of Brooklyn by an off-duty white police officer. Jack Newfield has written, "That gunshot signaled the end of the civil rights movement and the beginning of the long, hot summers."[55] Days of rioting ensued, and the following week violence broke out in Rochester, New York.

Other northern communities were also on the brink of rebellion that summer, and in late July, Lyndon Johnson called Kennedy to discuss what might be done to ease tensions. The attorney general cautioned the president that young urban residents had no faith in local black Democratic politicians and often considered them "Uncle Toms." Instead Kennedy suggested that a direct federal relationship with the grassroots in these communities seemed to offer more promise. He told Johnson of his work with young people in the capital and contended that it had given them "the feeling that there are people in government and in important places that are interested in them. Our experience . . . is that that makes a hell of a difference."[56]

As he prepared to leave Washington, Kennedy received a sendoff from local schoolchildren that seemed to bear out his assertion. Filling the football stadium at Cardozo High School, 3,500 students gave him a five-minute ovation and presented him with gifts, musical entertainment, and heartfelt speeches thanking him for his involvement with the community. Warming to signs that read "Hurry Back, Bobby" and "We'll Meet Again," Kennedy reiterated the message about the importance of inspiring hope, which he had shared privately with Lyndon Johnson. "If I and my brother had a role in that," he said, "that's our reward."[57]

On August 21, 1964, the front page of the *Washington Post* bore a photo of a smiling Robert Kennedy receiving a pen that Lyndon Johnson had used to sign the Economic Opportunity Act into law. The next day Kennedy formally entered the New York Senate race as the prohibitive favorite, with one poll giving him a seventeen-point lead over Keating.[58] His early campaigning in upstate New York drew enormous crowds. Along with the spectacle of the multitudes, media coverage focused on carpetbagger charges as the former attorney general attempted, unconvincingly, to claim New York as his native state.[59]

In spite of his huge crowds (which he suspected were really a tribute to his brother), he was not a skilled campaigner in the traditional sense. He did not enjoy being mobbed, and his speeches were halting.[60] Kenneth Keating had voted for the Economic Opportunity Act and a year earlier had even criticized John Kennedy for failing to fulfill his campaign pledges on poverty, so Robert Kennedy might have chosen another issue to distinguish himself from the incumbent.[61] He nevertheless discussed it regularly, employing Republican presidential candidate Barry Goldwater— who called the War on Poverty a "fake"—as his foil.[62] Kennedy also claimed credit, eschewing specifics, for the role the Justice Department had played in shaping the poverty program. Despite the new legislation, however, Kennedy addressed the problem almost as if the War on Poverty had yet to be declared.

His rhetoric was moralistic. In a book published in the middle of the campaign, Kennedy proclaimed poverty the main cause of "present discontents" and pronounced that "as long as there is plenty, poverty is evil. Government belongs wherever evil needs an adversary and there are people in distress who cannot help themselves."[63] He called for a moral commitment to a "living wage"—a term coined decades earlier by Catholic social thinker John A. Ryan which had entered the lexicon of labor and politics—and castigated Goldwater before a union audience as "a man who equates poverty with immorality, perhaps on the theory that all virtuous people inherit department stores."[64] The Republicans, the candidate charged, had "consciously decided that to act together, through the government, for the benefit of one's fellows, is a weak and immoral thing to do."[65] Kennedy, somewhat unfairly, linked Keating to these social Darwinist and Calvinist caricatures of Goldwater, even though the New York incumbent distanced himself from his party's nominee. Kennedy, in contrast, asserted repeatedly that the poor were victims who needed assistance, and that a large-scale federal role—"to the full extent it is needed"—was appropriate.[66]

Kennedy made two significant antipoverty policy proposals during the campaign. His housing proposal reflected his communitarian impulse. He called for a new federal commitment to public housing reliant not simply on structures but on "neighborhood and community development." Contending that "buildings do not make a viable neighborhood, but people do," he criticized the prevailing approach to urban renewal as bulldozing "blighted" areas and erecting new buildings without adequate attention to the social effects. Kennedy called for improved relocation allowances for those forced out of their neighborhoods (a major problem nationwide) and proposed rent assistance for those unable to afford increased rents resulting from neighborhood improvements. He disliked existing housing regulations that forced residents—often community leaders—out of neighborhoods when their earnings increased, which he felt ruined the chance for "responsible community action." Echoing the organic urban planning critiques of New York activist and author Jane Jacobs, Kennedy wanted to preserve the character of existing neighborhoods (and save money) by refurbishing structurally sound housing whenever possible. He also felt that housing policy had to provide for varied communities. "An urban renewal project," he said, "should not bring people of a single economic and racial background together in tall buildings."[67]

Kennedy's other antipoverty measure, which emerged in the closing days of the campaign, was less visionary. The Johnson administration had earlier proposed a $200 million Appalachian development bill and invited states in the impoverished region to participate upon its likely passage in 1965. New York had yet to enlist, and Kennedy lambasted Republican governor Nelson Rockefeller and Senator Keating for "air-tight partisanship" in not allowing the counties of the state's so-called Southern Tier—the portion of western New York State bordering Pennsylvania—to avail themselves of federal aid. It was a pork barrel campaign appeal, pledging to "bring New Yorkers the maximum return for their tax dollars," but it served his antipoverty goals as well.[68]

Whether his antipoverty themes helped Kennedy build political support during the campaign is unclear. A small but vocal group of prominent New York liberals, including writer Gore Vidal, journalist I. F. Stone, historian

Barbara Tuchman, and actor Paul Newman, formed a Democrats for Keating group, opposing Kennedy as, in the words of one member, "ruthless, reactionary, and dangerously authoritarian."[69] While he may have felt compelled to demonstrate that he was a liberal in the tradition of Eleanor Roosevelt and former senator Herbert Lehman, Kennedy had already exhibited a commitment to the issue by 1964, so even if he was using it to burnish his liberal credentials, his antipoverty focus was not simply opportunistic rhetoric.

Kennedy realized that the traditionally Democratic votes most essential to his success—and most apt to be influenced by his antipoverty rhetoric—were those of racial minorities. The poorest income group in New York City was Puerto Ricans, with a typical family earning less than 60 percent of the citywide average.[70] Because of their rapidly increasing numbers, Republicans hoped to make inroads with Puerto Rican voters in 1964.[71] John Kennedy won overwhelming majorities in Puerto Rican districts in 1960, and Robert Kennedy hoped to duplicate that success by speaking to their economic challenges and registering thousands of new voters (and doing so outside the uncooperative regular party machinery).[72] In addition to their prevailing Democratic disposition—Puerto Ricans generally identified the Republicans as the party of the wealthy—and loyalty to his brother (a Puerto Rican assistant to New York City mayor Robert Wagner asserted, "We are an emotional people" who "felt the Kennedy tragedy perhaps more deeply than others"), Kennedy had other advantages among Puerto Rican voters.[73] Business magnate O. Roy Chalk, who had funded Kennedy's elaborate D.C. playground, also owned both the airline most often used by Puerto Rican immigrants and the sole Spanish-language newspaper for the Puerto Rican community, El Diario–La Prensa.[74] The newspaper provided distinctly pro-Kennedy coverage, endorsing him as a "supporter of the underdog," prompting Republicans to complain of a "one-party press."[75]

His favorable treatment went deeper than his alliance with Chalk, however. Chalk hired Puerto Rican editors and wanted the paper to reflect community sentiments.[76] One Puerto Rican alderman declared that his people "loved" Kennedy, predicting that he might get 99 percent of the vote in his district. The most influential female writer for El Diario, Luisa Quintero, left the newspaper to work for Kennedy's campaign.[77] The most effective (and most repeated) Republican attack on Kennedy also likely fell flat among Puerto Ricans. Because so many were recent arrivals themselves, they were less likely to be repelled (and were perhaps even heartened) by repeated charges that Kennedy was not a true New Yorker.

Puerto Ricans had been slow to join the growing push for civil rights, but African American leaders in New York City began successfully joining forces with them in 1964. Their protests revolved around access to jobs and good schools. Robert Kennedy sought to reinforce that coalition, contending that while the Civil Rights Act would help liberate blacks in the South, "education, jobs, and decent housing . . . will emancipate the Negro and the Puerto Rican in the North."[78]

Some African American leaders initially feared that Kennedy was less concerned about education than about the likelihood of a predicted "white backlash" against civil rights.[79] Their worries appeared justified. Segregationist Alabama governor George Wallace had run up surprising vote totals as an insurgent Democratic presidential primary candidate in Indiana and Wisconsin, and according to a September New York Times poll, 54 percent of respondents believed that the civil rights movement was proceeding too fast.[80] Expectations of an anti-Kennedy groundswell among Italian Americans were spotlighted in an October New York Times article, as a reporter recorded the anger of restaurant patrons watching the candidate on television. "He pinched every Italian you know," one muttered, referring to Kennedy's aggressive pursuit of organized crime. "All he talks about is niggers and spics. Why don't you get a man on the TV?" In part because of embarrassment in the Italian American community over the negative light cast by the Valachi hearings, and in large measure because of backlash sentiments, political observers expected Keating to make major gains.[81]

African American commentators alleged that both Kennedy and Keating were appeasing backlash sentiments with their opposition to a limited New York City school board plan to "pair" white and predominantly minority schools (which consisted primarily of black and Puerto Rican children) and busing students between them to improve racial balance. The New York Amsterdam News pronounced its disappointment, contending that "Bobby sounds like Senator Goldwater on this one."[82] A Kennedy aide admitted to New York Times reporter R. W. Apple Jr. that the campaign wanted to avoid the "inflammatory" issue, preferring to leave decisions to local school districts. Kennedy's stated justification—that sending children "long distances away from schools in their own neighborhoods doesn't make any sense"—was vague and didn't speak to the actual plan, which did not involve lengthy trips. His position did square in principle with his communitarian impulse idealizing the local neighborhood, but it also reflected popular attitudes.[83] A New York Times poll found that 80 percent of respondents (including half of the African Americans surveyed) opposed the plan, and only about one quarter of black and Puerto Rican families accepted the invitations for their children to attend white schools.[84]

Kennedy was occasionally more daring on the stump. In Rochester, home of his opponent and site of the rioting that Kennedy and President Johnson had discussed two months earlier, the candidate disregarded the advice of a local official and addressed the racial tensions and the structural economic problems these created. "It would have been easier not to try to bring this matter up," Kennedy told the hushed audience, "but there are problems we are all going to have to face. I'm referring to the problem of the races living together." Kennedy then discussed the interrelationship of civil rights and economic problems: "In the South you can pass legislation to permit a Negro to have an ice cream cone at Howard Johnson's, but you *can't* pass legislation to automatically give a Negro an *education*. I believe the community must provide education so there can be *jobs*." Applause gradually broke the silence. "You have got to give Negroes some *hope*," Kennedy urged.[85]

Some African American voters were torn by the choice between Kennedy and Keating, who had established a progressive record on civil rights.[86] As James Baldwin, Jackie Robinson, and the NAACP's Clarence Mitchell came out for the incumbent, Keating sensed an opening and subtly accused Kennedy at the state NAACP convention of having bailed out on the civil rights movement when he resigned as attorney general.[87] Keating's attack barely had time to reverberate through the convention hall before Charles Evers stepped to the microphone and proclaimed that Kennedy "was the only man who ever did anything for Mississippi," throwing the convention up for grabs. When Kennedy spoke the next day, he received a considerably warmer reception than Keating, and any real challenge to Kennedy's hold on the African American vote ebbed.[88]

While the *New York Times* endorsed Keating, citing his solid record along with the editors' unease about Kennedy's lack of legislative experience and what they called his "relentless quest for political power," the *New York Amsterdam News* endorsed the challenger, contending that "no Attorney General in the history of America has more aggressively placed the weight of that great office behind the interests of fair play and the welfare of minority groups."[89] *Amsterdam News* editor James Hicks wrote a powerful election eve column explaining popular black support for Kennedy. Recounting his discussions with what he called the "night people" of Harlem—those whose work schedules were reversed—whom Hicks believed to be among the most reflective voters, the columnist summarized their feelings by quoting a bartender who said he was "going to get up out of my bed on Election Day and vote for Robert Kennedy—because his brother was a friend of mine!"[90]

On his first Election Day as a political candidate, Robert Kennedy could not even vote for himself (having only established official New York residency at the beginning of October), but the social and economic outsiders of the state—racial minorities—provided his margin of victory. While he defeated Keating by a less substantial margin than the historic mandate given President Johnson (who became the first presidential candidate to win every county in New York), he amassed the largest margin by a Democratic senatorial candidate since Herbert Lehman in 1938, winning the state by over 700,000 votes.[91] While Puerto Rican turnout was down nationwide from 1960, it stayed at its highest levels in New York City, giving Kennedy a large margin.[92] African American voters in New York City broke for Kennedy 80 percent to 20 percent, giving him a 400,000 vote margin there.[93] Also critically, a white backlash never really developed. Italian American margins remained where they had been in 1960, and Slavic voters supported Kennedy with record totals and similar percentages as among black voters.[94]

Kennedy toured the state in the weeks after the election, setting up listening sessions with municipal officials to introduce himself and hear more about local issues. Invariably the meetings were structured to focus on economic problems, with particular attention to the functioning of the nascent poverty program. Kennedy was surprised that few towns either understood or had organized Community Action Agencies to receive funding from the Title II provision of the Economic Opportunity Act. "This is a pile of money that's come along," he told the officials. "You ought to be taking advantage of it."[95] While all of the gatherings followed a similar template—eager local leaders pitching their hopes for federal assistance to their new celebrity senator on projects ranging from business development to urban renewal—two were particularly noteworthy as barometers of the shifting political winds in late 1964.

The first is interesting for symbolic reasons. Three years earlier the town of Newburgh had found itself at the center of a national firestorm over welfare when its city manager, Joseph Mitchell, implemented a plan to cut off welfare "chiselers," long the derogatory term for those considered able-bodied and therefore unworthy of public assistance.[96] In Newburgh that amounted primarily to black single mothers.[97] Mitchell became an iconic figure for conservatives (Barry Goldwater openly embraced him) and for disgruntled working- and middle-class whites in the early stages of the northern civil rights backlash.[98] As he grew in visibility, Mitchell blasted both the state government, which blocked his plan, and the Kennedy administration for its proposed "dictatorial" expansion of welfare.[99] After accusations of bribery and his acquittal on those charges, Mitchell eventually left in 1963 to work for the ultraconservative John Birch Society, and a new Democratic regime came into office. During Kennedy's meeting one official laid out in sympathetic detail the problems of the city's poor and pledged, upon Kennedy's inquiry, to apply for community action recognition. Another quoted Michael Harrington admiringly. Change had come to Newburgh.[100]

Many upstate cities were suffering from the beginnings of deindustrialization, and Syracuse was no different. What was unique about Kennedy's introductory meeting there was the forceful presentation of George Wiley, a chemistry professor at Syracuse University who had just been named second in command nationally at CORE. Wiley offered a pointed critique of urban renewal and the subsequent housing shortage in Syracuse, challenging the idea of investing federal money in local business in the hopes that it would "filter down" to all, including poor black families. Wiley proclaimed, "I'm here to tell you, that there are seven to ten thousand families in this area to whom not very much has filtered down."[101] Wiley's presentation brought the new senator into direct contact with the increasingly assertive tone of the northern civil rights movement, and Wiley himself would soon begin a journey on the issue of welfare that sought to go further than the regime change in Newburgh in burying the legacy of Joseph Mitchell.

Upon heading to the Senate, Kennedy hired two youthful Justice Department attorneys as legislative assistants. Each fit the model of his own legal pedigree. Peter Edelman was a studious, methodical Harvard Law School graduate from Minnesota who hadn't intended to stay in politics beyond the 1964 election. Adam Walinsky, a former marine and brash personality, had attended Yale Law School and was a wide-ranging thinker, gifted speechwriter, and gadfly to the senator. Both shared Kennedy's interest in poverty and would continue to influence his thinking on the topic, pressing him to take increasingly progressive positions throughout his senatorial career.

Walinsky was familiar with Kennedy's community-based approach to juvenile delinquency from his work in the Justice Department, and he shared Kennedy's emphasis on economic and psychological empowerment.[102] In the summer of 1964 Walinsky published an article in the *New Republic* arguing that middle-class opposition to a more aggressive attack on poverty was fueled by status fears. In addition to causing obvious material deprivation, Walinsky contended, poverty was also socially relative. "For both the old and new middle classes, the problem of preserving status becomes more acute in direct proportion to the technical ease with which poverty can be eliminated."[103] Still, Walinsky warned against condemning middle-class attitudes. In exchange for their support of a serious poverty program, middle-class Americans had to be offered answers to their own "poverty of satisfaction, purpose, and dignity."[104] It was a theme Kennedy would advance throughout his senatorial career, and this concern for the attitudes of middle- and working-class whites would to some extent gird him against charges of elitism that opponents inevitably leveled to discredit the wealthy politician's interest in the poor.

Perhaps even more than the proposals Kennedy espoused, the other factor that would to some extent shield him against charges of elitism as he became more visibly associated with the politics of poverty was his own ethnicity. As author Michael Novak would later contend, Robert Kennedy was widely perceived to be the most "ethnic" of the Kennedys because of "his bantamlike toughness, his large family, his intimate knowledge of personal suffering, even his sometimes choppy and almost inarticulate speech."[105] As the descendants of European immigrants became more entrenched components of the middle class in postwar America, and as they also felt the most threatened by urban social change, this identification would prove politically indispensable for Kennedy.[106]

Despite political fame that gave him disproportionate influence for a freshman senator, Kennedy still found himself in search of a role. Shortly after the election Walinsky sent his boss a memo outlining his possible strategic approaches in the Senate. As word of the president's plans to submit a flurry of liberal programs began to circulate on Capitol Hill, Walinsky cautioned Kennedy, "It will be relatively difficult for you to establish a reputation as an individual leader for progressive legislation." Kennedy could attempt to forge his own legislative path, but Walinsky warned that since the president would dominate the agenda of the Senate, "whatever its other advantages . . . the role of lonely spokesman would probably have serious adverse effects on your ability to 'do more for New York.'"[107]

Instead Kennedy adopted the strategy that both of his legislative aides recommended for his first session, supporting the president's Great Society legislation and occasionally proposing his own amendments. Kennedy made the inclusion of New York counties in the Appalachia bill his first legislative task. He met personally with senators from all of the states involved and considered other maneuvers.[108] After reading about Congressman John Quincy Adams's successful obstruction of a naval appropriations bill until he received assurance that the Boston Navy Yard would be kept open, he told his friend Richard Goodwin: "That's the great thing about politics . . . some things never change. And that's why I'm going to force them to put some New York counties in the bill for Appalachia."[109]

Although it was too late for New York to be included in the original bill, Kennedy somewhat haphazardly lobbied for the Southern Tier counties, calling in his first speech on the floor of the Senate for an amendment to study whether they could be added later. Opponents such as Rockefeller thought it rank opportunism on the part of Kennedy, harming the state's prosperous image for political gain. Republican Jacob Javits, the senior senator from New York, told his new colleague "in unmeasured terms and not without heat" that he had breached Senate etiquette by failing to consult him in advance to allow him to be part of the proposal.[110] The Appalachia legislation became the first measure of Johnson's Great Society adopted by the Eighty-ninth Congress. Buoyed by an overwhelmingly Democratic Senate, Kennedy's amendment passed, and in August the counties were officially included in the Appalachia program.

In the interim, local political leaders and newspaper editors in many of the heavily Republican Southern Tier counties, which were also home to ski resorts and wealthy residents, resisted federal assistance under the Appalachia act. One upstate leader suspected that some of the anti-aid sentiment was also "anti–Bobby Kennedy."[111] Denying the suggestion that there was a poverty problem, the mayor of Utica angrily declared: "I don't know who [Kennedy] talked to. This is a wonderful city."[112] A Tompkins County leader, saying he resented "being classed as a mendicant holding a tin cup," demanded, "Are we to advertise to tourists: 'Visit the Poverty-Stricken Finger Lakes and see America at its worst?"[113]

Kennedy grew frustrated with the fact that only two of the thirteen Southern Tier counties organized themselves to receive aid in the months after the passage of the bill. "One would expect that all responsible people in these counties would welcome this program as an opportunity," he told a Binghamton audience. "But instead," he continued, "we hear the voice of complacency, of neglect. 'We're doing fine' it says, 'we're not poor. No program like that for this community.' Such statements ignore the fact that in modern society plenty and poverty live side by side."[114]

Despite the resistance of some, those in the region who expressed their opinion to the new senator were generally pleased with his Appalachia initiative. Although one constituent called it "cheap politics," many more were supportive. One man wrote: "I usually vote Republican, but, first and always I'm an American. I wish to thank you for your attempt (so far) to aid the people in this area of New York State. I personally do not presently need Government support. However, due to mechanization and the failure of this area the future doesn't offer much." A self-described "grey haired Republican" from Otsego County assured him: "You have done the right and finest thing. . . . [M]any of us are in real need, but the rich in this county do not want to help us! They want it known that we are in a poverty stricken area!" A woman from Rochester confided: "Poor people believe you have the same thinking as our late beloved president. I know you do."[115]

Except for the prestigious Foreign Relations Committee, from which he was disqualified by seniority considerations, Kennedy's top choice for committee work in the Senate was Labor and Public Welfare.[116] Through the subcommittees of that body Kennedy would study the complexities of poverty from various angles. His principal antipoverty focus in early 1965 was education. President Johnson had decided to push for a major education initiative at the outset of the new Congress, and he attempted to link the bill to the War on Poverty. Unlike the National Defense Education Act of 1958, which offered general federal assistance, the proposed Elementary and Secondary Education Act of 1965 (ESEA) provided the first categorical federal aid to education. The bill was designed to channel federal funding, through the states, to "educationally deprived children"—most often those from poor families.

In spite of large Democratic majorities in both Houses, the ESEA was subject to contentious debate. Kennedy sat through hours of Senate hearings and pressed several concerns, revealing the contours of his antipoverty vision. Along with other senators, he believed that the age range of the bill should be expanded to include pre–school age children, and he wondered aloud on more than one occasion whether the overall amount of money being allotted was enough to make a difference.[117] His principal aim was ensuring that poor communities got the most bang for the buck from federal funds. Influenced by his distrust of local political bureaucracies and his PCJD perception that local school systems were frequently barriers to the advancement of needy students, Kennedy sought assurances that school boards would not waste the new funding by failing to innovate or to implement new technologies. He questioned Commissioner of Education Francis Keppel, the architect of the bill, along with HEW chief Anthony Celebrezze, about "one of the really great problems we have in the country," the inertia of some school boards. When Celebrezze protested that the risks inherent in local control were the price of democracy, Kennedy demurred: "We don't have to accept it. We can attempt to do better."[118] It was a somewhat radical position that again demonstrated his emerging conception of a direct federal relationship with poor grassroots communities to protect them against the broken bureaucratic structures there.

Throughout the hearings Kennedy explored a possible safeguard, "some kind of testing system," to gauge student progress and the effective use of federal funds. "I think it is very difficult for a person who lives in a community," Kennedy said, "to know whether, in fact, his educational system is what it should be, whether if you compare his community to a neighboring community they are doing everything they should do."[119] Despite his persistent inquiries, most witnesses doubted the availability of reliable tests.

Kennedy expressed skepticism when the superintendent of the Chicago public schools told the subcommittee that the safeguard was the community itself in the form of local groups of parents fighting against inadequate education. Speaking about poor children, Kennedy said:

> Many of them do not have parents. They do not have two parents anyway. They might have one parent, and maybe they have a group in the community that is going to come down and make their protest known, but a lot of times that is very difficult. They are working for $7 or $8 a day and making $40 or $50 a week. It is difficult to take off and go down and protest. . . . I think we have a special responsibility to those people who are less fortunate than we are, to make sure that the money that is being expended is going to be used so that the next generation will not have to have these kinds of hearings.[120]

Kennedy's concern for governmental coordination and efficiency emerged in pointed questioning of Sargent Shriver, who now headed the Office of Economic Opportunity (OEO), the agency created to direct the War on Poverty. Shriver tried to allay subcommittee fears about coordination between OEO and the Office of Education, which was charged with implementing the ESEA. When Shriver declared that his organization "could not care less" whether local requests for education aid came through community action agencies—and ultimately to OEO for funding—or through the Office of Education, since "the same people are going to look at it over there," the freshman senator objected. "That is not true," Kennedy said, exploring the complexities of the bureaucratic interplay and potential for conflict:

The representative of the community action program, which may be made up of 10 representatives in a community, might decide a particular action is necessary. Both of us have seen the struggles that have gone on in all these communities, Mr. Shriver, just continuously the struggles that go on. Of a 10-man committee, there might be one representative of the education board. The education board might feel strongly about a particular program, that it is worthwhile. The community action program might outvote that man 9 to 1 or 8 to 2. Then you are going to have a contest to see how the money is going to be handled. The Office of Education might feel the best way to handle it is through the education board and let them do it. And the Economic Opportunity Act people say, our operation is much better. And the fact that both of them are doing the same identical thing in a particular community, I think, in my judgment, is really asking for trouble.[121]

As in the PCJD model of the federal role in combating delinquency, Kennedy envisioned the federal government as an information clearinghouse for local communities wishing to explore the success of educational programs elsewhere. The New York senator was frustrated by the lack of existing research, however, and he feared the consequences. Discussing the variety of approaches described by community leaders with similar problems, he said: "Maybe we are going to find out a decade from now which group put in the right program. But by that time we have lost a good many lives."[122]

Aside from his doubts about local school systems, the overall urgency of the problem of educational deprivation was the main emphasis of Kennedy's questioning. Discussing his trip to West Virginia a year earlier, he repeated the story of how the few children able to attend school brought food home from their lunch program so their parents could eat at night. "With that kind of poverty," he said, "the poverty that exists now through no fault of anybody's, but because of the force of circumstances, the people must be helped."[123] He quoted from the letter of a young boy, whose decrepit New York City school he had visited: "Boom, your brother was killed, and you became a U.S. Senator. Boom, my brother was killed, and I ended up in a school."[124]

In the end, Kennedy's main contribution to the legislation was an amendment forcing the evaluation of local school systems' use of funds. "Look," Kennedy told Francis Keppel privately, "I want to change this bill because it doesn't have any way of measuring those damned educators like you, Frank, and we really ought to have some evaluation in there, some measurement as to whether any good is happening." Keppel agreed but warned Kennedy he couldn't change the bill that had come from the executive branch because "all those educators will scream bloody-murder." Keppel inquired about adding an amendment in Kennedy's name. "I don't want a Kennedy amendment," the New York senator insisted. "I want the damn thing amended."[125] Without fanfare, Keppel then asked Indiana Democrat John Brademas to attach the evaluation provision in his House committee, and it became part of the final bill signed by Lyndon Johnson in April 1965.[126]

Despite passage of the ESEA, Kennedy soon realized that education initiatives might mean little if they were stymied by more immediate problems. He visited Harlem and was repelled by the housing conditions. "The smell of rats was so strong," he told one audience, "that it was difficult to stay there for five minutes."[127] Touring a dilapidated tenement in Brooklyn where rat bites had disfigured the face of a Puerto Rican girl, the stunned senator wondered how such a thing could happen in the financial capital of the world.[128]

Elected on his own in a predominantly liberal state, having survived a threat of white backlash, Kennedy began, two years later in the context of another Alabama protest, to echo the "spirit of Birmingham" in his rhetoric. Although he had done nothing to support the school desegregation plan during the campaign, Kennedy condemned a white protest march (led by teachers and parents) against desegregation efforts, and wondered aloud why people weren't marching on City Hall to protest the quality of schools in ghetto areas or the dilapidated housing he had witnessed. He denounced backlash attitudes as a "new voice of intolerance" which proclaims that "this is a free country" and that African Americans "have the same chance as everyone else" and then uses "Negro poverty, Negro unemployment and lack of education as an excuse for not doing more." Citing statistics that poverty was the third leading cause of death in New York City, Kennedy noted the voting rights marches in Selma but asked, "Who marches for our own dead children?"[129] The urban poverty Kennedy condemned was about to result in an explosion.

In the pivotal summer of 1965 dramatic events would draw Kennedy beyond his modest strategic objectives in his first year in the Senate and help him begin to define a new, more independent political role. In May the Johnson administration sent U.S. forces into the Dominican Republic in an attempt to forestall a potential communist takeover, and Kennedy criticized the intervention. The first major troop increase in the Vietnam conflict occurred in July, and Kennedy offered a muted critique of military escalation there. Finally, in mid-August a traffic stop in the Watts section of Los Angeles triggered the first massive urban upheaval of the 1960s. After six days of violence, thirty-four people were dead, over one thousand had been wounded, and property damage exceeded $35 million. As clouds of smoke and weapons of war manned by a riot-control army rolled through the streets of Watts, Robert Kennedy was wrenched from the wilderness period of his public life and fired by a new sense of mission. His first objective was to make sense of the rebellion that the War on Poverty was, in part, meant to prevent.

5

THE EDUCATION

OF A SENATOR

SEEKING A

"GREATER SOCIETY"

The uprising in Watts shocked the nation, and leaders from across the social and political spectrum registered their opinions on the conflagration. Martin Luther King Jr. attributed the explosion to the kindling of "hunger and degradation . . . two diseases not uncommon to Negroes in other parts of America." An angry Dwight Eisenhower was roused from retirement to proclaim that he didn't "care what the condition of these people was. Those who started this . . . made the conditions far worse." The Reverend Billy Graham was confident that events were "definitely influenced by the communists" and worried that next time it would take "every military man in the country to," in Graham's words, "ease the tension." Adam Clayton Powell declared that the country had already seen the "Negro revolt" and was now witnessing "the revolt of the poor."[1]

Even though he had realized the potential for such an explosion years earlier, Robert Kennedy was dismayed by the violence in Watts. The scale of the rebellion would cause the New York senator to reassess a number of his assumptions about poverty in America. In the months and years after Watts, Kennedy became increasingly critical of President Johnson's War on Poverty, and he immersed himself in the issue seeking new answers to what increasingly seemed an intractable problem.

Both Johnson and Kennedy immediately realized the political danger Watts presented for Great Society programs. The private reaction of each man was overwrought. The president was initially stupefied by the uprising. "How is it possible," he asked, "after all we've accomplished? How could it be?"[2] In a heated moment, fearful that his monumental legislative triumphs were suddenly in peril, he told top domestic aide Joseph Califano that he feared "Negroes will end up pissing in the aisles of the Senate" as they had during Reconstruction, discrediting his attempts to help them.[3] Although he cloaked the package in the angry intonations of the backlash, calling the rioters lawbreakers on a par with Klansmen, Johnson nevertheless directed nearly $30 million in federal assistance to Watts in the weeks after the rioting.[4]

On hearing of the events in Los Angeles, Robert Kennedy confided to aides: "A lot of those looters are just kids in trouble. I got in trouble when I was that age."[5] While the comparison was plainly implausible on a number of levels, it demonstrated Kennedy's continuing attempt to identify with marginalized young people such as those he had met while chairing the juvenile delinquency committee. Having developed his own understanding of the relationship between poverty and crime, when Eisenhower attributed the Watts uprising to the nation's "becoming atmosphered . . . in a policy of lawlessness," Kennedy felt compelled to present an alternative view.[6]

With fires in the Los Angeles ghetto still blazing, Kennedy told a Milwaukee audience, "The country has turned away, I hope forever, from those whose hearts are dry as summer dust, who feel that the poor are evil, that security is weakening, and that every man should fend for himself."[7] A few days later he gained national attention when he asked attendees at the Independent Order of Odd Fellows convention in upstate New York to consider the plight of blacks who had left the South.[8] African Americans seeking the "promised land" in northern and western cities as part of the second Great Migration, Kennedy said, found "too many people full of hate and bitterness crowded into a dirty, stinky, uncared-for closet-size section of a great city." He warned that appeals for obedience to the law would be ineffective since the legal system had not protected poor blacks "from paying too much money for inferior goods, from having their furniture repossessed," or "from having to keep lights turned on the feet of children at night, to keep them from being gnawed by rats."[9]

The intensity of the upheaval in Watts caused Kennedy to abandon any remaining wariness about an expansive federal role. The New York senator attributed the tinderbox conditions in Watts to structural poverty created in large part by racism, and he pronounced the existing poverty war a mere first step, asserting that increased short-term antipoverty spending for the urban poor would create long-term progress. He suggested a massive jobs program to relieve the strains on the welfare system and on tax revenues. Kennedy's call for a limited study-action program was a distant memory by the fall of 1965, by which time he was instead arguing for the social welfare equivalent of the cold war foreign policy strategy of peace through massive military buildup.

At the same time, he told an interviewer that a conventional top-down programmatic approach would be ineffective. Northern white politicians, he insisted, were oblivious to the trials of urban blacks, and too content to deal with them in the old way (which he understood well) of purchasing bloc votes with "a smattering of political jobs and a few specified sums of money."[10] All of the lessons Kennedy had been learning through the previous five years were about to be tested as he struggled to shape a new kind of political response to poverty in the United States.

Watts was deluged by observers in the aftermath of the upheaval, but Kennedy waited until November to return and see things for himself. His initial diagnosis of the problem was reaffirmed when he and aide Peter Edelman spoke with local residents. Edelman asked a seemingly healthy middle-aged man about his challenges in Watts, and he replied, "Flustration." "Excuse me?" asked Kennedy, puzzled by the colloquialism. "Flustration," the man again replied. "What do you mean?" the senator asked. "Well man, when you's fifty and you is black, you can't get a job nohow."[11] The New York senator later heard the same message from young people: in the face of chronic joblessness, appeals to the values of education, thrift, and hard work seemed pointless.

Shortly after the riot former PCJD director David Hackett and Kennedy's New York City office chief, Tom Johnston, outlined possible reasons why a similar upheaval had not engulfed Harlem. Not surprisingly, Hackett argued that the ongoing organizational effort to fight delinquency (the PCJD had funded the Harlem Youth Opportunities Unlimited program there, which was controlled from start to finish by African American residents) had provided some hope for urban youth.[12] Nevertheless, they warned, there was "a large discrepancy between these hopes and the facts." Optimism had been generated not so much by programs already operating but by "the expectations of a radical change in the quality of individual and community life." Without a massive increase in aid for employment, housing, education, health, and recreation, Hackett and Johnston predicted "a form of lawlessness quite unlike anything in the past."[13]

At the same time, events in Watts and elsewhere were leading Lyndon Johnson, in the words of biographer Robert Dallek, to "temporarily put aside" a public focus on African American problems in "a tactical pause" that would "serve the larger cause of long term advance."[14] By late 1965 Johnson had grown frustrated with the controversy that the Office of Economic Opportunity—and principally the Community Action Program—was generating. Even before the Watts uprising, the administration had been feeling intense mayoral pressures to curb community action. Months earlier Los Angeles mayor Sam Yorty and Chicago boss Richard Daley had protested vehemently against the routing of OEO money past city hall. "What in the hell are you people doing," Daley asked Johnson aide Bill Moyers. "Does the president know he's putting M-O-N-E-Y in the hands of subversives? To poor people who aren't part of the organization?"[15] Yorty was battling local community representatives over control of OEO funds, and as a result, much-anticipated federal antipoverty money had failed to flow into the nation's third largest city, contributing considerably to the rising tensions in Watts.[16] Because it was becoming such a political lightning rod, Johnson seriously considered dismantling OEO in late 1965.[17]

Kennedy briefly addressed the controversy over participation by the poor in his Odd Fellows speech. He discussed rising impatience with the new political role of the poor without mentioning the Community Action Program by name, and cautioned that "poor people and Negro leaders will make mistakes; there will be graft and waste." In a warning with which he and his staff would later grapple, Kennedy said, "We will be tempted to run these programs for their benefit," meaning the benefit of the poor, whereas "it is only by inviting their active participation . . . that we can help them develop leaders who make the difference between political force—with which we can deal—and a headless mob."[18]

By year's end the political mood of the nation had changed dramatically. The war in Vietnam was bogging down, and Senator J. William Fulbright was about to initiate hearings to examine Johnson's Vietnam policy. The many fault lines in the fragile coalition for an assault on poverty in America were also apparent. In the most strident attack, community organizer Saul Alinsky, unconvinced that OEO was pressing for maximum feasible participation of the poor, called the War on Poverty a "macabre masquerade" and an example of "political pornography."[19]

Other critics on the left—including formerly close allies—emerged in 1965. Even before Watts, some African Americans had begun to question the War on Poverty more insistently. The Organization for Black Power, a forerunner of the Black Power movement initially identified with Stokely Carmichael, charged that the War on Poverty offered "little more than a bonanza . . . for the nation's social workers."[20] Labor leader Walter Reuther had formed the Citizens' Crusade Against Poverty (CCAP) a year earlier as a supportive liaison between OEO and the grassroots in poor communities. The group, which had the support of a wide array of prominent liberals and civil rights leaders, increasingly saw its role as the conscience of OEO, pressing for greater participation by the poor.[21] CCAP was headed by former Justice Department aide (and first director of the Community Action Program at OEO) Richard Boone. Boone stayed in regular contact with Kennedy and his office, providing intelligence on grassroots developments around the nation. He would remain as influential as anyone in Kennedy's evolving thinking about poverty.[22]

Perhaps no other event so exposed the fading liberal consensus as reaction to the government report *The Negro Family: The Case for Action* in the heated racial climate after Watts. Authored by former Labor Department official Daniel Patrick Moynihan, the study asserted that poor African American communities experienced a historically rooted pathology, which led to the "crumbling" of black families. While Moynihan also explored the role of socioeconomic discrimination, critics charged that the report fixed the blame for poverty on African Americans themselves. Many liberals, scholars, and black leaders were outraged. CORE leaders Floyd McKissick and James Farmer condemned the report, with McKissick denouncing its blanket imposition of a white middle-class template on African American life, and Farmer insisting that it provided "a massive academic cop-out for the white conscience."[23] Others, including some social scientists, black journalists, and even student radical Tom Hayden, agreed with Moynihan's basic analysis.[24]

If Kennedy's public statements in the months after Watts suggested that he was moving to the left of Lyndon Johnson, not all of his positions squared with such an assessment. Upon the release of the McCone Commission report on the causes of the Watts riots, Kennedy challenged all elements of society, including prominent African Americans, to demonstrate a greater commitment to the problems of the ghettos. "Too many Negroes who have already climbed the ladder of success," Kennedy chided, "have not extended their hands to help their kinsmen on the rungs below." No other white political leader could have offered such a reproof in the charged atmosphere of late 1965, after Watts and the Moynihan Report, without inviting scorn.[25] He also accepted the basic findings of the

McCone Commission, which most African American leaders considered a whitewash.[26] While it did attribute the uprising to racial tensions fueled by unemployment and poor educational and health care systems, and it discussed local animosity toward the police, the report also minimized the number of residents who were actively involved in the uprising—categorizing them as a criminal element—and it absolved police chief William Parker, who was deeply distrusted in the black community, from charges of racism. Kennedy and Parker had a friendship that dated to Kennedy's years on the Senate Rackets Committee, and the New York senator still considered Parker the best police chief in the nation. Friend and former OEO official Jack Conway was so concerned that Kennedy and his wife, Ethel, were "infatuated" with the authoritarian Parker that before Kennedy toured South Central Los Angeles, Conway sent the senator a collection of inflammatory statements uttered by the chief.[27]

Kennedy sidestepped the debate over the black family provoked by the Moynihan Report, but he did begin to criticize the impact of welfare on poor families. In the symbolic venue of a January 1966 Roosevelt Day dinner, the New York senator told Americans for Democratic Action, the preeminent liberal establishment group in American politics, that while the New Deal order had accomplished vital reforms, "welfare has also destroyed self-respect and encouraged family disintegration." Kennedy argued that the overriding goal instead had to be finding ways to integrate poor Americans "into full participation in the life of our communities."[28] As the speech went unreported by the major media, including the *New York Times*, Kennedy's anti-welfare sentiments generated no public controversy at the time.

In the weeks after Watts, Kennedy had set Walinsky and Edelman to work on new proposals to address conditions in poor urban areas. He told them that he was unafraid of prospective costs but wanted specifics on where the money would come from and what the programs would accomplish.[29] The results of Edelman and Walinsky's labors were three lengthy addresses delivered at the end of January 1966. The proposals in those speeches blended liberal and conservative ideas in a communitarian vision that would serve as the broad framework of Kennedy's approach to what was branded, in the wake of Watts, the "urban crisis."

The first speech, packed with statistics illustrating the continuing social isolation and inferior economic status of ghetto residents, emphasized the need for African American mobility. Calling the ghetto an absence of community, a "vast undifferentiated mass," Kennedy said that freedom for the inner city resident "to move if he wants to and where he wants to" was the first step in a strategy for breaking up urban slums. To that end he criticized public housing efforts for trapping urban residents in segregated areas and supported a Johnson proposal for new town developments outside cities with a percentage requirement for low-income housing. He also returned to familiar themes with roots in the PCJD model. The federal government should play the role of information clearinghouse for local communities, accumulating successful examples of desegregation. Federal grants could be targeted toward both public and private agencies, this time as a stimulant for fair housing efforts. In two more improbable proposals, he discussed using the model of immigrant employment centers that Israel had established to screen and help settle "migrants to our cities," and suggested consideration of boarding urban students in suburban school settings as "an introduction to life outside the ghetto."[30]

In his second address Kennedy declared that breaking up the ghetto was his ultimate goal but cautioned that it would take many years to accomplish. Disavowing the either-or proposition of ghetto dispersal or reconstruction, Kennedy called for a "total effort" aimed at the "regeneration" of inner city communities. His proposal made employment the centerpiece while renouncing a number of prevailing liberal orthodoxies. Despite citing education as critical to economic progress, Kennedy emphasized the seeming futility of schooling without jobs at the end of the process. He rejected both job training (a liberal, service-oriented approach embodied in the Job Corps) and "general prosperity" (the aggregationist or economic growth approach) as primary solutions, believing both had been tried and found inadequate.

Kennedy called instead for a massive rebuilding effort, staffed by inner city residents themselves. Workers would be trained and guided by labor unions and universities. The projects would be funded and advised by the government and the business community, but most important, local black leaders themselves would guide each effort. The projects would be "consciously directed at the creation of communities," addressing "unmet social needs" as well as physical reconstruction. He conceded that the costs would be great, but after outlining how such plans might be financed (he asserted, probably unrealistically, that most of the resources could be redirected from existing programs), Kennedy declared that the "returns in human spirit," including self-confidence and lessened dependency on welfare, would be immeasurable.[31]

The final speech, delivered before the United Auto Workers, promised increased economic and educational opportunities for working-class Americans. Continuing the themes of the social relativity of poverty and middle-class anxiety that Walinsky had first explored in his 1964 *New Republic* article, the speech was, in effect, an attempt to secure middle-class support for an escalation of the War on Poverty.[32] Kennedy called for measures to facilitate further education for workers who wished to "move up the occupational ladder," job retraining for those who wanted to find more satisfying careers, and government insurance programs for the transfer of pensions from one job to another.[33]

Despite his reputation as a political realist, Kennedy's array of proposals had a brainstorming quality. Some were politically impracticable, and many were less than fully developed. As in the community action projects, roles for state and local government were basically left unspecified, which undoubtedly would have created political problems for the overall strategy, given the tension that community action was already creating in many cities. The speeches are nevertheless significant because they provided the broad schema for all of Kennedy's subsequent urban proposals, and they offer insights into his evolving conception of how the War on Poverty could be waged more effectively.

Assessments of the speeches have varied widely. Michael Knox Beran, who has contended that Kennedy was moving toward more conservative remedies for poverty, calls them "as momentous an event in the history of the welfare state as any" for their emphasis on individual initiative and the concession that government programs had failed.[34] In contrast, journalist and Kennedy biographer Evan Thomas argues that they amounted to "a good deal of 1960s liberal boilerplate."[35]

In actuality, Kennedy's rhetoric was neither the dawn of "compassionate conservatism" nor a serving of warmed-over New Deal liberalism. The speeches instead further developed his communitarian vision for an assault on poverty. Unlike both conservatives and liberals, Kennedy did not pit public against private spheres in American society; for him, all sectors of the economy, all important institutions in a position to do so—including the federal government, labor unions, and universities—simply needed to pitch in and create jobs, because their failure to do so would invite more riots. This attempt to find cooperative roles for the other powerful institutional pillars of American life reflected an organic or corporatist conception of society in which individuals and institutions functioned best in cooperative partnerships rather than in regulated atomistic competition.[36] The vision he presented in the speeches retained the PCJD emphasis on opening the opportunity structures of the local community and allowing localities to direct the effort with outside support.

The speeches reveal other important ways in which Kennedy was moving beyond conventional liberal thought. Despite the fact that temporary work relief had been central to Franklin Roosevelt's New Deal, programs based on that principle had been largely dismantled before the United States entered World War II. Critics in the 1960s saw the remaining New Deal legacy as a bloated welfare system and the top-down management of social programs. Kennedy's analysis of welfare dependency and his insistence that the poor themselves play the preeminent role in the physical construction projects, providing the "man's work" that would be "hard and exacting" but also dignified and meaningful to the surrounding community, constituted an implicit critique of the remnants of the New Deal order.[37]

Another significant legacy of the New Deal—the managed economy—did find wide acceptance in postwar America. The 1960s were marked by a broadening consensus among economists and political leaders—including both liberal Keynesians and conservative monetarists—that overall economic growth, guided by federal policy, was the best answer to social and economic problems.[38] Despite the fact that it was John Kennedy who uttered the signature phrase of the Keynesian aggregationists—"a rising tide lifts all boats"—Robert Kennedy never embraced economic growth as the sole answer to poverty. He had been the lone significant dissenter in the Kennedy administration regarding the wisdom of a tax cut to stimulate the economy, and his reasons were grounded in his political faith in communitarian cooperation. He contended that a tax increase in the period after the Berlin crisis would provide an opportunity to extend the New Frontier principle to "ask what you can do for your country." He thought, Kennedy said later, that "it would bring home to the American people . . . the crisis, and the importance, and the fact everybody was making a sacrifice. Economists generally were against it."[39]

Perhaps even more than most politicians, Robert Kennedy had only a very limited understanding of theoretical economics. When journalist and friend Charles Bartlett wrote Kennedy suggesting that he might begin thawing his icy relationship with the business community by appearing before the Economic Club "to show that he knew what he was talking about," Kennedy scrawled in response, "In this area at the moment I don't."[40] He nevertheless basically accepted Roosevelt's admonition that "economic laws are not made by nature" but "by human beings" and that economic problems were matters of distribution that more properly fell into the purview of political and social pressure (in the interrelationship that constitutes political economy).[41] Kennedy continued to see poverty as structural and resistant to the aggregationist remedy of economic growth. In the coming years he would speak out against measuring the success of the nation's economy by the single most celebrated yet equally facile indicator, the gross national product, which focused solely on aggregate growth.

The urban plan that Robert Kennedy presented in early 1966 rested on provocative assumptions: that the nation had been sufficiently shaken by the Watts rebellion to do whatever it would take to get at the roots of the problem and prevent another such incident, that such large-scale cooperation motivated by this concern was possible, and that most Americans had a generous spirit and were still willing to expend resources on the urban poor. While in his third speech he attempted to enlist the working and middle classes in the effort with promises of federal assistance for their concerns, the measures he offered them were far from breathtaking. To some opponents who did not share Kennedy's assumptions, the plan for pouring vast resources into the nation's inner cities looked like the manifestation of a command economy.[42]

In fact the violence in Watts began to strain popular sympathy for poor African Americans, a trend that would intensify in the coming year. The uprising did, however, give antipoverty politics a new urgency because of increased anxiety about further eruptions. As hope gave way to fear, a flurry of activity ensued. Just days after the last of Kennedy's three addresses, President Johnson's new proposal for urban aid—later dubbed "Model Cities"—arrived on Capitol Hill. The bill was designed as an experimental attempt to bring all government antipoverty initiatives to bear in a coordinated way on selected cities. It was reminiscent of the PCJD approach, and Kennedy supported the measure. That same week Martin Luther King Jr. rented an apartment in a poor Chicago neighborhood as his focus shifted to the northern black freedom struggle. Reflecting the prominence of the issue at the time, politicians sometimes tripped over one another in an attempt to advance antipoverty initiatives. A minor dustup between Kennedy and recently elected New York City mayor John Lindsay arose in late January over a vacant South Bronx lot which both men planned to turn into a playground. One bemused liberal columnist observed, "NEVER have we seen white politicians so deeply engrossed with the problems of minority groups, after elections were over."[43]

Kennedy was determined to translate his urban speeches into action, so Walinsky began drafting a Ford Foundation proposal to fund a project based on the ideas he had outlined. Typically, Kennedy wanted to see his

Robert Kennedy first witnessed grinding poverty in the mountains of West Virginia while managing his brother's Democratic primary campaign there. Here he meets with miners in the coal fields near Bluefield in May 1960. Copyright Bob Lerner, LOOK Magazine / John F. Kennedy Presidential Library and Museum, Boston.

The President's Committee on Juvenile Delinquency (PCJD) would be an important pathway for RFK's understanding of urban poverty. David Hackett (at far left), RFK's lifelong friend and operational head of the committee, and Abraham Ribicoff, HEW secretary (second from right), attend the ceremony as John Kennedy announces a PCJD grant to New York City on May 31, 1962. Photo by Abbie Rowe. Courtesy John F. Kennedy Presidential Library and Museum, Boston.

As chair of the PCJD, RFK inspects educational materials at a youth center (date unknown). Courtesy John F. Kennedy Presidential Library and Museum, Boston.

Kennedy, TV star Chuck Connors (on RFK's right), and SCLC minister Walter Fauntroy (on Connors's right) attend the reopening of a swimming pool at Dunbar High School in Washington, September 11, 1963. Courtesy the Charles Sumner School Museum and Archives, Washington, D.C.

Kennedy is named an honorary Sioux and given the name "Brave Heart" at the 1963 conference of the National Congress of American Indians in Bismarck, South Dakota. Photo by Francis Miller / Time Life Pictures / Getty Images. Reproduced with permission.

The personal rift between RFK and LBJ would have significant ramifications for the nation's war against poverty. The tension seems evident at this June 4, 1963, White House gathering designed to urge southern business leaders to play a moderating role in the desegregation of public facilities. AP / Wide World Photos. Reproduced with permission.

Kennedy greets a crowd in Harlem during his victorious 1964 Senate campaign. Favorable perceptions of his efforts as attorney general brought Kennedy overwhelmi support from African Americc voters. Photo by Burton Berinsky / Landov. Reproducec with permission.

Kennedy helped launch the nation's first major community development corporation in the Bedford-Stuyvesant section of Brooklyn, which he tours here with Donald Benjamin of the Central Brooklyn Coordinating Council on February 4, 1966. Photo by Dick DeMarsico / World Telegram & Sun / Library of Congress.

While some Bed-Stuy residents were encouraged by RFK's visit, others, including frustrated local leaders who had seen many outsiders profess their interest, were not. Five-year-old Ricky Taggart was also unimpressed when Kennedy asked why he was not in school. Moments after this photo was taken, he slammed the door in the senator's face. Photo by Dick DeMarsico / World Telegram & Sun / Library of Congress.

On a Congressional fact-finding tour in April 1967, RFK and prominent activist Marian Wright learn about living conditions in the impoverished Mississippi Delta. CBS journalist Daniel Schorr takes notes beneath a portrait of President Kennedy. AP/Wide World Photos. Reproduced with permission.

Kennedy and Dolores Huerta of the UFW meet with the press in Delano, California, at the end of César Chávez's fast to pressure grape growers to recognize their union on March 10, 1968. Courtesy Walter P. Reuther Library, Wayne State University.

Kennedy and Chávez share communion at a mass celebrating the end of the fast, March 10, 1968. Courtesy Walter P. Reuther Library, Wayne State University.

Kennedy and Kentucky congressman Carl D. Perkins conduct hearings on the effectiveness of War on Poverty programs in a school gymnasium in Neon, Kentucky, on February 14, 1968. Berea College Special Collections and Archives, Appalachian Volunteers Collection. Reproduced with permission.

Kennedy campaigning among Mexican Americans in San Jose on March 23, 1968. His campaign focused heavily on gaining grassroots support from poor and minority groups. AP/World Wide Photos. Reproduced with permission.

The assassination of Martin Luther King Jr. on April 4, 1968, touched off urban uprisings in more than one hundred cities, including the nation's capital. Days later Kennedy toured the rubble with Walter Fauntroy (assisting Ethel Kennedy, in middle). Local residents, including one man who stumbled in his rush to shake the New York senator's hand, welcomed his concern. AP/World Wide Photos. Reproduced with permission.

Campaigning for the presidency in Watts, March 28, 1968.
AP/World Wide Photos. Reproduced with permission.

challenge firsthand. On an early February day in 1966 the winter air through which the senator strode was warmer than the welcome he received from his constituents in Bedford-Stuyvesant. During his visit to the Brooklyn ghetto Kennedy met icy responses from residents—one five-year-old boy slammed the door on him when the senator asked why he wasn't in school—and the disbelief of community leaders.[44]

Following his tour, Kennedy met with leaders of the Central Brooklyn Coordinating Council. The CBCC seemed to be exactly the type of broad-based, locally rooted organization Kennedy had been calling for in cities around the country, with representatives from municipal government, the business community, fraternal societies, labor unions, civil rights organizations, and churches.[45] Nevertheless, CBCC members took out their considerable frustrations on the senator.[46] He sputtered when meeting organizer Elsie Richardson irreverently declared: "We're tired of what we call 'getting the business.' . . . [W]e're here to hear from our senator what he plans to do." Civil Court judge Thomas Jones confided, "I'm weary of study, Senator, very weary." An assistant to the Brooklyn borough president insisted, "We got to have something concrete now, not tomorrow, yesterday."[47] Kennedy offered no solutions aside from suggesting a coordinated attack on the problem and the need for an official community spokesperson. Back at his New York apartment after the meeting, the dispirited senator grumbled: "I don't have to take that shit. I could be smoking a cigar in Palm Beach."[48] After his initial disillusionment, however, he directed Walinsky and Tom Johnston to continue work on more concrete plans for economic development in the inner city.

If his primary focus in early 1966 was urban poverty, the problems of another segment of the "other America" were brought to his attention in March when labor ally Jack Conway informed him of a grape pickers' strike in California. Having some familiarity with the issue from the planning stages of the National Service Corps, Kennedy had joined the Senate Subcommittee on Migratory Labor the previous summer.[49] He professed amazement at his first hearing when an official of the American Farm Bureau Federation testified against the right to minimum wages, collective bargaining, and limits on child labor for farm workers.[50] Conway called in the spring of 1966, on behalf of Walter Reuther, to request that the New York senator go to California for more hearings, as the AFL-CIO was attempting to help organize and support the farm workers. The subcommittee had been in existence for seven years, but it had never received the attention Kennedy's presence could bring to one of its field hearings. Reluctant to travel to the West Coast because of his breakneck schedule, he asked Peter Edelman repeatedly if he thought it worthwhile.[51] Grape growers were a powerful political force in California, and many were conservative Democrats. Author Michael Harrington reflected that "politically speaking . . . [the California trip] was probably a stupid thing to do."[52] Nevertheless, recalled Conway, "I really leaned on him. I just said, in effect, well, I've done things for you and I'm calling in chips on this one. He was mad at me, but he did it."[53]

Once he was there, Kennedy found the struggle of the farm workers compelling. The most poignant moment of the hearings was the testimony of Guadalupe Olivarez, an uneducated forty-four-year-old laborer and mother who told the subcommittee of her travails in the fields. Medical problems had forced her family to move around desperately trailing work. Fearful that her two children were too young to ride the school bus, she locked them in a car during the day after her employer informed her that school-aged children couldn't be in the fields. She told of farm workers who had been fired for voicing concerns and the fear this engendered. Her story appealed to Kennedy's sense of injustice. "Do your fellow farm workers feel they have any friends among those in authority," he asked, "or do they feel they're by themselves?"[54] Olivarez said she did not know, and was afraid to say anything lest she incriminate herself. It was a question Kennedy would revisit with many witnesses in poverty hearings over the next two years.

Kennedy's inquiry revolved around problems related to the unionization of migrant labor and a minimum wage for farm workers. Witnesses discussed the challenges of organizing a transient group of laborers, and Kennedy explored potential pitfalls while expressing his support for a union. He probed the moral imperatives for employers during the testimony of a longtime Catholic priest in the San Joaquin Valley, who conceded that employers had a responsibility to agree to a plebiscite for pickers on the question of unionization.[55] Kennedy later told a reporter: "Bishops should encourage their priests to work with the farm laborer. They themselves should leave their homes and live among these workers."[56] It would not be the last time he would criticize the church for laxity on the issue of poverty.[57]

At a crowded high school gymnasium in Delano, headquarters for the striking grape pickers, the subcommittee questioned the local sheriff, whose officers had been photographing picketing farm workers. Kennedy asked about the practice:

KENNEDY: I can understand you want to take pictures if there's a riot going on but I don't understand why if someone is walking along with a sign you want to take pictures of them? I don't see how that helps.

SHERIFF GALYEN: Well, they might take pictures of us, too.

KENNEDY: Sheriff, I don't think it's responsive. It's not a question of them wanting to take pictures of you. You're a law enforcement official. It is in some way an act of intimidation to go around and be taking their pictures.

SHERIFF GALYEN: I've got to identify those people through my district attorney. I've got to identify, that is the man.

KENNEDY: That is the man that what?

SHERIFF GALYEN: That caused this trouble.

KENNEDY: Let's separate the two points. I'm not suggesting that you not take pictures of the trouble that's occurring. We're talking about taking pictures of somebody walking along with a picket sign.

SHERIFF GALYEN: Well, he's a potential isn't he?

KENNEDY: Well, I mean, so am I.

Kennedy then inquired about the arrest of forty picketers for assembling illegally.

KENNEDY: Have you charged them with an offense?

SHERIFF GALYEN: It came up through the idea that we had news from the inside, that there was going to be some cutting done if they didn't stop saying certain things, so I'm responsible to arrest them as well as anyone else.

KENNEDY: What did you arrest them for?

SHERIFF GALYEN: Why if they got into a riot and started cutting up the people—

KENNEDY: I'm not talking about that. Once you got into a riot, I understand that, but before, when they're just walking along, what did you arrest them for?

SHERIFF GALYEN: Well, if I have reason to believe that there's going to be a riot started and somebody tells me that there's going to be trouble if you don't stop them, it's my duty to stop them.

KENNEDY: Then do you go out and arrest them?

SHERIFF GALYEN: Yes.

KENNEDY: And charge them?

SHERIFF GALYEN: Charge them.

KENNEDY: What do you charge them with?

SHERIFF GALYEN: Violation of—unlawful assembly.

KENNEDY: I think that's most interesting. Who told you that they're going to riot?

SHERIFF GALYEN: The men right out in the field that they were talking to said, "If you don't get them out of here, we're going to cut their hearts out." So rather than let them get cut, we removed the cause.

Senator George Murphy of California interceded to ask the sheriff to clarify his precautionary tactics, at which point Galyen said: "You'll find nobody say we beat anyone or anything like that. This is not Selma, Alabama." Kennedy returned to his questioning:

KENNEDY: This is the most interesting concept, I think, that you suddenly hear or you talk about the fact that somebody makes a report about somebody going to get out of order, perhaps violate the law, and you go and arrest them, and they haven't done anything wrong. How can you arrest somebody if they haven't violated the law?

SHERIFF GALYEN: They're ready to violate the law.

SENATOR MURPHY: I think it's a shame you weren't there before the Watts riots.

SENATOR WILLIAMS: We will recess—

KENNEDY: Can I suggest in the interim period of time, the luncheon period of time, that the sheriff and the district attorney read the Constitution of the United States?[58]

The overflow audience of mostly farm workers erupted in applause.

During the lunchtime break Kennedy spoke with César Chávez, leader of the striking grape pickers, in the parking lot. He had first met Chávez briefly while plotting voter organization efforts in California during the 1960 campaign, and Chávez had been impressed by Kennedy's willingness to listen, but the men had had no association in the intervening years.[59] Peter Edelman saw their conversation as pivotal. "The two of them stood talking, eye to eye, in a low conversational tone that was barely audible even to the first ring of people around them," Edelman remembered. "It went on for maybe five minutes, maybe even ten. I don't know what they said to each other," the aide said, but "I do know that when it was over they were friends for life."[60]

Kennedy's appearance had a salutary effect on farm worker organizing efforts. Chávez recalled: "People that were afraid were coming [to the hearing] and they were saying, 'Senator Kennedy says that the union's a good thing.' And we were saying, 'We've always said that.' 'Well, he's saying it. I believe it now.'"[61] Chávez also felt that Kennedy's support ended "red-baiting" accusations against his organization, the National Farmworkers Association. Kennedy would press for Labor Department certification of the grape pickers' strike (the farm workers were not recognized under the National Labor Relations Act) and help raise funds for both a medical clinic in Delano and a union service center in San Francisco. A few weeks after the clash, Schenley Corporation, the target of the grape pickers' strike, became the first major grower to recognize a farm workers' union. From March 1966 to his death, Kennedy's Senate office became the Washington entrée to power for the farm workers.[62]

Kennedy's schedule remained unrelenting in the spring of 1966. He had spoken about poverty frequently during his first year in the Senate, but it now became his most common theme. From California, Kennedy headed to the site of an old battleground in Oxford, Mississippi. The law student association at Ole Miss had invited the New York senator to speak despite the animosity the former attorney general still generated among many Mississippians four years after his Justice Department had facilitated the enrollment of James Meredith.[63] In his address Kennedy held up the issue of poverty as a mutual enemy, telling law students, "Racial injustice and poverty, ignorance and hope for world peace are to be found in the streets of New York and Chicago and Los Angeles as well," though in an ill-informed attempt to deemphasize past differences, Kennedy announced prematurely that in the South "disease and hunger and ignorance . . . have been diminished and almost completely defeated."[64]

Kennedy's Ole Miss appearance received a surprisingly cordial response, awakening echoes of his briefly successful quest for unity at the University of Georgia in 1961.[65] But 1966 would not be a year for even fleeting consensus. Less than three months later and only sixty miles from where Kennedy spoke, James Meredith was shot by a sniper while on a one-man "March Against Fear" through the South. Racial tensions across the nation ran menacingly high. That summer rioting broke out in Cleveland, Brooklyn, Chicago, and elsewhere. Louis Harris polls revealed that 70 percent of white Americans believed the pace of the civil rights was moving too fast, a 20 percent increase from 1964.[66] The Watts uprising had been catalytic in the centrifugal political effect of the later 1960s, propelling citizens frustrated with the status quo farther toward either end of the political spectrum, and

1966 would reveal the irreparable fracturing of Lyndon Johnson's liberal consensus.[67] A much more powerful white backlash would arise, and the centrifugal effect on racial minority groups was manifested in a growing militancy in the civil rights movement—exemplified by the emergence of both the Black Power movement and the Black Panther Party for Self-Defense—and it would soon be mirrored in the activities of other minority groups, with Native Americans calling for Red Power and Latinos organizing the militant Brown Berets.

The changing milieu was also reflected in the rising impatience—which Kennedy had seen up close in Bedford-Stuyvesant—of poor people's groups. In April 1966 Sargent Shriver was shouted down by angry attendees at the Citizens' Crusade Against Poverty convention, and in October OEO incurred a firestorm for withdrawing support from the popular and effective Head Start organization Child Development Group of Mississippi. While white liberals began castigating Lyndon Johnson over what they saw as deliberate deception regarding the Vietnam War, African Americans were more troubled by what they saw as his credibility gap on poverty. Because of Vietnam expenditures, the administration announced proposed OEO budget cuts early in the year, prompting *Washington Afro-American* columnist James D. Williams to assert: "The poverty program is in trouble among the poor. They have to an extent lost faith. So many times have they been deceived in the past, that their faith is a fragile thing. . . . Never have so many been promised so much and given so little, and they don't like what has happened." Williams incisively explained the widening breach that was at the heart of the urban crisis: "People in the ghetto are so accustomed to being assailed by the great big outside world, they tend to cling together for their own survival. Outside the walls, the affluent world can shake its head in horror, it can condemn, it can criticize, but in so doing it reinforces the belief in the ghetto that nobody really cares what happens to the poor, nobody understands."[68]

Kennedy's first open critique of administration domestic policy came upon word of the proposed cuts. "There is cause to wonder whether we are yet facing up to our responsibilities" to the poor, Kennedy told an upstate audience, citing spending reductions for housing and neighborhood facilities, the Elementary and Secondary Education Act, and a milk program for students. He stated that the nation now had an increased obligation because "the poor man—the Negro, the Puerto Rican, the Spanish-American, the poor white—serves in Vietnam out of all proportion to his place in the population figures," contending that casualty lists reflected these numbers.

The United States, he said, had to "keep faith with the sacrifice they are making."[69]

Kennedy also addressed the dissension created by community action programs. Americans "should not be disappointed," he cautioned,

> that community action has not been an instant success. It has been a long time since most leadership in this country has spoken to the poor and tried to understand the problems of their existence. We should not be disillusioned because spokesmen for the poor have not appeared overnight. It takes time for genuine leadership capable of action and results to develop. Nor should we fear the conflicts that have arisen as new power groups contend with old, as political leaders are forced to meet the slum dwellers instead of the ward leaders. Every department of city government dealing with social welfare problems should feel challenged to justify their traditional response to the problems of the poor. They may not like it but the price of their discontent may be progress—and stronger and safer communities for our children and ourselves.[70]

It was a spirited defense of an idea he had guided from the halls of the Justice Department to the front ranks in the War on Poverty, but it probably came too late. The critical period in popular perceptions of community action had been the first year of operation, but the program had been mired in controversy in Chicago, Los Angeles, and elsewhere. Aside from an oblique reference in his Odd Fellows address, Kennedy had been conspicuously silent on community action when he might have provided political cover for the administration.

Why had he not spoken out sooner? Was Kennedy displeased with Johnson's expansion of the program beyond the limited demonstration projects he and Hackett had initially envisioned and therefore allowed the administration to reap what it had sown? Other than his January 1964 memo to Johnson, Kennedy made little effort during the planning stages to argue against the expansion of the program, and indeed fought to make it a large part of the War on Poverty. Once he became a senator he vigorously encouraged New York communities to organize themselves in order to receive federal money.

Had he lost faith in the concept? Aide Peter Edelman contended that Kennedy "always sort of kept community action as a part of a strategy, but always of a lesser priority" than education and jobs.[71] That may have been true, but in 1967 Kennedy would raise the issue of participation by the poor in War on Poverty programs more frequently than ever before.

Dismissing his attachment to the idea as secondary thus seems counterfactual.

Had Kennedy failed to foresee the political trouble community action would create? The record indicates otherwise. Edelman claimed that Kennedy expected the conflicts arising from the program but never discussed this explicitly in public "because that would have been rather damaging."[72] Given his animosity toward Johnson, Kennedy likely felt little empathy for the president as he faced the wrath of Mayor Daley and other city leaders. Edelman recalled that his boss often intimated that it would be an unpopular move "to have the Federal Government financing people to come down and tell City Hall that it's doing the wrong thing."[73] The aide opined that Kennedy may have decided that community action was not "the most attractive thing to go into."[74]

Kennedy's reticence thus stemmed from political calculation, and as a result he made little contribution to defusing the explosive climate from which the Johnson administration began to retreat. Because of his rivalry with the president, Kennedy remained on the sidelines as community action—which dominated newspaper headlines across the nation and became the face of the War on Poverty to many Americans—lost its best chance for success before popular sympathies began to ebb.

The proposed spending reductions for poverty programs may have finally spurred Kennedy's vigorous defense of community action, but they also led the New York senator to doubt the political likelihood of sufficient federal antipoverty funding across the board. When civil rights leaders Andrew Young and Walter Fauntroy urged him to propose a $100 billion urban Marshall Plan, Kennedy replied, "If the Vietnam war ends, maybe in five years we can think in those terms."[75]

Instead he increased his emphasis on nongovernmental support for antipoverty initiatives, testing his ideas in a number of speeches through the spring of 1966. Before the National Council of the Churches of Christ, Kennedy repeated his call for the business community, universities, and other elements of society to join in a partnership with government for "a total program to reconstruct our urban society," with direction of the program "not in City Hall, and not in Washington," but coming from "residents of the ghettoes themselves."[76] A week later he told an NAACP gathering: "Government can—and must—help. But I think we must frankly accept that government can do only part of the job." A true community, said Kennedy, is "not dependent on the largesse of government," adding, "What the people of our ghettoes need is not greater dependence, but full independence; not the charity and favor of their fellow citizens, but equal claims of right and equal power to enforce those claims."[77] He insisted that government efforts on unemployment, housing, education, and crime were failing in any case, and noted that President Johnson's Model Cities legislation was being gutted by congressional opponents.

His alternative to reliance on government was the coordinated urban regeneration initiative he had outlined in January, directed by an individual community itself through a new institution which was the fruit of Walinsky's efforts: the development corporation.

Kennedy's initial conception of a development corporation was sketchy, calling for funding by mortgage loans from banks and insurance companies, private foundations, universities, labor union welfare and pension funds, and industrial corporations. In the most important aspect of the proposal, Kennedy suggested that community residents would gain a stake in the corporation through a variety of means, such as the purchase of condominiums or cooperative apartments, or putting a portion of their wages in equity shares. "With such a participating interest," he said,

> the people of the ghetto would—by every tradition of our law—exercise significant control over the circumstances of their daily lives. They would be shareholders; they would elect officers and directors; they would rise to speak at corporate meetings, not as petitioners but as members with a legal *right* to be heard and to vote on policy. They would vote and speak on matters of immediate importance to their daily lives. . . . As the assets and properties of the corporation grew, and as the local participants were to gain more experience[,] . . . they might even develop for us a new kind of approach to government in the metropolis—a system in which all neighborhoods manage themselves as corporate entities.[78]

If community action had been conceived as a way to bring increased political democracy to the residents of the inner city, Kennedy's development corporation was an attempt to introduce greater economic democracy. The idea would continue to take shape through the summer and autumn of 1966.

While Kennedy's proposal indicated a heady new direction in his strategic evolution on the issue of poverty, he maintained an attitude of studied caution. As urban violence again erupted in the summer of 1966, he sensed that the nation was on the precipice of domestic catastrophe. In a late night conversation with his friend Richard Goodwin, the author of Johnson's "Great Society" speech, Kennedy shared his frustration, telling Goodwin that the worst effect of the war was the brake it was putting on domestic initiatives. He confided: "We have a real chance to do something about poverty, to get blacks out of the ghettoes, but we're paralyzed. I don't like Johnson, but he was doing some good things. Now there's no direction." When Goodwin observed that people seemed to be turning inward, Kennedy concurred. "They're afraid," he said.

> They don't understand the war or what's going to happen. The economy's shaky. They read about hippies and draft-card burners and riots. They feel something's happening in the country, something they don't understand or particularly like. They feel threatened, and if you're threatened, you withdraw. . . . They're willing to give a little, to help the less fortunate. We proved that with the Peace Corps, the poverty program. People are selfish, but they can also be compassionate and generous, and they care about the country. But not when they feel threatened. That's why this is such a crucial time. We can go in either direction. But if we don't make a choice soon, it will be too late to turn things around. I think people are willing to make the right choice. But they need leadership. They're hungry for leadership.[79]

He tried to deal with problems on a smaller scale. Despite the fact that most senators regarded the Committee on the District of Columbia as a political millstone, Kennedy maintained his interest in District affairs and relished the opportunity to take on negligent landlords or unscrupulous businessmen in the nation's capital. Joseph Tydings of Maryland, a Kennedy friend, would ask the New York senator to take over questioning for his subcommittee when the chance for a dramatic clash might spotlight abuses, and Kennedy was invariably willing.[80]

Beginning in August 1966, Kennedy would take part in much more highly publicized Senate hearings examining the causes of the urban crisis. Senator Abraham Ribicoff of Connecticut, former secretary of HEW under President Kennedy, began hearings on the federal role in American cities through his government operations subcommittee. Ribicoff sought Robert Kennedy's participation, recognizing the media coverage his presence would attract, and the New York senator saw the hearings as an opportunity to learn about the problem and get reactions to his community development corporation proposal. Kennedy testified early in the hearings, which would stretch over the better part of the coming year. Although the programmatic substance of his statement was largely a repackaging of his January speeches, Kennedy laid out a theoretical framework for understanding the modern city as a "vast sprawling organism . . . a living social and economic body."[81] Kennedy reemphasized the urgency of the crisis of urban poverty and framed the problem as primarily an absence of community. "The whole history of the human race," he contended, "has been the history of community. Yet this is disappearing." He argued that the measure of any program for urban aid would be "the extent to which it helps the ghetto become a community—a functioning unit, its people acting together on matters of mutual concern, with the power and resources to affect the conditions of their own lives."[82]

Kennedy focused on employment as the most important step toward progress, not least because of its political value to the national community as a whole, but also because of its palatability for whites, in contrast to other aspects of the black freedom struggle. "Whatever people may feel about open housing or open schools," Kennedy said, "there can be no argument at all, no sense for even a committed segregationist, in the maintenance of Negro unemployment." Kennedy also contended that there was "no government program now operating," citing the relative futility of job training programs such as the Manpower Development and Training Act, which offered the promise of connecting poor urban citizens to jobs.[83]

He drew on other sources to serve as moorings for his communitarian goal of providing a sense of place, a meaningful social role, and hope for poor urban citizens that they could improve conditions around them. Kennedy quoted Lewis Mumford, who idealized organic community as a counter to the maladies of the modern Western world, and he cited Thomas Jefferson's ideal of smaller-scale democracy—"elementary republics of the wards"—as a potential corrective to urban governance "using the same kind of organizational structure whether the city had 2,000 people or 2 million."[84] The senator contended that his community development corporation proposal "might return us part way toward the ideals of community on a human scale which is so easily lost in the metropolis." In language stronger than the ambiguous "maximum feasible participation" of his testimony on the Economic Opportunity Act two years earlier, Kennedy asserted that "the full and dominant participation by the residents of the community concerned" was crucial to any plan designed to lift them out of poverty.[85]

Nearly all the witnesses who discussed Kennedy's proposal lauded it. Several—including Labor Secretary Willard Wirtz, Detroit mayor Jerome Cavanagh, and fellow committee member and New York senator Jacob Javits—had been exploring similar public-private initiatives, but none had developed a vision as comprehensive as Kennedy's community development corporation.[86] Javits contrasted Kennedy's proposal with his own

plan for partnerships between the federal government and private industry to train workers. Javits disliked the mandatory use of ghetto residents
in the rebuilding effort. He had concerns about workmanship and cost,
and preferred "to give a free opportunity to all workers, wherever they
may be."[87] Historian Michael Katz describes a similar dilemma in the
work relief programs of the New Deal as "efficiency versus numbers or . . .
the quality of work versus the amount of relief."[88] Kennedy believed that
the involvement of local residents was as important as the resulting
construction.

The Ribicoff hearings did not build community between Kennedy and
the Johnson administration, as the New York senator showed minimal
patience with cabinet officials testifying before the subcommittee. He
asked Robert C. Weaver, head of the new Department of Housing and
Urban Development (HUD), why only forty thousand new low-income
housing units were under construction nationwide. When Weaver tried to
explain the operational difficulties of finding sites and the failure of cities, including New York, to fulfill contracts on allocated units, Kennedy
pounced. "I am not here defending New York," he insisted. "I am just here
saying that there is a problem[,] . . . and while the cities and the States
and the Federal government struggle about it, fight about it, and talk about
it, the people that are suffering are the people that live in the ghetto and
in the substandard housing."[89] He questioned administration priorities
with a sympathetic Sargent Shriver, calling it an "outrage" that the administration had requested $4 billion for the development of a supersonic
plane when a similar figure would have increased by hundreds of thousands the number of children covered by Head Start.[90] As Labor Secretary
Wirtz attempted to explain the failure of job training programs, Kennedy
lamented the lack of hope among young people in the inner cities. "We are
on a razor's edge," the New York senator said. Wirtz concurred, and the
two exchanged quotes from Lord Acton on hope and the meaning of law
to society's weakest members. "Without quoting a lot of poems," Kennedy
added, "Sophocles said: 'Joy is here day that follows day, some swift, some
slow, death the only goal.'" The out-quoted Wirtz declared, "I give up," as
the room broke into laughter.[91]

Not surprisingly, Lyndon Johnson found little humor in the hearings.[92]
Dun Gifford, an assistant in Weaver's office, complained to Kennedy aides
that Ribicoff and Kennedy were characterizing administration efforts unfairly. Walinsky and Edelman, who befriended Gifford, sent him in to see
their boss. Gifford argued his case at length, and Kennedy asked the HUD
official when he had last spent time in a ghetto. Gifford admitted that he

had not seen conditions firsthand, and he soon thereafter visited with residents in troubled areas of Washington and Baltimore. "I really was changed," Gifford reflected. "I went back and told Bob that he was right. I still did my job for HUD, but with considerably less enthusiasm."[93]

After the first round of hearings with administration officials, Kennedy subjected several mayors to persistent questioning on the financial role of the federal government in their cities. When John Lindsay estimated that New York would need $50 billion in the next decade to make the city "thoroughly livable," Kennedy called the figure "astronomical" and concluded, "I don't think the answer is going to be just with federal funds."[94] Detroit mayor Jerome Cavanagh told the subcommittee that his city would need $15 billion over the same period of time, testifying that cities had exhausted nearly all revenue sources other than increased state aid. Both agreed that private enterprise investment was the one remaining option.

The most publicized moment of the Ribicoff hearings occurred when Kennedy grilled Mayor Sam Yorty of Los Angeles. Kennedy's aides were urging him to put Yorty in the hot seat over his failure to head off the Watts uprising, but the junior New York senator needed little encouragement. Yorty was a maverick Democrat who had backed Richard Nixon in 1960, and when in his opening statement he blamed the Watts riots on the unrealistic promises of politicians, Kennedy entered the fray. "It is not just a question of the politician and going around and making a number of promises," the New York Democrat said. "I expect somebody reading the Declaration of Independence and the Constitution of the United States . . . would feel that he was entitled to move ahead in society." When Yorty defended his remarks, Kennedy said, "These people expect to have as much of a chance as you have had and I have had." Yorty snapped, "Well, certainly they will not have had the chance you have had, but I hope they have the one that I have had."[95]

Kennedy criticized Yorty for a lack of leadership in spite of his limited jurisdiction, for his having left the city for a brief period during the Watts riots, and for his inability to answer specific questions about unemployment and job training. Yorty retorted, "I do not need a lecture from you on how to run my city."[96] Kennedy later fired back, "The mayor of Los Angeles I would like to have stay here through all of these hearings, and I think he could safely do so, because as I understand from your testimony you have nothing to get back to."[97]

Kennedy's clash with Yorty did not help him in the mainstream press, as his dogged questioning reawakened old charges of ruthlessness. The

Washington Star editorialized that Kennedy "summoned cabinet members and the mayors of large cities before him as if they were errant schoolboys and he their properly indignant teacher."[98] When a staff memo informed him that his mail was running 90 percent sympathetic to Yorty, Kennedy jotted, "I am beginning to get the point."[99] A *Time* reporter observed that the Ribicoff subcommittee "obviously had not done its homework," and Henry Cohen, a deputy New York City administrator who had attended the hearings with Mayor Lindsay, reflected that Yorty's protestations of limited responsibility were accurate. Yorty, Cohen declared, "had a better understanding of what local government in Los Angeles was than Bob Kennedy did."[100]

If the Yorty incident generated more criticism than praise among white commentators, black Angelenos, whose votes had helped put Yorty in office, saw the incident differently. One letter to the editor of the *Los Angeles Sentinel* pronounced: "Sam Yorty has never admitted any mistake himself but blames someone else. Every word Senator Robert Kennedy and Senator Abraham Ribicoff stated is absolutely true." Publisher Leon H. Washington Jr. asserted: "The mayor is not as knowledgeable about conditions in our town's deprived area as he should be. . . . Senator Kennedy was right." And a *Sentinel* columnist reported that "a lot of people have stood up to say that Mayor Sam got what was coming to him."[101]

Ultimately the incident likely reinforced existing perceptions of Kennedy, and in the fall of 1966 he was at the height of his popularity. As the country headed into an election season characterized by a white backlash against urban violence, Kennedy ran ahead of Johnson in some polls. One national columnist informally surveyed midwesterners' attitudes and was perplexed to find that most respondents opposed more liberal positions on Vietnam and antipoverty spending, yet they still favored Kennedy over Johnson. "He's a fighter, a hero type," stated one man. "He's a Kennedy," said another.[102] When Kennedy visited Columbus, a local Ohio paper wrote, "In 35 years of reporting the local and national scene we have never seen such enthusiasm from a crowd. . . . [W]e have never witnessed such pure idolation [*sic*]."[103]

Kennedy put his popularity to work in the fall of 1966, stumping for Democratic candidates across the country including liberals such as old antipoverty ally Paul Douglas of Illinois and California governor Pat Brown. Kennedy had been disappointed, however, by Brown's handling of the migrant labor issue, and as a result he did not attempt to influence California farm workers to support Brown.[104]

The political climate in the fall of 1966 was shaped by a public averse to the discussion of increased government spending for the War on Poverty.[105] A September Louis Harris poll found that 34 percent of respondents believed the War on Poverty was either somewhat or very successful, while 40 percent saw it as not very successful or a real failure.[106] Undeterred, Kennedy continued to call for greater outlays. Along with Pennsylvania Democrat Joseph Clark, Kennedy worked within the Labor and Public Welfare Committee to increase the budget recommendation for the poverty program by $750 million over the amount requested by the Johnson administration. "The War on Poverty, like it or not," Kennedy said in an early October Senate speech, "is the single outstanding commitment this Nation has made to the principle that poverty must be abolished." He conceded the possibility of a federal tax increase but argued that programs leading to work for those on relief rolls or living in subsidized housing would ease the local property tax burden. Kennedy discussed budgetary priorities, comparing antipoverty spending to other approved items such as $5 billion for the space program, $500,000 for free ammunition to gun clubs, $200,000 to promote the sale of cigarettes in Asian countries. "We have a greater responsibility," Kennedy declared, "to provide for those who cannot help themselves unless we help them do it."[107]

Kennedy called for an increased federal commitment on the Senate floor, but in speeches across the country that fall he focused on the potential of localities. He again placed the recent urban unrest in the context of a nationwide loss of community. "As cities get bigger and technologies more complex," he told one audience, "we seem to be losing the sense . . . of community, of human dialogue and mutual concern, the thousand invisible strands of common experience." Kennedy cited the much-publicized case of Kitty Genovese, a young New York woman whose neighbors heard her cries as she was stabbed repeatedly but did nothing. "The greatest threat," Kennedy said, "is that, too often, nobody cares; no one wants to get involved." He discussed the community development corporation as an alternative to entrusting one's problems "to some anonymous bureaucrat" and as a way to "return to our people significant control over the circumstances of their daily lives."[108]

At the dedication of a community college in Minnesota in September, Kennedy continued to downplay the role of the federal government and suggested instead a form of Wilsonian progressivism. "Bigness, loss of community, organizations and society grown far past the human scale," he said, "these are the besetting sins of the twentieth century, which threaten to paralyze our very capacity to act." He called for an active fight against "over-concentration" in order to "bring the engines of government, of technology, of the economy, fully under the control of our citizens, to recapture and reinforce the values of a more human time and place." He again quoted Thomas Jefferson on the importance of citizen participation and told the crowd, "Here you have shown that dedicated men and women need not wait for a faraway government to act." After grappling with urban problems in the Ribicoff hearings, Kennedy even made a desperate and impractical appeal to end the demographic shifts of preceding decades, stating, "The time has come to stem the flow [of population] to the cities—to prevent their further sprawling over the landscape, their further oppression of men's souls."[109]

Both Paul Douglas and Pat Brown would lose their races as the fall elections proved to be a Republican triumph. In the end, Kennedy's efforts to increase the poverty appropriation in the Senate also failed. A *Newsweek* article portrayed him as more concerned with the television coverage of the Ribicoff hearings and his own exposure on the campaign trail than with the poverty budget, quoting one colleague who called him a "hit-and-run" legislator. "If he really wanted to win that poverty fight," the off-the-record senatorial source said, "he'd have stayed right here in town for the past six weeks nailing down votes and coordinating pressure groups all over the country."[110]

The criticism of Kennedy's campaigning may have had some merit. Unlike Lyndon Johnson, Kennedy disdained the mechanics of the Senate and cloakroom politicking, preferring to create popular pressure through public appearances. But that fall the New York senator engaged in more than just attention seeking. He was at work developing plans for his own antipoverty initiative in Bedford-Stuyvesant. In a strategy memo Adam Walinsky cautioned his boss against giving in to pressures to take another overseas trip (Kennedy had gained considerable media attention and international stature from recent trips to Latin America and South Africa), writing: "There is a complete vacuum in the poverty leadership—black or white. You can seize the lead." Walinsky urged him to focus his energy on shaping his nascent urban project, and Kennedy agreed, returning the memo after scrawling: "I am not going anyplace this fall. I want to be with you walking side by side through the ghettos of N.Y."[111]

The Ribicoff hearings proved a helpful seminar on the urban crisis. Kennedy would learn from witnesses and test his own ideas for reshaping the War on Poverty. By the end of 1966 Kennedy's strategic approach had evolved considerably. He had moved from initiatives based on the principles of community action, volunteer service, and the need for better education to an alternative poverty war of his own. His escalating critiques of the Johnson administration would eventually lead the conservative *National Review* to label his efforts sarcastically "Bobby's Greater Society."[112] Kennedy had developed his own vision for a renewed assault on poverty, and he was poised to attempt his first offensive.

6

"BORN IN A STORM"

THE BEDFORD-STUYVESANT EXPERIMENT

By late 1966 community leaders in the Bedford-Stuyvesant section of Brooklyn were even more anxious than might have been expected after a year of escalating urban violence nationwide. The cause of their unease was the announced intention of their junior U.S. senator to implement a plan for the revitalization of their community. "They were still gun-shy," Civil Court judge Thomas R. Jones later reflected, "not sure either of how long our allies would stay with us, or where this [plan] was going, . . . or who the money would come from, or a number of things. . . . I knew little, they knew less." In short, the Bedford-Stuyvesant project was "born in a storm."[1]

Soon after he delivered his January 1966 urban development speeches, Robert Kennedy directed assistants Adam Walinsky and Thomas Johnston to shape an initiative based on them. When Kennedy visited Bedford-Stuyvesant two weeks later, Walinsky contended, the New York senator was there with a purpose, and his staff expected rough treatment from community leaders at a meeting held at the local YMCA. "He was looking around," Walinsky recalled, for a place to enact his community development plan. "And that's why we took him out there," the acerbic aide said. "So of course the liturgy in Bed-Stuy is that, you know, . . . 'We're tired, we want action, blah, blah, blah,' that was all planned. [At least] in our minds.'"[2]

Whatever the genesis of Kennedy's commitment to carrying out his experiment in Bedford-Stuyvesant—the challenge of local residents or the scouting of his aides—the choice was appropriate. Harlem was the most visible impoverished black community in the nation, but it was already the focus of high-profile antipoverty efforts. It also had strong-willed and well-entrenched political leaders, including the powerful congressman Adam Clayton Powell.[3] By contrast, Bedford-Stuyvesant had no congressional representative of its own, and its numerous community groups were diffuse, thus presenting a slightly less formidable political gauntlet for an externally initiated program to run. Perhaps most important, studies by the Pratt Institute revealed that Bedford-Stuyvesant had a less dilapidated housing stock than that of Harlem, a relatively high percentage of home ownership, and a significant number of longtime residents who could provide a foundation for economic redevelopment.[4]

Nevertheless, the challenge was daunting. With a population of over 400,000 and ever-expanding boundaries, "Bed-Stuy" was roughly as populous as Cincinnati and second only to the South Side of Chicago as the nation's largest ghetto. It was the most overcrowded area of New York City, and its median income was $1,500 below that of the city as a whole.[5] The nine-square-mile area contained no hospitals, colleges, or local newspapers. Riots in 1964 had elicited promises of help for the troubled neighborhood, but six months later, one newly paved vacant lot was the sum total of improvement.[6] Meanwhile, antipoverty money flowed into the borough of Manhattan, including Harlem, at a rate six times greater than into Brooklyn.[7]

After the dust settled from Kennedy's February visit, Walinsky and Johnston began their research. At first their work on the project was halting, as Kennedy maintained heavy involvement in other state and national issues. By the summer, however, both men estimated that they were spending half their time on Bedford-Stuyvesant. Through the course of the year they managed to confer with urban experts, business figures, and black community leaders nationwide in an effort to develop a program.[8]

Johnston, a thirty-year-old former television producer from a well-to-do Kentucky family, was given the pragmatic tasks of establishing necessary political and business contacts and of forging community ties. Kennedy had a poor reputation among business leaders, much of which derived from reports of his handling of the steel crisis as attorney general.[9] Johnston's urbane manner initially served him well in the diplomacy of coalition building. He contacted an old college friend, investment banker Eli S. Jacobs, to solicit ideas on approaching the business community.

Jacobs had served as Kenneth Keating's finance chairman in the 1964 Senate election and still distrusted Kennedy. Johnston nevertheless thought that the well-connected Jacobs might prove useful in the early stages of the project and contribute to its bipartisan appeal, so he arranged for the senator to meet him several times through the spring and summer of 1966.[10]

These personal encounters helped bring Jacobs on board. One April evening at a charitable event upstate Kennedy joked with Jacobs and other high-profile Republican business figures, who found the New York senator surprisingly likable. On another occasion Jacobs described a stare-down with Kennedy on an airplane. After a few minutes Jacobs had conceded, and when Kennedy told the young banker about a business luncheon he'd attended earlier in the day, Jacobs said, "I'll bet they were scared to death of you." "You know," Kennedy responded, "they were." The mock contest deflated Kennedy's ruthless reputation. "From that point forward," Jacobs reflected, "my views of him were caused to change."[11] Jacobs began to talk with friends in the business community about the Bedford-Stuyvesant effort and to work with Johnston on seeking potential business contributors.

Meanwhile, Johnston and other New York aides set out to solicit community support. The Kennedy assistant given principal responsibility for community contacts was an ambitious young African American named Earl Graves. Graves had been a real estate broker in Bedford-Stuyvesant, an occupation of ill repute among many community leaders, who had seen scare tactics disperse white homeowners during the postwar years.[12] Graves's first encounter with Kennedy was a Christmas party for underprivileged children that he had organized at the behest of the newly elected senator. Kennedy was impressed and brought Graves onto his staff.[13] While Kennedy's white aides found him a bit of a "hustler," his local roots and engaging personality generally helped Kennedy's relations with Bed-Stuy residents.[14]

Graves and Johnston focused most of their attention on the Central Brooklyn Coordinating Council, which had facilitated Kennedy's meeting at the YMCA. The CBCC was an umbrella organization for nearly one hundred community groups in the area. Although its leaders had greeted Kennedy with extreme skepticism, the CBCC and its principal offshoot, Youth In Action (the OEO-approved community action organization in Bedford-Stuyvesant), appeared to be the types of cooperative community organizations extolled by Kennedy for their capacity to build consensus and function in partnership with the federal government or other outside help.[15]

In fact, the CBCC leadership was polarizing, in no small part because its most influential voices were those of several respected (and sometimes feared) women whom critics derisively called "the matriarchy." Elsie Richardson was the most outspoken of these leaders, and she along with the others struggled to overcome sexism in the community, on one occasion chastising columnist Jackie Robinson for what she read as his celebration of ministers (all of whom were male) as the most important social leaders in the community. She told readers of the *Amsterdam News* that she was "sick and tired of having individuals do things for me rather than with me. Paternalism from within the community is no more desirable than from without."[16] CBCC leaders were resolved to shape the Kennedy effort, forming the Renewal and Rehabilitation Committee (R&R) to serve as the compass of the Bedford-Stuyvesant project. Kennedy and his staff committed early to the CBCC but failed to consult individuals within it or other organizations. An informal summer canvassing of Bedford-Stuyvesant residents by Kennedy's office portended trouble, hinting that neither that organization nor any other local groups had broad support.[17]

Judge Thomas Jones, who had also challenged the senator at the February meeting, remained unaware of the unfolding plans for his community. A Democratic state assemblyman who had campaigned for his judgeship with Kennedy in Bedford-Stuyvesant in 1964, Jones had amassed a following of his own. He'd had run-ins with the leaders of the CBCC, however, and the two political factions kept each other at arm's length. It was not until six months later that Kennedy contacted Jones personally and expressed surprise that he had not been included in the initial planning.[18] This poor communication did not anger Jones, but it did alienate another leader whom Kennedy failed either to consult or include, the sitting state assemblywoman for Bedford-Stuyvesant and another Jones rival, Shirley Chisholm. In embracing the CBCC to the exclusion of all other voices, Kennedy and his staff created a problem that would later threaten the viability of the project.[19]

This lack of communication indicates that Kennedy was not as engaged with the community aspect of the Bedford-Stuyvesant effort as he should have been. Throughout the formative period he would have to overcome his personal disdain—instilled by his father—for local political infighting. "It's an endless morass from which it is very difficult to extricate oneself. . . . [Y]ou always make enemies," the New York senator told an interviewer in a private oral history a year later.[20] All the Kennedys believed that national figures were weakened by getting involved in the struggles of local politics, yet that was exactly what the embryonic Bedford-Stuyvesant venture demanded.

By the late summer of 1966 Kennedy and his staff had already grown frustrated with CBCC leaders, and they began to search for more agreeable community leadership. "I have been working with these people in Bedford-Stuyvesant for six months and I can't get on track," Kennedy told Judge Jones. "Nobody'll take charge and nobody will do what has to be done and get going. . . . I can't waste any more time."[21] In a characteristic appeal he sought Jones's leadership on the community side of the project. "From what I hear," Kennedy confided, "you'll be able to do it, because you're tough enough to try to do it."[22] The judge accepted the summons and had Kennedy's staff inform CBCC leaders that he had the senator's confidence. They were thus forced to accept Jones's participation. The judge subsequently brought other community leaders into the R&R committee.

While Johnston labored on the functional side of the project, Walinsky continued to flesh out the idea for a community development corporation. Kennedy successfully sought federal funding for the initiative and others like it through a "special impact" amendment to the Economic Opportunity Act of 1964. Walinsky drafted the provision to funnel resources toward particularly impoverished inner city neighborhoods, based on the ideas outlined in Kennedy's January speeches: employment for ghetto residents on construction projects, public and private sector help in supporting locally owned businesses, and block grants for communities to streamline funding.

Learning from the Appalachia amendment of a year earlier, and seeking a bipartisan appeal, Kennedy asked Jacob Javits to cosponsor the legislation. After some initial disagreement over the funding request for $150 million, which Javits found exorbitant—he believed that his junior colleague "didn't have any real feeling for what a dollar meant"—and after his concern was assuaged that private enterprise involvement would not be sufficiently encouraged, Javits signed on. In the end, the House reduced the appropriation to $50 million over two years, but the Special Impact Program (SIP) passed in autumn 1966.[23]

The operational structure of the Bedford-Stuyvesant effort was as yet undetermined late into the summer. In September, Tom Johnston sent Kennedy a memo suggesting a framework that he felt addressed the need for a "constructive partnership with members of the white financial and business community." Johnston called for the formation of two boards, one composed of community leaders, the other a "Business Leaders Council" that would serve as "a loose form of a cabinet" to which the senator could turn for assistance. Johnston argued that within a year a large number of projects would be under way, and that the "firm and businesslike relationship" that would have been established between the two boards would allow the business leaders council to "be in a position to relinquish many of its responsibilities to the Development Corporation."[24] This two-board concept later became the organizational structure of the Bedford-Stuyvesant project, but not without controversy and confusion over the enduring role of each board.

Recruitment of prominent business executives began in earnest in the fall. Kennedy lunched with J. M. Kaplan of the Welch Company in September, and on one rainy October day he and Eli Jacobs visited eight other New York financial and political titans. Jacobs had suggested that they adopt a "domino theory" approach, obtaining support from the most respected figures first in the hope of influencing others to join the effort.[25]

Their first target was international banker and financier André Meyer, a longtime friend of the Kennedy family. Kennedy's pitch to Meyer and others was short on operational specifics but long on themes the high-powered business leaders could understand. Conceding that federal programs were not solving the problem of urban poverty, Kennedy presented the project as a chance to test both their abilities and their faith in private enterprise against the toughest domestic challenge facing the nation.[26] As expected, Meyer agreed to participate (while taking the opportunity to prod Kennedy to speak out more forcefully against the war).[27] IBM president Thomas Watson Jr., another Kennedy friend, and CBS head William S. Paley, whose stepdaughter was married to a Kennedy staffer, were next to accept. James Oates, president of Equitable Life, whom Jacobs considered the most respected figure in the insurance industry, pledged support, as did George Moore, president of First National City Bank, the second-largest banking institution in New York City.

As in Jacobs's case, the conservative Moore was won over by a personal meeting with the New York senator. Moore was mired at the time in struggles with Robert Moses, World's Fair planners, and the Metropolitan Opera, of which he was treasurer. Kennedy empathized with the embattled banking executive. He himself was concerned about the impending release of FBI documents revealing that he had authorized the wiretapping of Martin Luther King Jr., and was engaged in a highly publicized battle over William Manchester's forthcoming book on his brother's assassination.

When Moore complained that he was overburdened, Kennedy said: "Hell, Mr. Moore. That's nothing. I've got J. Edgar Hoover and William Manchester. Do you want to trade?"[28]

Kennedy and Jacobs also sought out former administration officials Douglas Dillon and Roswell Gilpatric. Gilpatric's law firm later provided pro bono legal counsel to the community corporation, and Dillon served as chair of the business board. David Lilienthal, former head of the Tennessee Valley Authority, was tapped for inclusion because of his experience with economic development. Lilienthal agreed to participate but cautioned Kennedy: "The success of the project would be endangered unless it is kept as nearly free of a partisan political coloration as is humanly possible. I am confident that this is your purpose."[29]

Kennedy fully agreed, but he handled the enlistment of business support with far greater aplomb than relations with prominent Republican political leaders. Senate colleague Jacob Javits still knew nothing of the project, and Mayor John Lindsay first learned of it as the result of a chance meeting with Kennedy on a street corner in early October.[30] Governor Nelson Rockefeller was never approached, although his brother David (then president of the Chase Manhattan Bank) was asked for assistance and declined formal participation.[31]

The final piece in the buildup to the program's inception was the search for foundation grants. Once Mrs. Vincent Astor was convinced that the program was a nonpartisan endeavor, the program was awarded its first sizable grant—$1 million—by the Astor Foundation.[32] The Stern Fund bestowed further grant money soon thereafter. Adam Walinsky then prepared a brief for the Ford Foundation, whose Gray Areas program had produced several of the concepts implemented by the PCJD. Paul Ylvisaker, a key architect of the Gray Areas project and then president of the public affairs group arising from it, was interested, but his vice president, Louis Winnick, was dubious. He thought the relationship between the business leaders and the community group an "untenable coalition" and found Walinsky's housing and relocation proposals impractical.[33] Nevertheless, because Winnick and Jacobs were old friends, and because he found the potential payoff exciting, he was willing to listen.

The new head of the Ford Foundation was former Kennedy White House adviser McGeorge Bundy. Bundy and Robert Kennedy were no longer close associates (before resigning Bundy had been a point man in the Johnson administration's counteroffensive against the senator's February 1966 speech, which was his first critique of Johnson's conduct of the Vietnam War). Kennedy had written Bundy soon after the former aide accepted his position with the Ford Foundation to make a case for his urban initiative, arguing, "No one—so far as I know—is presently thinking about using their housing or job programs as a lever for fundamental social change—for the building of community, for the reintegration of the Negro family, for the integration of the slum Negro into the ethos of private property, of self-government, of *doing* what is necessary instead of asking the government to do it."[34] Bundy told Eli Jacobs and others gathered at André Meyer's Manhattan apartment that he didn't care about the merits of the effort in Bedford-Stuyvesant, but it was worth "a reasonable amount" of Ford money to teach Kennedy that businessmen didn't have horns.[35]

After a spirited debate the foundation agreed to a grant on the condition that the two boards proposed by Johnston become incorporated, with funds flowing through the business leaders board (later named the Development and Services Corporation, or D&S).[36] Walinsky and Johnston solicited another $1 million, but Ford agreed to only $750,000, with an initial disbursement of $350,000 and the remainder to be released on a matching basis.

The final businessman recruited for the D&S board had the lowest profile, but he ultimately became the most involved. When Eli Jacobs first suggested him, Robert Kennedy and Tom Johnston had never heard of Benno Schmidt, a managing partner at the investment firm of John Hay Whitney & Company.[37] When Schmidt told the New York senator he'd voted for neither him nor his brother, Kennedy replied: "That doesn't make the slightest difference. I am extremely anxious that this *not* be a Robert Kennedy project."[38] Kennedy even suggested that he himself might not serve on D&S—a far cry from Johnston's memo suggesting that the board of business leaders serve as a "loose form of a cabinet" for the senator.[39] Kennedy described the D&S role as advisory; the board would work on problems "where and in the manner that the community corporation thought they should be attacked."[40] After John Lindsay and Jacob Javits (who by December had been made aware of the project) encouraged Schmidt to participate, the investment banker agreed to round out the D&S lineup.

Another addition to the project in late 1966 proved to be less fortunate. Edward Logue, who had an established national reputation as an authority on urban development, was working simultaneously as development director for the city of Boston and informal housing adviser to Mayor Lindsay. Logue vividly recalled Kennedy's appeal to him at their first meeting. "I don't know a fuckin' thing about housing, and neither does he," the senator began, nodding at aide Tom Johnston. "Maybe I never should have gotten into this. But . . . you do know something about it and I'd appreciate your help," he told Logue. "The bastard," Logue added. "He knew exactly how to get you."[41] In early December, Kennedy sent letters to board members announcing the hiring of Logue to "assume overall direction" of both the comprehensive plan and the specific programs of the project.[42]

Logue added credibility to the fledgling project; but while the appointment was hailed by some within D&S—J. M. Kaplan called it a "major coup"—his designation as chief planner ran counter to the organic genesis of programs that Kennedy had urged both privately and publicly.[43] As David Lilienthal wrote Kennedy: "The great emphasis you put upon action that wells up from within the community itself impressed me greatly. It was this very principle that enabled the TVA to succeed."[44] Nevertheless, other experts who were asked to develop plans also arrived on the scene, including architects I. M. Pei and David Crane, who were brought in to create new physical designs for the community. Kennedy's tendency to seek the "best brains" in a given field undoubtedly influenced these decisions, but they planted the seeds of future confusion and discord in the operation of the community development corporation.

As Kennedy concentrated his energies on assembling D&S and attracting other potential contributors, tensions within the community were threatening the viability of the R&R board. Kennedy facilitated the inclusion of Judge Thomas Jones, but CBCC leaders felt that the judge had been foisted upon them, and Jones found them impossible to deal with. He informed Kennedy that he could not work with them unless he was in charge. Desperate for stability and frustrated by his own experience with the CBCC, Kennedy gave Jones a blank check: "Whatever way you want to do it, you do it. I regard you as a man who is able to pull it together. Anything reasonable, I will do."[45]

Kennedy's backing gave Jones the authority to assume the chairmanship of R&R, overcoming the challenge of the CBCC. Nevertheless, Jones grew frustrated with Kennedy's staff, who he felt blocked his access to the senator. Whether it was a result of Jones's deferential personality or deliberate attempts by Johnston and Graves to play the role of surrogate, the situation ran counter to Kennedy's usual modus operandi of flattening bureaucratic hierarchies. The result was an increasingly frustrated head of R&R, and poor overall communication with the community side of the ledger.

Kennedy's handling of CBCC created another continuing problem. Because of his initially reposing trust in the group and then backing away, the organization justifiably felt that Kennedy and his staff had used them, and an already skeptical community organization became antagonistic.

This animosity was further exacerbated on the occasion of the official announcement of the Bedford-Stuyvesant project—an annual CBCC gathering to discuss housing problems. One CBCC leader angrily said later, "Kennedy took over *our* conference to launch *his* thing."[46]

Despite the tensions behind the scenes, Kennedy unveiled the initiative on December 10, at Public School 305 in Bedford-Stuyvesant. Seated behind him to symbolize the range of governmental support were Mayor Lindsay, HUD undersecretary Robert Wood, and Senator Jacob Javits, who had not been told of the project until shortly before the announcement but decided to support it on the assurance of Eli Jacobs and other friends on the D&S board that Kennedy had promised a nonpartisan operation. "The power to act," Kennedy told the crowd of about one thousand, "is the power to command resources of money, mind and skill." He continued, "The regeneration of the Bedford-Stuyvesant community must rest, therefore, not only on community action—but also on the acquisition and investment of substantial resources in the community." In closing, Kennedy cast the endeavor as a pivotal test, warning that "if this community fails, then others will falter, and a noble dream of equality and dignity in our cities will be sorely tried."[47]

The New York senator was well aware of the political stakes. Adam Walinsky cautioned, "This will be a difficult and costly venture—in time, in sweat, and in the penalties for failure"; but, he told Kennedy, "if you make this work, it will be the 'Kennedy plan' everywhere."[48] The Johnson administration, moving ahead with its Model Cities initiative, apparently did not feel threatened. Presidential assistant John Roche derided the New York senator as a "real-estate developer" in a memo to another top White House official.[49] Privately Kennedy had doubts of his own. He told writer Jack Newfield: "I'm not at all sure this is going to work. But it's going to test some new ideas, some new ways of doing this that are different from the government's."[50]

Coverage in the *Amsterdam News* was favorable, helping Kennedy recoup some community goodwill as the project got under way. "Santa Claus accelerated his schedule to arrive in God-forsaken Bedford-Stuyvesant 15 days ahead of time," wrote journalist Daphne Sheppard. The paper editorialized that the plan was "destined to be successful because the leaders are taking into consideration what the community thinks and wants."[51] Given that expectation, at the press conference following the announcement Judge Jones pledged that R&R members would go "house to house if necessary" to learn what the community desired.[52]

Jones also began an urgent search for an executive director to manage the day-to-day affairs of the community board and stabilize the situation. Jones conferred with Kennedy's staff, and they outlined the characteristics of the ideal executive: "He had to be an intellectual and he had to have proven his administrative ability, he had to be tough, he had to be honest. He had to be black. Preferably he had to come from the black community, locally."[53] Jones estimated that he interviewed about thirty candidates in a week before the emergence of Franklin Thomas, deputy police commissioner under Mayor Lindsay. Thomas had grown up in Bed-Stuy, went on to star as a basketball player at Columbia, and came with the highest recommendations from Lindsay and others.

The only problem was that Thomas was not certain he wanted the job. Unconvinced that the community rifts could be bridged, he found the project "awfully short on methodology, resources and all that stuff," and questioned the need for separate boards.[54] Jones persuaded Thomas to interview with the R&R board, but the CBCC representatives treated him shabbily, in Thomas's estimation, and declared that they would need to approve all his staff selections. Following the meeting Thomas told Jones, "I think you've got a hell of a problem in getting someone who has something to lose to come into this and take it on, given that kind of hostility that's there."[55]

After the interview Kennedy requested a meeting with Thomas at his New York apartment. Thomas described the treatment he had received, and Kennedy immediately called Jones. "You've just got to control that group. You're not going to get anybody to take this job if that's what they're demanding," an angry Kennedy told him. "We're beating our heads against a stone wall if that's the climate you're working with there."[56] Kennedy asked Thomas to wait before giving a definitive answer.

Tom Johnston tried to persuade Thomas to sign on, but Thomas fundamentally disagreed with the two-board structure. He felt that the boards would be insulated from each other. ("I think essentially the dual board structure," Thomas said later, "was to insure that at the first meeting of the board, if somebody said motherfucker, the white guys wouldn't all get up and run.")[57] He wanted access to the business leaders without having to go through Jacobs or Logue. Thomas remained uninterested in taking the job through February and March, as community disaffection mounted and CBCC leaders began calling him to ask if he'd made his decision. Nevertheless, he honored Kennedy's request and was noncommittal.

For two months Jones tried to build support and expand R&R, approaching young militant members of the Congress of Racial Equality, who had not been part of the debate, and even some moderate CBCC lead-ers.[58] Kennedy's staff recognized the critical status of the problem and the need for communication. "The Judge's relationship to his board is at an all time low," Graves advised in a memo to Johnston and Jacobs. "We must begin a sincere effort to give the Judge as much information as possible to give to his board. Even the ones who are on our side think we are doing nothing and saying less." According to Graves, "this project is identified as being Senator Kennedy's by everyone. We could not disown it, if we wanted to, therefore it behooves us to have the best possible image. The sooner we clean up the mess, the sooner we can begin to wear the 'white hats.' The people in the community and the board want to hear from the Senator!!"[59] Graves thought that Kennedy needed to call the "safe" board members per-sonally and "give them the facts of life regarding the executive director's job and the expansion of the board."[60]

In late March, Jones concluded that he and his allies on R&R had reached a complete impasse with the CBCC leaders. After obtaining the support of the mayor and Kennedy's staff, the judge issued an ultimatum: vote to expand the R&R board to include a wider range of community leaders and give him "carte blanche" for a three-week period to set up a feasible structure, or he would quit.[61] Jones lost by one vote, and an angry shouting match ensued in which the judge resigned, declaring that he would not be "emasculated" by the women leaders of the CBCC.[62]

The open fissure was the last thing the burgeoning project could afford. Jones, in frenetic consultation with the Kennedy and Lindsay staffs, decided to act. He put together a new board (later named the Bedford-Stuyvesant Restoration Corporation), excluding CBCC hard-liners and including figures who had been developing support of their own: the young, militant CORE leader Sonny Carson (who joined in spite of the fact that he had publicly called Kennedy a "colonialist" and Jones a "Tom"); Albert Vann, president of a radical Afro-American teachers' group; and local activist and minister Milton Galamison.[63] In the rush of events, one female board member joined Jones's forces believing that they were part of the expansion of R&R rather than an alternative board.[64] Lindsay was away at the time, and his urban adviser Mitchell Sviridoff was "surprised and somewhat annoyed" that Kennedy's staff had allowed matters to erupt as they had.[65] Nevertheless, he gave the imprimatur of City Hall to the new expanded board, and the announcement of its formation was made the next day.

CBCC leaders and their allies were predictably furious. They demanded a meeting with Kennedy, denied that they had resisted an expansion of the board, and called Jones's tactics "undemocratic."[66] The chairman of Youth In Action (YIA) asked, "Can an outside force enter into a community and dictate to it who its leaders should be?"[67]

Johnston responded with a letter to CBCC leaders contending that for several months the problem of an unrepresentative board had been expressed repeatedly by "many community leaders and representatives of diverse community groups not represented on the Board." In the end Johnston proclaimed the principle of maximum involvement "far more important than any other single issue," and insisted that "there will be more work for everyone who wants a share in it than they can do."[68] Johnston's arguments did nothing to ease tensions. The CBCC and YIA convened a protest meeting to denounce the actions of Kennedy and Jones. Five months after the program rollout at P.S. 305, signs reading "Go Home Mr. K, Because We Don't Need Your Kind of Help" and "Black Power Is Black Togetherness and You're Not with Us, Uncle Tom Jones" greeted a standing-room-only crowd at the same venue.[69]

Frank Thomas was still doubtful that he wanted to head the community board, even in its reconstituted state, but Kennedy and Benno Schmidt again began to press for his acceptance. When Thomas indicated his willingness to be part of the new group if given complete authority to shape the organization, Kennedy agreed. The senator told Thomas that he would regard his decision to take the job as a personal favor and assured him that he would help Thomas do whatever he wanted after he left the project.[70] There was some haggling on the D&S board over Thomas's salary, the type of vehicle he would be given, and a more formal contingency plan for a job should the project implode, but the problems were eventually ironed out, and Thomas became the first head of the Bedford-Stuyvesant Restoration Corporation.[71]

The seas were turbulent, but the vessel had been launched. Throughout the early months of 1967 planning efforts initiated by D&S had proceeded apace. Edward Logue had been allotted $300,000 in planning funds from the Astor Foundation grant, and by March, with the help of Philadelphia architect David Crane, he had developed a grand scheme for the physical reconstruction of Bedford-Stuyvesant. The heart of the effort was to be the redevelopment of a commercial zone two blocks in width between Atlantic and Fulton streets. Business and community facilities would be concentrated in this development area, providing a thriving center whose prosperity would, over time, radiate outward into the rest of Bedford-Stuyvesant. Logue identified a large number of underused streets in the area and proposed that they be replaced with landscaped walkways.[72]

Another element of the planning designed to enhance the quality of life for Bedford-Stuyvesant residents was architect I. M. Pei's concept of the "superblock." It would combine two or more existing blocks, replacing the streets between them with recreation areas for green space, play equipment, chess tables, swimming pools, or whatever else the community deemed useful. The major portion of the Astor grant, $700,000, was directed toward the development of two superblocks. In the Logue plan, over one hundred superblocks were anticipated. Although the plan called for local residents and contractors to do the work, there was community resistance. Many residents perceived it to be cosmetic, and believed that housing and larger-scale employment had to be the first priorities.[73] Pei contended that "once a block begins to show life and the evidence of development, things are bound to happen to the housing on the block."[74] His willingness to listen made him allies on the Restoration staff, and his plan later gained wider acceptance.[75]

The members of the D&S board were also set to work on general areas of their expertise in early 1967. Television mogul William S. Paley explored the development of communications infrastructure in Bedford-Stuyvesant, including cable television; banker George Moore focused on the financing of projects and mortgage pooling; Benno Schmidt concentrated on the development of small business; IBM's Thomas Watson spent time on job training and employment; and André Meyer worked on real estate problems and overall strategies of financing.[76]

In spite of the planning activity of the D&S board, one of the community complaints in the weeks leading up to the R&R split centered on the absence of a D&S presence in Bedford-Stuyvesant. Eli Jacobs, who was emerging as the functional head of the D&S board, had established an office for the corporation in Manhattan. "I developed a preference for us not being too intrusive, in a fear that we could be perceived to be colonials," Jacobs later explained, adding that recruitment would be easier in Manhattan.[77] In point of fact the decision, which Jacobs admitted was "never really well thought out," had the opposite effect. Judge Jones wrote Johnston in March that it was "urgent at this time that we establish the presence of staffs of these two corporations in the community." Jones warned, "In the absence of this, I fear that the development and services corporation will be forced into a position of planning for the community without being in the community, without hearing from the community, without being related directly enough to the renewal and rehabilitation corporation."[78]

The location of D&S offices was only one focus of rising criticism that the project was being imposed—planned "for" rather than "with" community residents. Another was the work of Ed Logue. As Jones's cautionary memorandum indicated, Logue was pressing ahead on planning without consulting R&R. After the Restoration board emerged, Logue took Jones and Thomas to see his earlier redevelopment efforts in New Haven, Connecticut. Jones was unimpressed. "I could see," Jones said, "that he was the kind of fellow who, like Robert Moses, would [proceed with his plan] without regard to what the people who he essayed to help thought about it."[79] The judge later reflected, "We were supposed to accept the gospel according to St. Logue, and we weren't ready to do that."[80]

Thomas also felt that Logue's effort was displaying signs of mission creep. He described weekend presentations for Restoration in which Logue tried to bring the community board up to speed on his planning efforts. Thomas told Logue that he had presented some good opportunities for action but had reached a logical point to suspend his efforts. According to Thomas, Logue "kicked and screamed and fought, . . . [but] it was clear to me that it had to happen, come to an end."[81]

Robert Kennedy also became disillusioned with Logue's go-it-alone tactics. At the first full-fledged D&S board meeting in early March, Logue laid out his wide-ranging concepts at length for the business leaders. Several board members grew impatient. George Moore said to him: "You just want us to listen at this stage and tell you we think it is a good idea. But what should we do?"[82] After the meeting Kennedy angrily told Jacobs: "Eli, get rid of Logue. I don't care what you have to do. Just get someone else."[83] Logue stayed on as a consultant for a few months, but the bulk of his plan was ignored.

The problem of Logue as "rogue elephant" was partly due to a lack of clear communication from Kennedy and a similar ambiguity to that which had surrounded the idea of community action. Seven months into the effort Jacobs claimed: "If you asked ten of the participants to define things, you would have gotten ten different conceptions of it. In some respects that was desirable, that people would have different impressions, until that had to change, and did, roughly in August and September, as the Restoration and D&S became more highly institutionalized and developed a pattern of working closely together." As a result, he recalled, "Logue's conception of the project was different from Tom Johnston's, which was probably different than mine, which was different from X's and Y's and Z's."[84]

The urban redevelopment vision as laid out by Kennedy in the January 1966 speeches and in his December 1966 announcement was comprehensive, and Logue had adopted a similarly expansive approach. Logue later contended that the Bedford-Stuyvesant program "needed a plan big enough and significant enough to make a real difference—or stop kidding the folks."[85] Kennedy had delegated the development of programmatic specifics to Logue, Jacobs, and his New York staff without ever clearly delineating his vision. The resulting ambiguity strained the relationships between the two boards and between Logue and community leaders. Logue departed during the summer of 1967 to run for mayor of Boston.

As the boards began to work together more closely, it became apparent that Jacobs's conception of the project exaggerated the role of D&S and was contributing to community antipathy. "I think we all knew," asserted Thomas, "that Eli Jacobs was not the right person for the job he had."[86] Judge Jones considered Jacobs an elitist who "spent most of the time talking about his ambitions to be a very successful stockbroker" and evidenced "no desire to come into the black community whatsoever."[87] Jacobs conceded that "not all the people who worked for me were consummate diplomats." The project "did have the aura of colonialism."[88] He tried to shield D&S members from the realities of community politics, maintaining that "this was their first introduction into the inner city for most of them, and you had to do it in stages. I mean if you put them in the same room so they were privy to the fights between Judge Jones and some of the women on the board, then you would have lost every one of them."[89]

Jacobs further implied that some of the charges of colonialism stemmed from Kennedy's demand for results. "It was not pleasant to be on the receiving end of his pressure," noted the young banker.[90] Kennedy, according to Jacobs, "would see a vacant block in Brooklyn, and he would say, 'I want a building there.'"[91] Jacobs questioned whether the senator "really knew what he wanted, other than to see a city where formerly there was a desert."[92] In Jacobs's estimation, Kennedy was "never responsive to complex explanations" and saw problem solving as a question of will on the part of his staff. As a result, Jacobs felt that he had to rely on the "ablest people"— D&S members—to make progress quickly.[93]

The political clock was ticking. Just as Kennedy had been unwilling to allow a prolonged debate over community differences for a resolution that might never come, he also refused to allow the bureaucratic problems of urban construction or anything else to slow the initiative. On one occasion the senator was angered by the trash collection problem in Bedford-Stuyvesant. "I want something done about garbage now," he told Jacobs and Thomas.[94] For the very reasons that had led him to embrace the potential of community action as an end run around city hall, Kennedy was uninterested in Eli Jacobs's discussion of the ingrained institutional memory of the New York City sanitation department, which made ghetto garbage pickup a low priority. Thus, while Frank Thomas had a direct line to the senator, Jacobs would be routed through Tom Johnston for the rest of his tenure as D&S executive director. He left the post in December 1967 feeling unappreciated and misunderstood.[95]

By the summer of 1967 Restoration was beginning to assume the leading role. In July the project received its first special impact grant, and a portion of the $7 million awarded by the Labor Department was used to conduct a house-to-house survey of community preferences for the project.[96] The canvassing found better housing, increased employment opportunities, and education to be the top priorities of Bedford-Stuyvesant residents.[97]

Frank Thomas, dealing with the fallout from the April realignment on top of preexisting skepticism among Bed-Stuy residents, believed that gaining the confidence of the community was as important as long-range planning. His first undertaking was the Community Home Improvement Program (CHIP), designed to put unemployed young men to work quickly on refurbishing the exteriors of homes and, in the process, giving them a sense that they had a stake in the community.[98] Homeowners were to contribute twenty-five dollars, maintain their property, and commit money for labor and materials for the interior improvement of their homes over the next year (with the work to be done, preferably, by local businesses).[99] Thomas met opposition from Jones, among others, who saw the project as superficial. Nevertheless, the plan went into effect, received a $500,000 federal special impact grant, and became tremendously popular. Restoration had to hold annual lotteries to determine which blocks would be renovated, and CHIP workers even began wearing their hard hats during off-hours as badges of pride. Through 1981 the program had worked on over 4,200 homes on 150 blocks.[100]

The shifting balance of power became evident in other ways. Thomas pushed to end D&S control over incoming funds and established a joint account for the two boards.[101] In December, Kennedy persuaded former Justice Department official John Doar to assume the reins as permanent executive director of D&S. Doar moved the offices of D&S into the same building as those of Restoration, the Granada Hotel in Bedford-Stuyvesant. While Thomas and Doar would spar in the years ahead over the need for a D&S executive or a large D&S staff, the men were generally able to work together.

The tendency toward D&S supremacy, however, did not disappear overnight. In the fall of 1967 William Birenbaum, a former provost of Long Island University, was hired to develop a four-year college in

Bedford-Stuyvesant. Thomas believed that Birenbaum felt uneasy with the notion that he was working for Restoration, so a new group under the nominal direction of D&S—the Educational Affiliate—was created with Birenbaum as its head.[102] At one working lunch Birenbaum offered Thomas and Kennedy a long-winded explanation of why African Americans should ultimately assume leadership of the Educational Affiliate. "Well, I don't see what the issue is," Kennedy said. "Frank heads the project and he's black, right?" Thomas felt that Kennedy's response "cut right through all of this elaborate bubble that Bill [Birenbaum] had been building up about his own independence and separateness, and all the rest of it." According to Thomas, "As Bob [Kennedy] said it he was looking right at Bill and straight in the eye and never stopped looking at him. Bill swallowed whatever he had in his mouth and said, 'Well, yes, that's right.'"[103]

The main purpose of D&S had been to help increase the appeal of private investment and economic development in New York's largest ghetto. In mid-1967 Tom Johnston outlined the two development options for Kennedy. One potential avenue was to bring in "branch enterprises of well-established commercial, industrial and financial companies"; the other called for the formation of new businesses with "maximum involvement of the residents of that community in the ownership, management and work force."[104] Johnston deemed the second option preferable for the long run but noted that the first would more likely yield immediate results.

The D&S board members had been recruited on the basis of a personal commitment, not an institutional one, and while several of them put the resources of their companies at the disposal of the project, none jumped at the chance to make a major investment in Bedford-Stuyvesant. At one D&S meeting in the CBS boardroom, a frustrated Kennedy, in the words of Frank Thomas, "just really gave them hell." Thomas described Kennedy's impassioned challenge to the board members: "They just were not doing what they'd said they were going to do, and . . . it wasn't a problem that was going to go away, it was going to get worse[,] and if this group couldn't come to grips with it and do the things asked of it, then what the hell was going to happen to the country? And[,] you know, what kind of representatives were they, of the best that the business world could produce? He really went right at them."[105] The corporate leaders listened without protest, and many made new pledges of assistance. D&S board member Tom Watson did approve an IBM contract with a metal assembling firm in Bedford-Stuyvesant. Given the potential among those on the board, however, this was a minimal commitment.

Kennedy tried to recruit other corporations but to little avail. The chairman of General Electric told him that the obstacles were too formidable, and the head of another corporation confided, "Senator, the afternoon I walk into my board of directors and tell them that Bobby Kennedy was here today, and he thinks we should put a plant in Bedford-Stuyvesant, that is the afternoon they'll have me committed."[106] Throughout the fall of 1967 Kennedy continued to press for business participation in inner city rehabilitation, in Bed-Stuy and elsewhere. The New York senator and his staff also worked at promoting another new strategy, based on tax incentives to increase private investment.

With Kennedy's approval, Johnston wrote André Meyer in late 1967 to urge greater involvement by D&S. The two agreed that board members should personally recruit ten to fifteen companies each.[107] Once again the only major corporation to come forward was Watson's. In April 1968 IBM announced that it would convert an old warehouse into a computer cable factory that would eventually employ four hundred local residents. Watson insisted that there was no pressure from Kennedy to open a plant in Bed-Stuy, but Frank Thomas and Kennedy aide Carter Burden contended that there were intense lobbying efforts to change IBM's original plan to put the factory elsewhere.[108] Burke Marshall, then general counsel for IBM and an informal Kennedy adviser, later asserted, "We got the people who were making the recommendation to change their minds," adding that the corporation wouldn't have located its factory in Bedford-Stuyvesant "if it hadn't been for that project and Senator Kennedy's involvement."[109]

Throughout Kennedy's direction of the initiative, nearly all of its funding came from either government grants or tax-exempt private foundations. This was not unexpected, as the plan was based on the premise that considerable planning efforts would be needed before the venture appeared viable to potential investors. Nevertheless, Kennedy was disappointed in the lack of commitment from the business community and remained skeptical that large-scale investment was in the offing.[110]

In reflecting on the early stages of the project, Eli Jacobs concluded that the most important contribution of the D&S board was to impose a "sense of marketplace reality" by limiting the number and types of projects called for by community leaders.[111] Robert Kennedy would have disagreed with Jacobs's assessment. D&S members had not been recruited principally to teach ghetto residents the middle-class virtues of the market system, although managerial expertise was part of the equation. Kennedy had begun the undertaking with the belief that private enterprise was an untapped resource to be placed at the disposal of a poor urban community.

The timidity of investors raised questions. Was business a force that could be trained like a weapon on the problem of urban poverty? Were the marketplace realities and limitations that Jacobs celebrated part of what caused urban poverty in the first place?[112] Some Kennedy allies had serious doubts. Sargent Shriver called the plan "impractical," and John Kenneth Galbraith, a structuralist on the question of antipoverty measures, disparaged the private enterprise approach, stating that the Bedford-Stuyvesant initiative would be successful "only so far as public money is available."[113] Michael Harrington contended that "the slums are, in business terms, a bad risk." Only government agencies might choose, "in the name of public social priorities, to make an 'uneconomic' investment of money. A private enterprise will not and cannot." Harrington felt that business could play "a subordinate role as the contractor for the popular will" but would not carry the lion's share of the burden. In the end, he declared, "it will not work. . . . [T]here can be no creative federalist panacea, enlisting business in a social crusade."[114]

Nevertheless, the Bedford-Stuyvesant project produced some early successes. Edward Logue's most important contribution was the discovery of the abandoned Sheffield Farms bottling plant. With a loan from George Moore's bank, D&S purchased the building in March 1967. It was renovated with special impact funds, employed local contractors, and became the eventual site of both the Restoration and D&S offices in the heart of the proposed redevelopment zone.[115] Ebbets Field Dodge, the first black-owned automobile dealership in the state of New York, was established with the help of D&S and Restoration. Moore, a D&S board member, coordinated a mortgage pool of nearly eighty banks and insurance companies. Announced in April 1968, it was viewed favorably by many in Bed-Stuy, including radical leaders. The mortgage pool reduced housing down payments and made Federal Housing Administration loans more accessible.[116] Also in early 1968 plans were finalized to press ahead with a City University of New York branch located in Bedford-Stuyvesant. In 1970 it became Medgar Evers College.[117]

There were short- and long-term disappointments as well. Two major corporations that had shown early interest, Xerox and U.S. Gypsum, decided against investing in Bed-Stuy. D&S members continued to make important contributions to the endeavor, but the project remained dependent, through the 1970s, principally on government funding. In the long run, the development corporation did not remake Bedford-Stuyvesant.

Nearly all eastern and midwestern U.S. cities suffered a devastating loss of manufacturing jobs in the 1970s, and while Restoration helped to hold the line on housing in the area and built the first new shopping center in Bed-Stuy in decades, it was fighting an uphill battle. If the 1970s were a period of steadily reduced expectations for the development corporation, by the 1980s the organization was saddled with debt and fighting for survival. Because of its inability to attract diverse revenue streams, the cuts in social spending during the Reagan administration would prove debilitating to Restoration.[118]

In 1978 Michael Harrington examined the efforts of Restoration and found that for each small victory won, the well-connected community development corporation had to bring a tremendous amount of political and financial power to bear—a luxury most lower-profile CDCs would not have at their disposal. Nevertheless, Harrington found reason to reassess his prediction of a decade earlier. "Something good is happening in Bedford-Stuyvesant," he wrote. If the community development corporation was "conceived of not as a panacea which will bring capitalist wealth or socialist justice to the poor, but as an important technique to mobilize people on their own behalf[,] . . . then it has relevance," he asserted. "For all the criticisms and limitations of the Bed-Stuy experiment, it is extremely satisfying to witness a social idea that works."[119]

Despite these struggles, Restoration endures. The first high-profile community development corporation, it established an approach to dealing with urban poverty that became pervasive in the 1980s and 1990s. The total number of presently functioning CDCs is estimated to be anywhere from two thousand to eight thousand.[120] Although the Bedford-Stuyvesant example was not the only spur to this growth, one study has contended that in both its failures and successes, "Restoration served as the pathbreaker for the community development movement."[121]

Robert Kennedy's participation in the day-to-day operations in Bedford-Stuyvesant diminished later in 1967 and came to a complete halt with the beginning of his presidential campaign in March 1968. In spite of his own doubts about the initiative, he continued to discuss the endeavor with anyone who would listen. According to campaign aide John Bartlow Martin, Kennedy talked about the Restoration project "endlessly."[122] Kennedy told John Doar, "If I wasn't a United States senator, I'd rather be working in Bedford-Stuyvesant than any place I know."[123]

In the end, what can be said of Robert Kennedy's role in the formation of the Bedford-Stuyvesant Restoration Corporation? The project itself was buoyed the rising tide of political support for public-private partnerships, and it was informed by the communitarian and corporatist aspects of Kennedy's political worldview. In a letter to Ford Foundation president McGeorge Bundy, Kennedy wrote, "The central problem of the ghetto is a want of useful function, of the opportunity to contribute to oneself, one's family, or one's community."[124] As Kennedy's proposal for the participation of the Ford Foundation asserted, the project's "success rests not only on the vitality of a single part of the American community but perhaps the very fact of that community itself."[125] The Bedford-Stuyvesant initiative exemplified a public partnership between various elements of a local community and the power centers of the larger national community.

The Ford proposal referred to the relationship between the business and community boards as a "delicate marriage . . . often contemplated but never consummated."[126] Robert Kennedy was the matchmaker and counselor who encouraged and, at times, forced the improbable union to work in its pivotal early stages. If elements of its framework and even some of the attitudes of its participants were incompatible with its ideal, over time those obstacles were reduced, and it became a vital social and economic organism.

By and large Kennedy was able to overcome the skepticism of Bedford-Stuyvesant residents. Outspoken CORE leader Sonny Carson recalled the senator's appearance at a 1967 community meeting at a church in Bed-Stuy: "Man, it was like the Pope walked in. . . . I thought, Oh my God if I interrupt him, people will look at me like, 'What the fuck are you doing, man? You can't do that! That's Robert Kennedy!'"[127] Carson went on to serve sixteen years on the Restoration board. As Benno Schmidt reflected: "Nobody, in my experience, had the standing in the Negro community, in the ghetto community, and among the poor that Bob Kennedy had. And nobody inspired their confidence and nobody had their all-out following to the degree he had."[128]

Those involved in the project are nearly unanimous in their assessment of Kennedy's importance to the experiment. Asked how vital his leadership was, Eli Jacobs responded: "Total. Without Robert Kennedy there would have been no Bedford-Stuyvesant project."[129] Frank Thomas considered Kennedy "very critical to the whole process."[130] Judge Jones told an interviewer, "The intensive concern and activities of Robert Kennedy . . . in the day-to-day problems which arose in trying to create such an organization, as small a scale as it had, the kind of work that was involved, I don't see anybody else doing."[131] Adam Walinsky expressed a similar sentiment: "I don't know any other United States senator who was going to go out, who could or would devote that kind of time and attention and effort and energy and produce those kinds of results, to create a project like that out of nothing."[132] Even Jacob Javits, a less biased observer, said, "I think it was his finest hour."[133]

A few months prior to the announcement of Kennedy's Bedford-Stuyvesant project, aide Tom Johnston predicted, "If in 18 months it is possible to begin in every area of the community's life constructive and well-thought-out programs, it should assure that in three to five years this would become one of the most vigorous and livable communities in New York City."[134] Measured against the optimistic prediction of his youthful aide or the overall ambition of his January 1966 urban speeches, the initiative was a resounding failure.

Nevertheless, while Kennedy had presented Bedford-Stuyvesant as an urban laboratory, he understood that its success was contingent on many factors. In late 1967 Kennedy wrote that the initiative was "far more than an experiment in slum self-regeneration. It is a demonstration in political change that could enhance the power, the sense of community of all of us. Its effects will not be felt overnight; to do what I have outlined will take time. And the idea of new community institutions is no guaranteed panacea. It must be part of a program that involves government at all levels, together with other private institutions in the society."[135]

The mechanism of the community development corporation was one new tactical approach in the struggle against poverty, yet Kennedy rarely placed great faith in structural or institutional solutions. He already realized that if business leaders chose not to invest, and if government support was not forthcoming, the CDC would be an empty shell. Popular will was the indispensable element in any major antipoverty initiative; building this support became the major task of his remaining political career.

7

"IT BECAME

HIS ISSUE"

FIGHTING FOR

THE WAR ON

POVERTY

Nineteen sixty-six was a Republican year, as the GOP gained forty-seven House seats, three Senate seats, and eight statehouses. With the nation's social divide widening and the center of the political spectrum moving to the right, two developments provide interesting illustrations of the changing political landscape. In New York City, a civilian police review board recently launched by liberal mayor John Lindsay was eliminated by an overwhelming referendum vote. Despite support from every major state official except Republican governor Nelson Rockefeller, the board, designed to provide a check on multiplying concerns about police brutality against African Americans and Latinos, was routed in the all-white districts of the city, and the far higher turnout in those areas than in minority precincts sealed its fate.[1] In October, James Meredith, one of the most powerful national symbols of integration, now pronounced it "another way of effecting white superiority." Meredith, recently wounded in a sniper attack, called instead for the freedom of blacks to remain apart from white America, and even appreciatively noted George Wallace's salesmanship on behalf of racial separatism. Meredith declared the Alabama governor "second only to Robert F. Kennedy in being the most astute politician in the country."[2]

In December of that year another, much more local African American activist offered a similar assessment of the junior senator from New York. Washington residents were testifying before Abraham Ribicoff's Senate subcommittee on the impact of the War on Poverty in their community, and most expressed concern over reduced funding for the program.[3] Katie Ridley, a District resident, directed her comments exclusively to Robert Kennedy. "I believe through you," she said, "it could be possible to keep this program going." Senator Ribicoff interrupted, reminding the witness that Kennedy was only one senator. Ridley responded: "The reason I say this is because of all the speeches I have heard from Mr. Kennedy. . . . I feel that Mr. Kennedy is one of the poor man's friends. I do not think this of our president."[4] Room 318 of the Old Senate Office Building, crowded with residents of the nation's capital, erupted in applause. Many poor Americans had begun to regard Robert Kennedy as their champion, and their cause would dominate his last full year in the Senate. In 1967 Kennedy would emerge as the most forceful advocate of a renewed national attack on poverty, in the process forging bonds with Americans who feared that the war being waged on their behalf was fading as a national priority.

While the most publicized round of the Ribicoff hearings had been the testimony of administration officials in the late summer of 1966, the Senate inquiry resumed in November. This time the proceedings focused on the views of the "private sector" of American life: business leaders, academics, urban planners, civil rights leaders, and city dwellers themselves. Kennedy explored two main themes with his questioning: the effects of social alienation on impoverished urban youth and the capacity of business to make a contribution to solving the problem.

Harvard child psychiatrist Robert Coles, who had studied poor children across the country, testified in December. Kennedy asked him how society could best help young ghetto residents. When Coles responded that he was troubled by the rising disillusionment of black teenagers, Kennedy recalled "walking along Fifth Avenue and seeing the faces of children between the ages of 6 and 12 who come from very wealthy homes," adding, "I don't know, but my impression, strong impression, is that the ones who . . . come from these ghetto areas, are much, much happier than the ones who are being pushed along in their prams."[5] Coles, while cautioning against romanticizing the plight of the poor, agreed and suggested that suffering might develop psychological strength and vitality in the young. Kennedy then observed that among inner city youth around the ages of twelve through fifteen, "sort of a castration begins, caused by the whole system." This sense that they would not be able to escape the ghetto, Kennedy believed, created an "absolutely explosive" situation.[6]

Coles's testimony reaffirmed Kennedy's acceptance of Ohlin and Cloward's opportunity theory—the idea that blocked social and economic outlets lead to delinquency. Kennedy felt that urban black youth no longer trusted anyone, including civil rights leaders. In the midst of rising militancy among young blacks, NAACP head Roy Wilkins admitted that he had been booed off a platform in Harlem, to which Kennedy responded, "I think many national leaders, both white and colored, would find it very difficult to go into a ghetto area and make a speech to a cross section of people."[7] Other civil rights leaders testifying before the committee, including Martin Luther King Jr., A. Philip Randolph, and Bayard Rustin, agreed. Rustin played upon President Eisenhower's famous warning in his farewell address to attribute the rising hostility and threat of violence to an increasing "fear-frustration complex."[8]

Kennedy had sensed this for some time, but he boldly framed the problem in cold war terms that would have been impolitic just a few years earlier. "These young people," Kennedy proclaimed," are further removed and further alienated from the older generation, white and Negro, than we are removed and differ within our own society from the Soviet Union. They are as apart within this country, alienated and separate to a much greater degree than we are from the philosophy that exists in what we now consider our adversaries."[9]

One African American leader Kennedy recognized as having credibility with young people in northern black communities was Floyd McKissick, leader of CORE. McKissick, a World War II veteran, emerged in 1966 as the second-most influential spokesperson for the shifting emphasis in the civil rights movement toward Black Power.

Black Power was amorphous; historian Thomas Sugrue has written that it "had nearly as many definitions as it did adherents."[10] For many African Americans it embodied their frustrations with the pace of progress and with the limited successes generated by nonviolent protest. It also suggested a new racial pride and even racial nationalism—a declaration that they would reshape the life of their community, if necessary, without white help and by rejecting nonviolence. For anxious whites, Black Power was an alarming specter, magnetizing media attention and evoking fears of a race war.[11]

At the outset of McKissick's testimony Kennedy probed the meaning and value of Black Power to the civil rights movement. "I don't think we have any more civil rights movement," McKissick said, charging that it had died with the second great "reneging" after the 1963 March on Washington, the failure to follow through on truly providing first-class citizenship (the first broken promise having been the denial of the promised "40 acres and a mule" to freed slaves after the Civil War). Kennedy thought that the "Black Power" slogan had not only set the civil rights movement back but also pushed the midterm election results rightward because it scared whites. The two sparred sharply over the importance of an interracial effort on civil rights, with McKissick insisting that CORE had not foreclosed that strategy.[12]

Kennedy's interrogation was not, however, merely a "Sister Souljah moment."[13] With the announcement of his Bedford-Stuyvesant initiative less than forty-eight hours away, the New York senator professed "a great deal of sympathy" for McKissick's emphasis on black pride and on community control. "We know the ghetto," McKissick told the committee.

> Most of the people in the ghetto, in spite of the fact it is the ghetto and it has got a whole lot of faults[,] . . . it is the only home that they have got. It is the only home that a black man who works all day as a porter . . . the only place that [he] can come home to and be a man. If he wears overalls all week, he would put on his suit on Sunday, he can be the deacon or trustee in his church or an usher, and that is his only place of hope where he is an individual and a man, and that . . . is the reason that he wants to live in Harlem.

The headlines would focus on their clash, but Kennedy slipped out of his seat and was shaking McKissick's hand before Ribicoff had a chance to call a recess, and the two men would go on to develop a mutual respect.[14]

The Ribicoff hearings were critical to Kennedy's evolution on the poverty issue.[15] He learned a great deal about prevailing thinking on the urban crisis and gained insights into what changes poor residents themselves believed necessary. Still, he wasn't satisfied with increased awareness. Kennedy prodded his aides to help him develop tangible results from the hours he spent in the Senate hearing room.[16]

The first of the political tools he took from the hearings was an idea for enticing private enterprise into the inner city. Kennedy had been intrigued by the potential role for business throughout the preparations for the community development corporation in Bedford-Stuyvesant, and he understood that profitability would be the main concern for corporations. Corporate leaders David Rockefeller of the Chase Manhattan Bank and G. L. Phillippe of General Electric underscored this point during the hearings. In his testimony before the subcommittee, urban expert Edward Logue—recently hired by the Bedford-Stuyvesant D&S Corporation—offered a possible strategy. "The surest way to get a man or a business to do socially useful things," Logue said, "is to make it a little more worth-while taxwise." Therefore, he said, "I urge that every possible tax incentive be given private enterprise to join in the war against poverty."[17]

Kennedy found the idea intriguing. As attorney general he had shown little compunction about finessing the tax code to encourage corporations to contribute humanitarian aid to Cuba in exchange for the release of Bay of Pigs prisoners in 1962.[18] In discussing the idea with a friend he admitted: "I've learned you can't rely on altruism or morality. People just aren't built that way."[19] Nevertheless, the proposal was risky. The political climate of the period favored the closing of tax loopholes. Aide Peter Edelman cautioned Kennedy, "The whole idea of using the tax code is at least somewhat inconsistent with your tentative thinking about trying to simplify the Internal Revenue Code and eliminate tax preferences."[20]

Around the same time Herbert Sturz of the Vera Institute, with whom Kennedy had worked on bail reform as attorney general, supplied the senator's staff with information on the Puerto Rican industrialization program known as Operation Bootstrap.[21] It had been initiated in the postwar period to provide tax incentives to American industry to locate plants in Puerto Rico, and it had achieved some impressive results through the 1950s and early 1960s.[22] Kennedy agreed that the principle behind it might be transplanted to ghetto areas, and he had aide Myron Curzan, a young Columbia Law graduate with no expertise on the issue, look into potential legislation for offering tax breaks to American corporations that invested in the inner city.

The other insight Kennedy gleaned from the Ribicoff proceedings was that such hearings, given his own ability to draw media attention, were a useful vehicle for continuing to highlight the problem of poverty and bring it home to both average Americans and opinion makers. Adam Walinsky later asserted that Kennedy's unique stature allowed him to "change, to some degree, the climate of public discussion, of scholarly discussion, of research, and all the rest, and really change the way people acted about a problem."[23] While this may have been an overstatement, the hearings had clearly helped Kennedy to emerge as a leader on the issue.

Along with new visibility came new criticism. SNCC leader Stokely Carmichael charged that Kennedy had a self-serving "plan for power" in black communities and had already purchased several prominent black newspapers to provide "a ready-made voice" when he ran for president.[24] New Left activist Robert Scheer wrote in the radical journal *Ramparts*, "The solutions which [Kennedy] has begun to propose would not be likely to shock even the more conservative members of the Senate."[25] Scheer called the

Bedford-Stuyvesant initiative "more reminiscent of Ronald Reagan than Herbert Lehman," and concluded: "This is not a serious program for the Negro poor. It comes no closer to the 'social revolution' that Kennedy sometimes talks about than the work of the Salvation Army."[26]

New Left leaders had been trying to keep Kennedy at arm's length for fear that he would co-opt their issues. As Scheer wrote, "The Kennedy rhetoric is dangerous precisely because it provides the illusion of dissent without its substance." He continued, "At hearings of his subcommittee, his tours through New York ghettos, and during speeches before scores of college audiences, [Kennedy has] hooked onto the mood of crisis and, as with everything else, come to use it." After observing the senator at close range, Scheer concluded that "Bobby Kennedy, for all his youth, charm and spontaneity, remains a very orthodox political figure."[27]

Student radicals intrigued Kennedy, however, and he and his staff tentatively reached out to movement leaders. New Left author and *Village Voice* reporter Jack Newfield, who spent a good deal of time with the New York senator through 1966 and 1967, was convinced that Kennedy was genuinely interested in doing something about poverty.[28] In January 1967 Newfield gave Kennedy a book by Students for a Democratic Society (SDS) leader Tom Hayden describing his attempt to help establish a black community union in Newark. Kennedy later told Newfield that he was impressed by Hayden's "feeling and honesty" but disliked parts of his book that "seemed sympathetic to violence."[29] Newfield and Walinsky both encouraged Kennedy to meet Hayden, and the senator obliged because, as Newfield put it, "he was curious to meet someone with a college degree who had voluntarily spent the last four years working with the wretched of Newark."[30]

Kennedy met with Hayden and historian-activist Staughton Lynd at his New York apartment in February 1967. While much of the discussion turned on the war in Vietnam, Kennedy asked about Hayden's work in Newark, and the three discussed the effects of Vietnam on antipoverty initiatives. Kennedy detailed his Bedford-Stuyvesant efforts. Hayden later reflected that "he was approaching the vision I had taken to Newark in 1964, one of uniting blacks and whites around an economic populism, finding a strategy of reform for the alienated through localized participatory democracy."[31] If Hayden retained doubts about Kennedy—fellow SDS leader Todd Gitlin recalls Hayden calling the New York senator "a little fascist" just days before he was killed—he was also struck by his conception of presidential potentialities. Kennedy assured him that if he were elected, he would pressure the television networks to air a documentary

that realistically portrayed the ghetto experience, publicize poverty statistics by city, and call local leaders to the White House to hash out "real
solutions."[32] Kennedy would quietly contact Hayden again to discuss both
Vietnam and his presidential campaign, and Hayden later pronounced
him "the only politician who interested me."[33]

For nearly three years the poverty issue had been identified almost
completely with the Democratic Party, and even more exclusively with the
Johnson White House. The early critiques of organizations on the left
such as SDS and the Citizens' Crusade Against Poverty first chipped into
Johnson's control of the issue. In 1966 the War on Poverty began to take
fire from elsewhere in the Democratic Party. Mississippi senator John
Stennis led southern Democratic opposition to the Head Start program
run by the Child Development Group of Mississippi (CDGM), which
he and others believed was dominated by radical civil rights activists.
Johnson and OEO caved in under this political pressure and funded a new
organization run by local moderates, to the consternation of most antipoverty leaders.[34] The critiques raised by Kennedy and Ribicoff during the
Senate hearings on the cities revealed an even more problematic Democratic split. Liberals such as Kennedy and Ribicoff wanted to escalate the
war against poverty, while Democratic moderates were increasingly willing to retreat.

Heavily outnumbered in the Eighty-ninth Congress, Republicans had
been relegated to playing a bit part in the poverty debate. In early 1967,
however, with a diminished Democratic majority in the new Congress and
increasing media accounts of mismanagement in War on Poverty programs, newly elected Republican senator Charles Percy (who had defeated
Paul Douglas in Illinois) proposed a bill designed to minimize the federal
role in creating housing. He called for a foundation, to be capitalized by
the sale of tax-free bonds, which would distribute resources to local non-
profit housing associations. In April 1967 House Republicans led by Albert
Quie of Minnesota and Charles Goodell of New York called for an alternative to the Economic Opportunity Act dubbed the "Opportunity Crusade."
They urged an end to the Office of Economic Opportunity and the Job
Corps, greater state contributions to the Community Action Program
(CAP), and tax credits for private industry to train youth.[35] The new political winds, as Kennedy had anticipated, were shifting in the direction of an
increasingly privatized war against poverty.

The cities had been the primary focus of the national debate on poverty
in 1966, but in 1967 the spectrum of discussion about the "other America"
would broaden. In part because of the emerging voices of assertive leaders

calling for self-determination, and in part because the highly visible youth counterculture was drawn to American Indian culture, the plight of Native Americans received perhaps the most increased media attention in 1967.[36] While Kennedy had developed an interest in Native American affairs during his years in the Justice Department, he had paid scant attention to the matter during his first two years in the Senate. Now Kennedy began revisiting the issue with friend and fellow freshman senator Fred Harris of Oklahoma. Harris's wife, LaDonna, was a Comanche, and she headed Oklahomans for Indian Opportunity, an advocacy group for young Native Americans. Fred Harris found Kennedy knowledgeable and surmised that his concern "was probably intensified by LaDonna."[37] Together Kennedy and Harris explored the possibility of a Senate inquiry into problems in Indian education.

LaDonna Harris wondered about Kennedy's motives. His sister Eunice Shriver told her that both President Kennedy and Attorney General Kennedy had regretted their roles in the Kinzua Dam project in upstate New York, which resulted in the relocation of Seneca families.[38] It was thus likely more than a coincidence that the first of Kennedy's many visits to Native American reservations in 1967 and 1968 was to the Seneca reservation south of Buffalo, where he participated in a powwow and toured a fabrics plant. Tribal leaders requested greater federal assistance for their attempts to bring manufacturing to the reservation, but Kennedy told them that the odds of receiving more money from the Bureau of Indian Affairs were "quite slim" because of budget pressures due to increasing expenditures in Vietnam.[39]

In March 1967 Kennedy traveled to Oklahoma to speak before LaDonna Harris's organization. "In every set of poverty figures," Kennedy noted, "the Indian emerges as the poorest."[40] He discussed the effects of the social alienation of Native American youth and urged efforts to renew their self-confidence. He praised the culture and historical contributions of the Plains Indians and encouraged young Native Americans in the audience not "to become a kind of button-down American." War on Poverty programs would be meaningful, he said, only if Native Americans fought to have their needs addressed.[41]

The New York senator got the biggest response for a statement during the question-and-answer session afterward. "I wish," Kennedy said, "I had been born an Indian." To critics it might have sounded like the worst kind of political pandering, but Fred Harris reflected: "He said it in a joking way but serious. The phrase itself in print sounded rather vacuous. . . . But [in person] it sounded so real and also kind of wistfully funny that every-body laughed and applauded overwhelmingly."[42]

Whatever the motive for his identification with them—and Ramsey Clark later suggested that it was because the federal government had "pushed them around"—Native Americans seemed to believe Kennedy.[43] Senator George McGovern of South Dakota, who had seen many candidates campaign among Native Americans in his own state, remarked, "The Indians had a special response to him that I never detected with any other politician."[44]

For his part, Kennedy pressed ahead on the formation of an Indian education subcommittee and began to "badger" NBC news producer Lucy Jarvis to air a documentary on Native Americans that would make the conditions of their poverty more visible.[45] Peter Edelman and new press secretary Frank Mankiewicz also remembered Kennedy's exploring the idea of television programs on poverty.[46] "You don't know," Kennedy told a friend, "unless you *see*."[47]

The Economic Opportunity Act of 1964 was up for renewal in 1967, and another forum for increasing the visibility of the poverty issue emerged when Pennsylvania Democrat Joseph Clark began Senate hearings aimed at assessing the effectiveness of War on Poverty programs. The liberal Clark, one of Kennedy's few good friends in the Senate, was running for reelection in 1968. Like Abraham Ribicoff, Clark realized the New York senator's likely impact on publicity for the hearings.

The subcommittee planned field hearings across the nation in 1967, and the first trip was scheduled for the Mississippi Delta in April. Mississippi had been the battleground for much African American political activism, including controversies that particularly nettled President Johnson. Aside from the recent CDGM affair, Johnson had been enraged by the attempt of the Mississippi Freedom Democratic Party, led by civil rights activist Fannie Lou Hamer and others, to replace the all-white Mississippi delegation to the 1964 Democratic National Convention.

The choice of Mississippi as the site of the first field hearing was less the product of any political desire to agitate the president further than evidence of a realization that the Magnolia State had already become a focus for antipoverty activism. A year earlier, congressional Democrat Joseph Resnick of New York had visited the area and attempted to alert the rest of the nation to the grinding poverty there, but he received no substantial coverage.[48] The National Council of Churches was discussing possible action in Mississippi, and leaders of the Field Foundation contemplated a research tour.[49] The Citizens' Crusade Against Poverty had also become involved in publicizing starvation conditions in the delta, and CCAP head and former PCJD hand Richard Boone suggested potential contacts in the state to Kennedy aides.[50]

Principally because of Kennedy, the Clark committee—which also included Jacob Javits and California Republican George Murphy—did attract national attention to conditions in the region. The hearings began with Kennedy and Javits challenging the testimony of John Stennis, who charged that the War on Poverty was the "most poorly managed federal program" he'd seen in his two decades in the Senate.[51] Local leaders who testified disagreed with Stennis. One told the senators that community action was "the real genius of the poverty program."[52] Kennedy asked other local officials about the extent of participation by the poor in the shaping of programs, and he was told that despite apathy or exclusion in some communities, poor residents were contributing to the boards of Head Start and several adult education programs.[53]

When the head of the state employment commission reported that 5 percent of graduates in an adult education program—hailed by many as a success—had found jobs and that the program had "improved" many of its participants, Kennedy responded, "You are pretty far down to say your life is improved but not so much that you can get a job." When the official replied that the result was "discouraging to us," Kennedy snapped, "I would think it might be discouraging to us but it is a little bit more discouraging to them who participate."[54]

Residents conveyed stories of suffering from hunger; one local leader estimated that 95 percent of children in the area were malnourished. Unita Blackwell of MFDP told the subcommittee that free food stamps or commodities were a necessity. A young civil rights attorney and activist named Marian Wright testified that starving and desperate families were helpless. "There is nowhere to go," she warned, "and somebody must begin to respond to them. I wish the Senators would have a chance to go and just look at the empty cupboards in the Delta and the number of people who are going around begging just to feed their children."[55] Kennedy and Clark planned to tour some of the "pockets of poverty" in the area the next day.

With television and print reporters in tow, longtime Mississippi civil rights leader Amzie Moore guided Kennedy and Clark around the hamlet of Cleveland. Looking inside the refrigerator of the first home they entered, the visitors saw only a jar of peanut butter. Outside, several barefoot children in tattered clothes were lined up next to one another. When Kennedy asked if they'd eaten lunch, the eldest indicated they had not.

Kennedy moved down the line and brushed a few on the cheek. A weathered, heavyset African American woman then approached the New York senator and thanked him for coming, proclaiming that she was too old to be helped but that his visit brought hope for the children. When Kennedy asked her age she said, "I'm thirty-three."[56] Walking to the next house, Kennedy told Peter Edelman that he thought he had seen the worst poverty in the nation in West Virginia, but it paled by comparison to this.[57]

While television crews were interviewing Clark, Kennedy went into the next house with Edelman and Marian Wright. The senator saw a small child seated on the floor and tried to evoke a response. "Hello . . . Hi . . . Hi, baby," Kennedy said, as he stroked her hair and rubbed her distended belly. He spent several minutes with the toddler, but the vacant expression never left her face.[58]

The delta experience shook Kennedy. Veteran CBS newsman Daniel Schorr observed, "At one point I thought he was close to tears."[59] When he returned to New York, he told Amanda Burden, the wife of aide Carter Burden: "You don't know what I saw! I have done nothing in my life! Everything I have done was a waste! Everything I have done was worthless!"[60] Melody Miller, a part-time staffer in the Washington office, recalled her boss pulling scraps of paper from his jacket pockets, calling friends, and urging them to send canned goods to the addresses he had recorded.[61]

The other senators were appalled as well, and before leaving Mississippi, George Murphy suggested that the subcommittee send a letter to the president requesting emergency food aid. Hunger, as distinct in its gravity from the political debate over the management of the War on Poverty, had emerged as a political issue.[62] Kennedy's office would be in the thick of the fight; from the Mississippi trip to the presidential campaign, Peter Edelman estimated that he spent 20 percent of his time on the issue.[63]

The day after returning to Washington, Kennedy and Clark saw Secretary of Agriculture Orville Freeman about the possibility of supplying free food stamps and/or increased surplus commodities for poor Mississippians. Kennedy respected Freeman, a holdover from his brother's administration, but he grew impatient when the secretary explained the restrictions on his department's latitude in the matter, including the right of localities to refuse federal assistance and the prohibition on providing both food stamps and surplus commodities in the same county. "I don't know[,] Orville," Kennedy urged, "I'd just get some food down there."[64]

Freeman was unconvinced that there were significant numbers of Mississippians with no income at all, so he sent his own representatives on a fact-finding mission to the delta. Peter Edelman served as guide, leading Freeman's aides through the same areas Kennedy and Clark had seen. They reported back to the agriculture secretary that the situation was indeed dire.[65] Federal nutritionists sent by Freeman concluded that participants in both the food stamp and commodity programs were receiving a diet inferior to that of poor southerners a decade earlier.[66]

Members of the Clark subcommittee, with new leverage as a result of the Agriculture Department findings, sent a formal request for emergency action to President Johnson. Kennedy was in a Senate hearing room when the subcommittee counsel informed Peter Edelman that Johnson aide Joseph Califano wanted the letter routed to the Office of Economic Opportunity. Edelman whispered the news to Kennedy, who, in Edelman's words, "just exploded. He said, 'You tell [Johnson's staff] to take the letter. The United States Senate can send a letter to the President of the United States.'"[67]

More than any bureaucratic restriction, the real brake on Freeman's activity was the power of southern Democrats on the committees that oversaw agricultural appropriations. The chair of the House agricultural appropriations subcommittee, Mississippi Democrat Jamie Whitten, disliked the congressional and media attention on poverty in his state, and he opposed anything that smacked of welfare handouts. The food stamp program had been able to survive and gradually expand from 1964 to 1967 only as a result of legislative trade-offs aiding the agricultural interests of conservative southern congressmen such as Whitten.[68]

In late April, Kennedy tried to persuade the subcommittee of another southern conservative, Louisiana Democrat Allen Ellender, to expand the food stamp program further. Kennedy contended that hunger was a problem that went beyond Mississippi, citing inadequate access to food stamps or commodity distribution in South Carolina, Alabama, Virginia, and New York. He discussed his delta trip, asserting, "Here in the United States in 1967 we saw a lot of children with swollen stomachs just as you see them in India or Africa." North Carolina Democrat Everett Jordan countered: "That might be [the result of] overeating. You cannot tell." Kennedy would not let this stand. "No, no it wasn't," he insisted, "because I asked them what they ate. . . . [I]t is a serious problem as to how they are going to get any food."[69]

After the dramatic spectacle of the delta tour, Leslie Dunbar of the Field Foundation called four doctors to schedule an examination of Head Start centers in Mississippi over the Memorial Day weekend. Among those in the contingent was Robert Coles, who had testified before the

Ribicoff committee just a few months earlier. The Third World diseases the group witnessed—scurvy, rickets, and beriberi—stunned them.[70]

Coles and his colleagues went to Washington in mid-June and reported their findings to administration officials Freeman, Sargent Shriver, and HEW secretary John Gardner. None gave them much hope for federal action. Kennedy requested a meeting with the group when he learned they'd been rebuffed. One member, a dejected Yale University pediatrician named Milton Senn, told Kennedy that his group had done all it could do. After a few awkward moments of silence, the New York senator said, "I'm not so sure."[71] Soon Kennedy was on the phone, and the Clark subcommittee had scheduled mid-July hearings in an effort to make the doctors' discoveries, in Kennedy's words, "available to people."[72]

Kennedy met with the physicians several times to prepare for the hearings. Coles later described the tutorial the senator gave them on the realities of Washington politics. Kennedy suggested that, given his manner and background, Raymond Wheeler, a soft-spoken southern doctor in the group, should be their primary media spokesman. During another meeting Kennedy was briefed on the symptoms of vitamin-deficiency diseases. Coles was disheartened when the seemingly uncomprehending senator said that the children in photographs he was shown looked fat. No doubt mindful of his recent testimony before the food stamp committee, Kennedy then explained the importance of perception in politics and the need to anticipate criticism.

The Field Foundation doctors influenced the New York senator as well. On one occasion they protested his warning that leveling a strong moral condemnation could have an adverse effect. Kennedy countered that if the doctors wanted their message to survive the hearings, they needed to understand the resistance they would face as perceived self-righteous outsiders. Given his own confrontational and moralistic tendencies, perhaps Kennedy sensed the irony in cautioning the doctors against adopting a Manichaean tone. Whatever the cause, he soon warmed to their approach. "You guys won't just be holding up your stethoscopes," he told them. "You'll be wagging your fingers—and I guess we have to figure out how you do both. . . . I suppose you *do* have two hands, each of you."[73]

Heading into the July hearings, Kennedy tried to lower the expectations of the doctors, reminding them of "the capacity of this town to shrug its shoulders at anything."[74] Nevertheless, he promised them his best effort, pledging, "We'll get through this struggle, and I expect that if we do, some children will eat better than before."[75] The testimony of the doctors did receive significant media coverage, but not as much as the shouting match between Jacob Javits and Orville Freeman on the second day of the hearings.[76] Kennedy, growing increasingly frustrated with the inability of administration officials to ascertain the scope of the problem, urged a national survey on malnutrition. He also tired of descriptions of bureaucratic red tape. "It seems to me," Kennedy complained, "we are floundering around a great deal.'"[77]

In the end Kennedy was able to amend a health bill to provide for a national nutrition survey. Another positive result of the pressure of the Clark hunger hearings, and particularly the effective testimony of the doctors, was Senator Stennis's proposal for a $10 million emergency hunger and medical bill to deal with the situation in the Mississippi Delta. Other committee members quickly signed on as cosponsors, and despite the nearly debilitating obstructionism of southern congressmen and the lack of support from the White House, it passed as part of the larger renewal of the Economic Opportunity Act in November (although emergency funds would not flow until April 1968, one full year after the Mississippi field hearings).

Hunger was only one aspect of the poverty issue that occupied Kennedy through the spring and summer of 1967. At the same time he attended further Clark committee field hearings across the country, his office proceeded with the development of tax incentive legislation, and he continued to oversee the transition to the new Restoration board in Bedford-Stuyvesant. Joseph Dolan, head of Kennedy's Senate office and his principal consultant on the political ramifications of his day-to-day activities, feared that Kennedy's immersion in the issue was beginning to create problems. Dolan got an earful of complaints about his boss at a dinner for Brooklyn political leaders, where one person asked: "So why does he always go to all the rallies in the Negro neighborhoods, and not to ours? White people vote too."[78]

If there was some concern that Kennedy was committing too much time to the issue, his involvement was also beginning to win new allies. Marian Wright was one former skeptic who viewed Kennedy differently after he came to the delta. She told Roger Wilkins, a friend in the Johnson administration: "He did things that I hadn't done. He went into the *dirtiest, filthiest, poorest* black homes, places with barely any floor, and only potbellied stoves; and he would sit with a baby who had open sores and whose belly was bloated from malnutrition, and he'd sit and touch and hold those babies.... I didn't do that! I didn't do that! But he did."[79] Wright stayed in touch with Kennedy and his office. When she mentioned an upcoming meeting with Martin Luther King to discuss the next major initiative for the Southern Christian Leadership Conference, Kennedy suggested that King "bring poor people to Washington to stay until Congress is so uncomfortable that it does what they want just to get them to go home."[80] He had learned the power of the "discomfort" generated by direct action protests as attorney general. Kennedy was perhaps now conveying to Wright that he had the mastered lesson—and now understood the story of Cinderlilly. His recommendation planted an important seed for the SCLC's Poor People's Campaign of 1968.[81]

Legislative aide Peter Edelman kept Kennedy informed about emerging grassroots organizations and community leaders nationwide, but the New York senator sought his own understanding while on the road for the Clark committee hearings.[82] Tired of what he viewed as the often self-serving testimony of official witnesses—which became a point of contention with Clark and his aides—Kennedy regularly wandered away from the official Senate entourage to talk with needy citizens.[83]

In Stockton, California, he scrambled down an embankment to chat with migrant families living in vehicles parked in a riverbed. A reporter recorded how one mother "accepted the visit of the junior senator from New York to her weedy temporary front door with perfect aplomb." "Karen," she asked her small daughter, "do you know who this is? This is President Kennedy's brother." Kennedy learned that the laborers, like delta residents, were existing on surplus commodities of peanut butter, flour, and grease, and were sustained by the hope that work picking cherries—delayed by excessive spring rain—was imminent. He squatted to chat with one shoeless little girl and was able to elicit a smile as photographers captured the moment.[84]

In Los Angeles the *Sentinel* reported that Kennedy gave "lengthy audience to the gripes of the angry and frustrated among the poor. His willingness to hear out the complaints, and his seeming concern for the problems of the deprived areas, led one wag in Watts to bestow upon him the affectionate and esteemed label of 'boss cat.' In the community it was a high honor, indeed, even for a man who is being touted as a presidential candidate."[85] Kennedy was "frequently lost" by an OEO escort hoping to show off a new facility in the San Joaquin Valley as the senator stopped to chat with Mexican American teens, and he was embraced by a Mexican American crowd on the streets of East Los Angeles after visiting a youth employment and training facility there.[86]

Because of East L.A.'s symbolic importance as the most influential Mexican American community in the nation, what might otherwise have been considered local matters there took on national significance. Schools would be at the heart of the tensions between Latinos and whites in the city. During his interrogation of Sam Yorty a year earlier, Kennedy had noted the McCone Commission's condemnation of the limited access to cafeterias in Mexican American schools.[87] In the spring of 1967 he (along with Mayor Yorty) would endorse the pivotal and successful school board candidacy of Mexican American leader Julian Nava. In the fall of that year Kennedy met with two emerging student groups, United Mexican-American Students (UMAS) and the Mexican American Student Association (MASA), to learn about and encourage their push for public school reform.[88]

Kennedy had been concerned about the problem of student dropouts since his work on juvenile delinquency, and in East Los Angeles rates often topped a shocking 50 percent.[89] He listened to the students' assessment of the schools and the continuing problem of police brutality, but a new Chicano newspaper, La Raza, reported that the main point conveyed by the young people revolved around self-identity. "We are Americans," one student said, "but we are chicanos also, we are not going to become anglo and the anglos have to realize that." Kennedy encouraged the students to "make use of the tremendous power potentially available to them in order to force real reform" and insisted that "real change won't come from Washington. . . . [Y]ou will have to do yourselves."[90]

In addition to his other activities, Kennedy took on another major factor in the poverty equation in early May. In a speech before the Day Care Council of New York, he criticized the welfare system at length, branding it "a second-rate set of social services which damages and demeans its recipients" and "destroys any semblance of human dignity."[91] Kennedy had employed similar rhetoric a year earlier without controversy, so the front-page New York Times coverage and ensuing fallout surprised him.[92] The Times editorial page blasted the junior senator for blaming all family problems on welfare; liberals contended that Kennedy was providing fodder to conservative critics of the system; and others, including New York governor Nelson Rockefeller, chastised him for not offering an alternative.[93]

Through his first two years in the Senate, Kennedy had not studied the welfare system in depth.[94] He held general principles and intuitions—jobs were good and handouts were bad, the misshapen incentives of the system pulled families apart, welfare was humiliating to those forced into it—but during the Ribicoff and Clark hearings he confronted the issue more concretely. Welfare recipients testifying before the committees conveyed near-universal disdain for the system. "All your dignity be took away from you in the welfare office," one witness had told him, and in June, Kennedy responded by calling for "welfare dignity reform." He proposed an end to general searches and "midnight raids" to determine if mothers were abiding by the "man-in-the-house" rule that limited AFDC (Aid to Families with Dependent Children) assistance to single women. He suggested that neighborhood centers replace centralized welfare offices and that client advisory councils be created to help recipients navigate the system and make it more responsive.[95]

Kennedy also focused his welfare critique on the continuing theme of participation. The welfare system, he said, should give recipients "a voice in shaping the program which is their sole sustenance."[96] Despite the fact that the Community Action Program, and its legislative clause requiring maximum feasible participation by the community, was coming under increasingly heavy attack, Kennedy publicly defended the provision more vigorously in 1967 than ever before. He repeatedly asked Clark committee witnesses about the roles of the poor in local programs. Nationwide, the meaning of participation was being debated more fully than ever before. According to Adam Yarmolinsky, the original intention of the participation clause was not that the poor should be involved in policymaking but that they should be helping to administer programs.[97] Kennedy disagreed. "The intention," he said, "was to give them power."[98]

An exchange with Oakland mayor John Reading revealed the heart of the political dispute over community action. Kennedy contended that the funds allotted for community action were "a drop in the bucket" compared to the size of overall budgets for each city, and sending federal money to city hall had not improved the situation in the past. "The philosophy really was to try to deal with it in a different way," Kennedy argued. "If you gave money regularly to the poor, the poor in turn could expect and have their voices listened to." Reading accepted the idea of participation but felt that if city government was to be ultimately responsible for the outcome, it had to have the power to delegate funds. Kennedy suggested that if poor citizens were unhappy with the mayor and decided to march on city hall in protest, their funds could be cut off to penalize them. Reading protested that local government had to be responsive, but Kennedy charged that it was not.[99]

The clash was similar to Kennedy's discussion with Anthony Celebrezze regarding the efficacy of local school boards during the education hearings of early 1965. Kennedy had objected similarly when the HEW secretary called the risk of unresponsiveness the "the price of local democracy." At the center of the debate was the question of whether local governments and agencies could be trusted to be effective or were more frequently stagnant bureaucracies. If the latter were the case, could anything really be done about such a fundamental element of American representative democracy? Daniel Patrick Moynihan, an informal Kennedy adviser and ally, was a persistent and influential critic of community action and called it "fascist" because, he contended, it delegitimized the ordinary channels of democratic representation by saying, in effect, "Let's not just have the city councilmen represent the neighborhood, but elect people to represent the poor of the neighborhood too." Asked privately what he thought of Moynihan, Kennedy confided, "He knows all the facts, and he's against all the solutions."[100]

The other pertinent question that arises from Kennedy's renewed promotion of community action has to do with whether there were local communities that were immune from turf wars or special interests. The ideal behind community action assumed that such a situation was possible, but Kennedy's own experience in Bedford-Stuyvesant had recently indicated otherwise. Despite his call for local control, Kennedy's unique notion of federalism was not based on faith in state or city government. Instead it hinged on the vitality of a direct relationship between the federal government and an imagined community of those in need who were kept from power at the grassroots level. "Kennedy federalism" on the problem of poverty thus sought to bypass the conventional machinery of representative democracy (and other entrenched social institutions) that continued to render the poor powerless. While other elements of Kennedy's approach to poverty had traditional roots, this conception of federalism had truly radical implications.

Despite his increased candor regarding the original intentions of community action and the boldness of his vision, Kennedy at times resorted to political maneuvering that betrayed his ideals. In Chicago, Republican colleague Jacob Javits rigorously interrogated Richard Daley on his use of poverty funds and asked if the mayor was meeting the OEO standard of one third poor residents on each community action board.[101] Daley, with the tacit acceptance of President Johnson, had steadfastly refused to take his marching orders from OEO and insisted on dispensing poverty funds himself.[102] Kennedy sought to derail Javits's attack by hinting that his line of questioning was partisan, informed by a document titled "Republican Party Memo to Republican Members of the Senate Poverty Committee." When Javits called Kennedy's insinuation "bad manners," Kennedy jabbed, "They missed me on the mailing list from the Republican National Committee."[103] If Kennedy was capable of putting other Democratic mayors in the hot seat, he was unwilling to challenge the most influential of them all.

Kennedy's political dexterity was tested by another tactical decision. Despite the pronouncement of *Fortune* magazine that no potential presidential candidate had generated as much antipathy from business since the 1930s, he made a concerted attempt to improve his image in the corporate world.[104] During the Clark hearings he lauded U. S. Chamber of Commerce plans to enlist businesses in fighting poverty, and he disingenuously claimed that he had supported his brother's tax cut proposal.[105] Kennedy also had former Justice Department aide Barrett Prettyman draft an article in his name titled "Government Injustice to Business," arguing that business deserved greater fairness and dispatch from federal administrative and regulatory agencies. The piece infuriated Walinsky and Edelman, who saw it as transparent pandering.[106]

Prettyman also introduced Kennedy to prominent executives. While many corporate leaders found the senator compelling in his attempts to enlist them in the Bedford-Stuyvesant initiative, the social visits arranged by Prettyman often resulted in uncomfortable silence. "The business thing was a problem. He never understood them," reflected Kennedy's friend and sometime adviser about the senator's relationship with businesspeople. "It wasn't that Bob disliked them," Prettyman believed, "so much as that he felt their view of life was somewhat alien to his." Prettyman felt that if Kennedy were a businessman he would have focused less on profits and "would have directed much more of his energies toward plans to benefit the community."[107]

In addition to any potential long-term political calculations, Kennedy's attempts to improve his reputation in the business world had a more pressing motive. The tax incentive bills he had directed Myron Curzan to develop were nearing completion, and in early July one of the many experts Curzan had consulted leaked them to the *New York Times*. Forced to announce them, a week later Kennedy called the bills new departures in housing and job creation because of their capacity to draw private investment into the ghetto. To ignore the possible contribution of business, Kennedy said on the Senate floor, was "to fight the war on poverty with a single platoon, while great armies are left to stand aside."[108]

The employment bill offered tax credits for new plant construction in poor urban areas, raised the tax deduction for new machinery and equipment in those same areas, and provided a special deduction for approximately one fourth of the wages paid to those considered the hardcore poor. Businesses were required to create at least fifty new jobs, fill two thirds of those positions with local residents, and maintain their investment for at least ten years. The housing bill pledged tax credits and rapid tax write-offs for the construction or rehabilitation of 300,000 to 400,000 units of low-rent housing over a period of seven years, and low-interest loans that would keep rents below $100 monthly.[109] Kennedy also called for a fund that would support "management corporations" to allow poor residents to participate in the management and maintenance of residential buildings. His office sent copies of the legislation to the five hundred largest corporations in the country to get reactions and build support.[110]

Events in the weeks surrounding the unveiling of the bills would add extra urgency to their objectives. On July 13, 1967, the city of Newark erupted in a murderous inner city riot that left 23 dead and 725 injured. Ten days later Detroit was engulfed in the largest conflagration of the decade, as 43 people were killed and nearly 1,200 injured in rioting there. In all it would be the worst summer of racial violence in postwar American history. As President Johnson announced that he was sending the National Guard into Detroit—in a statement that Kennedy found icily detached—the New York senator told his press secretary, Frank Mankiewicz: "That's it. He's through with domestic problems, with the cities. . . . He's not going to do anything. And he's the only man who can."[111]

Kennedy continued his own legislative push but found the road obstructed by the White House.[112] He discussed the proposed tax bills with Labor Department head Willard Wirtz during the Clark hearings. The secretary contended that tax credits were inappropriate, profiting "those operations which do not make the maximum contribution to the particular problem."[113] Wirtz argued that his figures showed more jobs were available than was popularly understood, that training needed to remain the major focus, and that the Special Impact Program was the best way to create jobs effectively. Kennedy was beside himself. He insisted that joblessness was the root cause of the recent riots, and that while the Bedford-Stuyvesant model was important, it would not attract industry "in a major way."[114] He contended that the administration was offering no new proposals. "The patient is dying," he said, "and we are still using the same medicine."[115]

Away from the spotlight, Kennedy's relationship with another administration official was also strained. The Office of Economic Opportunity was on the ropes in 1967, with Sargent Shriver under fire for alleged local mismanagement of War on Poverty programs, and for the perception by some of the continued politicization of the Community Action Program.

The latest riots seemed to confirm for critics the ineptitude of the agency. When Bill Mullins, a frustrated OEO official and former liaison to Kennedy's office, read a newspaper account of the senator's speech introducing his tax incentive bills in which Kennedy was quoted as calling existing antipoverty programs "degrading," an angered Mullins sent a personal letter to Frank Mankiewicz. Calling the speech "How to Turn a Profit on Poverty," he joked that Kennedy "had zoomed to the top of OEO's 'Big Time Bastard of the Week' list."[116] Kennedy demanded an apology from Shriver, who obliged.

Kennedy's relationship with Shriver had been a complex one. While they shared a similar can-do spirit, their personalities were divergent. In contrast to the laconic Kennedy, Shriver was loquacious, as eager to discuss the philosophy of Jacques Maritain as he was to massage the egos of congressmen. Their paths crossed often. Kennedy's office dealt with OEO regularly in attempts to secure funding for New York antipoverty programs, and the senator was unafraid to challenge his brother-in-law during congressional hearings. Kennedy did not, however, criticize Shriver before his Senate staff, and he deliberately stayed out of the CDGM Head Start controversy when he might have denounced the OEO's retreat there.[117] While Kennedy maintained warm relations with other Kennedy administration holdovers such as Robert McNamara, it seems likely that Shriver's willingness to go to work for Johnson in the aftermath of Dallas, in a position Kennedy himself had wanted, cast a pall over their relationship. In the end, Peter Edelman was left with the impression that his boss "never was very hot on Shriver."[118]

In September, Kennedy's housing bill came before the Senate Finance Committee because of its proposed alterations to the tax code, and its sponsor labored to master the complexities of the dauntingly intricate legislation.[119] The devil would lurk not in the details, however, but in new administration arguments against the bill. A treasury official asserted that the tax code should not be used for narrow purposes, and that incentives for housing construction should not be confined to ghetto areas. HUD secretary Robert Weaver then claimed that existing programs would do the job of providing housing more cost-effectively, making the Kennedy bill "superfluous."[120] Kennedy tried to counter the assault. He cited the existence of several federal tax incentives, including tax credits to promote investment in Israel and Thailand. He argued, with the support of several witnesses, that his bill would be both less costly to the federal treasury than existing subsidy and rent supplement programs and more likely to lure investors.[121] The New York senator also contended that housing had to be targeted for existing poor neighborhoods. Exaggerating for effect, he said, "If you take people out of Harlem and build a big housing project on 50th Street and Madison Avenue, you create a lot of problems as to where they are going to get jobs in the highly skilled area."[122]

In spite of his efforts, the White House had more weapons at its disposal, including the ability to stall. The administration created a presidential commission headed by industrialist Edgar Kaiser to study the role of private enterprise in urban housing, but it was to present no new proposals until late in the year. Those in the Kennedy camp suspected an orchestrated attempt to bottle up his bills, and the usually unsympathetic *National Review* and *Wall Street Journal* agreed.[123] William F. Buckley called the Johnson administration intellectually exhausted and declared, "There is no surer way of getting upstaged than unimaginatively turning down a scheme which enjoys deserved public support."[124]

Kennedy was increasingly frustrated by the president's priorities. While visiting economically troubled Allegany County in upstate New York, he chatted with a tenant farmer. On the wall of her spare dirt-floored shack hung a picture of her son, who was serving in Vietnam. The senator asked what he would do for a living when he returned, and the woman told him he would help her tend sheep. Driving away, Kennedy raged: "That's all we have to offer? I just can't believe this administration! I can't believe [Johnson] doesn't realize what is happening to the poverty programs because of Vietnam! Doesn't he see that he could help these people out of poverty by putting the money from that war into these people's lives? And there is not a damn thing I can do to stop it!"[125]

The war was not the only threat to the poverty program. The renewal of the Economic Opportunity Act was in jeopardy, as many southern Democrats and Republicans in Congress seemed disinclined to support the bill. Much of the effort to save the legislation devolved upon the Senate Labor and Public Welfare Committee, where Kennedy fought diligently to preserve as much of the original act as possible.[126] In the end Congresswoman Edith Green, who had opposed community action from its earliest PCJD manifestation, gained support for an amendment that mandated the flow of CAP funds through local government, assuaging the concerns of big city mayors and southern Democrats alike. Angry Republicans called it the "bosses and boll weevils" amendment. It would facilitate the survival of OEO and the renewal of the War on Poverty programs, but it eliminated the direct relationship of the federal government with the community action boards that Kennedy had believed so critical.[127]

By the fall of 1967 the War on Poverty had become at best a holding action, and Kennedy was one of the few national political leaders still calling for an advance. Other programs assisting the poor came under siege. In spite of his critiques of the welfare system, he believed that the social safety net had to be strengthened, and he was determined to fight proposed House limits on the welfare program which he called "a grim joke" and "reminiscent of medieval poor law philosophy."[128] Kennedy and Fred Harris allied to propose their own amendments, increasing monthly benefits by 20 percent and linking public assistance to work incentives while eliminating the coercion of mothers to find employment. They also called for cost-of-living adjustments for benefits and recommended that the increases be paid out of general revenue financing.[129]

Several of the Kennedy-Harris amendments passed individually, but when the conference committee dropped them all, Kennedy tried to rally sympathetic senators to make a stand. "Now is the time for some moxie," he said, urging a filibuster to block the House bill.[130] The House legislation still allowed for a marginal social security benefit increase, so pressure built on Kennedy and Harris to abandon their effort as the session neared an end. Majority leader Mike Mansfield warned that if they persisted, they would get many of their colleagues defeated in the next election, and the Johnson administration also urged Harris to relent. Kennedy and Harris nevertheless lined up a series of senators for a filibuster, which they began in mid-December.

On the beginning of the second day, although Kennedy had obtained an agreement from Finance Committee chair Russell Long to allow the senators opposed to the conference report the chance to speak, Long and majority whip Robert Byrd quietly introduced the measure for approval. Maryland senator Joseph Tydings, scheduled to continue to hold the floor, missed his opportunity to object. The filibuster was over. Kennedy was incensed when he heard the news. He disliked both Long and Byrd, and he laced into them in the Senate chamber, muttering, "I thought I was dealing with men."[131] He slammed the House legislation, calling it a "retreat into brutality," and stated that in over two thousand pages of hearings on the bill, only ten pages contained testimony from welfare recipients. "Is this the way the democratic system is supposed to work?" he asked angrily.[132] The legislation nevertheless passed by a margin of 62 to 14.

In spite of White House resistance, Kennedy forged ahead with the promotion of his tax incentive bills through the fall. He spoke before Rotary Clubs and chambers of commerce across the nation, employing themes that appealed to business groups—the limits of federal effectiveness, the destruction of initiative by welfare, the need for law and order—while at the same time stressing the needs of the poor and urging government to do more. He told an audience of young CEOs that "the blight of American poverty" was the most pressing domestic problem in a century (inexplicably omitting the Great Depression), and contended that the time had come to end the "gap between private enterprise and public crisis."[133] The New York senator cautioned against a desire merely to punish the rioters of the previous summer. "We must give encouragement to those who still believe progress is possible within our democratic system," Kennedy pleaded. "We cannot denounce those extremists who reject it if we do not prove that our society is capable of helping people lead a better life—in our urban ghettoes, in our areas of rural poverty, and on our Indian reservations as well."[134]

Kennedy was fighting an uphill battle as the summer's riots—two full years after Watts and two unsuccessful attempts to avoid long, hot summers later—further sapped popular sympathies for federal assistance. The *Wall Street Journal* surveyed the potential for progress in urban America and gave a thumbs-down to a proposed massive aid program. "The human soil for an internal Marshall Plan," the editors wrote, "is unfortunately not especially fertile."[135]

Throughout 1967 Kennedy continued to seek out manifestations of poverty beyond the ghetto in his ever-deepening involvement with the problem. He attended hearings on migrant labor and continued to push for the extension of the minimum wage and collective bargaining to migrant farm workers. Kennedy got into a verbal wrestling match with the counsel for a Texas agribusiness during an August hearing, challenging him to allow the local Catholic archbishop (known to be sympathetic to the migrants) to oversee a vote on whether the farm workers wanted a union.[136]

Kennedy also arranged a field visit to a farm labor camp near Rochester, New York, in September. The subcommittee contingent, including Jacob Javits, union officials, and reporters, was met with a sign reading "Anyone Entering or Trespassing Will Be Shot If Caught." Kennedy walked ahead. He proceeded to board a broken-down bus with the seats removed and cardboard for windows. Inside the odious vehicle—home for three families of migrant workers—were a half-dozen children with open sores and runny noses. Kennedy inspected another bus before confronting the farm owner. "You are something out of the nineteenth century," he said. "I wouldn't put an animal in those buses." The owner responded, "It's like camping out," as the two stared at each other. In the car afterward Kennedy muttered, "This is why you go into politics, because you can use your position to help people in trouble."[137]

Kennedy also remained interested in the problems of Native Americans throughout 1967. "He really got hooked on the Indian thing in a big way," friend and informal adviser Pierre Salinger reflected.[138] After the New York senator took a break from a summer vacation to visit a Head Start program for Navajos in Arizona, he told the Clark committee that he had found starvation conditions on the reservation.[139] In January 1968 Kennedy concluded a skiing vacation with a visit to an Indian school in California. Salinger's wife, Nicole, accompanied him and was struck by Kennedy's ability to connect with teenagers there, in spite of the fact that the children at the school seemed painfully distant and lifeless. "His selection of questions just showed that he put himself in the place of those children," she remembered.[140]

Kennedy's trip to the school was an informal extension of new senatorial duties, as his subcommittee on Indian education had held its first hearings in December. He was horrified to hear about the psychological impact of Indian boarding schools, a legacy of the nineteenth century, which were still the principal mode of education among Navajos. Kennedy called the practice of putting six-year-olds in faraway schools "barbaric," saying, "I cannot believe in a country with a Gross National Product of $800 billion that we cannot provide even a one-class school room for children closer to home."[141] At another hearing he described a visit to a public school library in Idaho, located in a school district that was 80 percent Shoshone, where the closest thing to a book on Native American history pictured a white child being scalped. When Kennedy asked the superintendent about the absence of history books, he replied that the Shoshone had no history. "Perhaps for older people," the senator told the subcommittee, "having had to deal with that kind of a problem for your whole lives you can accept it. For a child who is 7, 8, 9, 10, 11 years of age it seems to me an almost impossible burden."[142] The hearings gained sufficient publicity that sympathetic schoolchildren began writing Kennedy to offer their assistance to Native American youngsters.

Between Bedford-Stuyvesant, the debates and legislative fights over welfare and hunger, the Clark and migrant labor hearings and field visits, his tax incentive legislation, and the Indian education subcommittee, Kennedy spent a tremendous amount of time on the multifaceted problem of poverty in 1967. One day—December 14—was a microcosm of his activities. He opened the Indian education subcommittee hearings in the morning, took to the Senate floor to castigate the welfare bill maneuverings of

Byrd and Long in the afternoon, and spoke about poverty before the Citizens Union of New York in the evening. As the year came to a close, Joe Dolan was again concerned that Kennedy was narrowing his political base. "Don Quixote may have been a likeable fellow," Dolan wrote the senator, but "work on these issues consumes almost all of the time of your Legislative Assistants to the point where business men and labor leaders from the state are not seen, V.I.P. mail is not answered, etc.'"[143]

Kennedy had recently seen the musical *Man of La Mancha* three times, however, and he listened frequently to its theme song, "The Impossible Dream."[144] Though he had been politically schooled to pick winners, he spent the majority of his time in the latter half of 1967 fighting for anti-poverty legislation that seemed doomed by White House and congressional opposition. If a critical number of middle-class Americans had already abandoned the War on Poverty after Watts, more had certainly lost sympathy after the far greater upheavals of 1967. Kennedy nevertheless continued to ask audiences like the one at the Citizens Union to try to see the world "through the eyes of the young slum dweller," for "all of us, from the wealthiest to the young children I have seen in this nation, bloated by starvation, we all share one precious possession: the name 'American.' It is not easy to know what that means. But in part to be an American means to have been an outcast and a stranger, to have come to the exiles' country, and to know that he who denies the outcast and the stranger among us, he also denies America."[145] Whether Kennedy was tilting at windmills or moving toward a newly viable politics of the marginalized was unclear as the United States moved into the presidential election year of 1968.

8

"YOU CAN'T DENY THESE PEOPLE THE PRESIDENCY"

THE 1968 CAMPAIGN

While it seemed highly unlikely to most observers in the fall of 1967 that any Democrat would be able to wrest the nomination away from the incumbent president, liberal activist Allard Lowenstein had been at work organizing a "Dump Johnson" movement and targeted Kennedy as the candidate to lead the charge. Kennedy was sympathetic but thought the proposition unrealistic. In late September, Lowenstein, Arthur Schlesinger Jr., and others met at Kennedy's suburban Virginia home to discuss the election. Kennedy contended that if he were the first announced candidate, the campaign would be deemed personal. "No one would believe I was doing it because of how I felt about Vietnam and poor people," Kennedy said.[1]

Despite the fact that he demurred during the Lowenstein meeting and on subsequent occasions, Kennedy instructed aides to begin quietly surveying the national party landscape to test the viability of his candidacy. Joe Dolan was orchestrating the behind-the-scenes effort, and the cautionary November memo he had sent his boss warning him against spending too much time on poverty and related issues—thus narrowing his political base—might have been expected to carry significant weight.

Nevertheless, Kennedy's schedule showed little winnowing of his antipoverty activities. In January he was discouraged by what he saw and heard on a visit to the

South Bronx. Amidst mounds of garbage and rusted-out automobiles, local women complained about the dilapidated housing and lack of police protection, and borough politicians told him of bitter fights over anti-poverty funds. Kennedy's Indian education subcommittee also convened early in the year, and he heard testimony about the absence of schools in remote areas. After listening to the accounts of Native Americans, Kennedy declared, "I recognize that the poor child in the rural area is suffering, but I gathered from the unique problems that exist for the Indian child that the Indian child suffers even more."[2]

The new year thus began as 1967 had ended, but a significant change in the national political calculus occurred at the end of January. After repeated administration assurances that the war in Vietnam was moving toward a victorious conclusion, the Tet Offensive and brief seizure of the American embassy in Saigon by Viet Cong forces stunned many Americans. In late 1967 Democrat Eugene McCarthy agreed to become the antiwar candidate that Allard Lowenstein and others had sought, and after Tet his candidacy began to make strides in New Hampshire. Despite appeals from friends and advisers, Kennedy had serious reservations about McCarthy and refused to endorse the Minnesota senator. Kennedy's tortured thoughts for the next several weeks returned to his own potential candidacy.

Asked by an oral history interviewer whether Kennedy's ongoing debate over running influenced his willingness to remain involved in the various antipoverty initiatives he had begun in 1967, Peter Edelman contended that it increased Kennedy's sense of urgency to get things done before entering the race.[3] Kennedy arranged to chair Clark subcommittee hearings on hunger in eastern Kentucky in mid-February. The *Lexington Herald* portrayed the arrival of the New York senator, the only committee member to make the trip, as the fulfillment of a promise President Kennedy had made to Governor Edward Breathitt to visit the region in December 1963.[4]

Employment opportunities in the coal mining counties of Kentucky had been decimated by mechanization in the industry during the 1950s, and a steady stream of residents fled to Chicago, Detroit, and Cincinnati in search of work. Between 15 and 30 percent of the population in the region had left in the "great migration" of those years, leaving those who stayed behind even more impoverished.[5] While Appalachia received about one third of the dollars allocated by the Area Redevelopment Act of 1961, funding for the program had not been sufficient to make a significant impact.[6] Additional federal aid arrived in the form of the Appalachia

Regional Development Act in 1965, but it was directed toward infrastructure rather than job creation, so unemployment remained a critical problem in 1968.[7]

During the hearings Kennedy learned about the low-protein diets common to the region, which sometimes led to the same Third World diseases found in the Mississippi Delta. Harry Caudill, whose book *Night Comes to the Cumberlands* introduced many to the suffering in the region, outlined the problems of strip mining and absentee ownership. Caudill juxtaposed information about the profits of companies with heavy investments in the area, such as U.S. Steel and the Kentucky River Coal Corporation, with the fact that two thirds of the nation's most deprived counties were in that part of the state. "The poorest people and the most prosperous corporations in the United States are found right here in eastern Kentucky," he declared.[8]

The hearings consisted principally of local residents describing the challenges they faced. Witnesses explained how job-training programs had become ends in themselves, with the checks participants received becoming their sole income, and many told of their ebbing hopes that real employment awaited. Others attested to the high percentage of income that went toward food stamps and the common experience of running out of food before the end of the month. Cliston "Clickbird" Johnson, the father of a very large family, invited Kennedy to visit his home. "Did you ever see fifteen kids in three beds?" he asked. With ten children of his own, Kennedy joked, "I'm moving in that direction." Johnson tragicomically confided: "I just want to give you a little tip. The more children you've got, you just add a little more water to the gravy."[9] While Johnson's story seemed to provide sad but almost quaint regional (and stereotypical) color to the field hearing, he was no backwoods rube. By the spring of that year, when grassroots uprisings were taking place across the globe, Cliston Johnson had been radicalized. He would later be named to the national coordinating committee for the Poor People's Campaign by the Southern Christian Leadership Conference and bring a group from Harlan and Letcher counties to Washington.[10]

The radicalization of young people was also evident in the hearings in the Appalachian hollows. A high school student named Tommy Duff came with a group of students to inform Kennedy that he had been "indefinitely suspended" for taking photos and producing a newsletter to document the woeful physical condition of their school. He told the senator that his principal had threatened to report him to the local draft board if he didn't stop. When Duff asked if he should continue, and whether

Kennedy "would fight with me," the New York senator tacitly indicated his support. "Perhaps the principal would reconsider," Kennedy said, to loud applause. "I would think that you would be a student that would be worthwhile having in school."[11]

Not everyone greeted Kennedy warmly. One reporter called the decision to hold some of the hearings in a one-room schoolhouse when a new elementary school was available a "gimmick." Local politicians castigated Kennedy for "blackening" the image of their state and urged him to study poverty in New York City and Boston instead. One letter to the editor in a Louisville newspaper called Kennedy "the bushy-headed, self-appointed expert on all subjects" who offered false hopes to Kentuckians.[12]

Kennedy made no promises, however, announcing to those in a makeshift hearing room at a high school gymnasium, "I can't come and tell you all these problems will disappear." Instead he declared conditions in the region "unacceptable," pledged to focus attention on them, and insisted that if industry could not provide jobs for the region (he repeatedly recommended his tax incentive idea during the hearings as a means to that end), the federal government should serve as the employer of last resort.[13]

The real story of the eastern Kentucky visit was the response of the local people. As Kennedy walked through the hollows and small towns on his tour, throngs of area residents, particularly children, followed along. One southern journalist wrote: "The numberless poor and unemployed looked upon his car not as a modern machine loaned in Frankfort but as a white charger from a King Arthur stable. . . . Kennedy has identified himself with the poverty, and all its miseries, that besets so many millions in this country. He is now one of the faceless hungry. More than that, he is also their new-found champion. Not since the days of FDR's depression-day campaigns in Dixie had so many forlorn turned out with such hopeful enthusiasm to see a top political figure."[14] Seventy-year-old Orville Rogers spoke for many eastern Kentuckians when he wrote Kennedy: "I know you understand what kind of conditions I am living in. . . . Please keep on helping us poor folks all you can. . . . You can count on my vote what ever you run for."[15]

Kennedy also convinced other more discriminating observers of his concern. William Greider, a formerly skeptical reporter for the *Louisville Courier-Journal*, wrote that the media spotlight following the New York senator had given poor Kentuckians the chance to share their stories, and concluded, "I came away convinced that Kennedy's interest was genuine and that in some small measure the people of the mountains may be better off" for his visit.[16] Harry Caudill's wife, Anne, who was also an antipoverty activist, wrote a friend, "Granting the fact that he is a public figure a-building, there can be no mistake after hearing his public statements, his astute questions, and his private comments, that he understands that we have here a real American problem, and that *he* is on our side."[17] The progressive *Mountain Eagle* of Whitesburg concluded similarly, editorializing: "We were convinced that the senator felt so strongly about the plight of some of the families he visited that they, and their troubles, have become a permanent part of his subconscious. The senator will never be able to forget Eastern Kentucky . . . and both he and Eastern Kentucky will be the better for it."[18]

The pace of events accelerated after Kennedy's Kentucky trip. Back in Washington briefly, he followed up on his Appalachian tour with Orville Freeman, pressing the agriculture secretary about an unused fund dealing with surplus commodities. "You have several million dollars there," Kennedy insisted. "Why don't you use it? Why can't you use it? Why haven't you used it?" Kentucky senator John Sherman Cooper remembered that Freeman's face grew flushed as he protested that Congress had to grant authority for reapportioning the funds. According to Cooper, Kennedy then "got very angry and told him he *could* do something if he tried to do it and if he would take some initiative himself and not just wait 'til the Congress did something."[19] It did not occur until several months later, but eventually funding was freed up to supply increased commodities in the region.

Within days Kennedy was off to Oklahoma for more Indian education hearings, where he bridled upon hearing that local educational reform efforts were being called communist-inspired, even by those in Cherokee tribal government. "Changes should be welcomed," Kennedy chided, "and certainly not opposed on the basis of a person being a Communist because he wants to read a book about Indians. You know, somebody said every time you have a fight between the Indians and the white man, if the white man wins it's a victory and if the Indian wins it's a massacre. I remember that President Kennedy was made an honorary Indian on one occasion, and then he said from now on as he looked at television, he was going to cheer for the other side. I think we should start cheering a little bit for the other side."[20]

In Delano, California, César Chávez began a hunger strike in February to urge continued nonviolence by the striking farm workers in their confrontations with local police and security guards hired by growers. As the weeks dragged on, those close to Chávez worried about his health and asked if Kennedy might do something to help end his fast. Kennedy and

Chávez spoke at least once, and when Chávez agreed to end the strike, Kennedy said that he would be there for the occasion. Peter Edelman was concerned that the event might seem transparently political, but he later wrote that the New York senator "never let on that he saw it as anything but a mission to support his friend."[21]

Kennedy arrived on March 10 for a Catholic mass of thanksgiving and was mobbed by the farm workers. Organizer Dolores Huerta called the scene "absolute bedlam" and remembered people "coming up to him, and they would grab him and hug him and kiss him on the mouth!"[22] "We're pretty lousy in controlling crowds," the weak and frail Chávez told Kennedy. "The important thing is they're here," Kennedy replied.[23] Kennedy stood atop a car after the mass and uttered the rallying cry of the farm workers—"Viva la Huelga!"—in Boston-tinged Spanish that brought both cheers and laughter. The moment was a humble echo of his brother's speech at the height of the cold war in which he declared himself at one with Berliners, in the same Boston accent that evoked both adulation and good humor. Chávez later described the religious intensity of the response to the New York senator, stating that the farm workers felt "the kind of closeness that creates tearing him to pieces, little by little just wanting him all for you."[24] Kennedy left with cuts on his hands and torn jacket sleeves, but the experience inspired him. On the drive back to the airport he told a Chávez confidant, "Maybe I'll run."[25]

Aides Peter Edelman and Adam Walinsky pushed for Kennedy to make the race, as did Paul Schrade, the western director of the United Auto Workers, who accompanied Kennedy to Delano. Schrade was guiding UAW efforts to support both the farm workers and the Watts Labor Community Action Committee (WLCAC), which was created in the wake of the 1965 uprising to serve as a more broadly representative community action agency in the troubled area.[26] At the airport after his visit, Schrade seized his opportunity to "zero in on" the New York senator and pleaded: "You know, you can't deny these people the presidency. There's just too much at stake here."[27]

Vietnam was the issue that ultimately drew Robert Kennedy into the presidential race, but his frustration with the Johnson administration's handling of the poverty issue was also a decisive factor. In early March the Kerner Commission Report on the disorders in the nation's cities was released. The report pointed to the oppressive effects of "white racism"— the social and economic isolation of blacks—as the chief cause. Kennedy was pleasantly surprised by some of what he saw as the bold conclusions of the commission, but he quickly grew despondent as a week passed before any administration spokesman acknowledged the report. When Vice President Hubert Humphrey became the first to do so, he cautioned against both the commission's findings and its recommendations.[28]

It is unclear precisely when Kennedy decided to enter the race. Along with his frustration over Vietnam and problems at home, a complex combination of factors—the increasingly apparent success of Eugene McCarthy in New Hampshire, the changing attitudes of influential Kennedy advisers, the resurgence of Richard Nixon in the Republican Party—all conspired to make the previously politically untenable decision compelling. In the March 12 New Hampshire primary Johnson defeated McCarthy by only seven percentage points. The next day, when Kennedy told a reporter he was "reassessing" whether he would run, it confirmed for many the image of the senator as a ruthless opportunist.[29] He announced his candidacy on March 16, urging new policies to "end the bloodshed in Vietnam and in our cities" and "to close the gap between black and white, between rich and poor."[30]

The timing and manner of his entrance created problems. Kennedy's great fear had been that his presidential run would be interpreted as an extension of his longtime feud with Johnson, but he also worried about the effect of entering the race so soon after McCarthy's showing, repeatedly telling Paul Schrade, "The young people are going to hate me for this."[31] Nevertheless, he rationalized that McCarthy's performance had demonstrated that a party rift already existed, and his candidacy might thus be more readily justified on the basis of the issues. He miscalculated badly. Kennedy spent a considerable amount of time in the campaign answering charges of opportunism. "I can't believe that anybody thinks that this is a pleasant struggle from now on, that I am asking for a free ride," he told a television panel after he made his announcement. "I've got five months ahead of me."[32] In actuality he would have fewer than three months.

Kennedy brought in trusted White House aides from his brother's administration—Ted Sorensen, Larry O'Brien, Fred Dutton, and Kenny O'Donnell—whose political judgment he valued more than that of his young staffers, to lend stability to the whirlwind chase for delegates. As Dolan had done earlier, they urged the candidate to broaden his political base beyond his core constituency.[33]

Because of his credibility with African Americans, Kennedy had broader latitude than other candidates in employing the rhetoric of law and order. John Bartlow Martin reflected: "He was the only white man in America that Negroes trusted. They didn't care if he talked backlash to the Kokomo autoworkers. They knew that in his heart he was for them."[34]

Martin, a journalist, former speechwriter for Adlai Stevenson, and ambassador, was recruited to help shape the primary campaign in his native state of Indiana.[35] Kennedy spent most of his time in the Hoosier State trying to win ethnic and working-class white votes, and Martin coached Kennedy on the subtleties of this constituency. According to Martin, northern towns such as Hammond and Gary had an "ethnic backlash" vote, often driven by Polish Americans who feared the increasing political power of blacks (Gary had recently elected African American Richard Hatcher as mayor), while southern towns such as Kokomo were populated by former Tennesseans and Kentuckians who had come north seeking work during World War II. Before a campaign stop in Marion, Martin told Kennedy that blacks had been lynched in the town as recently as 1930. Nonplussed, the New York senator asked, "Why am I going there then?"[36] Martin told him of potential Democratic votes there, and suggested that Kennedy emphasize his role as the former "chief law enforcement officer of the United States," to imply that he could restore order in the cities. "I can go pretty far in that direction," Kennedy said.[37]

In California, Kennedy also listened when Fred Dutton, who traveled with the candidate, argued that he needed to spend less time with Mexican Americans and blacks and more time in the suburbs. Edelman and Walinsky, however, thought he was tacking too far to the right in his campaign rhetoric, and Kennedy also had doubts. "When do I get to have a liberal day?" he asked on one frustrating occasion.[38] Nevertheless, his pragmatic side and will to win led him frequently to heed the advice of his more experienced aides.

By the same token, Kennedy spent precious time during the campaign on poverty-related events that were not politically essential. After a rousing first day on the campaign trail at the two major universities in Kansas, he made an unscheduled stop at a trade school for Native Americans. Journalist Jules Witcover later called the appearance a "deplorable lapse" and portrayed it as shameless politicking at the expense of a troubled constituency.[39] Advance man Jim Tolan, who scheduled the stop, said it was intended as a statement that Kennedy would not forget Native Americans despite having embarked on his new endeavor.[40] "Knowing his feelings towards the Indians, it would have been absolutely incredible for me . . . when he was out there and it was only a fifteen minute ride, to leave that place and not go and visit those Indians," Tolan said.[41]

Four days after entering the race Kennedy set aside time to testify before the Senate Banking Committee to promote once again the idea of tax incentives for targeted housing in the inner city. He argued against the provisions of a pending bill that encouraged affordable housing in the suburbs. Wisconsin senator William Proxmire challenged Kennedy on the wisdom of building in the ghetto when economists were suggesting that jobs were moving out of the city, but Kennedy contended that despite the trend, ghettos would continue to exist. As he had proposed in the first of his three January 1966 speeches, he conceded that mobility for blacks was vital but asserted: "For a long time to come in the future there are just going to be very, very few Negroes who are going to be in a class where they are able to move out of the ghettos. . . . It will be hard for them to know how to find jobs [in the suburbs] and for their children to keep up in these schools." As he had during the tax incentive hearings the previous September, he exaggerated for effect. "Just looking at it practically, you are not going to be able to move 100,000 Negroes out of Harlem into Westchester, Nassau, or Suffolk," he said, referring to the suburban counties surrounding New York City.[42] Kennedy's own housing bill was still mired in committee.

In late March the candidate chaired more Indian education field hearings. He told one audience in Flagstaff, Arizona, that although he would "rather be with the Indians" than on the campaign trail, "it is very likely I could do more for the Indians as President of the United States."[43] Kennedy again heard dismal statistics about life on reservations, including a 10 percent infant mortality rate (twice that of the nation's inner cities and four times the national average), unemployment rates in excess of 50 percent, high school dropout rates approaching 70 percent, and a life expectancy of forty-two years. "I just think with all the problems we have here at home," the New York Democrat said, "the tremendous needs that exist here and that we have seen elsewhere around the country with Indians and other minority groups, it is a very strong argument [for] ending the [Vietnam] conflict that now takes $30 billion a year."[44]

In April, Kennedy went to the Pine Ridge Reservation in South Dakota for another education hearing. The South Dakota primary was on June 4, so the trip assumed greater political significance than the Arizona hearings. Kennedy visited Calico Village, the poorest area on the reservation, and was visibly moved by conditions there. Local residents were initially overwhelmed by the press gaggle, and Kennedy sought to comfort one scared six-year-old girl whose one-room shack (housing her family of eleven) he poked his nose in to visit.[45]

During the brief Pine Ridge hearing, the director of the planning office for the Oglala Sioux, Sam Deloria, told the subcommittee that Native Americans had to have community control over their schools and no longer wanted to wait "for an Indian expert to adopt us so that we may go through the motions of being involved."[46] His statement was exemplary of the movement toward Indian self-determination that had grown throughout the 1960s, in the wake of the Eisenhower era policy that had sought a termination of federal responsibility over Indian affairs. A 1961 report from the Commission on the Rights, Liberties, and Responsibilities of the American Indian urged a government policy of planning programs together with Native Americans to help them advance "from their present poverty to a decent standard of living" so they would no longer need federal assistance.[47] The report captured the tone of the burgeoning self-determination movement, but many older tribal leaders feared any shift in their established relationship with the federal government, which Deloria characterized as "You be the dumb guy and I'll protect you."[48] Kennedy found the testimony compelling; it undoubtedly resonated with his own assessment of the problems of the inner city. "What it finally comes down to, from your statement," he said to Deloria, "is that people want control over their lives. What we have done over a period of time is put control in the hands of the white man."[49]

Kennedy cut the hearing short in order to visit Wounded Knee, site of the final crushing Indian defeat of the nineteenth century. "The Germans show Dachau as a reminder" of past wrongs, Kennedy told reporters. "This was just as cruel, just as ruthless."[50] South Dakota senator George McGovern, who accompanied Kennedy, noted that Native Americans needed no explanation, and recognized the candidate's sensitivity.[51] Whatever the political calculation that may have factored into Kennedy's decision to spend time on Indian affairs in the midst of the primary races, it was certainly unconventional. When aide Fred Dutton tried to convince him that the Native American vote was insubstantial, telling him "he should knock off the Injuns," the candidate dashed off a note in response: "Those of you who think you're running my campaign don't love Indians the way I do. You're a bunch of bastards."[52]

Kennedy also disregarded Dutton and his more experienced advisers when he authorized David Hackett to establish a "grass roots development" initiative that sought to link his campaign with antipoverty community organizations and racial minority groups. The grassroots effort embodied Kennedy's ideal of a direct, responsive relationship between the federal level and the local residents of poor communities, and he clearly envisioned the strategy as important not only for the primaries but also for a potential fall campaign.[53] He sought in part to reactivate the formula for voter organizing and registration that had been so successful in 1960, often tapping the same leaders and groups to mount the effort. The initiative went further, however, probing for ways to connect with and energize individuals in groups that had been institutionally connected to the federal War on Poverty.

Local community action agencies were the most natural place to begin the search for support. Because the Green amendment of the previous fall, mandating the flow of CAP funds through local government, had delivered control over community action funds back to the nation's mayors, many groups were concerned about losing the political power they had only begun to wield, and were likely sympathetic toward the renewed potential for empowerment. The campaign also made contact with local VISTA leaders, who were in a position to introduce them to poor people's groups, and hired George Woodring, formerly an assistant director of the Appalachian Volunteers (AV) program (who, while in that capacity, had helped advance Kennedy's eastern Kentucky trip), to work on organizing and voter registration among poor people in West Virginia, eastern Kentucky, and elsewhere in the region, tapping into "the existing AV network."[54]

Dun Gifford, the former HUD official who had taken exception to Kennedy's criticisms of the department during the Ribicoff hearings, coordinated registration and get-out-the-vote drives for the grassroots effort, which he believed "had a very decided impact in terms of generating activity."[55] According to Gifford, the campaign effort to organize poor people's groups was left deliberately "amorphous and flexible" and kept "quiet, out of the way, and behind the scenes," but the political activism that the operation encouraged created tensions with old guard advisers such as Dutton, Larry O'Brien, and Kenny O'Donnell. On one occasion an O'Donnell assistant concerned about irritating Mayor Daley called Gifford to urge him to "get those poor people out of the mayor's office because we're going to lose every fucking delegate vote in the state if you don't."[56]

The grassroots initiative was kept out of sight not merely because of potential friction with the old school pols like Daley. It carried other considerable risks, including the perception that the poor were Kennedy's only energized constituency. More serious was the potential allegation that OEO-funded organizations had been handed over to the Kennedy campaign in violation of the Hatch Act, which proscribed political activity on the part of government employees.[57]

The figure who was perhaps most important to the start-up of the grassroots effort needed to operate most covertly. The organizational components of the War on Poverty from which Kennedy sought individuals' support—CAP, VISTA, and AV—were shaped largely by the work of

Richard Boone. Boone, who had strongly influenced Kennedy's views on grassroots empowerment during the planning for the committee on juvenile delinquency and the National Service Corps, utilized the considerable array of contacts he had developed through his years both in Washington and as director of the nonpartisan, tax-exempt Citizens' Crusade Against Poverty to suggest potential allies.[58] Both Boone and David Hackett—the most prominent of the Justice Department's "guerrillas"—eagerly resumed their service to their old boss for an even bigger objective, utilizing their hard-won expertise in asymmetric political warfare in Kennedy's unconventional quest for the presidency.

In early April, Boone brought key leaders to Hickory Hill, Kennedy's estate in Virginia, to meet with the senator, Hackett, and other aides to discuss funding and how they fit into the campaign. Without explicitly addressing the legality of using OEO-funded groups for political work, Kennedy emphasized to local and regional leaders in attendance—including Marian Wright, the Reverend Arthur Brazier of the Woodlawn Organization in Chicago, Ted Watkins of the Watts Labor Community Action Council, Albert Peña of the Political Association of Spanish-Speaking Organizations, and Grace Olivarez (former OEO director for the state of Arizona)—that it was their constitutional right as individuals to engage in coordinated political activity.[59] Peter Edelman believed that the potential impact of the community leaders was "much more important than getting the endorsement of a national leader, because these were the fellows who . . . if they wanted to, really had local organizations and could command a tremendous number of supporters at the local level."[60]

The campaign also successfully recruited César Chávez to serve on the California delegation, and Kennedy gained the support of the Mexican American Political Association (MAPA) and its president, Bert Corona, whom one aide astutely recognized as "probably the single most important figure in RFK's effort to gain massive Mexican American support."[61] MAPA was the largest group of its kind in the nation, and it established new Viva Kennedy offices in California, the Midwest, the Southwest, and the Pacific Northwest. As would occur in other places, traditional party and labor bosses chafed at the organizing activity of poor people's groups. Corona bridled at attempts by Jesse Unruh, speaker of the state assembly, who was Kennedy's most influential California ally, to control the activities and funding of MAPA and asked the candidate to intercede, which Kennedy did.[62]

Many contemporary observers dubbed the 1968 election the dawn of the "New Politics," a phenomenon characterized by greater reliance on television and personal organizations than on traditional party bosses and machinery.[63] Kennedy's campaign toed the line between this new orientation and the recognition that traditional Democratic connections still mattered. The attempt to meld the two approaches was manifested in the uneasy coexistence of former John Kennedy advisers with Robert Kennedy's younger Senate staffers, and in the candidate's willingness to employ both conventional politicking and a covert effort to gain the grass-roots support of community-based poor people's organizations. Nowhere were the challenges and inconsistencies of this balancing act more apparent, however, than in his decision to allow longtime Oregon congresswoman Edith Green to run his Oregon primary campaign.

Kennedy's partnership with Green flew in the face of his antipoverty objectives. She had been a formidable opponent of the President's Committee on Juvenile Delinquency, and she despised David Hackett (she agreed to run Kennedy's campaign only on the condition that Hackett stay out of her state). Green had opposed a minimum wage for farm workers and engineered the compromise that threatened whatever power the poor could bring to bear on the Community Action Program.[64] When a Kennedy strategist asked Green if the state's ghettos were organized, she defiantly pronounced, "There are no ghettos in Oregon."[65] Kennedy's Senate aides were horrified by her selection, and Green herself was less than enthusiastic.[66] Nevertheless, she had been instrumental in John Kennedy's 1960 Oregon campaign, and Robert Kennedy's first Senate press secretary, Wesley Barthelmes, had been a Green protégé. While it likely did not cost him political support among disadvantaged Americans elsewhere—Green was hardly a household name—her role in the campaign revealed Kennedy's capacity to be self-contradictory and politically expedient.[67] When Kennedy lost the Oregon primary by six percentage points, he blamed the loss not on Green's failure but on his own inadequate effort and the nature of the state, which he privately called "one giant suburb."[68] "Let's face it," Kennedy told friends, "I appeal best to people who have problems."[69]

Kennedy introduced no new antipoverty proposals during the presidential campaign. Peter Edelman tried to get him to support the increasingly influential idea of a guaranteed minimum income for families, but Kennedy insisted that work had to be central to any program of aid to the poor, contending that if the federal government should guarantee anything, it was jobs.[70] On another occasion Edelman drafted a social security proposal for low-wage employees whereby the employer would be required to pay both the employer and employee contributions. Kennedy read part of it and said, "You're trying to make a socialist out of me." He read further and joked, "Why, if my father read this, he'd talk again."[71] Most frequently he discussed the initiatives on which he was already at work—hunger, community development corporations, and tax incentives to industry for investing in poverty-stricken areas.

To those unfamiliar with Kennedy's emerging antipoverty plans, his rhetoric of community control and an expanded role for business, coupled with his new emphasis on his law enforcement experience, made him sound as though he was pandering to conservative audiences. Jules Witcover called the themes Kennedy's "Wall Street litany," and conservative California governor Ronald Reagan joked that Kennedy was sounding more like him every day.[72] Even ally Paul Schrade, who incurred the wrath of Walter Reuther for breaking from UAW support for the administration to back Kennedy, considered it "irresponsible" for the candidate to emphasize work over welfare and leave the impression that he was calling for bootstraps individualism.[73]

These more conservative themes had nevertheless been strands of Kennedy's thought for some time, but they were counterbalanced by liberal and even radical signals. Kennedy's emphasis on dignity and meaningful remuneration for welfare recipients, along with his visible fight against the social security amendments the previous fall, impressed welfare rights leader George Wiley, who sent word to Kennedy's wife, Ethel, that he was "personally very much in favor of his candidacy."[74] While Kennedy had not publicly aligned with National Welfare Rights Organization (which Wiley led, along with Johnnie Tillmon and Lillian Craig), the candidate's wife offered a powerful symbol of support by participating in a Mother's Day march from the Kennedy Playground in Washington, D.C., to a rally at the Cardozo High School stadium.[75]

Kennedy openly identified with other groups deemed militant, particularly the young. Campaigning before a tumultuous South Central Los Angeles crowd in late March, Kennedy wore a "Sons of Watts" pin, and his security was handled by the group. The Sons of Watts, an informal fraternal society created by former gang members after the 1965 uprising, provided community service work—often taking the lead in identifying and addressing community needs—and a sense of identity for its members.[76] The organization had received a considerable amount of favorable publicity, and Kennedy was undoubtedly drawn to its emphases on community self-help and racial pride, the elements of the Black Power movement that he found most valuable.

Weeks earlier, while in town to support César Chávez, Kennedy had also received a call from a Chicano leader seeking his support for the controversial walkout protests undertaken by thousands of East Los Angeles high school students. Sal Castro, a Lincoln High School teacher who had encouraged the students, phoned Kennedy's office in an attempt to gain the New York senator's endorsement for their protests seeking better schools. Chicano student leaders were frustrated and discouraged that no public officials—neither sympathetic white leaders nor even elected Mexican American officeholders—openly supported their efforts. It was "amazing," Castro recalled, "our own community would not touch it."[77] Castro, who had worked for the Viva Kennedy initiative in 1960 and even advanced a major Kennedy Los Angeles campaign event in the weeks before the 1960 election, thought the New York senator might be their best hope. Kennedy agreed to meet with the students.[78]

As he descended the steps of his plane at Los Angeles International Airport, Kennedy unfurled a poster of Mexican revolutionary Emiliano Zapata, whom the young activists had embraced as a hero.[79] Governor Reagan and Los Angeles police chief Thomas Reddin blamed these "blowouts" on outside agitators. The meeting and a picture of Kennedy with student leaders—emblazoned with the caption "Bobbie Joins the Blowout Committee—Outside Agitator?"—emboldened the students, who were facing increasing pressure to relent.[80] The *Chicano Student News* reprinted a telegram from Kennedy expressing his full support. "The *future president* of the U.S. is telling us," the newspaper urged, "that he supports Blowouts as an excellent method of getting reforms for education. Now are we going to let some 2 bit mayor, police chief, racist administrators . . . and a ridiculous Vaudeville team that poses for a Board of Education say we are wrong?!"[81]

Kennedy expected his popularity among Latinos to be critical to his chances in the California primary, and while the Latino press wasn't as far-reaching as the black media, his candidacy was bolstered by Mexican American newspaper coverage. *El Informador*, a Spanish-language newspaper published in conjunction with the African American–owned *Oakland Post*, endorsed Kennedy as "the ONLY candidate who has shown continuing interest" in the "special problems of Mexican Americans, Puerto Rican Americans, etc., in this country. He has given these groups, at a minimum, the feeling of 'being taken into account.'"[82] The newspaper proclaimed that it was not merely swooning over Kennedy's attention to the community, although it was "undeniably" part of his political strategy to "woo Hispanic Americans." Pronouncing a clear-eyed assessment that Kennedy was "also perhaps the first to have noticed the POWER that Hispanic Americans are gaining," *El Informador* nevertheless declared that because of "his views on domestic issues, minority groups support him."[83]

At the same time, Kennedy aide Adam Walinsky emphasized that another group needed a champion. "The danger group," according to Walinsky, was working-class whites, who were feeling in their own way excluded, increasingly concerned about their economic, social, and even physical security. When the Kerner Commission report was released, Walinsky privately wrote his boss that he found its emphasis on white racism inflammatory and counterproductive. "The blue collar worker, worried about his daughter getting . . . raped by a black kid," Walinsky warned, "or about his block deteriorating when the drunks move in, is not going to be suddenly overcome with a rush of guilt." Working-class whites, Walinsky argued, were "crying out for attention . . . for a role," but felt lost in the headlines given to minority grievances.[84]

An April 1968 poll suggested that Kennedy's popularity among blue-collar whites in Indiana depended less on his more conservative stances on some issues than on an affinity for his image as a fighter. In the Oliver Quayle survey, Kennedy led both Eugene McCarthy and Indiana governor Roger Branigin by a three-to-one margin, and in the two most decisive totals of the poll, respondents overwhelmingly rejected the charges that Kennedy was untrustworthy and "too tough and ruthless."[85] There were misperceptions of Kennedy's positions among those who supported him, as several believed, for example, that Kennedy was willing to use any means short of nuclear weapons to win in Vietnam. This, however, also reflected the perception that Kennedy was tougher than any other candidate. Journalists Rowland Evans and Robert Novak, who accompanied the pollster through a working-class suburb of Indianapolis, inexplicably attributed Kennedy's popularity to his family identification despite the fact that by a two-to-one margin, likely Kennedy voters indicated that their support was *not* based principally on that factor.[86]

It was the allure of Kennedy as a bare-knuckles advocate for their interests that led some of these same white voters to support the insurgent candidacy of George Wallace in the fall of 1968.[87] An internal campaign memo based on canvassing in central Indiana also confirmed Kennedy's popularity among whites holding favorable views of Wallace.[88] Their faith in Kennedy also allowed some working-class whites to suspend their animosity toward blacks. When television correspondent Charles Quinn confronted white Kennedy voters in Gary with the candidate's progressive positions regarding African Americans and asked how they could vote for the New York senator, one of them responded: "I don't know. Just like him."[89] An unlikely motorcade through Gary featuring Kennedy, African American mayor Richard Hatcher, and former middleweight boxing champion and white ethnic hero Tony Zale embodied Kennedy's potential coalition.[90]

If Kennedy did evince a pragmatic willingness to accentuate the more conservative elements of his domestic vision in communities such as those studied by the Quayle poll, he was at the same time unafraid to challenge his crowds. He addressed a local businessmen's club in Vincennes, Indiana, on the need for contributions by private enterprise to solving the problem of poverty, and was afterward peppered with questions unrelated to the topic, such as his position on government-imposed daylight saving time, which was troubling area farmers far more than urban poverty. Kennedy had no stance on the issue and tried to change the subject, asking whether the crowd was aware that rats outnumbered people in New York City. Several in the southern Indiana audience chuckled at the thought, as it confirmed their distasteful images of the nation's largest city. Kennedy sternly admonished them not to laugh.[91] He ended the appearance shortly thereafter and received a less than fond farewell.

The candidate repeatedly told jeering student audiences that he opposed draft deferments. At Creighton University in Omaha, Kennedy contended that blacks were serving as paratroopers in Vietnam at a rate four times their representation in the population at large. One student asked, "Isn't the Army one way of getting young people out of the ghettos?" Kennedy countered, "Here at a Catholic university, how can you say that we can deal with the problems of the poor by sending them to Vietnam?"[92]

At Indiana University Medical School he discussed the need for more affordable health care to avoid "condemning the poor to illness and the average American to the whim of fate."[93] Students questioned the feasibility of his proposals, and one asked where he would get the money for new federally funded programs. "From you," Kennedy snapped. In other speeches and other settings he had discussed specific cuts in supersonic transport and the space program, but on this occasion Kennedy was irritated and launched into an extended homily:

> I look around this room today and I don't see many black faces who will become doctors. You can talk about where the money will come from. . . . Part of civilized society is to let people go to medical school who come from ghettos. You don't see many people coming out of the

ghettos or off the Indian reservations to medical school. You are the privileged ones here. It's easy to sit back and say it's the fault of the federal government, but it's our responsibility too. It's our society, not just our government that spends twice as much on pets as on the poverty program.[94]

Kennedy was also willing to challenge minority groups. In Oakland he scheduled a meeting with the militant Bay Area Black Caucus, which included representatives of the Black Panthers. California assemblyman and Kennedy supporter Willie Brown convened the forum, which grew to nearly three hundred people and included what according to Brown was "practically every element of a black ghettoized community . . . that one could think of."[95] The meeting quickly became hostile and ran until late into the evening. The candidate was on the receiving end of derisive epithets and virulent accusations by frustrated attendees that he was only after their votes. Olympic decathlon champion Rafer Johnson came with Kennedy to show his support, and when Johnson declared that he was embarrassed by the behavior of the crowd, he was booed and called a "technicolor nigger and a middle class cat."[96]

Kennedy remained composed as the attacks grew harsher. Curtis Lee Baker, a charismatic local leader sometimes known as "Black Jesus," angrily proclaimed: "Look man, I don't want to hear none of your shit. . . . You bastards haven't did nothing for us." Finally Kennedy responded: "You scream at me, 'What are you doing?' All right, you're yelling and screaming. What are you doing for your own people? You expect us to do it all for you? What are you doing?"[97] When someone charged again that he wasn't really interested in blacks, Kennedy chided, "Well, you know better than that."[98]

By 1968 Robert Kennedy had been through many similar experiences, from the meeting with James Baldwin to tense exchanges with Bedford-Stuyvesant community leaders. After this one he told advance man Jim Tolan, who was shaken by the Oakland conclave, that people in the crowd were lashing out because "they just didn't want to look in the eyes of anybody else like they were Uncle Toms." He agreed that "these things are nasty, but you just have to do them," reassuring Tolan, "Things will be all right." The candidate was prescient. Without consulting the Kennedy campaign, the next day Baker and other meeting attendees functioned as advance men and informal security for huge Kennedy rallies in Oakland. Baker recalled, "I put a leaflet out that Kennedy was coming in this area and that I wanted him to be treated with the utmost respect."[99] According to Latino activist Hector Lopez, the Black Panthers "got out in front of the car and started shoving people aside . . . and that's how Bobby Kennedy got into West Oakland." Lopez called it "the first truly community event" he'd seen in his eight years in the city.[100]

Kennedy sometimes gained the grudging respect of militant black leaders who would not support him. Stokely Carmichael told a Kennedy aide that he recognized the senator's popularity and feared that Kennedy's candidacy would co-opt his own power in the black community. Black Panther Eldridge Cleaver considered Kennedy "too white to be alright" but mused that he "wore the aura of an idol-smasher."[101] Boxing champion Muhammad Ali told a college crowd that although his Black Muslim faith prohibited voting, "black and white youth are all for Robert Kennedy. He tells the truth about race, religion, and war."[102]

Other wary, far lesser known militant black leaders planned to meet with Kennedy in Indianapolis on April 4 to size up the candidate. The New York senator was scheduled to speak at a rally in the inner city of Indianapolis that night. After delivering a speech on hunger at the University of Notre Dame in South Bend, Kennedy was informed that Martin Luther King had been shot in Memphis. He boarded a plane for Indianapolis, and when he landed, Kennedy was told that King had died. Indianapolis mayor Richard Lugar warned the candidate against holding the rally, but a black assistant chief of police told Kennedy's advance men that the senator and his family could have slept outside all night in the Indianapolis ghetto and remained unharmed.[103] Without hesitation, Kennedy left the airport for the planned event at Seventeenth and Broadway.

The audience was still unaware of King's death when Kennedy mounted a flatbed truck that served as the stage. Speaking without notes, he informed the assembled crowd of King's death and tried to comfort those in attendance by confiding that he had felt the same anguish after a white man murdered his brother. It was the first time Kennedy publicly addressed his feelings about the assassination. "You can be filled with bitterness, with hatred, and a desire for revenge," Kennedy said. "We can move in that direction as a country, in great polarization—black people amongst black, white people amongst white, filled with hatred toward one another. Or we can make the effort, as Martin Luther King did, to understand and to comprehend, and to replace that violence, that stain of bloodshed that has spread across our land, with an effort to understand with compassion and love."[104] Rioting broke out in over one hundred cities that night, but Indianapolis was not one of them.[105]

In his hotel room after the speech, Kennedy met with a group of fourteen young black activists, leaders of a local group called the Radical

Action Program. They were upset about King's death, and one snapped at Kennedy: "You're all the same. . . . Our leader is dead tonight, and when we need you, we can't find you." Kennedy was also in a foul mood, telling the group that he had left home at five in the morning, his children pleading with him to stay, only to read criticism of his excessive affinity for minorities on the way to Indiana. "I have to laugh," he sniffed. "Big business is trying to defeat me because they think I am a friend of the Negro. You are down on me because you say I am part of the establishment." The group listened intently. "I happen to think I have something to offer you and your people," said Kennedy. After a lengthy discussion, he instructed them to contact his state campaign director if they needed him. They came away convinced, and the African American vote would prove essential to Kennedy's eventual victory in Indiana.[106]

The next day Kennedy decided to maintain one speaking engagement, addressing the Cleveland City Club on "the mindless menace of violence in America." In a moving speech that criticized a culture of violence in the country that honored "swagger and bluster and the wielders of force," he cautioned that there was

> another kind of violence, slower but just as deadly, destructive as the shot or the bomb in the night. This is the violence of institutions; indifference and inaction and slow decay. This is the violence that afflicts the poor, that poisons relations between men because their skin has different colors. This is a slow destruction of a child by hunger, and schools without books and homes without heat in the winter. This is the breaking of a man's spirit by denying him the chance to stand as a father and as a man among other men. And this too afflicts us all.[107]

Kennedy appealed for a renewal of community, saying, "We can perhaps remember—even if only for a time—that those who live with us are our brothers, that they share with us the same short moment of life, that they seek—as we do—nothing but the chance to live out their lives in purpose and happiness, winning what satisfaction and fulfillment they can."[108]

Kennedy attended King's funeral in Atlanta along with countless other dignitaries, including fellow candidates Eugene McCarthy and Richard Nixon. Absent, however, was President Johnson, who only days earlier had shocked the nation by withdrawing from the presidential race. Afterward Kennedy met with a group of King's aides and other prominent African Americans in his hotel suite. As in Indianapolis, the emotions of the day boiled over. "People were just angry and bitter and grieving. . . . [T]hey decided to take it out on him," Andrew Young recalled. One of the group,

James Bevel, said that King had had an economic program "to feed hungry people" and insisted that "the next President of the United States has got to have an economic program to bring poor people into the economy and into the society, and I just want to know[,] . . . Do you have a program or do you know anybody that does?"[109] Kennedy told him, "I do have one or two ideas," but he insisted that he "just came to pay tribute to a man I had a lot of respect for." Young, John Lewis, and others present were impressed with Kennedy's willingness to listen, and they began to transfer some of their hopes to his campaign.[110]

The day after King's death those aboard Kennedy's plane could see the smoke rising from the urban unrest as they flew back into the capital. By the spring of 1968 Kennedy had developed what Peter Edelman called "a personal messianic, somewhat egotistical, but . . . highly justified" confidence in his ability to move events by reaching people on an individual level.[111] He wanted to go into the heart of the rioting—"I think I can do something with these people," he told John Bartlow Martin—but he was dissuaded temporarily by advisers who feared it might be seen as grandstanding.[112] The following day Kennedy attended the Palm Sunday service at the church of the Reverend Walter Fauntroy, an important King ally. The Roman Catholic senator generated some controversy when he received communion at the Baptist church before walking the streets of the capital with Fauntroy. He occasionally sneezed from the still lingering tear gas and the smoke from smoldering buildings, but as Kennedy moved through the ravaged streets, a friendly crowd massed behind him. One woman took his hand and said, "I knew you would be the first to come here, darling," while another resident told the senator that he too was a father of ten children and wanted a better life for his family. Federal troops unaware of the cause for the commotion braced for another clash until they realized it was the New York senator. "They took off their masks and let us through," Fauntroy said. "They looked awfully relieved."[113]

Kennedy felt the weight of responsibility that came with his conviction that he was the candidate of poor Americans. "If I could just do it for *him*," Kennedy confided to Rafer Johnson, as he pointed out a black child with disheveled clothes and no shoelaces.[114] On the campaign plane leaving Omaha, he and reporter Jack Germond discussed particular children they had seen in that city's ghetto and wondered aloud what would happen to them when they realized the hopelessness of their surroundings. "This was not a case of a politician conning a reporter by showing how sensitive he was to the disadvantaged," Germond said of the off-the-record conversation.[115] On the way to speak the day after King's death, Kennedy told

Jim Tolan he hoped and prayed that he wouldn't disappoint people like those in the crowd at Seventeenth and Broadway and the black leaders he had met with afterwards.[116]

After his defeat in Oregon, Kennedy's back was against the wall in California. His best opportunity to challenge Hubert Humphrey was to demonstrate his national appeal through the primary process, and losses in the final contests would be devastating to his hopes. Kennedy's task was a delicate one. The mob scenes he generated seemed to be the popular stampede necessary for a candidate challenging an incumbent administration, but Jesse Unruh was opposed to the candidate's motorcading through black areas. In the aftermath of Watts and two subsequent years of rioting nationwide, Unruh and other advisers were fearful that the particularly fervent responses Kennedy evoked from blacks and Mexican Americans would alienate middle-class whites.[117]

A large turnout among minority and poor voters—who tended to vote far less regularly than any other group—was critical to Kennedy's success. With significant voices in his campaign urging him to limit his appearances among that constituency, other means were employed to encourage turnout covertly. Los Angeles mayor Sam Yorty charged that Kennedy's campaign was paying registrars thirty cents for each new black voter registered, a practice called "an old California custom" by journalist Carl Rowan.[118] When Delaware Republican senator John Williams asked the Justice Department to look into potential criminal activity, a Kennedy campaign official was sufficiently concerned that he sent a memo to Edward Kennedy and Ted Sorensen informing them that he would "see whether we have a problem."[119]

In fact Louis Martin had been given the task of distributing "walking around money" to black community leaders, and John Bartlow Martin recalled John Seigenthaler telling him he had been "buying Negro preachers" in the Bay Area to encourage their flocks to vote for Kennedy.[120] Seigenthaler later denied that this was the case and asserted that local assemblyman Willie Brown, who had arranged Kennedy's tempestuous meeting with the Black Caucus, was so impressed with his comportment that he rejected San Francisco congressman Phillip Burton's demand that the Kennedy campaign put up $20,000 to finance get-out-the-vote efforts, which would redound to the Democratic congressman's favor. "No, no Phil, not this time," Brown said. "This one's on the house for Bobby."[121]

Whatever the extent to which Kennedy's campaign resorted to under-the-table dealing to turn out minority voters, the candidate was unable to heed the warnings of his seasoned advisers and opted to energize his base—and himself after the disappointment of Oregon—by campaigning among Mexican Americans and blacks in San Francisco and Los Angeles. Great crowds greeted him in both cities. When the motorcade turned in to a Mexican American district in San Francisco, the candidate saw thousands of people rushing toward his vehicle. Smiling at advance man Jim Tolan, he said: "I'm home. I'm home."[122]

Despite the fact that Eugene McCarthy had chaired a committee on unemployment while in the Senate, he did not compete vigorously with Kennedy on the poverty issue or challenge him significantly for minority votes. "I couldn't get the Negro votes away from Bobby Kennedy. I could have moved into the ghettos and stayed in the whole campaign," McCarthy later said.[123] Nevertheless, the issue would provide one of the few contrasts that emerged from a much anticipated debate between the two men days before the primary.

McCarthy maintained that the ghettoes had to be broken up or else the nation would perpetuate a "practical apartheid" that would only grow more entrenched if low-cost housing was built in poor areas. "Most of the employment is now in the belt line outside of the cities," McCarthy said. It was the same argument that William Proxmire had made during Kennedy's testimony on the housing bill in March, and the New York senator now employed a similar rebuttal. "You say you are going to take 10,000 black people and move them into Orange County," Kennedy said. He then warned that to "put them in the suburbs where they can't afford the housing, where their children can't keep up with the schools, and where they don't have the skills for the jobs, it is just going to be catastrophic."[124]

Many contemporary observers (and later historians) considered Kennedy's election eve remark demagoguery, an appeal to the fears of middle- and upper-class whites in conservative Orange County. Kennedy's comment had indeed been strategically inserted; according to Adam Walinsky, Kennedy was "primed and ready for bear" in anticipation of McCarthy's critique.[125] His rejoinder was nevertheless consistent with his thinking on ghetto reconstruction as far back as his January 1966 speeches, of which journalists and even newly arrived campaign advisers had little grasp.[126] On other occasions the New York senator had used similarly overdrawn references to the difficulties blacks would face in the suburbs and wealthier areas to argue against a rapid dispersal strategy. Kennedy's characterization of the Minnesota senator leading an African American exodus to the conservative middle-class stronghold of the state was an objectionable distortion, but McCarthy's association of the term "apartheid" with Kennedy's position emphasizing the rebuilding of ghetto communities was at least as demagogic and perhaps more so.[127]

His popularity among minority and poor voters proved the decisive factor in his 46.3 to 41.8 percent victory over McCarthy. (Vice President Hubert Humphrey had not announced his candidacy until April and was not on the ballot.) An NBC voting analysis determined that 70 percent of low-income voters supported Kennedy. The survey also found that 75 percent of African American voters and nearly 90 percent of Mexican American voters cast ballots for the New York senator.[128] Overall, one out of every eight Kennedy voters was black, and César Chávez, whose farm workers' union had suspended an ongoing strike to concentrate on registering voters, reported that in Los Angeles there were Mexican American precincts with nearly 100 percent turnout, almost all of which went for Kennedy.[129] While McCarthy won two thirds of the counties in California, Kennedy won Los Angeles County by over 120,000 votes, and his large pluralities there and in San Francisco and Sacramento were decisive.[130]

Before Kennedy descended to thank supporters in the Ambassador Hotel ballroom in Los Angeles late on the night of the primary, he teased former SNCC president John Lewis that more Mexican Americans had turned out than blacks.[131] George McGovern called to inform him that he had won handily in the South Dakota primary. Kennedy believed that his victory in the rural state—which was also the boyhood home of the vice president—might send a strong signal to party bosses about his national appeal. Kennedy eagerly asked those gathered in his suite, "Do you want to hear about the Indians?" He relayed the news that he had won one Native American precinct with 878 votes, as compared to two for McCarthy and nine for a Humphrey slate.[132]

Dolores Huerta of the farm workers' union stood behind Kennedy once he reached the podium in the Embassy Ballroom. Kennedy thanked César Chávez and Bert Corona along with "friends in the black community" for their support. "With such a high percentage voting today," Kennedy said, "I think it really made a major difference."[133] He went on to reiterate that the objective of his candidacy was to end divisions in the country "between blacks and whites, between the poor and the more affluent, or between age groups or on the war in Vietnam."[134] As he turned from the podium to the celebratory cheers of the enthusiastic crowd, a radio reporter asked how he would overcome the delegate strength of the vice president. The candidate replied, "I'll just have to struggle for it."[135] They were Kennedy's last recorded words. As he proceeded slowly through the pantry of the hotel kitchen, he suddenly fell to the floor with gunshot wounds to his head and neck. A seventeen-year-old Mexican American busboy named Juan Romero, whose hand Kennedy had just shaken, knelt and gave him a rosary.[136] Twenty-five hours later Kennedy's struggle ended.

In a tragic and ironic coincidence, Robert Kennedy was dead at forty-two, the same painfully young age to which an American Indian could expect to live in 1968. His body was flown back to New York for a funeral at St. Patrick's Cathedral. The funeral train then wound its way down the eastern seaboard to Washington. Huge crowds of all kinds gathered along the route, but the working-class and poor people who tended to live along the rail lines in cities were particularly visible. They were Kennedy's core constituency, and they turned out in the thousands to say farewell. As he looked out from the train, civil rights activist Ivanhoe Donaldson saw several white policemen—many of whom were visibly moved—holding black children in their arms so they could get a better look at the coffin as it passed. "There was the dream, all along the train tracks," Donaldson reflected. "But yet, in the last car, in that caboose, was the reality."[137]

The funeral procession made three stops in the capital to recognize the phases of Kennedy's career, pausing first in front of the Justice Department and then at the Senate Office Building. Before crossing the bridge to Arlington National Cemetery, the hearse carrying Kennedy's body pulled up in front of the Lincoln Memorial to allow participants in the Poor People's Campaign to pay their respects.[138] Their encampment named Resurrection City, the basic idea of which Kennedy had suggested to Marian Wright a year earlier, stretched out on the Mall near the Memorial. As if on cue, the gentle evening rain that had been falling stopped, and a choir of schoolchildren began to sing the "Battle Hymn of the Republic." The residents of Resurrection City raised their hands in solidarity and joined in the song.[139]

CONCLUSION

Journalist J. Anthony Lukas was struck by the diversity of mourners who came to pay their respects at St. Patrick's Cathedral. "World statesmen in formal dark suits stood next to Harlem school boys in torn Levis and sneakers," Lukas reported. "Suburban housewives in trim fashionable suits waited side by side with young Puerto Rican girls who fingered worn rosary beads." The *New York Times* reporter was most taken with the turnout of the poor and the young. "At times every fourth or fifth face in the line seemed to be that of a Negro or a Puerto Rican," Lukas wrote, guessing that about a third of the mourners were twenty-one or younger.[1]

In the black community of Washington, D.C., where Kennedy had invested so much time and energy, a reporter described the reaction of African Americans as to "a great personal loss." Said one disconsolate woman, "We don't have nobody, now, nobody," while another declared, "To be like the Kennedys and speak out on the issue of poverty, you got to be ready to meet your maker."[2]

At San Quentin prison, a planned performance by Native American dancers from more than twenty tribes for the entertainment of 350 prison inmates was transformed into a mourning dance rite as a tribute to Kennedy as "a fallen warrior." The magazine *Indian Truth*, rushing out its obituary at the deadline for its summer issue, wrote: "Privately and in public gatherings, Indian people spoke of their loss and their sorrow. . . . He was, by most, considered to be a true friend of the Indian."[3]

The *Mountain Eagle* of Whitesburg, Kentucky, discussed Kennedy's ongoing contact with local officials after his visit to the region, suggesting "firm indications that the Senator was planning some major reform legislation, to be written with Eastern Kentucky in mind. Many Eastern Kentuckians who watched Kennedy while he was here and who were aware of his continuing interest in area problems believed his presidency would give the mountain man a valued friend in the White House."[4] A West Virginia columnist insisted that Kennedy "was ruthless because he fought desperately to eliminate the poverty he saw. . . . Not everyone who didn't like Robert Kennedy saw and heard and talked with him in West Virginia. Few who did walked away thinking his divisiveness, opportunism and ruthlessness were all so bad. I didn't."[5]

A young Latino singer named Hermanitos García recorded Spanish and English versions of a song called "Robert F. Kennedy Prayer," asking God "Why, if you are so good, do you permit them to harm . . . the best candidate?"[6] El Informador reflected: "Kennedy was especially worthy to be called a friend to the farm workers of California. . . . Perhaps this was because of his open admiration for César Chávez, a mutual admiration; perhaps because he was simply a good human being. In Delano they wept for Kennedy with more tears, with deeper pain, and for better cause."[7]

In the weeks after Robert Kennedy's entry into the presidential race, the oblivious cochairman of Eugene McCarthy's California campaign attributed Kennedy's popularity among racial minorities to "the celebrity factor."[8] True, as the brother of the recently martyred president, Robert Kennedy could boast of unrivaled celebrity status among those vying for the office in 1968. One U.S. senator had earlier famously quipped that he treated the junior senator from New York no differently than he would any future president. Nevertheless, this book has been an explication of the political alliance that ran deeper than Kennedy's political opponents or the majority of Americans likely realized.

In early 1968 journalist Pete Hamill wrote a still hesitant Kennedy, attempting to persuade him to challenge Lyndon Johnson for the Democratic nomination. "I wanted to remind you," Hamill wrote, "that in Watts I didn't see pictures of Malcolm X or Ron Karenga on the walls. I saw pictures of JFK. That is your capital in the most cynical sense; it is your obligation in another, the obligation of staying true to whatever it was that put those pictures on those walls."[9] In part, this book has also been an examination of how those pictures got there.

It was, of course, partly a matter of identity politics. As the first Irish Catholic president, John Kennedy, as biographer Robert Dallek has suggested, realized the dream of "hyphenated Americans" by ascending to the top of the social and political ladder.[10] And Catholics of all ethnicities likely nodded in agreement with the farewell message of a popular church weekly when it wrote, "Because of the faith and courage and example of

John Kennedy, a Catholic in the United States will never again have to be considered a 'second class citizen.' Because of him a Catholic school boy will never again have to feel that the highest office in the land is closed to him."[11]

There was not necessarily, however, a natural connection for racial minorities and poor people who did not share his faith. John Kennedy was as much Harvard-educated aristocrat as Catholic pol. His popularity also stemmed from the approach of his 1960 campaign, which was deliberately geared toward cultivating relationships that racial minority groups found both convincing and empowering. Both the candidate and his campaign manager worked to establish the outreach and the infrastructure for effective voter registration campaigns among Mexican Americans, Puerto Ricans, and African Americans that were essential to his victory. Among Mexican Americans especially, the process of being recruited and organized by their own leaders for the presidential campaign proved a major step toward political empowerment, even if they weren't always thrilled with the president's performance. John Kennedy also campaigned on economic issues, and specifically the problem of poverty, much more extensively than has been recognized. While the Democratic Party in the wake of the New Deal had something of a built-in coalition among minority groups and working-class whites, it took Kennedy's 1960 campaign to reenergize that coalition and expand it to new arrivals such as Puerto Ricans.

The crucible of his administration's flawed but ultimately responsive handling of the surging civil rights movement at the time when its momentum reached a tipping point would be the most important factor in the allegiance of African Americans. President Kennedy's death, which many African Americans interpreted as retribution from a racist society, elevated their esteem beyond the level of any conventional political admiration. Because of his obvious closeness to the president, but also because African Americans and other racial minorities (perhaps less justifiably) felt that he had stood with them in their drive for first-class citizenship in his pivotal role as attorney general, this affection readily transferred itself to Robert Kennedy.

Robert Kennedy began to examine poverty as a distinctive issue at the same time that he attempted to manage the political challenges of the civil rights movement. Initially his understanding was very limited, and the primary levers of change he attempted to manipulate were conventional ones. A donated public swimming pool was the result of calls to archbishops and rabbis; a playground emerged from the beneficence of a millionaire businessman. Over time, however, Kennedy's baptism in the power of social change from below generated by the direct action protests of the civil rights movement—as much as he tried to temper and guide them so that matters could be efficiently and quietly managed by judges and politicians—along with his desire to investigate issues related to delinquency and poverty up close, set him on course for a different vision of social change. Sometime PCJD "guerrilla" Leonard Duhl observed that Kennedy began moving from the cool, expert systems management approach to change, which he characterized as the "McNamara-Bundy approach," to the "Hackett-Boone-Walinsky and Edelman" approach of creating change from the grassroots up.[12]

Kennedy was only moving in that direction, however, and he tried to meld the two approaches. He understood the value of ready power— political or financial—so he never abandoned his belief in the need for swift top-down action. His communitarian impulse, which linked the grassroots local community to the federal power of the national community—as well as other sources of power in American life, from business, to organized labor, to universities—was what he had begun to work out in the vehicles of community action and community development corporations, but it is not clear that he was on the verge of a politically sustainable mechanism. The struggles of the Community Action Program and the divisions in Bedford-Stuyvesant, both of which were at times less than skillfully managed, bear this out.

If political cooperation was at the heart of Kennedy's vision of community, his own actions sometimes betrayed that ideal, with significant consequences. He recognized politics to be a blood sport, and his personal disdain for Lyndon Johnson, while substantive on a number of matters, manifestly contradicted his ideal of cooperation. His tug-of-war with the president became apparent in his lack of public support for the Community Action Program during the critical early months of the Office of Economic Opportunity. Out of political self-interest, Kennedy failed to defend vigorously the program of which he was the patron and instead allowed Johnson to take a political beating. This contributed to Johnson's scorn for the Office of Economic Opportunity and, to a certain extent, to his decreased willingness to fight for antipoverty funds. Vocal support by the New York senator would not have stopped press coverage of political conflict between city halls and CAPs, or allegations of misused community action funds, but it might have blunted their force and slowed the erosion of popular sympathy for the overall effort. White House domestic adviser Joseph Califano thought it the greatest of tragedies that Johnson, with his unparalleled legislative skills, and Kennedy, with a unique capacity to "inspire masses of people," were unable to join forces.[13] Instead, each at times worked against the efforts of the other and the larger cause of poor Americans. In the end, perhaps it is true, as Michael Harrington wrote, that "in protest there is the possibility of a beloved community; in politics there is not."[14]

In large part because of his communitarian disposition, Kennedy sometimes failed to choose what liberals saw as the most progressive antipoverty positions. He opposed a guaranteed income on the basis of the value he placed on the dignity of work. He criticized the welfare system despite the concerns of some liberals and moderates that this would provide fodder for conservatives looking to dismantle it. In this and other ways he also anticipated emerging conservative critiques and the likely limits on expenditures of public dollars to battle poverty. His tax bills were developed not out of any reverence for the market system in itself but as a corporatist attempt to coerce one of the most influential "organs" of American society—the business community—to assist the needier parts of the body social.

Aside from the political potential of some of his proposals to find centrist ground in a period when the first substantial experiments in public-private partnerships were being launched, there is real question whether they would have solved the poverty problem. His proposals precluded significant structural changes to the economy in spite of strong evidence that these were necessary. From the first, Kennedy instead focused on community- and place-based strategies. Community action and the community development corporation thus joined a list of localized proposals dating back to the Progressive Era which historian Alice O'Connor has described as being forced to "swim against the tide" of the larger national aggregate market forces that ultimately overwhelmed urban economic progress.[15] Even as Kennedy became convinced that larger infusions of federal dollars were necessary to address aspects of the poverty problem, he saw that budget constraints created by the Vietnam War and the increasingly conservative political climate in the United States would make sufficient federal funding politically untenable. Rather than fighting for structural changes such as income redistribution strategies, the New York senator turned to tax incentives in an attempt to draw private resources into poverty-stricken areas.

Kennedy's hope that private enterprise could be trained as a weapon on the problem of poverty demands analysis. Employing a corporeal analogy (befitting his organic conception of society), Kennedy was willing to loose the forces of self-interest in a diseased part of the body social in order to cure it, a process almost akin to using radiation on a cancerous growth. Could business be channeled by federal tax policies as a force for social good? One early economic assessment of the Kennedy plan found it to have only limited potential.[16] The idea nevertheless gained adherents as the popularity of market-based strategies to address poverty grew in the conservative milieu of the 1980s, and it was advocated again first in the "enterprise zone" initiative of Jack Kemp, former secretary of housing and urban development, and later enacted in the empowerment zone–enterprise community legislation of the Clinton administration. The initiative has received support from both sides of the political aisle, but its effects are as yet difficult to assess.[17]

While his tax incentive and community development corporation proposals are significant historical contributions, Kennedy did not develop a lengthy antipoverty legislative record as a senator. He was, however, to a large degree boxed out of doing so because of the blizzard of progressive legislation sent to Congress by Lyndon Johnson. From the first, Kennedy chose the strategy laid out by aide Adam Walinsky after his election to the Senate: to add amendments when appropriate and offer alternative proposals when necessary. Ultimately his most concerted antipoverty efforts in the Senate were his attempts to save or augment funding for Johnson's existing poverty programs (most of which had their genesis in the Kennedy administration), to learn how those programs were or were not working, and to build public pressure to sustain the waning national will for the War on Poverty.

He was most effective in the last of these efforts. Like all skilled political leaders, Kennedy took a conventional political medium and modernized it to connect with ordinary Americans. As Franklin Roosevelt had done with radio and his brother had with both the press conference and television, Robert Kennedy modernized the creaky political tool with which he had so much familiarity—and which first brought him public notice—the congressional hearing. It had been a locus of political energy in the 1950s (the power of which he saw up close), but in comparison with the dramatic events in the streets during the 1960s it seemed outmoded. Robert Kennedy's unparalleled ability to command media attention revived it. Conservative columnist Holmes Alexander described the phenomenon: "The ghetto hearings have been his from the start. . . . [I]t is only when Kennedy leans forward to question that the reporters lean hard on their pencils, and only when Kennedy pokes at the administration's sorry performance . . . that the news begins to churn."[18] In the videotape era which now facilitated nightly broadcasts of both troubling scenes from the field and dramatic confrontations with witnesses, Kennedy's star power made him a Jacob Riis for the jet age. And that traveling window into the world of the "the other half"—now the "other America"—created sustained popular interest in the issue, headaches for the Johnson administration, and, at times, pressure for political action. Perhaps most important, poor Americans might easily have viewed Kennedy's whirlwind antipoverty inspections as exploitative had he not established long-lasting political relationships (often dating back to the 1960 campaign) and a record of concern. Instead they were usually encouraged by his interest.[19]

While there is legitimate room for debate about the wisdom of Kennedy's antipoverty policy proposals and strategies, the fact that he had constructed by 1968 a rare coalition of historically marginalized and excluded Americans seems clear. In spite of Kennedy's unwillingness to embrace significant structural economic change, Michael Harrington decided to endorse his presidential candidacy. The two met only once, and as Harrington later described it, the New York senator "smiled very sort of mischievously or shamefacedly or a combination of both, and said, 'Well, I guess you don't like all this stuff I say about free enterprise, do you?'" Harrington responded, "I guess you don't like all the stuff I say about socialism," and the two laughed.[20] Ultimately Harrington came to believe that Kennedy's "almost religious identification with poor people," along with his potential "to go one step beyond the Roosevelt coalition" by bringing in blue-collar whites and politically active young people, was the last best hope for the War on Poverty. "There was," Harrington contended, "at least an outside chance" of putting such an electoral coalition together for a brief moment in 1968, but in Harrington's estimation, after Kennedy's death there was "no serious chance that [the] kind of massive programs and new departures that are required are going to be passed into law."[21]

In his classic study of the North Atlantic region, political scientist Karl Deutsch asserted that the political leader most likely to facilitate a movement of social integration was one who could unite the "most inside of the outsiders" and the "most outside of the insiders" in society.[22] John Kennedy, as the first Irish Catholic in the Oval Office, thus symbolized Deutsch's outsider as insider. Robert Kennedy inherited his brother's legacy, yet what he did with the stature afforded by his unique political status was more important than the fact of his outsized public platform. Even more energetically and deliberately, Robert Kennedy attempted to embrace those at the margins of American society. "I know in my experience that John Kennedy had a real good reception among the minorities," César Chávez said. But they looked at Robert Kennedy "as sort of the minority kind of person himself. I don't know; maybe I'm wrong, but with Bobby it was like an entirely different thing. With Senator Robert Kennedy it was like he was ours."[23]

National politicians in the post-Vietnam, post-Watergate era have frequently portrayed themselves as Washington outsiders. Robert Kennedy was certainly not a Washington outsider, yet beyond the ethno-cultural roots that Robert Dallek suggests drew minorities to President Kennedy, Robert Kennedy's very personality exuded discomfort with the prevailing social, economic, and political order. Tom Hayden later called the senator "an alienated man in the body of an American success story."[24] Kennedy's natural inclination was to focus on the nation's problems. He ridiculed Vice President Hubert Humphrey's call for the "politics of joy" in the 1968 campaign. The "Kennedy perspective," according to journalist and one-time Kennedy speechwriter Jeff Greenfield, was that America "was in a lot of trouble."[25] Another aide recalled Kennedy's self-observation that he easily retained troubling statistics about juvenile delinquency and other problems but struggled to remember "remedial statistics about how much is right or how much is being done."[26]

Drawn to problems and eager to see those in distress firsthand, by 1968 Robert Kennedy had been visiting the most destitute places in the country—often beyond the media spotlight—for eight years. The poor Americans he encountered were aware of Kennedy's potential motives; they were frequently suspicious, and told him so. During a visit to Spanish Harlem with Puerto Rican prizefighter José Torres, the former light heavyweight champion asked Kennedy why he wanted to spend time visiting barrios. The New York senator quietly responded: "Because I found out something I never knew. I found out that my world was not the real world."[27]

In meetings with poor and minority groups Kennedy invariably proclaimed his interest in their challenges, as their way of life was manifestly alien to his own. Lyndon Johnson had quickly embraced an attack on poverty, in part because of his own understanding of deprivation from his rural Texas upbringing. When Johnson decided to tour Appalachia in the spring of 1964, it was to dramatize rural poverty for the rest of the nation.[28] Kennedy, in contrast, realized that he did not yet understand. On one occasion he told Jack Newfield, who grew up in Bedford-Stuyvesant, that he was jealous of his experience.[29] When he toured troubled areas to meet with young gang members or unemployed miners, which he did frequently throughout his years in both the Justice Department and the Senate with the zeal known only to a new convert, he asked them to describe their daily struggles. Influenced by these experiences, Kennedy was drawn further into the problem. He listened as the frustrations, anger, and desperation of excluded Americans boiled over at his expense, and he returned to listen repeatedly. "A skilled politician wouldn't have exposed himself like that," *Ebony* journalist Simeon Booker said, "but Bobby did. . . . [T]hey cussed him out, and they told him he didn't know what the hell it was all about. I think it made him say, 'Well, we're not going in the right direction. There's some other things that we've got to explore.'"[30] At the same time, Kennedy was willing to challenge the leaders of poor and minority communities. Even former antagonists sensed his unique concern. James Baldwin told an oral history interviewer: "Unlike [with] most people in power, there was a way to talk to him; there was a way to reach him. Something might happen."[31] By the time he ran for president, Kennedy had achieved a political rarity—an honest dialogue with racial minorities and the poor in America.

What Robert Kennedy likely would have continued to offer, which few national politicians since have conveyed, was a sense of outrage at "poverty in the midst of plenty" that would not have been easily branded a class warfare, radical, or left-wing vision. Kennedy's established reputation as a ruthless political realist and determined anticommunist might have inoculated him against charges of softheaded tax-and-spend liberalism that have dogged the Democratic Party since the presidential campaign of George McGovern, and the conservative elements of his policy prescriptions would have been primarily directed toward the needs of the poor rather the reduction of federal welfare costs. While a continued attack on poverty would have been a much tougher political sell, Kennedy might have had the leadership capacity that Ronald Reagan showed in setting a national mood of outrage against taxation that has lasted for decades. At the very least, Kennedy's ability to connect with the white working-class Americans whom Richard Nixon successfully roused in opposition to Great Society programs might have bought more time for a sustained War on Poverty to take root and for experimentation with new approaches. Ultimately this abiding national dedication—rather than programs or even structural economic changes that could be dashed by political fluctuations—would have been the only real hope. The War on Poverty never received this long-term commitment.[32]

At a minimum, Kennedy's antipoverty efforts contributed something enduring to the nation's political culture. The images of the troubled New York senator communing with hungry children and migrant farm workers, along with his repeated protestations that their plight was "unacceptable," have served as a national measuring stick, and subsequent political leaders have retraced his steps in the hope of reinvigorating the national conversation about the issue.[33]

Robert Kennedy ran for the presidency at a pivotal moment in American history. Sympathy for the War on Poverty was dwindling. The frustrations of that tempestuous era were resulting in a rising tide of white backlash and increasingly strident racial and ethnic nationalism. The promise and appeal of integration—particularly for the young—were fading. In his book *To Seek a Newer World* Kennedy rendered his vision of the political moment:

> Great gulfs now yawn between black and white, right and left; the Minutemen share nothing with the Revolutionary Armed Movement—except a conviction of their own right to use guns and violence against fellow citizens with whom they disagree. These divisions spring from different causes, and may exist entirely apart from one another: The "hippie" rejecting affluence and action is far away from the Negro sharecropper or his unemployed brother in the city slums, who are in desperate need of action to achieve a minimum share of the affluence and acceptance the other scorns. But the effect of the two divisions is more than the sum of each. For at some point—who can say where, or under what strain—there is the danger that too many will not share the same goals, the same understanding of the present or vision of the future; that our politics and our life will lose much of their capacity to move forward, because we will not agree on where we want to go—or even where we are at the time.[34]

In his estimation, young people, to whom Kennedy was drawn and who constituted the uniquely engaged generation that quickened and often led the rights revolution, were the key to renewing the national community. Two snapshots of the hopes Kennedy inspired among youth are worth considering as this book draws to a close. Deborah Rooks was a Native American student at a Catholic mission school in South Dakota when Kennedy visited in April 1968. On an otherwise cool and gray day, the students at Red Cloud School brightened when the presidential candidate arrived. Rooks thought Kennedy looked "tired and sad," but when he urged the schoolchildren to be proud of their heritage and leaders like Crazy Horse, and as "he spoke of the good in the Indian people," Rooks thought some of her classmates were going to cry. "Here was someone great," Rooks later wrote, "who could help us and wanted to help us. . . . That day was one of the happiest days at Holy Rosary [Mission] because a dream came true. We wouldn't be labeled dirty Indians anymore because he cared."[35]

One evening during the final week of the California campaign, Kennedy called for room service at the Ambassador Hotel. Juan Romero made a deal with another busboy, promising to share his tips and pick up extra trays if he could be the one to assist the waiter with any calls from the senator's suite. Romero eagerly accompanied the waiter to room 511 when the call came. Kennedy waved them in and shook hands with both of them. "At that moment," Romero reflected, "nobody could tell me I was just a busboy, or just a Mexican. I felt like I was as American as apple pie."[36]

Robert Kennedy convinced a great many poor Americans that someone at the highest levels of government understood their challenges and was trying mightily to improve their lot. He was a political figure with stature and appeal not limited to those at the margins of American life, and as such, Kennedy offered all the more promise of bridging the nation's economic and racial divides. In the end, there is no way of knowing whether he would have disappointed his emerging constituency, but for a brief moment the hope that many excluded Americans vested in Robert Kennedy brought a greater sense of community to the United States. And that, as he once counseled, makes a hell of a difference.

NOTES

INTRODUCTION

1. Richard Harwood, "McCarthy and Kennedy: Philosopher vs. Evangelist," *Washington Post*, May 26, 1968.
2. Marie Ridder, "Many-Faceted Kennedy Wages Dynamic Campaign," *Independent Star-News*, April 21, 1968, www.newspaperarchive.com.
3. Jeff Greenfield, oral history interview by Roberta Greene, December 10, 1969, transcript, 5, John F. Kennedy Library. On crowd reactions, see Richard Harwood, "Kennedy's Words Miss Crowd Mood," *Washington Post*, April 20, 1968; Richard Harwood, "In Far West, He Stresses War, Slums," *Washington Post*, April 18, 1968; Pierre Salinger et al., eds., *"An Honorable Profession": A Tribute to Robert F. Kennedy* (Garden City, N.Y.: Doubleday, 1968), 99.
4. César Chávez, oral history interview by Dennis J. O'Brien, January 28, 1970, transcript, 16–17, John F. Kennedy Library.
5. Evan Thomas, *Robert Kennedy: His Life* (New York: Simon & Schuster, 2000), 341.
6. Vine Deloria Jr., *Custer Died for Your Sins: An Indian Manifesto* (New York: Avon, 1969), 192.
7. Arthur M. Schlesinger Jr., *Robert Kennedy and His Times* (Boston: Houghton Mifflin, 1978), 778.
8. The most critical book-length works that emphasized Kennedy's opportunism are by his contemporaries Victor Lasky, *Robert Kennedy: The Myth and the Man* (New York: Pocket Books, 1968); and Ralph de Toledano, *R.F.K.: The Man Who Would Be President* (New York: Putnam, 1967). A significant scholarly study which suggests that Kennedy moved left for opportunistic reasons is Gareth Davies, *From Opportunity to Entitlement: The Transformation and Decline of Great Society Liberalism* (Lawrence: University Press of Kansas, 1996). For a 1966 discussion of Kennedy's presumed opportunism between conservative William F. Buckley Jr. and liberal columnist Murray Kempton, see *Firing Line with William F. Buckley, Jr.: "Bobby Kennedy and Other Mixed Blessings,"* prod. William F. Buckley Jr., DVD (Hoover Institution, 2008).
9. *The Kennedys*, exec. prod. Elizabeth Deane, videocassette (PBS Video, 1992).
10. Sue G. Hall, ed., *The Spirit of Robert F. Kennedy* (New York: Grosset & Dunlap, 1968), 5–6. Kennedy was acutely aware of his public image and the perception of the changes in his political persona. When he saw a television interview with Ted Sorensen in which the former aide described his unfavorable first impressions of Robert Kennedy (Sorensen's subsequent comments on Kennedy's growth had been edited out), he sent Sorensen a note on a transcript of the show: "Teddy old pal—Perhaps we could keep down the number of adjectives and adverbs describing me in 1955 and use a few more in 1967." Theodore C. Sorensen, *The Kennedy Legacy: A Peaceful Revolution for the Seventies* (New York: Mentor, 1969), 30.

11. On the efforts of social scientists to define poverty, see Alice O'Connor, *Poverty Knowledge: Social Science, Social Policy, and the Poor in Twentieth-Century U.S. History* (Princeton: Princeton University Press, 2001). On the development of the poverty line, see Gordon M. Fisher, "The Development and History of the U.S. Poverty Thresholds: A Brief Overview," aspe.hhs.gov/poverty/papers/HPTGSSIV. htm. The initial poverty thresholds were based largely on food costs and family size.

12. Billy G. Smith, ed., *Down and Out in Early America* (University Park: Pennsylvania State University Press, 2004), xii–xiii.

13. Seymour Martin Lipset, *American Exceptionalism* (New York: W. W. Norton, 1996); Sacvan Bercovitch, *The Puritan Origins of the American Self* (New Haven: Yale University Press, 1975); Deborah L. Madsen, *American Exceptionalism* (Edinburgh: Edinburgh University Press, 1998).

14. Thomas Hine, *Populuxe* (New York: Knopf, 1987), 3.

15. Michael Harrington, *The Other America: Poverty in the United States* (1962; rpt., New York: Simon & Schuster, 1997), 179.

16. Ibid., 2, 9.

17. In recent years a growing number of influential historians have been reassessing the periodization of the movement and arguing for a "long civil rights movement" that dates to the increased influence of African Americans in organized labor in the 1930s. For the seminal article that makes this case, see Jacquelyn Dowd Hall, "The Long Civil Rights Movement and the Political Uses of the Past," *Journal of American History* 91 (March 2005): 1233–63.

18. For the pathbreaking studies on the western and northern civil rights movements, see Josh Sides, *L.A. City Limits* (Berkeley: University of California Press, 2003); Robert O. Self, *American Babylon: Race and the Struggle for Postwar Oakland* (Princeton: Princeton University Press, 2005); and Thomas J. Sugrue, *Sweet Land of Liberty* (New York: Random House, 2008).

19. Alan Brinkley, "Liberty, Community, and the National Idea," *American Prospect*, November 1, 1996, www.prospect.org/cs/articles?article=liberty_community_ and_the_national_idea.

20. As one indicator of the changing vocabulary, the first usage of the term "Freedom Struggle" by the *Chicago Defender* appeared in the summer of 1961; see "Baptists Raise $40,000 in SCLC Integration Fight," *Chicago Defender*, August 5, 1961.

21. For an important survey of African American attitudes, see "The Negro in America," *Newsweek*, July 29, 1963, 15–35.

22. Davies, *From Opportunity to Entitlement*.

23. Other important studies that have identified Kennedy's vision as communitarian are Michael J. Sandel, *Democracy's Discontent* (Cambridge: Harvard University Press, 1996), 299–304; and Michael Knox Beran, *The Last Patrician: Bobby Kennedy and the End of American Aristocracy* (New York: St. Martin's, 1998), 169–75.

24. Michael Kazin, *The Populist Persuasion: An American History* (New York: Basic Books, 1995).

25. *The Kennedys.*

26. See Lewis L. Gould, *1968: The Election That Changed America* (Chicago: Ivan R. Dee, 2003); and Michael Flamm, *Law and Order: Street Crime, Civil Unrest, and the Crisis of Liberalism in the 1960s* (New York: Columbia University Press, 2005).

27. "In RFK's Final Hours, an Interview," www.msnbc.msn.com/id/21134540/vp/24949903#24949903.

1. FROM THE NEW DEAL TO THE NEW FRONTIER

1. Jerome Beatty, "Nine Kennedys and How They Grew," *Reader's Digest*, April 1939, 83–85; Wilhela Cushman, "With the Kennedy Family in London Town," *Ladies' Home Journal*, October 1938, 30–31; H. H. Hallinan, "Nine Young U.S. Ambassadors," *Parents Magazine*, September 1939, 26–27.

2. Amanda Smith, ed., *Hostage to Fortune: The Letters of Joseph P. Kennedy* (New York: Viking, 2001), 270–71.

3. *Bobby Kennedy in His Own Words*, exec. prod. Peter W. Kunhardt, videocassette (HBO Home Video, 1990).

4. Evan Thomas, *Robert Kennedy: His Life* (New York: Simon & Schuster, 2000), 39.

5. Nigel Hamilton, *JFK: Reckless Youth* (New York: Random House, 1992), 627, 665, 766; Helen O'Donnell, *A Common Good: The Friendship of Robert F. Kennedy and Kenneth P. O'Donnell* (New York: Morrow, 1998), 15.

6. Rose Kennedy, *Times to Remember* (Garden City, N.Y.: Doubleday, 1974), 103. A book that explores this topic in some depth, while not probing the ramifications of his Catholicism more particularly, is Konstantin Sidorenko, *Robert F. Kennedy: A Spiritual Biography* (New York: Crossroad, 2000).

7. Peter Collier and David Horowitz, *The Kennedys: An American Drama* (New York: Summit, 1984), 119.

8. David Hackett, oral history interview by John Douglas, July 22, 1970, transcript, 4, John F. Kennedy Library.

9. Ibid., 65.

10. Robert E. Thompson and Hortense Myers, *Robert F. Kennedy: The Brother Within* (New York: Dell, 1962), 112; Peter Edelman, oral history interview by Roberta Greene, July 15, 1969, transcript, 98, John F. Kennedy Library; Gerald Tremblay, oral history interview by Roberta Greene, January 8, 1970, transcript, 11, John F. Kennedy Library.

11. James T. Patterson, *America's Struggle against Poverty in the Twentieth Century* (Cambridge: Harvard University Press, 2000), 77.

12. Herbert J. Gans, "The Failure of Urban Renewal: A Critique and Some Proposals," *Commentary*, April 1965, 29–37.

13. Theodore Andrews, "John F. Kennedy, Lyndon Johnson, and the Politics of Poverty, 1960–1967" (Ph.D. diss., Stanford University, 1997), 30.

14. Ibid., 44.

15. Ibid., 47.

16. Ibid., 48–50.

17. For a thorough and incisive study on the role of social scientists, see Alice O'Connor, *Poverty Knowledge: Social Science, Social Policy, and the Poor in Twentieth-Century U.S. History* (Princeton: Princeton University Press, 2001).

18. Michael B. Katz, *The Undeserving Poor: From the War on Poverty to the War on Welfare* (New York: Pantheon Books, 1989), 9.

19. Even in 1964, the year the War on Poverty would be declared by President Johnson, a Gallup poll of middle-class Americans revealed that by a narrow margin more respondents believed that "lack of effort" was more to blame for an individual's poverty than "circumstances beyond his control." Cited in Patterson, *America's Struggle*, 106.

20. Ibid., 88–93; Alice O'Connor, "Neither Charity nor Relief: The War on Poverty and the Effort to Redefine the Basis of Social Provision," in *With Us Always: A History of Private Charity and Public Welfare*, ed. Donald T. Critchlow and Charles H. Parker (Lanham, Md.: Rowman & Littlefield, 1998), 194.

21. For one example of incremental reform, see Edward D. Berkowitz and Kim McQuaid, "Welfare Reform in the 1950s," in *Poverty and Public Policy in Modern America*, ed. Donald T. Critchlow and Ellis W. Hawley (Chicago: Dorsey Press, 1989), 200–210.

22. Michael Harrington, *The Other America: Poverty in the United States* (1962; rpt. New York: Simon & Schuster, 1997), 17.

23. Thomas Hine, *Populuxe* (New York: Knopf, 1987), 3.

24. Jean Stein and George Plimpton, eds., *American Journey: The Times of Robert Kennedy* (New York: Harcourt Brace Jovanovich, 1970), 50.

25. "A Look behind Those Russian Smiles," *U.S. News & World Report*, October 21, 1955, 137–38.

26. James W. Hilty, *Robert Kennedy: Brother Protector* (Philadelphia: Temple University Press, 1997), 99.

27. Robert F. Kennedy, *The Enemy Within* (New York: Popular Library, 1960), 137.

28. Murray Kempton, "The Uncommitted," *The Progressive*, September 1960, 17.

29. David J. O'Brien, "Social Teaching, Social Action, Social Gospel," *U.S. Catholic Historian* 5, no. 2 (1986): 199.

30. Athan G. Theoharis and John Stuart Cox, *The Boss: J. Edgar Hoover and the Great American Inquisition* (New York: Bantam, 1990), 233–34.

31. Andrew Greeley, *The Catholic Imagination* (Berkeley: University of California Press, 2000); Andrew Greeley, "Protestant and Catholic: Is the Analogical Imagination Extinct?" *American Sociological Review* 54 (August 1989): 485–502; John E. Tropman, *The Catholic Ethic and the Spirit of Community* (Washington, D.C.: Georgetown University Press, 2002); Mary E. Bendyna, "The Catholic Ethic in American Politics" (Ph.D. diss., Georgetown University, 2000).

32. William Lee Miller, "Religion and Political Attitudes," in *Religious Perspectives in American Culture*, ed. James Ward Smith and A. Leland Jamison (Princeton: Princeton University Press, 1961), 87.

33. Greeley, *Catholic Imagination*, 130; John T. McGreevy, *Catholicism and American Freedom: A History* (New York: W. W. Norton, 2003), 126–70.

34. Kennedy, *Enemy Within*, 306.

35. For the best study on Kennedy as his brother's keeper, see Hilty, *Brother Protector*.

36. "A Look behind Those Russian Smiles," 146.

37. Ibid. The Globetrotters were used as cultural ambassadors throughout the cold war, most famously playing before 75,000 fans in Berlin in 1951.

38. Scott Stossel, *Sarge: The Life and Times of Sargent Shriver* (Washington, D.C.: Smithsonian Books, 2004), 119–23; Anthony Lewis, "What Drives Bobby Kennedy," *New York Times Sunday Magazine*, April 7, 1963, 59.

39. Andrews, "Kennedy, Johnson," 31.

40. Address by Robert F. Kennedy at Georgetown University, March 15, 1958; and Address by Robert F. Kennedy at Universal Notre Dame Night in Detroit, April 9, 1958, Robert F. Kennedy Pre-Administration Papers, Working Files, Select Committee, Speech File, 1957–1959, box 114, John F. Kennedy Library.

41. Carl M. Brauer, *John F. Kennedy and the Second Reconstruction* (New York: Columbia University Press, 1977), 20–29; Nick Bryant, *The Bystander: John F. Kennedy and the Struggle for Black Equality* (New York: Basic Books, 2006), 86.

42. Bryant, *Bystander*, 63; "Sen. Kennedy Takes Exception," *Chicago Defender*, April 6, 1957.

43. "Whispering Breezes," *Chicago Defender*, August 3, 1957; Lester Granger, "Manhattan and Beyond," *New York Amsterdam News*, November 30, 1957.

44. "'Christmas Seal' Fails to Stick," *Chicago Defender*, December 15, 1959.

45. Brauer, *Second Reconstruction*, 27–28; Hilty, *Brother Protector*, 169–70.

46. Brauer, *Second Reconstruction*, 30.

47. See Daniel B. Fleming Jr., *Kennedy vs. Humphrey, West Virginia, 1960: The Pivotal Battle for the Democratic Presidential Nomination* (Jefferson, N.C.: MacFarland, 1992).

48. Alfred Chapman, oral history interview by William L. Young, February 15, 1965, transcript, John F. Kennedy Library.

49. "The Democratic Pollster," *Time*, April 6, 1962, 21.

50. Arthur M. Schlesinger Jr., *Robert Kennedy and His Times* (Boston: Houghton Mifflin, 1978), 198. When Robert Kennedy consulted with the head of West Virginia's Junior Chamber of Commerce, Frank Fischer, he urged a fourth "F": "Franklin." Robert Dallek, *An Unfinished Life: John F. Kennedy, 1917–1963* (Boston: Little, Brown, 2003), 252.

51. According to historian Richard Drake, well over half of those employed as coal miners in the Appalachian region in 1950 had lost their jobs to automation by the middle of the decade. Richard B. Drake, *A History of Appalachia* (Lexington: University Press of Kentucky, 2001), 207.

52. Joseph Alsop, "Slab Fork," *Victoria Advocate*, April 17, 1960, www.newspaperarchive.com.

53. "Kennedy Sights Opposition Plot," *Beckley Post-Herald*, April 12, 1960, www.newspaperarchive.com. The campaign ran an advertisement in West Virginia newspapers reminding residents that Kennedy cared about them. "For weeks," proclaimed the ad, Kennedy "lived among you," witnessing firsthand "idle mines and deserted plants" along with "'Eisenhower curtains' row on row." The advertisement called Humphrey a "tool of a cynical 'Gang-Up'" and a "front man." "Who Cares? Kennedy Cares!" advertisement, *Charleston Daily Mail*, May 4, 1960, www.newspaperarchive.com.

54. Theodore H. White, *The Making of the President, 1960* (New York: Pocket Books, 1961), 127.

55. Richard N. Goodwin, *Remembering America: A Voice from the Sixties* (Boston: Little, Brown, 1988), 88. For further analysis of Humphrey's style, see David Halberstam, *The Powers That Be* (New York: Knopf, 1979), 324.

56. White, *Making of the President*, 127; Goodwin, *Remembering America*, 86.

57. Topper Sherwood, "Kennedy in West Virginia," *Goldenseal*, Fall 2000, 15.

58. On Kennedy and coal miners, see "Kennedy Had 2 Close Calls at Itmann Mine," *Raleigh Register*, April 28, 1960, www.newspaperarchive.com; Herb Little, "Roosevelt Joins Kennedy Caravan on Southern Trip," *Charleston Daily Mail*, April 26, 1960; Anthony W. Ponton, "John F. Kennedy in West Virginia, 1960–1963" (M.A. thesis, Marshall University, 2004), 43–50. Kennedy won McDowell County, one of the poorest in the coal region, by a five-to-one margin. "Kennedy Scores Sweep in West Virginia Vote," *Bridgeport Post*, May 11, 1960, www.newspaperarchive.com. For oral history examples, see John Amos, oral history interview by William L. Young, August 6, 1965, transcript, John F. Kennedy Library; and Rev. Harley Bailey, oral history interview by William L. Young, December 5, 1964, transcript, John F. Kennedy Library. West Virginia journalist Thomas Stafford, who covered the campaign, contended that "in the end money provided the winning edge." Thomas F. Stafford, *Afflicting the Comfortable: Journalism and Politics in West Virginia* (Morgantown: West Virginia University Press, 2005), 76. Conversely, biographer Evan Thomas asserts that "the money was not decisive." See Thomas, *Robert Kennedy*, 95; Stafford, *Afflicting the Comfortable*, 78; and Peter Edelman, oral history interview by Larry Hackman, March 13, 1974, transcript, 18, John F. Kennedy Library.

59. William Walton, oral history interview by Jean Stein, transcript, Jean Stein Papers, box 9, John F. Kennedy Library.

60. Edelman, oral history interview by Hackman, 18.

61. Hackett, oral history interview, 64.

62. Stafford, *Afflicting the Comfortable*, 78–79. According to Stafford, they did not; in large part because of various forms of federal assistance, the state would make significant economic progress during the Kennedy presidency. See also Fleming, *Kennedy vs. Humphrey*, 166–69.

63. Schlesinger, *Robert Kennedy*, 215; Alex Poinsett, *Walking with Presidents: Louis Martin and the Rise of Black Political Power* (Lanham, Md.: Madison Books, 1997), 62.

64. On registration efforts, see Harris Wofford, *Of Kennedys and Kings: Making Sense of the Sixties* (Pittsburgh: University of Pittsburgh Press, 1980), 61; Poinsett, *Walking with Presidents*, 68; and Brauer, *Second Reconstruction*, 42. On the civil rights plank, see Brauer, *Second Reconstruction*, 42; and Schlesinger, *Robert Kennedy*, 215–16.

65. Brauer, *Second Reconstruction*, 36; "The Democratic Platform," *Washington Afro-American*, July 16, 1960; "At the Convention," *Washington Afro-American*, July 30, 1960.

66. Schlesinger, *Robert Kennedy*, 63.

67. Poinsett, *Walking with Presidents*, 63–64, 68–69.

68. Edwin O. Guthman and Jeffrey Shulman, eds., *Robert Kennedy: In His Own Words* (New York: Bantam, 1988), 72.

69. Hilty, *Robert Kennedy*, 171; Poinsett, *Walking with Presidents*, 73.

70. Guthman and Schulman, *In His Own Words*, 72.

71. Brauer, *Second Reconstruction*, 63. Editorials in the *Washington Afro-American* and *Chicago Defender* also noted Kennedy's statement. Carlos McCormick, a Kennedy campaign aide serving as a liaison to Mexican American groups, had also pushed for such a statement, which may have found an even more receptive hearing in the Latino community. "Kennedy-Nixon Debate," *Washington Afro-American*, October 1, 1960; "Kennedy Will Be Great President," *Chicago Defender*, November 19, 1960; Kenneth C. Burt, *The Search for a Civic Voice: California Latino Politics* (Claremont, Calif.: Regina Books, 2007), 189–90.

72. Wofford, *Of Kennedys and Kings*, 63.

73. Burt, *Search for a Civic Voice*, 190; Thomas W. Cowger, *The National Congress of American Indians: The Founding Years* (Lincoln: University of Nebraska Press, 2001), 130.

74. Poinsett, *Walking with Presidents*, 78.

75. James L. Hicks, "Running Backwards," *New York Amsterdam News*, October 13, 1960.

76. "Jackie Robinson Raps Kennedy," *Chicago Defender*, April 9, 1960.

77. "Jackie Robinson," *Chicago Defender*, August 30, 1960; "Jackie Robinson," *Los Angeles Sentinel*, October 13, 1960; "Jackie Says Kennedy Has Negro Vote Now," *New York Amsterdam News*, October 15, 1960. One Kennedy precinct worker said that the candidate's brother "must have had a hole in his head" to attack Robinson. Paul Duke, "New York and Religion: Issue May Aid Kennedy with Jews and Negroes as Well as Catholics," *Wall Street Journal*, September 15, 1960.

78. Robert Spivack, "Watch on the Potomac," *Chicago Daily Defender*, September 28, 1960.

79. Bryant, *Bystander*, 176–78.

80. For the best accounts of the King calls, see Wofford, *Of Kennedys and Kings*, 11–28; Thomas, *Robert Kennedy*, 100–104; Brauer, *Second Reconstruction*, 46–52; Hilty, *Brother Protector*, 171–75; Bryant, *Bystander*, 180–85.

81. Stephen B. Oates, *Let the Trumpet Sound: A Life of Martin Luther King, Jr.* (New York: Mentor, 1985), 159; Wofford, *Of Kennedys and Kings*, 22.

82. Wofford, *Of Kennedys and Kings*, 23.

83. Edward Peeks, "King Freed after Sen. Kennedy Intervenes," *Washington Afro-American*, October 29, 1960.

84. "Kennedy's Call to Mrs. King Won Votes," *New York Amsterdam News*, November 5, 1960; James L. Hicks, "All Together Again," *New York Amsterdam News*, November 5, 1960.

85. Hicks, "All Together Again." Among this group of advisers were Marjorie Lawson, Vel Phillips, and Frank Reeves. Brauer, *Second Reconstruction*, 44–45.

86. Marie Brookter, "Many Factors Turn Negroes to Kennedy," *Chicago Defender*, November 8, 1960.

87. For analysis of the African American vote, see Bryant, *Bystander*, 187; Associated Negro Press, "Negro, as Voter and as Issue Helped to Insure Kennedy Win," *New York Amsterdam News*, November 19, 1960; Anthony Lewis, "Negro Vote Held Vital to Kennedy Win," *New York Times*, November 27, 1960; James Booker, "Democrats Sweep Harlem by 3–1 Margin," *New York Amsterdam News*, November 12, 1960; Layhmond Robinson, "Negro Vote Kennedy Big Push," *New York Times*, November 11, 1960.

88. Les Matthews, "Reaction as Kennedy Won," *New York Amsterdam News*, November 12, 1960.

89. Wofford, *Of Kennedys and Kings*, 28; Layhmond Robinson, "Baltimore Study Uncovers Apathy," *New York Times*, October 23, 1960.

90. "It's Kennedy: AFRO's Choice for President," *Washington Afro-American*, October 29, 1960. In "hundreds of interviews in major Northern Negro population centers from coast to coast," the *Wall Street Journal* found "almost no discernible anti-Catholicism." An African American interviewee from Pittsburgh echoed the sentiments of *Washington Afro-American* editors: "Being a member of a minority group himself . . . I think [Kennedy would] be beneficial to the Negroes and more inclined to fight bigotry." Robert D. Novak, "The Negro Vote," *Wall Street Journal*, October 25, 1960.

91. Steven Mintz, ed., *Mexican American Voices* (St. James, N.Y.: Brandywine Press, 2000), 189.

92. Chávez met with John Kennedy in 1959 to discuss the registration efforts of the Community Service Organization (CSO) and requested a free hand from the campaign to register voters in the barrios. The Massachusetts senator agreed, over-riding concerns from staffers. Chávez ultimately saw the Viva Kennedy movement as "a big PR thing," while the real work was done by organizers such as those from the CSO. César Chávez, oral history interview by Dennis J. O'Brien, January 28, 1970, transcript, 3, John F. Kennedy Library.

93. Ignacio García, *Viva Kennedy: Mexican Americans in Search of Camelot* (College Station: Texas A&M University Press, 2000), 45.

94. Burt, *Search for a Civic Voice*, 185–94.

95. García, *Viva Kennedy*, 105. García notes that 91 percent of Mexican Americans in Texas voted for Kennedy, and Kennedy's margin of 200,000 among Mexican Americans there offset the 150,000 vote advantage Nixon amassed among white Texans. For further analysis, see Mark R. Levy and Michael S. Kramer, *The Ethnic Factor: How America's Minorities Decide Elections* (New York: Simon and Schuster, 1972), 78; Burt, *Search for a Civic Voice*, 193–94; Gladwin Hill, "Religious Factor Weighed in Texas," *New York Times*, November 10, 1960.

96. García, *Viva Kennedy*, 106.

97. Ibid., 57–58. García contends that Kennedy's Catholicism served as the "cultural bridge" to Mexican Americans.

98. Chávez, oral history interview, 16.

99. The advertisement also called Kennedy "the simple people's man." Campaign poster, copy in author's possession.

100. Peter Kihss, "City Spanish Vote at a Record High," *New York Times*, November 2, 1960.

101. Peter Kihss, "A Kennedy and a Rockefeller Seek Puerto Rican Votes Here," *New York Times*, August 25, 1960.

102. Kihss, "City Spanish Vote."

103. Thomas Sowell, *Ethnic America: A History* (New York: Basic Books, 1981), 239.

104. "Kennedy, Dems Bid for Indian Vote," *Arizona Daily Sun*, November 7, 1960, www .newspaperarchive.com. Kennedy had been working with George since the summer, when the NCAI leader was invited, somewhat strangely, to a gathering on the patio at the Kennedy Hyannis Port compound with other representatives of the "Nationalities Division" of the Democratic National Committee. The group planned outreach to recent immigrants and ethnic groups from eastern European nations, a sum total of twenty-two ethnic groups. While there George "told of Indian problems." "Kennedy Promised Support," *High Point Enterprise*, August 7, 1960, www.newspaperarchive.com; "American Indians 'Happy' over Democratic Platform," *Arizona Daily Sun*, August 18, 1960, www.newspaper archive.com.

105. "Indian Aid Pledged: Kennedy Vows to Develop Reservation Resources," *New York Times*, November 18, 1960.

106. "Kennedy, Dems Bid for Indian Vote."

107. On the economic situation in the weeks before the 1960 election, see "Consensus: Mild Recession," *Time*, October 31, 1960, 74; Richard Rutter, "Wanted: A Word for '60 Economy," *New York Times*, October 9, 1960; "Mueller Rejects Recession Talk," *New York Times*, October 22, 1960; Ann Mari May, "President Eisenhower, Economic Policy, and the 1960 Election," *Journal of Economic History* 50, no. 2 (June 1990): 417–24.

108. Kihss, "City Spanish Vote."

109. Austin C. Wehrwein, "Chicago District Sheds Its Apathy," *New York Times*, November 2, 1960. For further discussion of economic motives on the part of African Americans, see Anthony Lewis, "Negro Vote Held Vital to Kennedy," *New York Times*, November 27, 1960; "Why Kennedy Won?" *Chicago Defender*, December 1, 1960; Novak, "Negro Vote."

110. Novak, "Negro Vote."

111. Lester Granger, "Battleaxe and Bread," *California Eagle*, December 8, 1960.

112. "Why Kennedy Won?"

113. Advertisement, *New York Times*, September 14, 1960.

114. A. H. Raskin, "Labor Drive Aids Kennedy's Hopes," *New York Times*, November 6, 1960.

115. Dallek, *Unfinished Life*, 294.

116. John Alexander Williams, *Appalachia: A History* (Chapel Hill: University of North Carolina Press, 2002), 339.

117. Advertisement, *New York Times*, August 22, 1960; "Campaign Issues in the Words of the Two Candidates," *New York Times*, October 2, 1960; Patterson, *America's Struggle*, 122.

118. Julius Duscha, "Kennedy Says U.S. Will Need 3-Front Action Early in '61," *Washington Post*, September 21, 1960; Anthony Lewis, "Kennedy Pledges to 'Outdo' Soviet in 'First 90 Days,'" *New York Times*, September 21, 1960.

119. "Kennedy on the Move," *Washington Post*, September 22, 1960.

120. James L. Sundquist, *Politics and Policy: The Eisenhower, Kennedy, and Johnson Years* (Washington, D.C.: Brookings Institution, 1968), 72.

121. Ibid.; "Kennedy Pledges Help to Jobless," *New York Times*, September 20, 1960. For the political advantage Kennedy gained in one of the few West Virginia districts that had voted Republican in the previous election cycle, see A. H. Raskin, "See-Saw District Leans to Kennedy," *New York Times*, November 1, 1960.

122. "Text of the Debate between Kennedy and Nixon Held on Television in Chicago," *New York Times*, September 28, 1960.

123. "Nixon's Tone Gets Tougher," *Ada Daily News*, September 28, 1960, www .newspaperarchive.com.

124. Goodwin, *Remembering America*, 86.

125. John D. Morris, "Kennedy Unit Spurs Needy-Areas Drive," *New York Times*, December 10, 1960; Julius Duscha, "Depressed Area Report Asks Speed," *Washington Post*, January 2, 1960; Executive Order 10914, www.lib.umich.edu/govdocs/ jfkeo/eo/10914.htm.

126. See Laurence Stern, "Drive to Help Migrants Seen Won in Election: Meeting Told Kennedy Success Is 'Best Chance in Our Lifetime,'" *Washington Post*, November 18, 1960; "Kennedy Praised for Indian Stand," *New York Times*, November 17, 1960; "Indian Aid Pledged"; García, *Viva Kennedy*, 9.

127. Victor Riesel, "Sen. Douglas Kennedy's New Medicine Man," *Manitowoc Herald-Times*, December 16, 1960, www.newspaperarchive.com.

128. Hilty, *Brother Protector*, 186–90. Other campaign managers named attorney general in the twentieth century include Harry Daugherty (under Harding and Coolidge), Howard McGrath (Truman), Herbert Brownell (Eisenhower), and John Mitchell (Nixon).

129. Vincent J. Burke, "Fear Bobby May Hurt President Kennedy," *Chicago Defender*, December 31, 1960.

130. Poinsett, *Walking with Presidents*, 83, 87.

2. AT THE FULCRUM OF THE MOVEMENT

1. Godfrey Hodgson, *America in Our Time* (Princeton: Princeton University Press, 2005), 67–98.

2. Two outstanding recent studies which explore the depth of the national fissure are Maurice Isserman and Michael Kazin, *America Divided: The Civil War of the 1960s* (New York: Oxford University Press, 2004); and Rick Perlstein, *Nixonland: The Rise of a President and the Fracturing of America* (New York: Scribner, 2008).

3. Aldon Morris has noted that sit-ins were employed before the one in Greensboro, North Carolina, in 1960, but that is when the direct action protest tactic first received mass attention and began to multiply in unprecedented ways.

Aldon D. Morris, *The Origins of the Civil Rights Movement: Black Communities Organizing for Change* (New York: Free Press, 1984), 188–94.

4. James T. Patterson, *Grand Expectations: The United States, 1945–1974* (New York: Oxford University Press, 1996), 683.

5. Steven F. Lawson, *Running for Freedom: Civil Rights and Black Politics in America since 1941* (Philadelphia: Temple University Press, 1991), 40–41, 47–58. The Southern Manifesto was a pledge to employ "all lawful means" to overturn the *Brown* decision, and it became yet another symbol of the rising tide of white southern defiance. Eighty-two congressmen and nineteen senators—all but two were Democrats—signed the document.

6. Charlotte G. O'Kelly, "Black Newspapers and the Black Protest Movement, 1946–1972," *Phylon* 41, no. 4 (1980): 317.

7. Lawson, *Running for Freedom*, 51.

8. "No Longer Important," *Washington Afro-American*, December 24, 1960; "For the Undecided," *Washington Afro-American*, October 15, 1960. Expressions of disappointment and frustration with Eisenhower permeated African American newspapers in the final months of the administration. For other examples, see "Ike Gets It Said," *Washington Afro-American*, March 19, 1960; "It's Kennedy: The AFRO's Choice for President," *Washington Afro-American*, October 29, 1960; "Tuesday's Election as We See It," *Washington Afro-American*, November 12, 1960; "Too Little, Too Late," *California Eagle*, December 29, 1960; "The Eisenhower Years," *California Eagle*, January 19, 1961.

9. "Kennedy Will Be Great President," *Chicago Defender*, November 19, 1960; Simeon Booker, "What Negroes Can Expect from Kennedy," *Ebony*, January 1961, 33.

10. Edward Peeks, "President-Elect Shows He Can Handle Dixie," *Washington Afro-American*, November 12, 1960.

11. "The Kennedy Cabinet," *California Eagle*, December 22, 1960.

12. The best assessments of Robert Kennedy and the Kennedy administration on civil rights are James W. Hilty, *Robert Kennedy: Brother Protector* (Philadelphia: Temple University Press, 1997), 289–494; Carl M. Brauer, *John F. Kennedy and the Second Reconstruction* (New York: Columbia University Press, 1977); Taylor Branch, *Parting the Waters: America in the King Years, 1954–1963* (New York: Simon & Schuster, 1988); and Lawson, *Running for Freedom*, 66–95.

13. The hierarchical military metaphor is not entirely appropriate for the mass movement in the South and elsewhere, as several civil rights organizations—most notably SNCC—emphasized a bottom-up conception of leadership. See Wesley C. Hogan, *Many Minds, One Heart: SNCC's Dream for a New America* (Chapel Hill: University of North Carolina Press, 2007).

14. "All the Natives Are Restless," *Ebony*, January 1962, 80.

15. On the importance of African American publications to the civil rights movement and as windows into African American life generally, see Thomas J. Sugrue, *Sweet Land of Liberty* (New York: Random House, 2008), 47, 135–36.

16. The extent of Robert Kennedy's relationship with editors is unclear, but he did speak before the National Newspaper Publishers Association convention in 1962,

won their national award in 1963, and sent a letter complimenting the *Washington Afro-American* for "doing an excellent job of reporting the news in a responsible and fair manner." "We Get Letters from Such Interesting and Nice People," *Washington Afro-American*, February 16, 1963.

17. Louis Lautier, "Kennedy Faces Problems," *Atlanta Daily World*, January 18, 1961.

18. Louis Lautier, "Crystal Clear Strategy," *Atlanta Daily World*, May 13, 1961.

19. Alex Poinsett, *Walking with Presidents: Louis Martin and the Rise of Black Political Power* (Lanham, Md.: Madison Books, 1997), 87; Harris Wofford, *Of Kennedys and Kings: Making Sense of the Sixties* (Pittsburgh: University of Pittsburgh Press, 1980), 137.

20. Robert F. Kennedy, "Law Day Address at the University of Georgia Law School," www.americanrhetoric.com/speeches/rfkgeorgialawschool.htm.

21. Anthony Lewis, "Robert Kennedy Vows in Georgia to Act on Rights," *New York Times*, May 7, 1961. According to one student's account, the ovation Kennedy received "was as loud and as long as they give the football team for winning a game against Georgia Tech." Benjamin Mays, "My View," *Pittsburgh Courier*, June 3, 1961.

22. "Bob Kennedy Tells Dixie: I'll Enforce the Law; Harlem Lawyers Praise Speech," *New York Amsterdam News*, May 13, 1961; Jimmy Booker, "Uptown Lowdown," *New York Amsterdam News*, May 13, 1961. Martin wrote Kennedy privately: "Your speech in Georgia was a peach. Congratulations are pouring in from brothers everywhere, here and abroad. If you keep this up, one of these days I might be able to go back home. Seriously, you showed great statesmanship, and I am honored to call you 'honorary brother.'" Poinsett, *Walking with Presidents*, 103.

23. "Kennedy Speech on Civil Rights Wins Thanks of NAACP," *Washington Afro-American*, May 20, 1961.

24. Fred Shuttlesworth, "A Southerner Speaks," *Pittsburgh Courier*, April 15, 1961; Raymond Arsenault, *Freedom Riders: 1961 and the Struggle for Racial Justice* (New York: Oxford University Press, 2006), 78; Morris, *Origins of the Civil Rights Movement*, 45, 68–73; Hilty, *Brother Protector*, 318.

25. Hilty, *Brother Protector*, 317.

26. Edwin O. Guthman and Jeffrey Shulman, eds., *Robert Kennedy: In His Own Words* (New York: Bantam, 1988), 93.

27. "Attorney General's Pleas," *New York Times*, May 25, 1961.

28. Cartoon, *Washington Afro-American*, June 3, 1961; "Disappointing Advice," *Washington Afro-American*, May 27, 1961. See also "Ridiculous," *New York Amsterdam News*, June 24, 1961.

29. James L. Hicks, "The Proposition," *New York Amsterdam News*, June 10, 1961.

30. Louis Lautier, "The Impossible," *Washington Afro-American*, June 6, 1961.

31. "Pittsburghers Speak Up," *Pittsburgh Courier*, June 10, 1961.

32. "So True," *New York Amsterdam News*, July 21, 1961.

33. James L. Hicks, "Ride, Daddy, Ride," *New York Amsterdam News*, July 1, 1961. Loren Miller had recognized the emerging generational identity shift a year earlier in looking at students and the sit-in movement. Loren Miller, "Loren Miller Says . . . ," *California Eagle*, March 10, 1960.

34. Victor S. Navasky, *Kennedy Justice* (New York: Atheneum, 1971), 171. Navasky's study is the best analysis of Robert Kennedy's leadership in the Justice Department. For the clearest explication of the Justice Department's rationale, see Burke Marshall's comments in Wofford, *Of Kennedys and Kings*, 160.

35. Hilty, *Brother Protector*, 328; "Bob Kennedy Rejects Bid of Nonviolent Committee," *Chicago Daily Defender*, April 12, 1962. Robert Kennedy was also reluctant to give credit to the protesters when discussing the Freedom Rides at the national convention of African American insurance agents in the summer of 1962, attributing successes to "local officials and citizens." Robert F. Kennedy, "Kennedy Sums Up His Civil Rights Record," *Chicago Defender*, August 11, 1962.

36. Morris, *Origins of the Civil Rights Movement*, 235.

37. For the best analysis of the expectations engendered by the Justice Department to protect registration workers, see Charles M. Payne, *I've Got the Light of Freedom: The Organizing Tradition and the Mississippi Freedom Struggle* (Berkeley: University of California Press, 1996), 109–10.

38. Navasky, *Kennedy Justice*, 169; Wofford, *Of Kennedys and Kings*, 158–61; Poinsett, *Walking with Presidents*, 100–101; Lawson, *Running for Freedom*, 81. That was in fact what Justice Department official John Doar was working on in Birmingham when he telephoned the attorney general to warn him of the mob violence which soon incapacitated John Seigenthaler. Hilty, *Brother Protector*, 322.

39. Branch, *Parting the Waters*, 478–82; Lawson, *Running for Freedom*, 82–83.

40. "Arrest Mobsters Who Burned Freedom Ride," *New York Amsterdam News*, September 9, 1961; John Dittmer, *Local People: The Struggle for Civil Rights in Mississippi* (Urbana: University of Illinois Press, 1994), 95; "ICC Ruling: 'Sit Anywhere,'" *New York Amsterdam News*, September 30, 1961; "The End of Bus Jim Crow," *California Eagle*, September 28, 1961.

41. "Bobby Kennedy Kept Faith," *Washington Afro-American*, September 30, 1961. For another positive review, see Louis Lautier, "Definitive Action," *Atlanta Daily World*, August 10, 1961.

42. Jackie Robinson, "Our Big Stick," *New York Amsterdam News*, August 12, 1961. Robinson would continue to see the attorney general as more committed than the president to civil rights. See Jackie Robinson, "How the Average Negro Is Thinking," *New York Amsterdam News*, June 23, 1962.

43. Hilty, *Brother Protector*, 318.

44. *King: A Filmed Record . . . Montgomery to Memphis*, prod. Ely Landau, videocassette (Pacific Arts Video, 1988); "Wallace Cries Gov't. Got Talk on Segregation," *Atlanta Daily World*, December 14, 1962; Evan Thomas, *Robert Kennedy: His Life* (New York: Simon & Schuster, 2000), 274.

45. "Dixie Has Duty to Comply with School Desegregation Decision," *Atlanta Daily World*, May 3, 1962; "Little Rock to Get into Train Shipping Act," *Atlanta Daily World*, May 5, 1962; "Freedom Riding in Reverse," *Atlanta Daily World*, May 25, 1962. Fewer than twenty African Americans actually accepted the bus tickets, but the campaign got so much publicity that Gallup conducted a poll on the "Negro Resettlement" initiative; 71 percent of respondents had an "unfavorable" view and 9 percent

favored the project. George H. Gallup, ed., *The Gallup Poll* (Wilmington, Del.: Scholarly Resources, 1971), 1768.

46. "Secret Weapon," *New York Amsterdam News*, November 4, 1961; "SCLC Aide Likes Robert Kennedy," *Washington Afro-American*, January 6, 1962; Simeon Booker, "'Mr. Civil Rights' Goes to Africa," *Ebony*, October 1961, 89–91. *Ebony* was sometimes criticized as a lifestyle magazine for the black middle class, but Adam Green has forcefully argued that not only was it more socially conscious and perceptive than its critics allowed, but also the magazine is essential to understanding "modern black community and identity." Adam Green, *Selling the Race: Culture, Community, and Black Chicago, 1940–1955* (Chicago: University of Chicago Press, 2007), 131–32.

47. Chuck Stone, "Pres. Kennedy's Not Weak, Our Political System Is," *Washington Afro-American*, November 4, 1961. The *Afro*, which had a reputation as one of the most assertively progressive black newspapers, even ran a front-page photo referring to the president as "Our Man." "Whee! Our Man!" *Washington Afro-American*, May 26, 1962. On the reputation of the newspaper, see Chuck Stone, "Confession of an 'Angry Young Man' Who Is Neither Angry Nor Young," *Washington Afro-American*, January 5, 1963. For other positive assessments, see "Negro Progress in 1961," *Ebony*, January 1962, 21–28; and "Looking Ahead," *Los Angeles Sentinel*, December 28, 1961. The *Sentinel* called the attorney general's "fearless crusade against racial discrimination in all forms" a "signal achievement."

48. "Kennedy's Record Since '61," *Chicago Defender*, April 14, 1962.

49. Chuck Stone, "How Badly Does President Kennedy Want Civil Rights?" *Washington Afro-American*, May 26, 1962; Louis Lautier, "Says JFK in Trouble with Civil Righters," *Washington Afro-American*, April 21, 1962.

50. Josh Sides, *L.A. City Limits* (Berkeley: University of California Press, 2003), 100; "Pen Stroke Needed Now," *California Eagle*, August 10, 1961; "Time to Stroke That Pen," *California Eagle*, December 14, 1961; "Kennedy Breaks a Promise," *California Eagle*, January 11, 1962; "Is President Kennedy Backing Down?" *California Eagle*, April 26, 1962.

51. For an example, see "SNCC Challenges Atty. Gen. Kennedy to Protect Georgia Voter Registration," *Chicago Defender*, July 28, 1962.

52. "Kennedys Asked to View Bias in Mississippi," *Atlanta Daily World*, October 11, 1962; "NAACP Asks President to Visit Mississippi," *Atlanta Daily World*, October 18, 1962.

53. David Maddux, "New Registration March Broken Up by Delta Police," *Atlanta Daily World*, April 4, 1963.

54. Fleming, the former head of the SRC, had an instrumental role in shaping the Voter Education Project with the Justice Department. Navasky, *Kennedy Justice*, 118–19; David Garrow, *Bearing the Cross: Martin Luther King, Jr., and the Southern Christian Leadership Conference* (New York: HarperCollins, 2004), 162–63.

55. Jean Stein and George Plimpton, eds., *American Journey: The Times of Robert Kennedy* (New York: Harcourt Brace Jovanovich, 1970), 111–12.

56. "The Right to Vote," *Chicago Defender*, April 16, 1962; "The Poll Tax Issue," *Chicago Defender*, August 30, 1962. In this same period the *Defender* praised the attorney general for his effectiveness in desegregating the petroleum industry in the South.

"How to End Job Bias," *Chicago Defender*, August 22, 1962. For a critical exception on the protection of voter registration volunteers, see "Bob Kennedy Hit on Vote Lethargy," *Los Angeles Sentinel*, January 17, 1963.

57. "Slow Registration," *Chicago Defender*, October 31, 1962.

58. Hilty, *Brother Protector*, 333; "Good Old Days Are Dead," *California Eagle*, August 9, 1962.

59. "Attorney General Says U.S. Striving to Solve Segregation Problems," *Atlanta Daily World*, October 11, 1962; "Meredith Praised for Role in U.S. Struggle," *Atlanta Daily World*, October 11, 1962; "Fight Reds, Help Race Equality, Atty. Gen. Urges," *Atlanta Daily World*, October 31, 1962.

60. "Evers Urges 'Quarantining' of Mississippi," *California Eagle*, November 15, 1962.

61. "RFK Admits Our Linen Must Be Washed First," *Washington Afro-American*, November 3, 1962.

62. The *California Eagle*'s banner headline proclaimed, "YANKEE TROOPS DEFEAT MISSISSIPPI'S REBELS: Meredith's Enrollment a Victory for Negroes" (October 4, 1962), and *Ebony* called the "crushing of [the] Mississippi revolt" the "key accomplishment of the year." "Negro Progress in 1962," *Ebony*, February 1963, 84; "Kennedy 'Took Bull by Horns' to Force 'Ole Miss' to Obey," *Washington Afro-American*, October 6, 1962. See also Brauer, *Second Reconstruction*, 202. The *Chicago Defender* praised Kennedy's behind-the-scenes attempts to stimulate business and economic influence to increase compliance and acceptance among moderate whites. "Economic Pressure," *Chicago Daily Defender*, January 9, 1963.

63. "Narrowing the Gap," *Chicago Defender*, October 23, 1962. See also "Leaders Praise Big 3," *New York Amsterdam News*, October 20, 1962.

64. "U.S. Headed for 'Disaster' Unless Race Bias Wiped Out—R. Kennedy," *Chicago Daily Defender*, August 30, 1962; "RFK Plots Rights Progress," *New York Amsterdam News*, October 27, 1962; "Integration Foes Make Capital Time Bomb," *Chicago Daily Defender*, February 27, 1963; "Robert F. Kennedy Declares: Eliminating Discrimination 'A Need, Not a Choice," *Atlanta Daily World*, April 26, 1963. On northern segregation, see "Calls North's Bias 'More Sinister,'" *Chicago Defender*, May 5, 1962; "Robert Kennedy Calls for End to Labor Bias," *Chicago Daily Defender*, March 11, 1963; "Bobby Kennedy Admits U.S. Record 'Bad' on Race Relations," *Chicago Daily Defender*, June 5, 1963.

65. Poinsett, *Walking with Presidents*, 110–11; Brauer, *Second Reconstruction*, 219–20; Branch, *Parting the Waters*, 693.

66. "Mr. Lincoln and Mr. Kennedy," *Washington Afro-American*, February 16, 1963; Branch, *Parting the Waters*, 694; Jackie Robinson, "Master of Tokenism," *New York Amsterdam News*, February 16, 1963.

67. In the aftermath of John Kennedy's assassination, *Ebony* hailed this as among the slain president's most important achievements. Simeon Booker, "How JFK Surpassed Abraham Lincoln," *Ebony*, February 1964, 33–34; "Biggest Reception Ever," *Ebony*, May 1963, 89. One example of John Kennedy's felicitous social relationship with African Americans that received considerable media coverage involved his surprise appearance at a Los Angeles cotillion attended by the daughter

of entertainer Nat King Cole. The *California Eagle* reported, "For the first time ever, the President of the United States made his appearance at a debutante ball given by members of the Negro community . . . in the seemingly spontaneous manner that has gained him wide popularity." Grace E. Simons, "Kennedy 'Crashes' Links' Debutante Ball," *California Eagle*, November 23, 1961; "Cookie Cole Meets Society," *Ebony*, January 1962, 72–78. For an example of Robert Kennedy's similar activity, see "Deltas Hear Robert Kennedy Speak during Surprise Visit," *Pittsburgh Courier*, August 24, 1963. On John Kennedy's ability to connect with African Americans in a way that even the more progressive Hubert Humphrey could not, see Simeon Booker, oral history interview by John Stewart, April 24, 1967, transcript, 27, John F. Kennedy Library.

68. Gallup, *Gallup Poll*, 1769, 1789. The overall composition of respondents—particularly whether African Americans were even included—is not clear, as the only categories into which the Gallup data were subdivided were by political affiliation and "white Democrats outside South" and "white Republicans outside South."

69. Brauer, *Second Reconstruction*, 211.

70. Wofford, *Of Kennedys and Kings*, 170. For a powerful statement of the combined hopes and frustrations of African American commentators at this point, see "Pres. Kennedy, Civil Rights, and 'Dropping Our Buckets,'" *Washington Afro-American*, March 9, 1963.

71. Brauer, *Second Reconstruction*, 212; Chuck Stone, "Is JFK Losing Colored Vote?" *Washington Afro-American*, November 17, 1962. Even the ordinarily uncritical *Ebony* declared that there was "little doubt that much more was needed to realize America's promise of 'liberty and justice for all.'" "Negro Progress in 1962," *Ebony*, February 1963, 85.

72. "Housing Order: Little and Late," *California Eagle*, November 30, 1962.

73. Poinsett, *Walking with Presidents*, 111–12.

74. Wofford took the term from King's assessment of where the battle for civil rights stood in April 1963. Wofford, *Of Kennedys and Kings*, 170–71.

75. Stein and Plimpton, *American Journey*, 118; Brauer, *Second Reconstruction*, 249–50; Joseph D. Mathewson, "Kennedy, Businessmen Meet on Integration; Publicity Contrasts with Earlier Secrecy," *Wall Street Journal*, June 5, 1963.

76. Robert Kennedy to Averell Harriman, June 17, 1963, Averell Harriman Papers, Library of Congress.

77. Donald F. Martin, "Attorney General Calls on Wallace," *Atlanta Daily World*, April 26, 1963; Stanley S. Scott, "Kennedy Cites Need for Progress in Removing Racial Injustices," *Atlanta Daily World*, April 27, 1963.

78. Lawson, *Running for Freedom*, 93.

79. "Cleveland Council Urges JFK to Act in Birmingham," *Chicago Daily Defender*, May 8, 1963; "Bombings Upset Peace, Trigger Ala. Rioting," *Chicago Daily Defender*, May 13, 1963.

80. "The Mood in Alabama," *Chicago Defender*, May 11, 1963; "The Long Wait," *New York Amsterdam News*, May 18, 1963; cartoon, *Washington Afro-American*, May 18, 1963; "Time for Federal Action," *California Eagle*, May 9, 1963.

81. A Gallup poll found shifting perspectives on the integration struggle as a result of the Birmingham campaign, with the number of respondents viewing the administration as "pushing racial integration too fast" down six percentage points from the previous fall and those seeing the pace as "not fast enough" up six points. Gallup, *Gallup Poll*, 1823. For King's statement, see Guy Carawan, *Sing for Freedom: The Story of the Civil Rights Movement through Its Songs*, compact disc (Smithsonian/Folkways 40032).

82. Branch, *Parting the Waters*, 808–9.

83. Arthur M. Schlesinger Jr., *Robert Kennedy and His Times* (Boston: Houghton Mifflin, 1978), 330–31; Robert F. Kennedy and Burke Marshall, oral history interview by Anthony Lewis, December 22, 1964, transcript, 585, John F. Kennedy Library.

84. Stein and Plimpton, *American Journey*, 121.

85. The presence of Jones may have contributed to Kennedy's unease with the group. The FBI had learned that Jones was working closely with King aide Stanley Levison, who the Bureau had convinced Kennedy and Marshall was a "secret Communist." Levison resigned after King met with Kennedy in June 1963 and explained the risks of his involvement. Through the summer Jones functioned covertly as the go-between for King and Levison. Edward Schmitt, "The FBI and the SCLC, 1962–1965: From Surveillance to Counterintelligence" (M.A. thesis, Marquette University, 1996), 16.

86. Stein and Plimpton, *American Journey*, 119, 121.

87. Ibid., 120. James Baldwin, oral history interview by Jean Stein, transcript, box 1, Jean Stein Papers, John F. Kennedy Library.

88. For the best account of the meeting, see Hilty, *Brother Protector*, 354–59; Robert F. Kennedy, oral history interview by John Bartlow Martin, April 30, 1964, 288, John F. Kennedy Library.

89. Stein and Plimpton, *American Journey*, 121.

90. "News of the Week," *New York Amsterdam News*, June 1, 1963.

91. "Who's Bobby Kennedy Kidding?" *Washington Afro-American*, June 1, 1963; "Baldwin Clan Flops in Meet with RFK," *Pittsburgh Courier*, June 8, 1963.

92. Ralph Matthews, "The Civil Rights Explosion," *Washington Afro-American*, June 8, 1963; James L. Hicks, "Brains and Brawn," *New York Amsterdam News*, June 1, 1963. For other opinions on the Baldwin meeting, see George Schuyler, "Views and Reviews," *Pittsburgh Courier*, June 22, 1963; and Jackie Robinson, "Jim Baldwin and Bob Kennedy," *New York Amsterdam News*, June 8, 1963. Schuyler, among the more conservative of African American columnists, was alone among the newspaper commentary surveyed here in his criticism of what he considered the disrespectful treatment of the attorney general. Robinson, a cultural icon himself, praised the idea of dialogue but was unable to grasp why the Kennedys, "tremendously intelligent and sensitive people," found it "so difficult to understand our basic human yearnings." Robinson concluded that a Brooklyn schoolteacher got it right when she said: "Mr. Kennedy . . . would like to be right. But he'd rather be president." For a more favorable contemporary analysis of the role

of African American cultural leaders in the movement, see "Outgrowing the Ghetto Mind," *Ebony*, August 1963, 98.

93. In his 1964 oral history interviews on the Baldwin meeting, Kennedy proclaimed it "not really worth the time" to discuss, asserting that it had "accomplished no good." Kennedy, oral history interview by Martin, 289; Kennedy, oral history interview by Lewis, 586. According to Senate aide Peter Edelman, Kennedy "wasn't very forgiving about that meeting, ever." Peter Edelman, oral history interview by Larry Hackman, March 13, 1974, 29, John F. Kennedy Library. Kennedy even engaged in uncharacteristic pop psychologizing about the group, suggesting that the others felt compelled to join Smith's attack out of guilt that "they were not suffering like [other] Negroes were suffering," or perhaps had a "complex" resulting from the fact they were wealthy or married to white people (as several of those present were). Nevertheless, Kennedy ultimately blamed himself for getting involved with "that group" and stated that he remained unaffected in his feelings about the general struggle of blacks. Kennedy, oral history interview by Martin, 289–90. See also Thomas, *Robert Kennedy*, 244–45, on Kennedy's reactions to the meeting.

94. Edwin O. Guthman, *We Band of Brothers* (New York: Harper & Row), 221.

95. Schlesinger, *Robert Kennedy*, 908.

96. "Kennedy and Eisenhower on Civil Rights: In Perspective," *Washington Afro-American*, June 8, 1963.

97. See www.jfklibrary.org/Historical+Resources/Archives/Reference+Desk/Speeches/JFK/003POF03CivilRights06111963.htm.

98. For King's reaction, see Branch, *Parting the Waters*, 825; Thomas F. Jackson, *From Civil Rights to Human Rights: Martin Luther King, Jr., and the Struggle for Economic Justice* (Philadelphia: University of Pennsylvania Press, 2007), 168–69.

99. Jackie Robinson, "The President's Speech," *Washington Afro-American*, June 22, 1963.

100. "JFK Team Goes All Out for Civil Rights: 'A Profile of Courage,'" *New York Amsterdam News*, June 29, 1963.

101. "Major Poll Shows Kennedy Popular, Muslims Disliked," *Atlanta Daily World*, July 27, 1963. A September 8 Gallup poll echoed the numbers of the Harris survey, with 89 percent of African Americans approving President Kennedy's job performance and only 5 percent disapproving. Gallup, *Gallup Poll*, 1838.

102. Schlesinger, *Robert Kennedy*, 348–51; "Atty. General Robert F. Kennedy Takes Dim View of Mass March on Washington," *Atlanta Daily World*, June 27, 1963.

103. John Lewis, "Speech Prepared for the March on Washington, August 1963," www.hartford-hwp.com/archives/45a/641.html. For an incisive account of the changing dynamics in the planning of the event, see Jackson, *From Civil Rights to Human Rights*, 171–76. See also Sugrue, *Sweet Land of Liberty*, 306–9.

104. "JFK Urges Acceleration of Civil Rights Efforts," *Washington Afro-American*, August 31, 1963.

105. Samuel Hoskins, "Urgent Plea to President: Move Now Before It's Too Late," *Washington Afro-American*, September 21, 1963.

106. "Says B'Ham Bombing 'Organized Murder,'" *Atlanta Daily World*, September 26, 1963.

107. For the best account of the King meeting and White House responses to the Birmingham bombing, see Branch, *Parting the Waters*, 888–98; "Gregory at Meet, Gets SCLC Award," *Washington Afro-American*, September 28, 1963. Gregory had come to admire Robert Kennedy and told the audience: "Bobby Kennedy is about the greatest thing since Lincoln. I don't know what his brother is waiting for."

108. Gallup, *Gallup Poll*, 1844. Kennedy's disapproval ratings never reached substantial levels, but most observers traced the rising numbers at this point to his civil rights bill.

109. "Will Kennedy Get Soft?" *Washington Afro-American*, September 28, 1963.

110. "Bob Kennedy's Speech," *Chicago Daily Defender*, October 16, 1963.

111. "RFK Takes Blame in 'Sell-Out' of Rights Proposal," *Pittsburgh Courier*, October 26, 1963; "Bob Kennedy's Speech," *Chicago Daily Defender*, October 16, 1963. See also Chalmers M. Roberts, "'White Backlash' Leaves Many Scared: Politicians Taking a Wary Attitude toward the Civil Rights Question," *Washington Post*, October 20, 1963.

112. "Harrisburg Windmill," *Pittsburgh Courier*, October 26, 1963. The *Courier* reported that in response, what were called "Democratic Decontamination Teams" (DDT) were being sent through the city's black and Italian wards to correct the "distortions, untruths and misstatements of fact" which they accused the Republican workers of spreading. On Italian American perceptions, see Lee Bernstein, *The Greatest Menace: Organized Crime in Cold War America* (Amherst: University of Massachusetts Press, 2002).

113. "Group Plays 'Racist' Message in N.Y.," *Chicago Daily Defender*, June 3, 1964.

114. "Onion for the Day," *Chicago Defender*, October 16, 1963; "Bobby Kennedy Chickens Out," *Pittsburgh Courier*, October 26, 1963. For other criticism, see "NAACP's Mitchell Charges Sellout," *Atlanta Daily World*, October 17, 1963; "RFK Call for Right Bill Trim Sparks Curt Note by NAACP," *Washington Afro-American*, October 19, 1963; "King Rips Kennedy Rights Backdown," *Chicago Daily Defender*, October 22, 1963; Dawn Knight, "RFK Takes Blame in 'Sell-Out' of Rights Proposal,'" *Pittsburgh Courier*, October 26, 1963; "Wilkins Says Government Playing with Human Lives," *Chicago Defender*, October 26, 1963; "Mitchell Sees 'Incalculable Harm in Backdown on Civil Rights," *Atlanta Daily World*, October 27, 1963; "Demonstrators Hit Kennedy Position on Rights Bill," *Atlanta Daily World*, October 31, 1963; "Civil Rights Retreat," *California Eagle*, October 24, 1963; "The GOP Can't Be Blamed," *California Eagle*, October 31, 1963. For a more sympathetic reading of Kennedy's motives and the political realities in Congress, see Anthony Lewis, "Robert Kennedy Tries to Prevent Rights Deadlock," *New York Times*, October 16, 1963; Anthony Lewis, "In Washington: The Administration Moves to Reduce Opposition to Civil Rights Bill," *New York Times*, October 20, 1963; Chalmers M. Roberts, "Administration Must Take Rap as Bottled Rights Bill Is Uncorked," *Washington Post*, October 16, 1963; and the summary of other newspaper views in "Opinion of the Week: At Home and Abroad," *New York Times*, October 20, 1963.

115. Thomas, *Robert Kennedy*, 273–74.

116. "Texas Poll: Gov. Connally's Popularity Rises," *Del Rio News-Herald*, September 22, 1963, www.newspaperarchive.com.

117. Branch, *Parting the Waters*, 917; Schlesinger, *Robert Kennedy*, 606; Thomas, *Robert Kennedy*, 275. Months earlier, one southern paper called him the "worst enemy of the South since Thad Stevens." Hilty, *Brother Protector*, 363.

118. Grace E. Simons, "NEGROES DOUBT OFFICIAL STORY OF ASSASSINATION: Believe Murder Linked to Civil Rights," *California Eagle*, November 28, 1963.

119. Fred Porterfield, letter to the editor, *Washington Afro-American*, November 30, 1963. For another example, see Robert L. Robinson, "New York Negroes Have 'Mixed Emotions' over "Bobby' Kennedy's Bid for Senate," *Pittsburgh Courier*, September 5, 1964.

120. Oswald Sykes, "Lumumba, Evers, Kennedy, Must This Sad Circle Grow?" *Washington Afro-American*, December 7, 1963. For other accounts of popular grief, see "Woman with Rifle Mourns for President," *California Eagle*, November 28, 1963; "Child, 10, Sorry Kennedy Dies, Writes Lament," *California Eagle*, November 28, 1963; Simeon Booker, "How JFK Surpassed Abraham Lincoln," *Ebony* February 1964, 27.

121. "Mrs. Kennedy's Majesty Like That of Mrs. Medgar Evers," *Washington Afro-American*, December 7, 1963.

122. Photograph, *Chicago Daily Defender*, December 23, 1963.

123. Charles Evers, *Have No Fear: The Charles Evers Story* (New York: John Wiley & Sons, 1997), 157–58. Evers reported that he and Robert Kennedy spoke on a weekly basis. He also recalled John Kennedy telling him along with Myrlie Evers in the Oval Office after the murder of Medgar Evers, "You know, they'd kill me, too, if they could."

124. Kenneth M. Stampp, *1857: A Nation on the Brink* (New York: Oxford University Press, 1990), viii.

125. Ibid., 322–23, 328–31.

126. Booker, oral history interview, 37.

127. Ivanhoe Donaldson, oral history interview by Jean Stein, transcript, box 2, Jean Stein Papers,.

128. Brauer, *Second Reconstruction*, 220.

129. "Secret Weapon," *New York Amsterdam News*, November 4, 1961. An *Ebony* poll of over one hundred prominent African Americans in early 1964 found Robert Kennedy to be one of the three "most trusted whites" in America, finishing behind only *Brown* decision author and Supreme Court Chief Justice Earl Warren and the liberal publisher of the *Atlanta Journal-Constitution*, Ralph McGill. Finishing just behind the attorney general was Supreme Court Justice Hugo Black. Alex Poinsett, "The Ten Most Trusted Whites," *Ebony*, April 1964, 36–44.

130. "Robert Kennedy Role Is Questioned," *Chicago Defender*, January 4, 1964. Kennedy also placed third on the *Defender*'s "honor roll" for the year 1963, just behind Dick Gregory and ahead of Martin Luther King Jr. "Defender's 1963 Honor Roll: 10 Named," *Chicago Defender*, January 11, 1964.

3. POVERTY AND JUSTICE

1. James W. Hilty, *Robert Kennedy: Brother Protector* (Philadelphia: Temple University Press, 1997), 406.

2. Victor S. Navasky, *Kennedy Justice* (New York: Atheneum, 1971), 441; William Anderson, "Robert Kennedy Asks 8 Laws to Rout Crime," *Chicago Tribune*, April 7, 1961. For examples of media coverage, see "Robert Kennedy Urges New Laws to Fight Rackets," *New York Times*, April 7, 1961; and Susan Wagner, "Seek 8 Laws to Help FBI in War on Crime," *Atlanta Daily World*, April 7, 1961.

3. Nicholas Lemann, *Promised Land: The Great Black Migration and How It Changed America* (New York: Vintage, 1992), 124–25; Jean Stein and George Plimpton, eds., *American Journey: The Times of Robert Kennedy* (New York: Harcourt Brace Jovanovich, 1970), 77; Arthur M. Schlesinger Jr., *Robert Kennedy and His Times* (Boston: Houghton Mifflin, 1978), 413; David Hackett, oral history interview by John Douglas, July 22, 1970, transcript, 67, John F. Kennedy Library.

4. Hackett, oral history interview by Douglas, 4, 14; Allen J. Matusow, *The Unraveling of America: A History of Liberalism in the 1960s* (New York: Harper & Row, 1984), 108.

5. Hackett, oral history interview by Douglas, 68.

6. Richard Cloward and Lloyd Ohlin, *Delinquency and Opportunity: A Theory of Delinquent Gangs* (Glencoe, Ill.: Free Press, 1960); James T. Patterson, *America's Struggle against Poverty in the Twentieth Century* (Cambridge: Harvard University Press, 2000), 101. The other contemporaneous work that embodied the structural approach was John Kenneth Galbraith, *The Affluent Society* (Boston: Houghton Mifflin, 1958). Cottrell did not exercise as much influence early on as Ohlin, but ultimately his emphasis on participation of the poor in antipoverty efforts became the dominant theme in the PCJD. For a good summary of Cottrell's views and the ideological forces at work in the PCJD, see Leonard S. Cottrell Jr., "The Competent Community," Supplemental Materials to "Poverty and Urban Policy," John F. Kennedy Library; Daniel Knapp and Kenneth Polk, *Scouting the War on Poverty: Social Reform Politics in the Kennedy Administration* (Lexington, Mass.: D. C. Heath, 1971), 25–52; Alice O'Connor, *Poverty Knowledge: Social Science, Social Policy, and the Poor in Twentieth-Century U.S. History* (Princeton: Princeton University Press, 2001), 124–36.

7. Hackett, oral history interview by Douglas, 74–75. The meetings were intended to be kept below the media's radar, but a few newspaper reporters got wind of Kennedy's walking tour, which stretched forty blocks. John P. McKenzie, "Shirt-Sleeved Bob Kennedy Goes Slumming to Visit East Side Gangs," *Washington Post*, March 9, 1961.

8. "Robert Kennedy Polls Delinquents about Behavior," *Capital Times*, March 9, 1961, www.newspaperarchive.com. For evidence that Kennedy meant it when he said he understood their brawling, see Lance Morrow, "My Mixed Feelings about Bobby Kennedy," *Time*, June 7, 2000 (online edition only) www.time.com/time/nation/article/0 ,8599,46818,00.html.

9. Jim Myers, "RFK's Childhood Pal Carries On—Alone," *YouthToday*, www.youthtoday .org/publication/article.cfm?article_id=212. On the gangs and the dynamics of East

Harlem in this period, see Eric C. Schneider, *Vampires, Dragons, and Egyptian Kings: Youth Gangs in Postwar New York* (Princeton: Princeton University Press, 2001), 91–105.

10. Edwin Guthman, *We Band of Brothers* (New York: Harper & Row, 1969), 226–27; Hackett, oral history interview by Douglas, 74; McKenzie, "Shirt-Sleeved Bob Kennedy Goes Slumming"; Aaron Schmais, correspondence with author, May 16, 2001.

11. Schmais, correspondence with author.

12. "Poverty Seen Topping All D.C. Issues," *Washington Post*, December 9, 1960; Luther P. Jackson, "Capitol Is Heart of 'Poverty Row,'" *Washington Post*, January 1, 1961.

13. Edward Peeks, "A Rotten Deal: Colored Kids Stuck in D.C.'s Worst Schools— Physical Facilities 'Terrible,'" *Washington Afro-American*, May 13, 1961; Attorney General to Walter N. Tobriner, March 28, 1963, Robert F. Kennedy Attorney General Papers, Correspondence, Chronological, box 14, folder: 3/17/63–3/31/63, John F. Kennedy Library; Schlesinger, *Robert Kennedy*, 414–15.

14. "Cary Grant Comes to Shaw," *Washington Post*, September 28, 1963; "Cary Grant a Hit at Playground with Bob Kennedy as Co-Star," *Washington Post*, September 21, 1963; "R. Kennedy, Murrow Visit Schools Here," *Washington Post*, June 7, 1963; Charles Turner, "Shaw Is Symbol of Pride, Shame," *Washington Afro-American*, October 19, 1963; Ernest Lotito, "Kennedy Playground Has Grownups in a Tizzy," *Washington Post*, October 15, 1964.

15. Ronald L. Goldfarb, *Perfect Villains and Imperfect Heroes: Robert F. Kennedy's War against Organized Crime* (New York: Random House, 1995), 320.

16. Les Ledbetter, "Religious Groups, Attorney General Will Reopen Pool," *Washington Afro-American*, July 13, 1963; Eve Edstrom, "Donated Cash Opens School Pool," *Washington Post*, July 10, 1963.

17. E. Barrett Prettyman Jr., oral history interview by Larry Hackman, June 5, 1969, transcript, 8–9, John F. Kennedy Library. For another example of Kennedy's activity, see "Robert Kennedy Opens Lot for Night Recreation Area," *Washington Afro-American*, August 3, 1963.

18. "Playground Plan May Be Approved at Site of New Shaw Junior High," *Washington Post*, September 13, 1963; Burke Marshall, oral history interview by Larry Hackman, January 20, 1970, transcript, 11, John F. Kennedy Library.

19. "Chalk Leads Drive to Finance Playground Idea of R. Kennedy," *Washington Post*, December 1, 1963; "John F. Kennedy Playground Is Dedicated in Capital," *New York Times*, June 4, 1964; Jean M. White, "10,000 Children Christen Kennedy Playground Here," *Washington Post*, June 4, 1964.

20. Gerald Grant, "Where Would All the Students Go?" *Washington Post*, September 1, 1965; "L.A. May Get Playground of JFK Type," *Washington Post*, July 19, 1964; "Kennedy Playground Dedicated in D.C.," *Atlanta Daily World*, June 9, 1964. Chalk initially hoped to reproduce this success with a company focused on similar urban conversions.

21. *West Side Story*, dir. Robert Wise and Jerome Robbins, DVD (MGM Home Entertainment, 2003). For an example of the debate over delinquency and the preva-

lence of the maladjustment diagnosis, see "Conformity and Delinquency," *Washington Post*, January 2, 1955.

22. Richard N. Goodwin, *Remembering America: A Voice from the Sixties* (Boston: Little, Brown, 1988), 447.

23. Lydia Katzenbach, oral history interview by Jean Stein, transcript, Jean Stein Papers, box 5, John F. Kennedy Library; Stein and Plimpton, *American Journey*, 166.

24. Lemann, *Promised Land*, 129. Kennedy's identification with the problems of juvenile delinquents was apparently enduring. Several years later, when writer and New Left activist Jack Newfield asked Kennedy what his vocation might have been had he not been born into his political family, the New York senator replied in earnest, "Perhaps a juvenile delinquent or a revolutionary." Jack Newfield, *Robert Kennedy: A Memoir* (New York: E. P. Dutton, 1969), 19.

25. U.S. House Special Subcommittee on Education, *Hearings on the Juvenile Delinquency Control Act*, 87th Cong., 1st sess. (Washington, D.C.: U.S. Government Printing Office, 1961), July 12, 1961, 109.

26. Hackett, oral history interview by Douglas, 93.

27. Ibid., 75, 93–94.

28. Quoted in Richard J. Whalen, *The Founding Father: The Story of Joseph P. Kennedy* (New York: New American Library, 1964), 403.

29. Ellis W. Hawley, "Herbert Hoover, the Commerce Secretariat, and the Vision of an 'Associative State,' 1921–28," *Journal of American History* 61, no. 1 (June 1974): 116–40; Ellis W. Hawley, "Hoover: Associationalism and the Relief Crisis," *With Us Always: A History of Private Charity and Public Welfare*, ed. Donald T. Critchlow and Charles H. Parker (Lanham Md.: Rowman & Littlefield, 1998), 161–90.

30. Bruce A. Lohof, "Herbert Hoover, Spokesman of Humane Efficiency: The Mississippi Flood of 1927," *American Quarterly* 22 (Fall 1970): 692.

31. Joan Hoff Wilson, *Herbert Hoover: Forgotten Progressive* (Boston: Little, Brown, 1975).

32. "Attorney General Kennedy, Re: Problems of Juveniles," NBC-TV, June 4, 1962, Robert F. Kennedy Attorney General Papers, Speeches, 1961–1964, box 1. For a similar statement, see Henry Keys, "Kennedy Sees Delinquency as Biggest Problem Facing U.S.," *Atlanta Daily World*, April 4, 1963.

33. Pope John XXIII, *Mater et Magistra*, May 15, 1961, www.vatican.va/holy_father/john_xxiii/encyclicals/documents/hf_j-xxiii_enc_15051961.

34. Historian Michael Katz has written: "The story of Catholic charity in America has hardly been told by historians, who usually ignore or slight its efforts. The Protestant coloration of the history of American social reform truly is remarkable." Michael B. Katz, *In the Shadow of the Poorhouse: A Social History of Welfare in America* (New York: Basic Books, 1996), 63–64, 342; John T. McGreevy, *Catholicism and American Freedom: A History* (New York: W. W. Norton, 2003), 130, 152–53; Neil Betten, "American Attitudes toward the Poor: A Historical Overview," *Current History* 65, no. 383 (July 1973): 4.

35. Dorothy M. Brown and Elizabeth McKeown, *The Poor Belong to Us: Catholic Charities and American Welfare* (Cambridge: Harvard University Press, 1997), 1. See also

Robert D. Cross, *The Emergence of Liberal Catholicism in America* (Cambridge: Harvard University Press, 1958), 108–15.

36. Pope Pius XI, *Quadragesimo Anno*, quoted in National Conference of Catholic Bishops, *Contemporary Catholic Social Teaching* (Washington, D.C.: United States Catholic Conference, 1991), 71. While Herbert Hoover fell from grace by contesting their coreligionist Al Smith in 1928 and in failing to deal more aggressively with the economic conditions of the Great Depression, Hoover's humanitarian efforts to relieve the hunger of postwar Europe and his efforts to craft an associative state made him popular with many American Catholics. Historian Steven Avella has argued that Hoover's associational efforts "bore a resemblance, to at least some Catholic observers, to the principle of subsidiarity and the organic social order" called for by Catholic social teaching. Steven M. Avella, "Before the Fall: American Catholic Attitudes toward Herbert Hoover," unpublished essay in author's possession. See also Ronald W. Schatz, "American Labor and the Catholic Church, 1919–1950," *U.S. Catholic Historian* 3 (Fall–Winter 1983): 183–85. John McGreevy calls Hoover's associationalism "a faint echo" of European reform efforts at corporatism and notes that "the Catholic vision of social reform, unlike the dominant non-Catholic alternative, saw no connection between social reform and individual autonomy." McGreevy, *Catholicism and American Freedom*, 146, 153.

37. McGreevy, *Catholicism and American Freedom*, 141–45, 150–54; Francis L. Broderick, *Right Reverend New Dealer, John A. Ryan* (New York: Macmillan, 1963); John A. Ryan, *Distributive Justice: The Right and Wrong of Our Present Distribution of Wealth* (New York: Macmillan, 1919).

38. John XXIII, *Mater et Magistra*; Richard P. McBrien, *Catholicism: Study Edition* (Minneapolis: Winston Press, 1981), 985; J. Bryan Hehir, "Catholic Social Teaching and the Challenge of the Future," *Woodstock Report* 54 (1998), www.woodstock .georgetown.edu/publications/report/r-fea54a.htm.

39. "For the Record," *National Review*, August 12, 1961, 77.

40. Andrew Greeley, *The Catholic Imagination* (Berkeley: University of California Press, 2000). For the reflections of one of Kennedy's daughters on the importance of Catholic social teaching to his family, see Kathleen Kennedy Townsend, *Failing America's Faithful: How Today's Churches Are Mixing God with Politics and Losing Their Way* (New York: Warner Books, 2007). See also Thomas Maier, *The Kennedys: America's Emerald Kings* (New York: Basic Books, 2003), 240–44, 490–510.

41. Hackett, oral history interview by Douglas, 71.

42. U.S. House Special Subcommittee, *Hearings on the Juvenile Delinquency Control Act*, 108.

43. "Poverty and Urban Policy: A Group Discussion of the Kennedy Administration Urban Poverty Programs and Policies," Brandeis University Conference, June 16–17, 1973, transcript, 359, John F. Kennedy Library. On the program's moorings in the Chicago School, see O'Connor, *Poverty Knowledge*, 45–54, 125–36.

44. The "guerrillas" were a fluid group. For the various individuals involved, see Knapp and Polk, *Scouting the War on Poverty*, 111; Myers, "RFK's Childhood Pal."

45. For a study and critique of Kennedy administration "action intellectuals" (or "thinker doers," in his phraseology), see David Halberstam, *The Best and the Brightest* (New York: Random House, 1969).

46. Knapp and Polk, *Scouting the War on Poverty*, 8.

47. Hackett, oral history interview by Douglas, 86.

48. Sam Roberts, *A Kind of Genius: Herb Sturz and Society's Toughest Problems* (New York: PublicAffairs, 2009), 53.

49. Francis Allen, oral history interview by author, June 16, 2006.

50. Ibid.; Anthony Lewis, "U.S. Favors Bail on Honor System," *New York Times*, March 25, 1963.

51. Allen, oral history interview. According to Allen, the attorney general received responses from 100 percent of the federal attorneys.

52. Lee S. Friedman, "The Evolution of a Bail Reform," *Policy Sciences* 7 (1976): 300.

53. "Address by Attorney General Robert F. Kennedy to the National Conference on Bail and Criminal Justice," May 29, 1964, Robert F. Kennedy Attorney General Papers, Speeches, 1961–1964, box 2.

54. While there had been important bail reform studies conducted in the 1950s, the Allen committee's report and the visibility of Robert Kennedy's push were key factors in the submission and passage of the 1964 bail reform legislation that became the new law in 1966. Wayne H. Thomas, *Bail Reform in America* (Berkeley: University of California Press, 1976), 162. See also Samuel Walker, *Popular Justice: A History of American Criminal Justice* (New York: Oxford University Press, 1998), 194–95.

55. One of the challenges the Allen committee faced was defining poverty. In the end, the committee concluded that "poverty must be viewed as a relative concept with the consequence that the poverty of accused must be measured in each case by reference to the particular need or service under consideration." *Report of the Attorney General's Committee on Poverty and the Administration of Federal Criminal Justice* (Washington, D.C.: U.S. Government Printing Office, 1963), 8.

56. U.S. Senate Subcommittee on Constitutional Rights and the Subcommittee on Improvements in Judicial Machinery, *Hearings on Federal Bail Procedures*, 88th Cong., 2d sess. (Washington, D.C.: U.S. Government Printing Office, 1964), August 4, 1964, 37; "Address by Robert F. Kennedy Prepared for Delivery before the New England Conference on the Defense of Indigent Persons Accused of Crime," November 1, 1963, Robert F. Kennedy Attorney General Papers, Speeches, 1961–1964, box 2.

57. Robert F. Kennedy, *The Pursuit of Justice* (New York: Harper & Row, 1964), 81.

58. Ronald Goldfarb, correspondence with author, January 19, 2009; Walker, *Popular Justice*, 194.

59. U.S. Senate Subcommittee, *Hearings on Federal Bail Procedures*, 37.

60. Virginia Burns, oral history interview by Daniel Knapp, November 28, 1967, Daniel Knapp Papers, John F. Kennedy Library; Lloyd Ohlin and Leonard Cottrell, oral history interview notes, February 21, 1969, Richardson White Papers, box 7, Notes: Misc., John F. Kennedy Library.

61. Hilty, *Brother Protector*, 314.

62. Kenneth C. Burt, *The Search for a Civic Voice: California Latino Politics* (Claremont, Calif.: Regina Books, 2007), 196–97; Ignacio García, *Viva Kennedy: Mexican Americans in Search of Camelot* (College Station: Texas A&M University Press, 2000), 110; Mario T. García, *Memories of Chicano History: The Life and Narrative of Bert Corona* (Berkeley: University of California Press, 1994), 232; "Raps Kennedy in Neglecting Campaign Vow," *Chicago Tribune*, November 10, 1963.

63. Rowland Evans and Robert Novak, "Inside Report . . . The Ethnic Clash," *Washington Post*, July 10, 1963.

64. For the best account of the Kinzua Dam episode, see Thomas Clarkin, *Federal Indian Policy in the Kennedy and Johnson Administrations, 1961–1969* (Albuquerque: University of New Mexico Press, 2001), 49–57. See also "A.C.L.U. Seeks Halt in Kinzua Dam Work," *New York Times*, December 27, 1960.

65. "President Kennedy Will Not Halt Kinzua Dam," *Indian Truth* 38, no. 2 (October 1961): 6–7.

66. Ramsey Clark, oral history interview by Larry Hackman, June 29, 1970, transcript, 12, John F. Kennedy Library.

67. Robert F. Kennedy, "Buying It Back from the Indians," *Life*, March 23, 1962, 17–19 (emphasis added).

68. Ibid.

69. Editorial from the *Ute Bulletin*, reprinted in the *NCAI Sentinel*, June 1962. The *Bulletin* proclaimed: "Whatever may be the purpose behind Mr. Kennedy's article, it only added to the confused image that the average American citizen has of his fellow citizen, the American Indian. He is too often viewed as anachronistic, comic, and a dull wit, relegated to a reservation which might be viewed as a haven for the mentally retarded, and someone who is separate and apart from every human being, in spite of the fact that he has been an American citizen since 1924 and has played a significant role in the progress of our country."

70. Clark, oral history interview, 13.

71. Opinion among scholars on the impact of the Indian Claims Commission, which was signed into law in 1946, has been generally critical. For a cogent critical appraisal, see Nancy Oestreich Lurie, "The Indian Claims Commission," *Annals of the American Academy of Political and Social Science* 436 (March 1978): 97–110. A more sympathetic yet balanced assessment is Francis Paul Prucha, *The Great Father: The United States Government and the American Indians* (Lincoln: University of Nebraska Press, 1984), 1022–23. The *Ute Bulletin*, in the same editorial chastising the Kennedys over the *Life* article, did assert that what it desired was faster processing of claims, an objective the administration met.

72. *NCAI Sentinel* 7, no. 2 (July–August 1962): 2; Robert Burnette, *The Tortured Americans* (Englewood, N.J.: Prentice-Hall, 1971), 73; Donald Janson, "Indian Group Is Ready to Take Court Action in Fight Against Discrimination," *New York Times*, September 19, 1963. Kennedy phoned the head of the Bureau of Indian Affairs, Philleo Nash, while Burnette was in his office and intoned, "Let's not take any little steps, shall we, Philleo?" Philleo Nash, oral history interview by William W. Moss, February 26, 1971, transcript, 54, John F. Kennedy Library.

73. Nash, oral history interview, 55–56; Memo, Burke Marshall to Robert Kennedy, September 6, 1963, Robert F. Kennedy Attorney General Papers, Trips, box 15. Burke Marshall advised Kennedy that he had looked into the twenty-five complaints of police brutality in the previous year and believed that none could be prosecuted under civil rights statutes "mainly because in those instances where injuries were suffered by the Indians they were invariably brought on by [the individual's] resistance or hostile action toward the police who were attempting to arrest him for drunkenness or other illegal behavior."

74. James L. Sundquist, *Politics and Policy: The Eisenhower, Kennedy, and Johnson Years* (Washington, D.C.: Brookings Institution, 1968), 85–86. The issue was of such mainstream concern that a July 1961 poll found that 67 percent of respondents were "willing to sacrifice" to pay for job retraining programs, more than twice the percentage of respondents willing to sacrifice for an improved military.

75. Patterson, *America's Struggle*, 123–25.

76. Clarkin, *Federal Indian Policy*, 71.

77. Patterson, *America's Struggle*, 123.

78. Eunice Kennedy Shriver, oral history interview by John Stewart, May 7, 1968, transcript, 21–22, John F. Kennedy Library; Edward Shorter, *The Kennedy Family and the Story of Mental Retardation* (Philadelphia: Temple University Press, 2000), 84. Eunice Kennedy Shriver most famously influenced her brother to create the President's Panel on Mental Retardation.

79. President's Study Group on National Voluntary Services, "In Consideration of a National Service Corps (Some Initial Staff Observations)," Records of the Secretary of Labor W. Willard Wirtz, 1962–1969, box 16, folder "1962–Committee-Task Force on National Service Corps," John F. Kennedy Library; William H. Crook and Ross Thomas, *Warriors for the Poor: The Story of VISTA, Volunteers in Service to America* (New York: William Morrow, 1969), 23–24.

80. In the same poll 74 percent of respondents gave the Peace Corps a favorable rating. See "6 of 10 Ask a Domestic Peace Corps," *Washington Post*, November 22, 1962. The proposal was little noted in the black press, but *Washington Afro-American* columnist Edward Peeks called for the African American community to rally to the proposal. Edward Peeks, "Peace Corps Urged in Rights Struggle," *Washington Afro American*, November 24, 1962.

81. Dr. Leonard Duhl, oral history interview by Jean Stein, transcript, Jean Stein Papers, box 2.

82. Ibid.; David Hackett, oral history interview by Jean Stein, transcript, Jean Stein Papers, box 4; "Poverty and Urban Policy," 185.

83. Teletype, SAC Chicago to Director, August 23, 1963; and memo, Courtney A. Evans to Assistant Director Alan Belmont, August 24, 1963, Robert F. Kennedy FBI File, copy in author's possession; "Robert Kennedy Drops in for Day," *New York Times*, August 15, 1963; "Meets Youth," *Atlanta Daily World*, August 18, 1963.

84. Hackett, oral history interview by Stein.

85. Richard W. Boone, correspondence with author, February 27, 2001; "Poverty and Urban Policy," 224–26, 245–46.

86. Memo, David Hackett to the Attorney General, Subj: Immediate Strategy on National Service Corps Legislation, April 25, 1963, Robert F. Kennedy Attorney General Papers, General Correspondence, box 41, National Service Corps.

87. U.S. Senate Subcommittee on the National Service Corps of the Committee on Labor and Public Welfare, *National Service Corps: Hearings on S. 1321*, 88th Cong., 1st sess. (Washington, D.C.: U.S. Government Printing Office, 1963), May 29, 1963, 44; U.S. House Special Subcommittee on Labor of the Committee on Education and Labor, *National Service Corps: Hearings on H.R. 5625*, 88th Cong., 1st sess. (Washington, D.C.: U.S. Government Printing Office, 1963), May 22, 1963, 13; William James, "The Moral Equivalent of War," www.barnard.columbia.edu/amstud/resources/nationalism/james.htm; Harris Wofford, *Of Kennedys and Kings: Making Sense of the Sixties* (Pittsburgh: University of Pittsburgh Press, 1980), 313–14. For an example of Kennedy's continuing ruminations on the topic, see "A Redbook Dialogue: Robert Kennedy and Oscar Lewis," *Redbook*, September 1967, 106.

88. "Statement by Attorney General Robert F. Kennedy before the Subcommittee on the National Service Corps of the Senate Committee on Labor and Public Welfare, May 29, 1963," Robert F. Kennedy Attorney General Papers, Speeches, 1961–1964, box 2.

89. "The Baby-Sitting Corps," *Chicago Tribune*, August 16, 1963; "Domestic Peace Corps," *New York Times*, August 5, 1963; "Corps for Service," *Washington Post*, August 10, 1963.

90. Stephen Pollak, correspondence with author, June 20, 2006; Phillip Warden, "House Snips $7,000 from Spending Bill," *Chicago Tribune*, May 1, 1963.

91. John Kennedy added a brief plug for the program to his American University address in June 1963, but it was overlooked in the discussion afterward of his nuclear test ban proposal. The president pointed to the nation's capital as a "prime example" of the need for assistance, asserting, "There is a good deal of poverty in the United States but not too many people see it." Memo, David Hackett to the Attorney General, Subj: National Service Corps, June 7, 1963, Robert F. Kennedy Attorney General Papers, General Correspondence, box 41, National Service Corps; "Kennedy Says D.C. Needs Peace Corps," *Washington Post*, July 18, 1963.

92. Memo, July 10, 1963, Robert F. Kennedy Attorney General Papers, Personal Correspondence, box 14, Notebook; "Citizens Press for National Service Corps," *Washington Post*, August 3, 1963; Drew Pearson, "The Peace Corps and a Kansas Town," *Washington Post*, July 16, 1963. The congressional party also visited a mental health facility in Kansas to examine the effectiveness of volunteers there.

93. For contemporary profiles of congressional dynamics, see John D. Morris, "Congress Facing a 'Hard Summer' as Logjam Grows," *New York Times*, July 1, 1963; Cabell Phillips, "Congress Lags Far Behind Its Schedule," *New York Times*, August 25, 1963; Paul Duke, "Reaction to Integration Drive: Dixie Democrats Threaten Most Kennedy Programs," *Wall Street Journal*, June 14, 1963; Jerry Landauer, "Civil Rights Push, Rebellious Congress Bedevil Kennedy Plans," *Wall Street Journal*, July 9, 1963.

94. Memo, Re: Meeting with Citizens Committee for a National Service Corps, September 12, 1963, Robert F. Kennedy Attorney General Papers, Personal Corre-

spondence, box 14, Notebook; "Address by Honorable Robert F. Kennedy, Attorney General of the United States, at the Commencement Exercises of Trinity College, Washington, D.C., June 2, 1963," Robert F. Kennedy Attorney General Papers, Speeches, 1961–1964, box 2.

95. "U.S. Indians Back Local Peace Corps," *Washington Post*, March 18, 1963. See also "LaFarge Hails Bill to Help Young Indians," *New York Amsterdam News*, February 16, 1963.

96. National Congress of American Indians to the Attorney General, May 2, 1963, Robert F. Kennedy Attorney General Papers, Trips, box 15.

97. Janson, "Indian Group Is Ready to Take Court Action."

98. "Remarks by Attorney General Robert F. Kennedy before the National Congress of American Indians, Bismarck, North Dakota, September 13, 1963," Robert F. Kennedy Attorney General Papers, Speeches, 1961–1964, box 2.

99. "Indians Victims, R. F. Kennedy Says," *New York Times*, September 14, 1963, 11.

100. Richard L. Lyons, "House Unit Hears Attorney General Appeal for Youth Employment Act," *Washington Post*, February 20, 1963; U.S. Senate Subcommittee on Employment and Manpower of the Committee on Labor and Public Welfare, *Youth Employment Act: Hearings on S. 1*, 88th Cong., 1st sess. (Washington, D.C.: U.S. Government Printing Office, 1963), February 26, 1963. Hackett, oral history interview by Douglas, 93; Gilbert Douglas, "D.C. Youth Must Be Offered More— RFK," *Washington Afro-American*, July 28, 1962; Louis Cassel, "Integration Foes Make Capital a Time Bomb," *Chicago Daily Defender*, February 27, 1963; "Robert F. Kennedy Declares: Eliminating Discrimination 'A Need, Not a Choice,'" *Atlanta Daily World*, April 26, 1963.

101. Memo, Louis Martin to Kenneth O'Donnell, April 19, 1963, Robert F. Kennedy Attorney General Papers, General Correspondence, White House Regional Conferences, 1963, box 67.

102. "'Spirit of Birmingham' Intensifies Integration Pushes Outside South," *Wall Street Journal*, May 17, 1963.

103. William G. Weart, "Negroes to Widen Protests on Jobs," *New York Times*, May 30, 1963; Robert E. Baker, "Negroes in Cambridge Tired of Waiting," *Washington Post*, April 21, 1963. See also Layhmond Robinson, "New York's Racial Unrest: Negro Anger Mounting," *New York Times*, August 12, 1963.

104. Lerone Bennett Jr., "The Mood of the Negro," *Ebony*, July 1963, 38.

105. See the transcript of this important May 20, 1963, meeting in Jonathan Rosenberg and Zachary Karabell, *Kennedy, Johnson, and the Quest for Justice: The Civil Rights Tapes* (New York: W. W. Norton, 2003), 116–20.

106. Dick Gregory, *Up from Nigger* (New York: Stein & Day, 1976), 131; Herb Lyon, "Tower Ticker," *Chicago Tribune*, January 31, 1963. On his relationship with Robert Kennedy, see also Dick Gregory, *Callus on My Soul: A Memoir* (New York: Kensington, 2003), 142; "Name Dick Gregory on Youth Committee," *Los Angeles Sentinel*, December 13, 1962; "Comic Gregory Files Assault Charge against His Master of Ceremonies," *Washington Post*, September 28, 1963.

107. Taylor Branch, *Parting the Waters: America in the King Years, 1954–1963* (New York: Simon & Schuster, 1988), 809; Rosenberg and Karabell, *Kennedy, Johnson*, 116–20.

108. Thomas J. Sugrue, *Sweet Land of Liberty* (New York: Random House, 2008), 267–69.

109. Jeff Shesol, *Mutual Contempt: Lyndon Johnson, Robert Kennedy, and the Feud That Defined a Decade* (New York: W. W. Norton, 1997), 83; Robert Kennedy, oral history interview by Anthony Lewis, December 4, 1964, transcript, 463, 466, John F. Kennedy Library.

110. Taylor Branch, *Pillar of Fire: America in the King Years, 1963–65* (New York: Touchstone, 1998), 90–91. Labor Secretary Willard Wirtz was caught in the crossfire between the two men, who he said were waging "all-out warfare as to who was the more active proponent of special opportunities for the employment of minority workers." Wirtz called the struggle "unseemly," suggesting that Kennedy made it personal and Johnson was "strongly inclined to exaggerate" the contributions of business leaders nominally working with the committee. Willard Wirtz, *In the Rear View Mirror* (Beloit, Wis.: Beloit College Press, 2008), 37.

111. "Economics Answer to Rights Woes—RFK," *Atlanta Daily World*, July 31, 1963; Robert Kennedy, oral history interview by John Bartlow Martin, April 30, 1964, transcript, 284–85, John F. Kennedy Library; Robert Kennedy, oral history interview by Lewis, December 4, 1964, 472–73.

112. Carl M. Brauer, *John F. Kennedy and the Second Reconstruction* (New York: Columbia University Press, 1977), 282–83; Hilty, *Brother Protector*, 387.

113. John F. Kennedy Library President's Office Files, Presidential Recordings Collection, tape 90, reel 2, June 1, 1963. On the debate over an accelerated public works bill, see Sundquist, *Politics and Policy*, 93–97. Labor Secretary Wirtz would push that fall for a major job creation bill that Bureau of the Budget official William Cannon called "a utopia, a five billion dollar-a-year job program. That wasn't in the works at all." William Cannon, oral history interview by Michael Gillette, May 21, 1982, Lyndon B. Johnson Library, Austin, Tex.

114. Nicholas Katzenbach, *Some of It Was Fun: Working for RFK and LBJ* (New York: W. W. Norton, 2008), 119–20.

115. On the limits of the existing PCEEO, see Brauer, *Second Reconstruction*, 80.

116. "'Spirit of Birmingham' Intensifies."

117. House Committee on the Judiciary, *Civil Rights: Hearings on Miscellaneous Proposals*, 88th Cong., 1st sess., 1963 (Washington, D.C.: U.S. Government Printing Office, 1963), 1373.

118. Carl Brauer, who interviewed Walter Heller and those closest to Kennedy in the Council of Economic Advisers and the Bureau of the Budget, was convinced that Kennedy had read both the book and Macdonald's review. Carl M. Brauer, "Kennedy, Johnson, and the War on Poverty," *Journal of American History* 69, no. 1 (June 1982): 103. See also "Poverty and Urban Policy," 52, 55; Adam Yarmolinsky, "Camelot Revisited," *Virginia Quarterly Review* 72, no. 4 (Autumn 1996): 659.

119. Theodore C. Sorensen, *Kennedy* (New York: Harper & Row, 1965), 405–8; Edward B. Claflin, ed., *JFK Wants to Know: Memos from the President, 1961–1963* (New York: William Morrow, 1991), 180; William S. Borden, "Defending Hegemony: American Foreign Economic Policy," in *Kennedy's Quest for Victory: American Foreign Policy, 1961–1963*, ed. Thomas Paterson (New York: Oxford University Press, 1989), 63–64.

120. Sorensen, *Kennedy*, 407. Historian Maurice Isserman notes that conservative Republicans and southern Democrats were more numerous in Kennedy's first Congress than in Eisenhower's last. Maurice Isserman, *The Other American* (New York: PublicAffairs, 2000), 192.

121. Brauer, "Kennedy, Johnson," 103.

122. Memo, Louis Martin to Kenneth O'Donnell, April 19, 1963, Robert F. Kennedy Attorney General Papers, General Correspondence, White House Regional Conferences, 1963, box 67.

123. Brauer, "Kennedy, Johnson," 103; Layhmond Robinson, "Rockefeller Says Kennedy Wavers," *New York Times*, June 7, 1963.

124. Michael L. Gillette, *Launching the War on Poverty: An Oral History* (New York: Twayne Publishers, 1996), 1–17; "Poverty and Urban Policy," 173. See also Patterson, *America's Struggle*, 134–38, on Heller's antipoverty initiatives. Heller's antipoverty work actually began before the inception of a formal task force, in a series of informal Saturday discussions with economic advisers and economists outside the government such as Robert Lampman of the University of Wisconsin. A major debate over the administration's motives for civil rights and antipoverty initiatives emerged early on, as Frances Fox Piven and Richard Cloward contend that the administration had political motives and was trying to increase black support for the Democratic Party. Francis Fox Piven and Richard Cloward, *Regulating the Poor: The Functions of Public Welfare* (New York: Pantheon, 1971). By contrast, Adam Yarmolinsky contended that in his experience, the Kennedys' motives were dictated by "99 and 44/100 percent noblesse oblige and that there was no concern whatsoever about holding on to the black vote." "Poverty and Urban Policy," 193–94. David Hackett also asserted, "If it had been a political program and if the administration wanted to cater to the blacks and to the black vote, we would have done it completely different[ly]. . . . Bob Kennedy is certainly a political animal . . . [but] he never had one discussion, never thought about it in those terms." "Poverty and Urban Policy," 201, 205.

125. Green was convinced that excessive planning was a waste of time and money. She was also unhappy with Hackett's leadership of the PCJD. "I thought he used it as a political vehicle," she told an interviewer later. "He had no competence to administer that program at all." Edith Green, oral history interview by Roberta Greene, February 27, 1974, transcript, 2, John F. Kennedy Library; "Poverty and Urban Policy," 225. See Knapp and Polk, *Scouting the War on Poverty*, 117–27, on the problems in Cleveland.

126. Lillian B. Rubin, "Maximum Feasible Participation: The Origins, Implications, and Present Status," *Annals of the American Academy of Political and Social Science*

385 (September 1969): 14–29. On the Gray Areas project, see Alice O'Connor, "Community Action, Urban Reform, and the Fight against Poverty: The Ford Foundation's Gray Areas Program," *Journal of Urban History* 22 (July 1996): 586–625; O'Connor, *Poverty Knowledge*.

127. Richard Boone, oral history interview by Richardson White, January 30, 1969, Richardson White Papers, box 7, Notes: Misc.

128. Robert Kennedy, oral history interview by Lewis, December 4, 1964, 394; Robert Kennedy, oral history interview by Anthony Lewis, December 22, 1964, transcript, 548, John F. Kennedy Library; Edwin O. Guthman and C. Richard Allen, eds., *RFK: Collected Speeches* (New York: Viking, 1993), 129.

129. Memo, David L. Hackett to the Attorney General, Re: Participation in the Heller Study of Poverty, November 6, 1963, Supplemental Materials to "Poverty and Urban Policy," John F. Kennedy Library.

130. Ibid.

131. Daniel Patrick Moynihan, *Maximum Feasible Misunderstanding* (New York: Free Press, 1969), 77–79; "Poverty and Urban Policy," 151; Hackett, oral history interview by Douglas, 90, 92. William Cannon was perhaps the biggest supporter of community action in the Bureau of the Budget and believed strongly in its capacity for flexibility and adaptability. Cannon, oral history interview.

132. "Poverty and Urban Policy," 228, 231–32.

133. Ibid.; Hackett to Heller, Re: 1964 Legislative Programs for "Wider Participation in Prosperity."

134. "Poverty and Urban Policy," 145; James L. Sundquist, oral history interview by Stephen Goodell, April 7, 1969, transcript, 32–33, Lyndon B. Johnson Library.

135. Sorensen, *Kennedy*, 404.

136. Homer Bigart, "Kentucky Miners: A Grim Winter," *New York Times*, October 20, 1963.

137. Memo, R. W. Boone to Franklin D. Roosevelt Jr., n.d., Theodore C. Sorensen Papers, box 37, Poverty: Eastern Kentucky, John F. Kennedy Library. On the genesis and evolution of the AVs, see Thomas J. Kiffmeyer, *Reformers to Radicals: The Appalachian Volunteers and the War on Poverty* (Lexington: University Press of Kentucky, 2008).

138. Brauer, "Kennedy, Johnson," 111–12.

139. Discussing the likelihood of an antipoverty legislative program, William Cannon told an oral history interviewer: "There was kind of an implicit responsibility in the [Bureau of the Budget] office to be a ramrod for the White House, which is to keep the process moving fast enough to the end. So it was from that angle that we began to get concerned if the president really wanted a program like this. That wasn't clear. That was not at all clear." Cannon, oral history interview.

140. Gillette, *Launching the War on Poverty*, 15.

141. Bernard Russell, oral history interview by Daniel Knapp, November 29, 1967, Daniel Knapp Papers, John F. Kennedy Library; Richardson White Jr. and Beryl A. Radin, "Youth and Opportunity: The Federal Anti-Delinquency Program," unpublished ms., 256–57, Richardson White Papers, box 1, file: Manuscript. For

more on the tension between Washington Action for Youth (WAY), the juvenile delinquency agency funded by the PCJD, and Superintendent Carl F. Hansen, see Maurine Hoffman, "D.C. School Staff Reacts Coolly to 'WAY' Ideas," *Washington Post*, January 10, 1964.

4. TROUBLES AND TRIALS

1. Lester David and Irene David, *Bobby Kennedy: The Making of a Folk Hero* (New York: PaperJacks, 1988), 217.
2. David Hackett, oral history interview by John Douglas, July 22, 1970, transcript, 97, John F. Kennedy Library; David and David, *Bobby Kennedy*, 217. See also Nicholas Katzenbach, *Some of It Was Fun: Working for RFK and LBJ* (New York: W. W. Norton, 2008), 134.
3. Jean Stein and George Plimpton, eds., *American Journey: The Times of Robert Kennedy* (New York: Harcourt Brace Jovanovich, 1970), 147.
4. Gerald Grant, "Justice Dept. Is Santa to School Children," *Washington Post*, December 21, 1963; "Good to See Our Man Smile Again," *Chicago Defender*, December 23, 1963.
5. William vanden Heuvel and Milton Gwirtzman, *On His Own: Robert F. Kennedy, 1964–1968* (New York: Doubleday, 1970), 23.
6. "Harlem Youths Urge Lawmen 'Get Busy,'" *New York Amsterdam News*, February 29, 1964.
7. Bernard Russell, oral history interview by Daniel Knapp, November 29, 1967, Daniel Knapp Papers, John F. Kennedy Library; Sanford Kravitz, oral history interview by Daniel Knapp, February 11, 1969, John F. Kennedy Library.
8. Richardson White Jr. and Beryl A. Radin, "Youth and Opportunity: The Federal Anti-Delinquency Program," unpublished ms., 258, Richardson White Papers, box 1, file: Manuscript, John F. Kennedy Library.
9. Arthur M. Schlesinger Jr., *Robert Kennedy and His Times* (Boston: Houghton Mifflin, 1978), 631.
10. Katzenbach, *Some of It Was Fun*, 134–36.
11. Dick Schaap, *R.F.K.* (New York: New American Library, 1967), 194. The notes hung on the walls of Kennedy's Justice Department and Senate offices.
12. William Cannon, oral history interview by Michael Gillette, May 21, 1982, Lyndon B. Johnson Library, Austin, Tex.
13. Michael L. Gillette, *Launching the War on Poverty: An Oral History* (New York: Twayne Publishers, 1996), 16; Nicholas Lemann, *Promised Land: The Great Black Migration and How It Changed America* (New York: Vintage, 1992), 141.
14. Dick Gregory would joke that when Lyndon Johnson embraced Kennedy's agenda, "twenty million Negroes unpacked." Nick Kotz, *Judgment Days: Lyndon Baines Johnson, Martin Luther King, Jr., and the Laws That Changed America* (Boston: Houghton Mifflin, 2006), 34.
15. Nicholas de B. Katzenbach, oral history interview by Larry Hackman, October 8, 1969, transcript, 1, John F. Kennedy Library; William Cannon, oral history interview; Schlesinger, *Robert Kennedy*, 638. Further confirmation of the seriousness

of Kennedy's interest in the post can be found in a late December memo Hackett sent to Kennedy, listing as the top recommendation for the poverty program "that the attorney general be named chairman of a cabinet committee responsible for administering a major attack on poverty." Memo, David L. Hackett to the Attorney General, Re: Administration Attack on Poverty, December 30, 1963, Adam Walinsky Papers, box 33, folder: Poverty: Hackett, John F. Kennedy Library. When Robert Kennedy ran for president in 1968, his campaign prepared a brief on his record that claimed he had chaired "the Special Cabinet Committee on Poverty" which "led the government's effort to formulate the war on poverty, which led to the Economic Opportunity Act." Such a formal committee never actually materialized as the motive force behind War on Poverty planning. That role would be left to the Shriver Task Force. "Robert F. Kennedy: The Record and the Program," Peter Edelman Papers, box 8, folder: Misc. 1968 (Campaign Materials), John F. Kennedy Library.

16. Memo, Robert F. Kennedy to Theodore C. Sorensen, December 16, 1963, Theodore C. Sorensen Papers, box 37, Attack on Poverty Program, John F. Kennedy Library.

17. This understanding of Kennedy's use of "self-help" appears to be borne out by the use of the term in Boone's memo to Franklin Roosevelt Jr. regarding flood relief in Kentucky. Boone was the foremost advocate for participatory democracy among Hackett's "guerrillas." Richard Boone, correspondence with the author, June 21, 2001; memo, R. W. Boone to Franklin D. Roosevelt Jr., n.d., Theodore C. Sorensen Papers, box 37, Poverty: Eastern Kentucky. See also "Citizens Press for National Service Corps," *Washington Post*, August 3, 1963.

18. Memo, Robert F. Kennedy to Theodore C. Sorensen, December 16, 1963, Theodore C. Sorensen Papers, box 37, Attack on Poverty Program.

19. David Hackett, oral history interview by author, May 5, 2001. Hackett's testimony before the Senate on behalf of the Economic Opportunity Act was revealing in this regard. Rep. Charles Goodell pressed Hackett to admit that there weren't sufficient data to support the expansion of community action to a $300 million program. Hackett avoided a direct answer but contended that the PCJD experience demonstrated the viability of federal-local coordination—a great achievement in Hackett's mind—a process change that would in time undoubtedly produce appropriate local solutions to reduce delinquency. U.S. House Subcommittee on the War on Poverty of the Committee on Education and Labor, *Hearings on the Economic Opportunity Act of 1964*, 88th Cong., 2d sess. (Washington, D.C.: U.S. Government Printing Office, 1964), April 22, 1964, 1235–59.

20. Memo, Robert F. Kennedy to Theodore C. Sorensen, December 16, 1963, Theodore C. Sorensen Papers, box 37, Attack on Poverty Program.Hackett, oral history interview by author.

21. Memo, the Attorney General to the President, January 16, 1964, Theodore C. Sorensen Papers, box 37, Attack on Poverty Program, John F. Kennedy Library. Kennedy was actually on a Far East trip, meeting with Sukarno in Indonesia on that day.

22. Quoted in Lemann, *Promised Land*, 149.

23. Ibid., 87, 61; Michael Beschloss, ed., *Taking Charge: The Johnson White House Tapes, 1963–1964* (New York: Simon & Schuster), 244.

24. Beschloss, *Taking Charge*, 204, 209.

25. Marjorie Hunter, "Johnson Signs Bill to Fight Poverty; Pledges New Era," *New York Times*, August 21, 1964, 11.

26. Gerald Tremblay, oral history interview by Roberta Greene, January 8, 1970, transcript, 27, 43, John F. Kennedy Library; Jeff Shesol, *Mutual Contempt: Lyndon Johnson, Robert Kennedy, and the Feud That Defined a Decade* (New York: W. W. Norton, 1997), 169–70; Hackett, oral history interview by Douglas, 91, 97–107; Peter Edelman, oral history interview by Larry Hackman, March 13, 1974, 138, John F. Kennedy Library. According to Office of Economic Opportunity official Frederick Hayes, there was tension between Hackett and Shriver as well. David Grossman and Fred Hayes, oral history interview by Richardson White, notes, February 6, 1969, Richardson White Papers, box 7, Notes: Misc.

27. Frank Mankiewicz, oral history interview by Stephen Goodell, April 18, 1969, transcript, 17, Lyndon B. Johnson Library. In a much later interview by Nicholas Lemann, Mankiewicz said that David Hackett and several others may have been with him during this meeting, but it seems unlikely that, given Hackett's displeasure with the expansion of community action, he would have concurred that the program was taking shape along PCJD lines. Lemann, *Promised Land*, 149. Of course President Kennedy himself had no clear conception of a poverty program in late 1963, so Robert Kennedy's question seems mainly to be indicative of a desire to find solace in his brother's memory.

28. Adam Yarmolinsky, "The Beginnings of OEO," in *On Fighting Poverty: Perspectives from Experience*, ed. James L. Sundquist (New York: Basic Books, 1969), 40.

29. Ibid., 43; Cannon, oral history interview. A December 1963 draft memo for Kennedy to send to Johnson called the program "an effective adjunct of the overall attack on poverty" and proposed a potential compromise with Republicans that would limit its purview to "Indians, migrant farm workers, the District of Columbia and specified areas of mental health," none of which could create much of a political base. Memo, William R. Anderson to the Attorney General, December 5, 1963, Robert F. Kennedy Attorney General Papers, General Correspondence, National Service Corps, 8/63–9/63, 12/63, John F. Kennedy Library. See also "Domestic Peace Corps Voted by House Panel; Changes Held Needed," *Wall Street Journal*, December 12, 1963.

30. Marjorie Hunter, "Robert Kennedy Asks G.O.P. Aid in Pushing for Home Peace Corps," *New York Times*, February 21, 1964; "Robert Kennedy Pushes Domestic Peace Corps," *Barnard Bulletin*, March 2, 1964, www.newspaperarchive.com; Mrs. Oscar Chapman to the Attorney General, February 28, 1964, Robert F. Kennedy Attorney General Papers, General Correspondence, National Service Corps, 2/64–3/64, box 41.

31. Gillette, *Launching the War on Poverty*, 240–41; Hackett, oral history interview by Douglas, 103.

32. Richard Boone, interview notes, January 30, 1969, Richardson White Papers.

33. White and Radin, "Youth and Opportunity," 162; Gillette, *Launching the War on Poverty*, 77; Adam Yarmolinsky, oral history interview by Michael L. Gillette, October 22, 1980, transcript, 17, Lyndon B. Johnson Library.

34. Norbert A. Schlei, oral history interview by Michael L. Gillette, May 15, 1980, transcript, 17, Lyndon B. Johnson Library.

35. "Poverty and Urban Policy: A Group Discussion of the Kennedy Administration Urban Poverty Programs and Policies," Brandeis University Conference, June 16–17, 1973, transcript, 229, John F. Kennedy Library. James Sundquist has asserted that during the planning process he was the only member of the Shriver Task Force who was giving the coordination aspect of community action serious attention. James Sundquist, oral history interview by Stephen Goodell, April 7, 1969, transcript, 44, Lyndon B. Johnson Library.

36. Gordon J. Davis and Amanda Hawes, "Toward an Understanding of Decision Making in the Office of Economic Opportunity: The CDGM Affair," *Harvard Civil Rights–Civil Liberties Law Review* 2 (Spring 1967): 266.

37. Leonard S. Cottrell, "The Competent Community," Supplemental Materials to "Poverty and Urban Policy," John F. Kennedy Library.

38. Lemann, *Promised Land*, 152.

39. Hackett, oral history interview by Douglas, 103. William Cannon would later contend that he and others supportive of community action prevailed upon Hackett and Boone for help fearing it was going to be dropped from the legislation. "I firmly believe that the major reason Community Action survived was because David Hackett prevailed upon Attorney General Kennedy to intercede with Mr. Shriver." Quoted in Schlesinger, *Robert Kennedy*, 638–39. On Shriver's resistance to the PCJD model, see "Poverty and Urban Policy," 240.

40. Richard W. Boone, correspondence with author, March 12, 2001; "Poverty and Urban Policy," 238–39. Shriver later protested to author Nicholas Lemann, however, that he did not need to be sold on community action. Lemann, *Promised Land*, 153, 379.

41. Lemann, *Promised Land*, 149.

42. Ibid., 153.

43. Henry Kissinger, *The White House Years* (Boston: Little, Brown, 1979), 54. On Chicago School precursors to community action, see Noel A. Cazenave, "Chicago Influences on the War on Poverty," *Journal of Policy History* 5, no. 1 (1993): 52–68.

44. Quoted in Robert Dallek, *Flawed Giant: Lyndon Johnson and His Times* (New York: Oxford University Press, 1998), 657; "Poverty and Urban Policy," 70–71.

45. U.S. House of Representatives Subcommittee on the War on Poverty Program, *Hearings on the Economic Opportunity Act of 1964*, 88th Cong., 2d sess. (Washington, D.C.: U.S. Government Printing Office, 1964), April 7, 1964, 330.

46. Ibid., 305; emphasis added. It is uncertain who authored the phrase "maximum feasible participation," but the best evidence seems to suggest it was Harold Horowitz.

47. Ibid. 331–33.

48. Ibid., 329.

49. Ibid., 317.

50. Address by Attorney General Robert F. Kennedy to the Friendly Sons of St. Patrick of Lackawanna County, Scranton, Pa., March 17, 1964, Robert F. Kennedy Attorney General Papers, Speeches, 1961–1964, box 2.

51. "Bobby Kennedy Visits City, County Impoverished Areas," *Charleston Daily Mail*, April 29, 1964, www.newspaperarchive.com; Edwin Guthman, *We Band of Brothers* (New York: Harper & Row, 1969), 271.

52. Guthman, *Band of Brothers*, 271; Robert F. Kennedy, *The Pursuit of Justice* (New York: Harper & Row, 1964), 16. Kennedy also later discussed his West Virginia experience during the Senate hearings for the Elementary and Secondary Education Act. U.S. Senate Subcommittee on Education, *Hearings on the Elementary and Secondary Education Act*, 89th Cong., 1st sess. (Washington, D.C.: U.S. Government Printing Office, 1965), February 2, 1965, 2604–5.

53. Marquette University Commencement Address, June 7, 1964, Robert F. Kennedy Attorney General Papers, Speeches and Press Releases, 1961–1964, box 3.

54. Jon Margolis, *The Last Innocent Year: America in 1964* (New York: William Morrow, 1999).

55. Jack Newfield, *Robert Kennedy: A Memoir* (New York: E. P. Dutton, 1969), 98.

56. Beschloss, *Taking Charge*, 475.

57. Phil Casey, "Students Steal Show as Kennedy Resigns," *Washington Post*, September 4, 1964.

58. Schlesinger, *Robert Kennedy*, 666; vanden Heuvel and Gwirtzman, *On His Own*, 39.

59. See, e.g., Martin Arnold, "Kennedy Mobbed in Grand Central," *New York Times*, September 5, 1964.

60. "Kennedy Discusses Campaign Tactics," *New York Times*, November 5, 1964.

61. On Keating's support for a federal poverty effort, see Marjorie Hunter, "Keating, Javits Unite on Poverty," *New York Times*, March 29, 1964.

62. Robert E. Baker, "War on Poverty a Fake, Goldwater Says," *Washington Post*, September 19, 1964.

63. Kennedy, *Pursuit of Justice*, 9.

64. Goldwater's grandfather built the largest department store in Phoenix, Arizona. Statement on Minimum Wage, September 19, 1964, Robert F. Kennedy Senate Papers, 1964 Campaign, Speeches and Press Releases, box 20; "Liberals Call for a 'Just Society' Achieved by Government Action," *New York Times*, September 20, 1964, 73. In his call for a minimum wage hike Kennedy did not, however, recommend as large an increase as other liberals. The minimum wage in 1964 stood at $1.25. Kennedy called for a raise to $1.50 an hour, while the Liberal Party of New York sought $2.00.

65. Address by Robert F. Kennedy to Shop Stewards, Amalgamated Clothing Workers Union, September 23, 1964, Robert F. Kennedy Senate Papers, 1964 Campaign, Speeches and Press Releases, box 20.

66. Vanden Heuvel and Gwirtzman, *On His Own*, 79.

67. "Statement on a Housing Program for New York and the Nation," October 6, 1964, Robert F. Kennedy Senate Papers, 1964 Campaign, Speeches and Press

Releases, box 20; Martin Arnold, "Kennedy Pledges Attack on Slums," *New York Times*, October 7, 1964. Kennedy proposed that residents who began to earn more income might be charged an affordable rent to encourage them to stay in the community.

68. "Appalachian Development Program," October 25, 1964, Robert F. Kennedy Senate Papers, 1964 Campaign, Speeches and Press Releases, box 21.

69. Schlesinger, *Robert Kennedy and His Times*, 669; Layhmond Robinson, "Democrats Form a Keating Group," *New York Times*, September 13, 1964.

70. Sydney H. Schanberg, "Kennedy Favored by Puerto Ricans," *New York Times*, October 18, 1964; Neil Sheehan, "Lower East Side: Profile of a Slum," *New York Times*, August 25, 1964.

71. Peter Kihss, "City's Puerto Rican Voters Appear Heavily Pro-Johnson, but G.O.P. Believes It Can Cut Margin," *New York Times*, September 15, 1964.

72. Ronald Sullivan, "Kennedy Aides Say Many Party Leaders Have Not Helped in Registration," *New York Times*, October 7, 1964; Ronald Sullivan, "Buckley Avoiding Kennedy Tours," *New York Times*, September 26, 1964.

73. Sydney H. Schanberg, "Kennedy Favored by Puerto Ricans," *New York Times*, October 18, 1964.

74. "The World of Roy Chalk," *Time*, June 8, 1962, 84–86; "Sparks & Machete Blows," *Time*, February 18, 1966, 41.

75. "Sparks & Machete Blows"; Schanberg, "Kennedy Favored."

76. Sally M. Miller, *The Ethnic Press in the United States* (New York: Greenwood, 1987), 306–10.

77. Vicki Ruíz and Virginia Sánchez Korrol, *Latinas in the United States* (Bloomington: Indiana University Press, 2006), 356–57, 602.

78. Layhmond Robinson, "New York's Racial Unrest: Negro Anger Mounting," *New York Times*, August 12, 1963; Layhmond Robinson, "Puerto Rico Bid on Rights Is Made," *New York Times*, January 3, 1964; Peter Kihss, "Puerto Ricans Gain," *New York Times*, February 6, 1964; Fred Powledge, "1,800 Join March for Better Schools for Puerto Ricans," *New York Times*, March 2, 1964; Sydney H. Schanberg, "Pickets Blockade Plumbers' Office," *New York Times*, May 13, 1964; "The Thin Red Line Emotional Experience," *New York Amsterdam News*, October 31, 1964.

79. Anthony Lewis, "Concern Grows over 'White Backlash,'" *New York Times*, May 10, 1964; "Ofay Backlash Would Hurt Dems: RFK," *Chicago Defender*, August 8, 1964.

80. "Y'All Moving Too Fast Says NY Times Poll," *Chicago Daily Defender*, September 22, 1964.

81. Douglas Robinson, "Kennedy in Trouble with Italian-Americans in City about Two Issues," *New York Times*, October 13, 1964. In 1960 John Kennedy won 64 percent of the Italian American vote in New York State, taking upstate by a three-to-one margin, but some were predicting only a minimal advantage there for Robert Kennedy. Mark R. Levy and Michael S. Kramer, *The Ethnic Factor: How America's Minorities Decide Elections* (New York: Simon and Schuster, 1972), 170.

82. "Surprised and Disappointed," *New York Amsterdam News*, September 12, 1964; "AJC Wants Issues Discussed Clearly," *New York Amsterdam News*, September 26,

1964. The liberal American Jewish Congress also castigated both Keating and Kennedy for their stances.

83. In actuality the plan would not have required sending students any farther than ten minutes from their home by bus, but Kennedy preferred not to reopen the discussion during the campaign. Kennedy had indicated his opposition to busing in principle a year earlier, so while there was undoubtedly political calculation in his handling of the issue, it was not entirely born of the moment. Cabell Phillips, "Robert Kennedy and Senator Ervin Almost Agree," *New York Times*, August 9, 1963; R. W. Apple Jr., "Kennedy Says He Opposes Distant Busing of Students," *New York Times*, September 9, 1964; "Surprised and Disappointed," *New York Amsterdam News*, September 12, 1964; Robert H. Terte, "Donovan Assails Busing as Issue," *New York Times*, September 9, 1964.

84. "Y'All Moving Too Fast Says NY Times Poll"; Robert H. Terte, "Pupils in Imbalanced Schools Are Found Declining Transfers," *New York Times*, August 8, 1964.

85. Gerald Gardner, *Robert Kennedy in New York* (New York: Random House, 1965), 71–72.

86. Robert L. Robinson, "New York Negroes Have 'Mixed Emotions' over 'Bobby' Kennedy's Bid for Senate," *Pittsburgh Courier*, September 5, 1964; Fred Powledge, "Negroes for Kennedy in Mild Fashion," *New York Times*, October 11, 1964.

87. Layhmond Robinson, "Keating Speaks at Negro Session," *New York Times*, October 3, 1964. Keating's advance text—which he later stood by—used tougher language than his delivered remarks. Nevertheless, he had made the charge on other occasions.

88. James Booker, "Evers' RFK Praise Sparked NAACP Row," *New York Amsterdam News*, October 17, 1964.

89. "Keating vs. Kennedy," *New York Times*, October 18, 1964; "For Robert F. Kennedy," *New York Amsterdam News*, October 10, 1964.

90. James L. Hicks, "His Brother Was a Friend of Mine!" *New York Amsterdam News*, October 31, 1964. On African Americans' loyalty to John Kennedy and their enduring sense that he had paid the ultimate price for his civil rights initiative, see also Robinson, "New York Negroes Have 'Mixed Emotions.'"

91. Vanden Heuvel and Gwirtzman, *On His Own*, 54; Byron Porterfield, "Johnson Reverses History in Republican Suffolk," *New York Times*, November 5, 1964; Earl Mazo, "Support from All Ethnic Groups Shown in Tristate Johnson Vote," *New York Times*, November 4, 1964.

92. Levy and Kramer, *Ethnic Factor*, 78–79.

93. M. S. Handler, "Negroes, a Major Factor in Johnson Victory, Viewed as Abandoning the G.O.P.," *New York Times*, November 5, 1964.

94. R. W. Apple Jr., "Kennedy Edge 6–5," *New York Times*, November 4, 1964; Anthony Lewis, "White Backlash Doesn't Develop," *New York Times*, November 4, 1964; Levy and Kramer, *Ethnic Factor*, 151. The only ethnic group with whom Kennedy lagged significantly behind recent Democratic percentages was Jewish Americans, who remained loyal to Keating. Julius Duscha, "LBJ Vote Credited for Bob Kennedy's Defeat of Keating," *Washington Post*, November 4, 1964.

95. Edelman, oral history interview, March 13, 1974, 121; Milton Gwirtzman, oral history interview by Roberta Greene, February 10, 1972, transcript, 50–52, John F. Kennedy Library. See also Helen O'Donnell, *A Common Good: The Friendship of Robert F. Kennedy and Kenneth P. O'Donnell* (New York: William Morrow, 1998), 358; Dick Hendrickson, "RFK Says New York Slow to Begin Poverty Programs," *Syracuse Post-Standard*, December 16, 1964, www.newspaperarchive.com.

96. See "The Welfare City," *Time*, July 28, 1961, 17; "Newburgh Stirs New Relief Rift," *New York Times*, May 19, 1961; James T. Patterson, *America's Struggle against Poverty in the Twentieth Century* (Cambridge: Harvard University Press, 2000), 104–6.

97. For the social dynamics in the city, see Joseph P. Ritz, *The Despised Poor: Newburgh's War on Welfare* (Boston: Beacon Press, 1966).

98. "Goldwater Hails Newburgh Plan as Ideal for All Cities," *New York Times*, July 19, 1961.

99. "Mitchell Assails U.S. Welfare Plan," *New York Times*, February 4, 1962.

100. Robert Kennedy at a community meeting in Newburgh, N.Y., January 13, 1965, audio recording R-14, John F. Kennedy Library.

101. Robert Kennedy at a community meeting in Syracuse, N.Y., December 11, 1964, audio recording R-6, John F. Kennedy Library.

102. Vanden Heuvel and Gwirtzman, *On His Own*, 88–89.

103. Adam Walinsky, "Keeping the Poor in Their Place: Notes on the Importance of Being One-Up," *New Republic*, July 4, 1964, 16.

104. Ibid., 18.

105. Michael Novak, *The Rise of the Unmeltable Ethnics: Politics and Culture in the Seventies* (New York: Macmillan, 1972), 18; Adam Walinsky, oral history interview byLarry Hackman, May 22, 1972, 155, John F. Kennedy Library.

106. The best study on the reactions of white ethnics to urban social and economic change in the period leading up to the urban tumult of the 1960s is Thomas J. Sugrue, *The Origins of the Urban Crisis: Race and Inequality in Postwar Detroit* (Princeton: Princeton University Press, 1996). While a substantive debate has emerged among historians as to whether European immigrants had to work toward racial acceptance or were "white on arrival," by the 1960s the descendants of southern and eastern European immigrants were accepted members of the American middle class.

107. Memo, Adam Walinsky to Robert F. Kennedy, Re: Legislative programs and strategy for new session, November 7, 1964, Peter Edelman Papers, box 7, folder: November 1964.

108. Joseph F. Dolan, correspondence with author, May 6, 2001.

109. Richard N. Goodwin, *Remembering America: A Voice from the Sixties* (Boston: Little, Brown, 1988), 450.

110. William V. Shannon, *The Heir Apparent: Robert Kennedy and the Struggle for Power* (New York: Macmillan, 1967), 85; Jacob Javits, oral history interview by William vanden Heuvel, June 19, 1970, transcript, 11, John F. Kennedy Library; Peter Edelman, oral history interview by Larry Hackman, January 3, 1970, transcript, 33–51,

John F. Kennedy Library. Ron Linton, a Kennedy staffer in the chamber with him before his statement, contended that Kennedy wanted to present the amendment in conjunction with Javits but went ahead without him when the senior senator failed to arrive in the chamber. O'Donnell, *A Common Good*, 357–58.

111. Homer Bigart, "'Gateway to the Finger Lakes' Stubbornly Fights Poverty Aid," *New York Times*, February 26, 1965.

112. Homer Bigart, "Utica Unifying Forces to Lead Mohawk Valley's Fight on Poverty," *New York Times*, December 22, 1964.

113. Bigart, "'Gateway to the Finger Lakes.'"

114. Homer Bigart, "Upstate Apathy Annoys Kennedy," *New York Times*, March 30, 1965.

115. Telegram, Robert E. Hammer to Robert F. Kennedy, February 2, 1965; James E. Furman to Robert F. Kennedy, February 3, 1965; Loretta Dunham to Robert F. Kennedy, February 28, 1965; and Ann Culhane to Robert F. Kennedy, September 3, 1965, Robert F. Kennedy Senate Papers, Correspondence, 1965, Poverty, box 15, John F. Kennedy Library.

116. Robert F. Kennedy to Mike Mansfield, December 18, 1964, Robert F. Kennedy Senate Papers, Correspondence, Subject File: Senate, box 12. The bureau chief in Washington, D.C., for a Syracuse newspaper reported that Kennedy chose Labor and Public Welfare in order "to pursue his special interests of the poor and uneducated." Don Bacon, "Stuffy Senate Awaits Kennedy Brothers and New Life," *Syracuse Post-Standard*, December 22, 1964, www.newspaperarchive.com.

117. U.S. Senate Subcommittee on Education, *Hearings on the Elementary and Secondary Education Act*, 89th Cong., 1st sess. (Washington, D.C.: U.S. Government Printing Office, 1965), January 29, 1965, 1235, 1282.

118. Ibid., January 26, 1965, 513.

119. Ibid., 514.

120. Ibid., January 29, 1965, 1298.

121. Ibid., February 2, 1965, 2625. James Sundquist asserts that Shriver was never very interested in the coordinating aspect of running OEO. Sundquist, oral history interview, 40–41. The Kennedy-Hackett conception of OEO director had given primary importance to the role of coordinator in chief.

122. U.S. Senate Subcommittee on Education, *Hearings on the Elementary and Secondary Education Act*, 89th Cong., 1st sess. (Washington, D.C.: U.S. Government Printing Office, 1965), February 2, 1965, 2543.

123. Ibid., 2605.

124. Ibid., February 11, 1965, 3014. Senior New York senator Jacob Javits, not wanting to be upstaged, responded, "A few of us started off our lives in just that way and carry that vision in our hearts, right here, I can assure the Senator." Ibid.

125. Hugh Davis Graham, *The Uncertain Triumph: Federal Education Policy in the Kennedy and Johnson Years* (Chapel Hill: University of North Carolina Press, 1984), 79. Kennedy did claim credit for the amendment in his 1967 book *To Seek a Newer World*, but he expressed frustration with its lack of implementation. Robert F. Kennedy, *To Seek a Newer World* (Garden City, N.Y.: Doubleday, 1967), 31.

126. Peter Edelman, oral history interview by Roberta Greene, January 3, 1970, transcript, 163, John F. Kennedy Library. According to Edelman, Adam Walinsky drafted the amendment that was implemented by the House committee. Adam Walinsky, oral history interview by Thomas Johnston, November 29, 1969, transcript, 48–49, John F. Kennedy Library.

127. Address by Senator Robert F. Kennedy, National Council of Christians and Jews, April 28, 1965, Robert F. Kennedy Senate Papers, Speeches and Press Releases, box 1.

128. Schlesinger, *Robert Kennedy*, 111–12.

129. "RFK Hits Northern Teachers, Marchers," *New York Amsterdam News*, May 8, 1965.

5. THE EDUCATION OF A SENATOR

1. "Leaders at Odds over L.A. Riot," *Chicago Defender*, August 21, 1965.

2. Doris Kearns, *Lyndon Johnson and the American Dream* (New York: Harper & Row, 1976), 305.

3. Robert Dallek, *Flawed Giant: Lyndon Johnson and His Times* (New York: Oxford University Press, 1998), 223.

4. Ibid., 224.

5. William vanden Heuvel and Milton Gwirtzman, *On His Own: Robert F. Kennedy, 1964–1968* (New York: Doubleday, 1970), 80.

6. David S. Broder, "Yorty and Shriver Disagree on Riots," *Washington Post*, August 18, 1965.

7. Quoted in Douglas Ross, *Robert F. Kennedy: Apostle of Change* (New York: Pocket Books, 1968), 11.

8. Founded in seventeenth-century England, the Odd Fellows had the largest African American membership among fraternal mutual aid societies in the United States by the early twentieth century.

9. Address by Senator Robert F. Kennedy, Independent Order of Odd Fellows, Spring Valley, N.Y., August 18, 1965, Robert F. Kennedy Senate Papers, Speeches and Press Releases, box 1, John F. Kennedy Library. In the assessment of Michael Knox Beran, the real significance of Kennedy's Odd Fellows address was his acknowledgment that the welfare state was bloated. Beran attributes Kennedy's expressed concern about wasted human resources and financial drain on the community to "the existing welfare regime" rather than to the problem of poverty that created the need for a social safety net. While Kennedy did indeed see problems with the welfare system and would later critique it forcefully, Beran ignores Kennedy's insistence that "the Poverty Program—and other vital efforts, such as Aid to Education—must and will expand. But we need to do far more—in a far more urgent fashion." Michael Knox Beran, *Last Patrician: Bobby Kennedy and the End of American Aristocracy* (New York: St. Martin's, 1998), 103.

10. "Leaders at Odds over L.A. Riot."

11. Peter Edelman, oral history interview by Larry Hackman, January 3, 1970, transcript, 104, John F. Kennedy Library.

12. Most of the projects funded by the PCJD had been absorbed into OEO antipoverty efforts, and many served as the initial Community Action Program in their community.

13. Memo, Dave Hackett and Tom Johnston to Senator Robert F. Kennedy, August 27, 1965, Milton Gwirtzman Papers, Publications: *On His Own* Subject File, box 5: Memoranda, 8/1964–3/1968, John F. Kennedy Library. On the Harlem youth program, HARYOU-ACT, see Daniel Knapp and Kenneth Polk, *Scouting the War on Poverty: Social Reform Politics in the Kennedy Administration* (Lexington, Mass.: D. C. Heath, 1971), 9–11.

14. Dallek, *Flawed Giant*, 226. For an interpretation of the administration's inactivity as a retreat rather than a tactical pause, see William C. Selover, "The View from Capitol Hill: Harassment and Survival," in *On Fighting Poverty: Perspectives from Experience*, ed. James L. Sundquist (New York: Basic Books, 1969), 158–87. Selover argues that Johnson was fed up with the War on Poverty and his silence left a vacuum that for the first time allowed Congress to enter significantly into the debate.

15. Nicholas Lemann, *Promised Land: The Great Black Migration and How It Changed America* (New York: Vintage, 1992), 167.

16. Samuel F. Yette, *The Choice: The Issue of Black Survival in America* (New York: G. P. Putnam's Sons, 1971), 69–70; Robert A. Bauman, "Race, Class, and Political Power: The Implementation of the War on Poverty in Los Angeles" (Ph.D. diss., University of California–Santa Barbara, 1998), 150–87. Yette and Bauman both contend that Yorty's obstructionist stance contributed to the frustrations that erupted in Watts.

17. Lemann, *Promised Land*, 165; Dallek, *Flawed Giant*, 223–26, 329–34. On Johnson's early concerns about the Community Action Program, see William Cannon, oral history interview by Michael Gillette, May 21, 1982, 34, Lyndon B. Johnson Library.

18. Address by Senator Robert F. Kennedy, Independent Order of Odd Fellows.

19. Quoted in James T. Patterson, *America's Struggle against Poverty in the Twentieth Century* (Cambridge: Harvard University Press, 2000), 140.

20. Irwin Unger, *The Best of Intentions: The Triumphs and Failures of the Great Society under Kennedy, Johnson, and Nixon* (New York: Doubleday, 1996), 170.

21. Kevin Boyle, *The UAW and the Heyday of American Liberalism* (Ithaca: Cornell University Press, 1995), 189–91, 216; Kenneth B. Clark and Jeannette Hopkins, *A Relevant War against Poverty* (New York: Harper & Row, 1970), 198–204; John C. Donovan, *The Politics of Poverty*, 3d ed. (Washington, D.C.: University Press of America, 1980), 57–58; Unger, *Best of Intentions*, 168–70. Among those who supported or played a role in CCAP were two critical influences on the PCJD— Richard Boone, who served as its executive director, and Richard Cloward. Others who supported the organization included Michael Harrington, Paul Potter (a founder of Students for a Democratic Society), Richard Goodwin, A. Philip Randolph, and Martin Luther King Jr.

22. See the comments of Kennedy adviser Frank Mankiewicz in Center on Budget and Policy Priorities, "Tribute to Richard W. Boone," www.cbpp.org/boone-video.htm.

23. Thomas J. Sugrue, *Sweet Land of Liberty* (New York: Random House, 2008), 379. McKissick would later assert that he was angered by the insubstantial White House conference at which the report was discussed, but that the report "was absolutely correct" in its assertion that "we need male symbols." U.S. Senate Subcommittee on Executive Reorganization of the Committee on Government Operations, *Hearings on Federal Role in Urban Affairs*, 89th Cong., 2d sess. (Washington, D.C.: U.S. Government Printing Office, 1966), August 23, 1966, 2318.

24. Daryl Michael Scott, "The Politics of Pathology: The Ideological Origins of the Moynihan Controversy," *Journal of Policy History* 8, no. 1 (1996): 92–96; Tom Hayden, *Reunion: A Memoir* (New York: Random House, 1988), 148–49; Sugrue, *Sweet Land of Liberty*, 379. Hayden did not publicize his views at the time.

25. Address by Senator Robert F. Kennedy, Long Island University, December 16, 1965, Robert F. Kennedy Senate Papers, Speeches and Press Releases, box 2.

26. "Watts Riot Study Depicted as Weak," *New York Times*, January 23, 1966, 71. During the Senate hearings on the problems of urban America, chaired by Abraham A. Ribicoff of Connecticut, Kennedy said, "I know there is a great deal of controversy about [the McCone Commission], but in my judgment it was a major step forward and highlighted some of the needs not only in Watts but elsewhere across the country." U.S. Senate Subcommittee, *Hearings on Federal Role in Urban Affairs*, 778.

27. Jack T. Conway, oral history interview by Larry Hackman, April 11, 1972, transcript, 92, John F. Kennedy Library; John Nolan, oral history interview by Roberta Greene, July 24, 1970, transcript, 105, John F. Kennedy Library. On one occasion Parker referred to Mexican Americans as only "one step removed from the wild tribes of Mexico." For examples of other inflammatory comments and African American reactions, see "Parker Raps Brotherhood," *California Eagle*, September 15, 1960; "The Road to Understanding," *California Eagle*, May 17, 1962. Kennedy's assessment of Parker was not widely known, but he did discuss his friendship with the recently deceased chief during Los Angeles mayor Sam Yorty's testimony before the Ribicoff Committee on the Federal Role in Urban Affairs in August 1966. U.S. Senate Subcommittee, *Hearings on Federal Role in Urban Affairs*, 766.

28. Address, Senator Robert F. Kennedy, ADA National Roosevelt Day Dinner, January 27, 1966, Robert F. Kennedy Senate Papers, Speeches and Press Releases, box 2.

29. Edwin O. Guthman and C. Richard Allen, eds., *RFK: Collected Speeches* (New York: Viking, 1993), 165.

30. Address by Senator Robert F. Kennedy, Federation of Jewish Philanthropies, New York, January 20, 1966, Robert F. Kennedy Senate Papers, Speeches and Press Releases, box 2.

31. Address by Senator Robert F. Kennedy, Conference on the Revitalization of Harlem, January 21, 1966, New York, Robert F. Kennedy Senate Papers, Speeches and Press Releases, box 2.

32. Adam Walinsky, "Keeping the Poor in Their Place: Notes on the Importance of Being One-Up," *New Republic*, July 4, 1964, 15–18; Adam Walinsky, oral history

interview by Roberta Greene, November 22, 1976, transcript, 656, and September 7, 1979, 769, John F. Kennedy Library.

33. Address by Senator Robert F. Kennedy, Regional Conference of the United Auto Workers, New York, January 22, 1966, Robert F. Kennedy Senate Papers, Speeches and Press Releases, box 2.

34. Beran, *Last Patrician*, 104.

35. Evan Thomas, *Robert Kennedy: His Life* (New York: Simon & Schuster, 2000), 318.

36. For further evidence of this perspective, see Robert F. Kennedy, *The Cities: Pressure Points in Our Society,* sound cassette (Washington, D.C.: Washington Tapes, 1967). Kennedy said: "Communities compete with one another. They compete with one another for industry, for recreational purposes, for education, instead of trying to work out their problems together. Maybe it would be better if one community concentrated on education, another community concentrated on areas of homes and living units, and another on the field of business. But at least there should be an overall plan and program to try to develop an area with all the governmental units cooperating with one another. And that does not exist, not only between the states, but between counties and between communities." On corporatism as a distinctive perspective on society, see Ellis W. Hawley, "The Discovery and Study of a Corporate Liberalism," *Business History Review* 52, no. 3 (Autumn 1978): 309–20; and Michael J. Hogan, "Corporatism," *Journal of American History* 77, no. 1 (June 1990): 153–60. Hogan defines corporatism as "a system that is founded on officially recognized functional groups, such as organized labor, business, and agriculture. In such a system, institutional regulating and coordinating mechanisms work to integrate the groups into an organic whole, elites in the private and public sectors collaborate to guarantee stability and harmony, and that collaboration creates a pattern of interpenetration and power sharing that often makes it difficult to determine where one sector leaves off and the other begins" (154). Similarly, Rhys Williams has written: "A traditional theme in Catholicism is the image of the Church—and of the well-ordered society—as the 'body of Christ.' Different 'organs' or 'appendages' play different roles in the functioning of the whole. The whole of society is the reality, with the various parts or elements having distinct and complementary obligations and contributions to make." Rhys H. Williams, "Visions of the Good Society and the Religious Roots of American Political Culture," *Sociology of Religion* 60, no. 1 (Spring 1999): 19.

37. Address, Conference on the Revitalization of Harlem.

38. See Robert Collins, *More: The Politics of Economic Growth in Postwar America* (London: Oxford University Press, 2000).

39. Robert Kennedy, oral history interview by Anthony Lewis, April 13, 1964, transcript, 147–48, John F. Kennedy Library; James W. Hilty, *Robert Kennedy: Brother Protector* (Philadelphia: Temple University Press, 1997), 275.

40. Charles Bartlett to Robert F. Kennedy, March 2, 1966, Robert F. Kennedy Senate Papers, Correspondence, Personal, B: 1966, Baggs–Bassett.

41. Peter Edelman said of Kennedy, "If there was any area that he looked on as being Greek to him, it was economics." On Kennedy's limited understanding of and

interest in economic theory, see Edelman, oral history interview by Hackman, July 15, 1969, 72–73; Adam Walinsky, oral history interview by Thomas Johnston, November 29, 1969, transcript, 45, John F. Kennedy Library. The Franklin Roosevelt quote is cited in William E. Leuchtenberg, *Franklin D. Roosevelt and the New Deal* (New York: Harper & Row, 1963), 344.

42. For examples of far right opposition that adopted this view of Kennedy's willingness to use federal power in civil rights and the War on Poverty, see Medford Evans, *The Usurpers* (Belmont, Mass: Western Islands, 1968), 220–21, 246; and Frank A. Capell, *Robert F. Kennedy: Emerging American Dictator* (Zarephath, N.J.: Herald of Freedom, 1968).

43. "Kennedy Amazed by City Park Plan," *New York Times*, January 24, 1966; Gertrude Wilson, "Where the Action Is," *New York Amsterdam News*, January 8, 1966. See also "Officials across Nation Battle to Remove Slum," *Chicago Defender*, February 26, 1966.

44. Ralph Blumenthal, "Brooklyn Negroes Harass Kennedy," *New York Times*, February 5, 1966. The *Times* headline might have been reversed, given the community's growing exasperation with purported helpers from the outside.

45. Donald Webster, "The Web Must Be Grasped Whole": The Bedford-Stuyvesant Restoration Corporation, 1967–1988" (M.A. thesis, University of Virginia, 1991); "Restoration: We Made Sure Everybody Had a Voice," brooklynhistory.org/podcast/BHSpodcast/Brooklyn_Historical_Society.xml.

46. Kennedy had actually encouraged the foundling organization's youth program while attorney general, but along with the major task of making progress on a dire economic situation, the CBCC had become embroiled in a battle for funding with the OEO-recognized antipoverty group in Bedford-Stuyvesant, Youth In Action. "Council's Youth Service's Project Gets in Motion," *New York Amsterdam News*, August 24, 1963. On the challenges facing CBCC, see "Boro Council Opposes New Anti-Poverty Unit," *New York Amsterdam News*, July 10, 1965; "King's Diary," *New York Amsterdam News*, October 2, 1965; "Renewal 'Trickle' Irks Coordinating Council," *New York Amsterdam News*, January 1, 1966.

47. "Boro Cry to RFK, JVL: 'We're Tired of Waiting,'" *New York Amsterdam News*, February 12, 1966; "Brooklyn Negroes Harass Kennedy."

48. Thomas, *Robert Kennedy*, 319.

49. Kennedy maintained a particular interest in the children of migrant laborers and had made a specific inquiry into conditions for them in the fall of 1963. George H. Weber to Thompson Powers, November 7, 1963, Robert F. Kennedy Attorney General Papers, General Correspondence, box 38.

50. U.S. Senate Committee on Labor and Public Welfare Subcommittee on Migratory Labor, *Hearings on Amending Migratory Labor Laws*, 89th Cong., 1st sess. (Washington, D.C.: U.S. Government Printing Office, 1965), July 8, 1965, 93–95, 100–101.

51. Edelman, oral history interview by Hackman, July 15, 1969, 125–26.

52. Jean Stein and George Plimpton, eds., *American Journey: The Times of Robert Kennedy* (New York: Harcourt Brace Jovanovich, 1970), 280.

53. Conway, oral history interview, 93. See also John Barnard, *Walter Reuther and the Rise of the Auto Workers* (Boston: Little, Brown, 1983), 181–82; and Victor G. Reuther, *The Brothers Reuther and the Story of the UAW* (Boston: Houghton Mifflin, 1976), 367–70, on the interest of Reuther and the UAW.

54. U.S. Senate Committee on Labor and Public Welfare Subcommittee on Migratory Labor, *Hearings on Amending Migratory Labor Laws*, 89th Cong., 2d sess. (Washington, D.C.: U.S. Government Printing Office, 1966), March 15, 1966, 529–37.

55. Catholic bishops in California affirmed this position later in the hearings. In his questioning of farm workers Kennedy explored whether the clergy had been helpful enough.

56. A.V. Krebs Jr., "Grape Strikers Begin 300-Mile Pilgrimage," *National Catholic Reporter*, March 23, 1966.

57. Having grown up in regular contact with clergy and the church hierarchy, Kennedy would take his complaints to the highest levels, privately telling Pope Paul VI that the American church needed to become "the foremost champion for changing this kind of difficult, poverty-stricken life," and that it should broaden beyond its largely Italian and Irish American parishioners to reach out to Latinos. In August 1967 he delivered a stinging critique of the church hierarchy before the National Catholic Conference for Interracial Justice. "Those churches who have ministered to an affluent flock while ignoring the hungry, the jobless, and the unclothed[,] . . . who have compromised the moral imperatives of equality to win the support of their complacent followers[,] . . . who have ignored the plight of the migrant worker . . . have not aided our security, they have hurt it." Address by Senator Robert F. Kennedy, National Catholic Conference for Interracial Justice, August 17, 1967, Robert F. Kennedy Senate Papers, Speeches and Press Releases, box 2.

58. U.S. Senate Committee on Labor and Public Welfare, *Hearings on Amending Migratory Labor Laws*, March 16, 1966, 626–30.

59. César Chávez, oral history interview by Dennis J. O'Brien, January 28, 1970, transcript, 2, John F. Kennedy Library.

60. Peter B. Edelman, *Searching for America's Heart: RFK and the Renewal of Hope* (Boston: Houghton Mifflin, 2001), 45.

61. Chávez, oral history interview, 7.

62. Jack Conway, oral history interview by Jean Stein, September 21, 1968, transcript, Jean Stein Papers, box 1, John F. Kennedy Library; Edelman, *Searching for America's Heart*, 46; Mario T. García, *Memories of Chicano History: The Life and Narrative of Bert Corona* (Berkeley: University of California Press, 1994), 233. On Kennedy's continuing interest in unionizing efforts, see Joint Statement of Senator Harrison A. Williams Jr., Chairman, Senate Subcommittee on Migratory Labor, and Senator Robert F. Kennedy, Member of the Subcommittee, June 28, 1966, Robert F. Kennedy Senate Papers, Speeches and Press Releases, box 2.

63. Nadine Cahodas, *The Band Played Dixie* (New York: Free Press, 1997), 122–24; "Miss. Bigots to Stage 'Ride-In' against Bobby," *Chicago Defender*, February 15, 1966.

64. Address by Senator Robert F. Kennedy, University of Mississippi, March 18, 1966, Robert F. Kennedy Senate Papers, Speeches and Press Releases, box 2.

65. Gertrude Wilson, "A Milestone," *New York Amsterdam News*, April 2, 1966.

66. *CBS Reports: Black Power, White Backlash*, exec. prod. Leslie Midgely, videocassette (Films for the Humanities & Sciences, 2000).

67. Bruce J. Schulman, *The Seventies: The Great Shift in American Culture, Society, and Politics* (New York: Simon & Schuster, 2001); Rick Perlstein, *Nixonland: The Rise of a President and the Fracturing of America* (New York: Scribner, 2008). Perlstein contends that August 1966 was the turning point for Republicans in abandoning centrism and a stake in the liberal consensus. Schulman carries the centrifuge argument further into the 1970s, contending that the whirlwind social forces of the previous decade had sent many individuals and groups off the political and civic spectrum entirely and into the solitary pursuits of the "Me Decade."

68. James D. Williams, "Sightseeing," *Washington Afro-American*, April 30, 1966. See also "Poverty War and Vietnam," *Washington Afro-American*, January 8, 1966; "Washington Notebook," *Washington Afro-American*, February 19, 1966; Baker E. Morton, "Pie-In-the-Sky, That's a Lie," *Washington Afro-American*, October 1, 1966; "A Cry of Pain," *Washington Afro-American*, December 24, 1966.

69. Address by Senator Robert F. Kennedy, WGHQ Human Relations Dinner, Ellenville, N.Y., April 19, 1966, Robert F. Kennedy Senate Papers, Speeches and Press Releases, Reading Copies 3/66–6/66, box 4.

70. Ibid.

71. Edelman, oral history interview by Hackman, January 3, 1970, 142. Former Justice Department aide Ed Guthman has written that "within two years Bob [Kennedy] was recognizing the limitations in the Community Action approach that he had recommended. . . . [H]owever, unlike many leading political figures in both parties, he did not react with rancor or criticism, but spoke about facts and needs and proposed new approaches." Edwin Guthman, *We Band of Brothers* (New York: Harper & Row, 1969), 228. This incorrectly absolves Kennedy of not clearly defining, defending, or working to shore up community action earlier, and it also runs counter to his continuing call for participation by the poor.

72. Edelman, oral history interview by Hackman, January 3, 1970, 136.

73. Ibid., 134–35.

74. Ibid., 141.

75. As quoted in Brian Dooley, *Robert Kennedy: The Final Years* (Staffordshire: Keele University Press, 1995), 31.

76. Address of Senator Robert F. Kennedy, National Council of the Churches of Christ: Pre–White House Conference on Civil Rights, May 11, 1966, Robert F. Kennedy Senate Papers, Speeches and Press Releases, box 2.

77. Address by Senator Robert F. Kennedy, NAACP Legal Defense Fund Banquet, May 18, 1966, Robert F. Kennedy Senate Papers, Speeches and Press Releases, box 2.

78. Ibid.

79. Richard N. Goodwin, *Remembering America: A Voice from the Sixties* (Boston: Little, Brown, 1988), 464.

80. Tydings later recalled that Kennedy was the only senator who volunteered to serve on the D.C. committee he chaired. Joseph D. Tydings, oral history

interview by Roberta Greene, May 3, 1971, transcript, 34, John F. Kennedy Library; Joseph D. Tydings, correspondence with author, July 23, 2002. For an example, see Kennedy's questioning of landlord Nathan Habib, U.S. Senate Subcommittee on Business and Commerce of the Committee on the District of Columbia, *Hearings on Housing in the District of Columbia*, 89th Cong., 2d sess. (Washington, D.C.: U.S. Government Printing Office, 1966), July 19, 1966, 165–92. On Kennedy's involvement with D.C. affairs, see Peter Edelman, oral history interview by Roberta Greene, transcript, 277–79, John F. Kennedy Library; and memo, Peter Edelman to Senator Kennedy, Re: Upcoming Matters on Your Return, June 15, 1966, Robert F. Kennedy Senate Papers, Correspondence: Personal File, 1964–1968, box 3.

81. U.S. Senate Subcommittee, *Hearings on Federal Role in Urban Affairs*, August 15, 1966, 26–27.

82. Ibid., 28.

83. Ibid., 32–33.

84. Ibid., 26, 38–39. Adam Walinsky had begun regularly sprinkling Mumford quotes into Kennedy's speeches, and the author would testify before the committee the following spring, telling Kennedy: "There is a residue of community life, at least in poor neighborhoods. . . . [T]hese elementary human relationships are important and we must preserve them." U.S. Senate Subcommittee on Executive Reorganization of the Committee on Government Operations, *Hearings on Federal Role in Urban Affairs*, 90th Cong., 1st sess. (Washington, D.C.: U.S. Government Printing Office, 1967), April 20, 1967, 3614–16. On Mumford's organicist, communitarian philosophy, see Casey Nelson Blake, *Beloved Community: The Cultural Criticism of Randolph Bourne, Van Wyck Brooks, Waldo Frank, and Lewis Mumford* (Chapel Hill: University of North Carolina Press, 1990), 212, 266–95. The most complete statement of Kennedy's organic, communitarian vision for urban America can be found in Robert F. Kennedy, *To Seek a Newer World* (Garden City, N.Y.: Doubleday, 1967), 19–62.

85. U.S. Senate Subcommittee, *Hearings on Federal Role in Urban Affairs*, August 15, 1966, 38.

86. On the growing popularity of the idea of public-private partnerships, see Joseph W. Sullivan, "GOP on the Offense: Revived Party Seeking More Positive Image with 'New Federalism,'" *Wall Street Journal*, November 18, 1966; Arlen J. Large, "'Just Like Comsat': That's What Public-Private Antipoverty Firms Wouldn't Be," *Wall Street Journal*, December 7, 1966.

87. U.S. Senate Subcommittee, *Hearings on Federal Role in Urban Affairs*, August 15, 1966, 46.

88. Michael B. Katz, *In the Shadow of the Poorhouse: A Social History of Welfare in America* (New York: BasicBooks, 1996), 238–39.

89. U.S. Senate Subcommittee, *Hearings on Federal Role in Urban Affairs*, August 16, 1966, 195.

90. Ibid., 429.

91. Ibid., 516–17.

92. Gareth Davies, *From Opportunity to Entitlement: The Transformation and Decline of Great Society Liberalism* (Lawrence: University Press of Kansas, 1996), 138–39; Jeff Shesol, *Mutual Contempt: Lyndon Johnson, Robert Kennedy, and the Feud That Defined a Decade* (New York: W. W. Norton, 1997), 138–39, 246.

93. K. Dun Gifford, oral history interview by Larry Hackman, November 22, 1971, transcript, 6–7, John F. Kennedy Library.

94. U.S. Senate Subcommittee, *Hearings on Federal Role in Urban Affairs*, August 22, 1966, 582, 598.

95. U.S. Senate Subcommittee, *Hearings on Federal Role in Urban Affairs*, August 23, 1966, 771.

96. Ibid., 764.

97. Ibid., 777.

98. Shesol, *Mutual Contempt*, 246.

99. Memo, Carl (not further specified) to Senator, August 31, 1966, Joseph Dolan Papers, John F. Kennedy Library. One typical critical letter read: "Your brother had depth and tenderness. As for you, your liberalism is phony, and you are a cut-throat, obnoxious politician in the very worst sense. Sam Yorty may not be a Thomas Jefferson or an Abe Lincoln but neither are you by one hell of a way. I sincerely hope that Yorty may turn your very cheap, purely political remarks into a boomerang." The writer also enclosed three dollars for Kennedy to get a hair-cut—a regular occurrence in his unfriendly correspondence. H. E. Jennings to Senator Robert Kennedy, August 23, 1966, Robert F. Kennedy Papers, Senate File, Correspondence: Subject File, 1966, box 91.

100. "Poverty and Urban Policy: A Group Discussion of the Kennedy Administration Urban Poverty Programs and Policies," Brandeis University Conference, June 16–17, 1973, transcript, 316, John F. Kennedy Library; "Magnet in the West," *Time*, September 2, 1966, 14–15. *Time* called the clash "a minus for Bobby Kennedy's political fortunes in California."

101. D. Tubbs, letter to the editor, *Los Angeles Sentinel*, September 1, 1966; Leon H. Washington Jr., "Mayor Yorty Needs to Know 'Watts Happening,'" *Los Angeles Sentinel*, September 1, 1966; Bill Lane, "The Inside Story," *Los Angeles Sentinel*, September 1, 1966.

102. Ted Knap, "Why Iowa Prefers RFK to Johnson," *Washington Daily News*, August 25, 1966.

103. J. Hull Wilson, "Ohio Democrats Like RFK for President," *Elyria Chronicle-Telegram*, October 10, 1966.

104. Chávez, oral history interview, 9.

105. "LBJ's Poverty Bill on Shaky Ground," *Chicago Daily Defender*, September 13, 1966.

106. Polling data also revealed a large divide between African Americans' and low-income whites' perceptions of the poverty war, as blacks supported the program by a five-to-one margin, while fewer than one third of poor or working-class whites saw it as successful. Cited in Bauman, "Race, Class, and Political Power," 75.

107. Senate Speech on the War on Poverty, October 3, 1966, Robert F. Kennedy Senate Papers, Speeches and Press Releases, box 3.

108. Address by Senator Robert F. Kennedy, Civic Center Club Ray Corbett Dinner, September 10, 1966, Robert F. Kennedy Senate Papers, Speeches and Press Releases, Reading Copies 6/66–10/66, box 5.
109. Address by Senator Robert F. Kennedy, Community College Dedication, Worthington, Minn., September 17, 1966, Robert F. Kennedy Senate Papers, Speeches and Press Releases, box 3. At the same time, of course, a demographic reversal was about to begin, but not along the lines Kennedy suggested, as many white Americans started relocating to the suburban areas of the nation's Sun Belt.
110. Quoted in "The Bobby Phenomenon," *Newsweek*, October 24, 1966, 36.
111. Memo, Adam to RFK, Re: Program for the fall, n.d., Adam Walinsky Papers, box 26, John F. Kennedy Library.
112. "Stick-in-the-HUDs," *National Review*, October 3, 1967, 1056.

6. "BORN IN A STORM"

1. Thomas R. Jones, oral history interview by Roberta Greene, November 26, 1971, transcript, 40, John F. Kennedy Library.
2. Adam Walinsky, oral history interview by Roberta Greene, September 7, 1979, transcript, 778–79, John F. Kennedy Library.
3. Ibid., 780.
4. Jack Newfield, *Robert Kennedy: A Memoir* (New York: E. P. Dutton, 1969), 100–101; "Performance in Black and White: An Appraisal of the Development and Record of the Bedford-Stuyvesant Restoration and Development and Services Corporations," Burke Marshall Papers, box 39, 4, John F. Kennedy Library.
5. "Performance in Black and White," 4. By way of comparison, the national median income in 1965 was $6700, and the median income in Harlem in 1966 was less than $4000. "The Merchant's View," *New York Times*, September 4, 1966; Thomas A. Johnson, "Harlem Likened to a New Nation," *New York Times*, December 11, 1966.
6. Newfield, *Robert Kennedy*, 100; Jones, oral history interview, 4.
7. "Performance in Black and White," 8.
8. Newfield, *Robert Kennedy*, 104; "Performance in Black and White," 12.
9. Newspapers reported that Kennedy had ordered FBI agents to wake steel executives and the press in the middle of the night. This led to the widespread notion that Kennedy had used "Gestapo tactics" against corporate leaders. Kennedy denied ordering the agents to wake anyone in the middle of the night, and Justice Department assistant Edwin Guthman claimed some responsibility for the affair. Evan Thomas asserts that J. Edgar Hoover deliberately waited to have agents notify the executives for maximum negative publicity to be directed at Kennedy. Nevertheless, as is often the case in politics, the perception was more important than the reality. Evan Thomas, *Robert Kennedy: His Life* (New York: Simon & Schuster, 2000), 170–71; Edwin Guthman, *We Band of Brothers* (New York: Harper & Row, 1969), 233–34; Victor S. Navasky, *Kennedy Justice* (New York: Atheneum, 1971), 352–53; Robert Kennedy, oral history interview by Anthony Lewis, December 6, 1964, transcript, 510, John F. Kennedy Library. On attitudes of the business

community toward RFK, see Gerald Rosen, "Bobby Kennedy and the Businessmen," *Dun's Review*, October 1966, 33, 89–90.

10. Eli S. Jacobs, oral history interview by Roberta Greene, October 27, 1976, transcript, 1–3, John F. Kennedy Library.

11. Ibid., 2–3.

12. Jones, oral history interview, 12; "Performance in Black and White," 4, 92–93; Newfield, *Robert Kennedy*, 97–98; Carter Burden, oral history interview by Roberta Greene, February 13, 1974, transcript, 4–7, John F. Kennedy Library.

13. Earl G. Graves, *How to Succeed in Business without Being White* (New York: HarperBusiness, 1997), 11–12.

14. Burden, oral history interview, 4–7; Walinsky, oral history interview by Greene, 243–44.

15. Pratt Institute for Community and Environmental Development, "CDC Oral History Project, Bedford-Stuyvesant Restoration Corporation," www.picced.org/advocacy/bsrc.htm; memo, Tom Johnston to RFK, n.d., Thomas Johnston Papers, box 3, Bedford-Stuyvesant, Programs, John F. Kennedy Library. Johnston used the same term to describe the community board that Leonard Cottrell had with regard to the PCJD: "The Board which will be headed by Judge Tom Jones," Johnston wrote, "represents a strong and competent community group with which all of Senator Kennedy's work in Bedford-Stuyvesant can be coordinated."

16. Elsie Richardson, letter to the editor, *New York Amsterdam News*, July 30, 1966.

17. Memo, Vernon Rutherford to Thomas Johnston, n.d. but later identified by Johnston as summer 1966, Thomas Johnston Papers, box 2, Memoranda: Miscellaneous, 8/27/65–4/10/67.

18. Jones, oral history interview, 6–7. In New York State, judges are elected to the bench.

19. "Performance in Black and White," 24–25; Susan Brownmiller, "This Is Fighting Shirley Chishom," *New York Times*, April 13, 1969. "Kennedy didn't understand the district," Chisholm told Brownmiller. "I was the top vote-getter, but Kennedy never sought me out."

20. Robert F. Kennedy, oral history interview by John F. Stewart, August 1, 1967, transcript, 663, John F. Kennedy Library. He was discussing John Kennedy's involvement in local Massachusetts politics as senator, but the power struggles of Bedford-Stuyvesant in 1966–67 could not have been far from his thoughts.

21. Jones, oral history interview, 7.

22. Ibid., 8.

23. Jacob Javits, oral history interview by William vanden Heuvel, June 19, 1970, transcript, 13, John F. Kennedy Library; Walinsky, oral history interview by Greene, 255. Not surprisingly, Kennedy and Javits aides present different explanations of the momentary disagreement. Walinsky argued that Javits misread the amendment with regard to attracting private enterprise and protested needlessly until Kennedy got angry and "threw the thing down on the table and the committee was sitting there and he read it to them and he said, 'Well it's right there senator and the statement you're making just isn't true.'" Walinsky contends that Javits felt

that Kennedy was trying to steal his idea of incentives for business investment in ghetto areas. Javits aide Robert Patricelli contended that Kennedy staffers failed to emphasize the centrality of private enterprise, and that Javits's sensitivity was owed to the fact that he had to weigh whether to abandon his own contemplated technical assistance initiative for ghetto areas. The Kennedy staff also neglected to inform Javits until much later that they were developing a program in Bedford-Stuyvesant toward which Kennedy hoped to direct SIP money, and this later caused tension at the staff level. "Performance in Black and White," 14–16.

24. Memo, Tom Johnston to RFK, n.d., Thomas Johnston Papers, box 3, Bedford-Stuyvesant, Programs. Johnston later identified the date of the memo as October 1966, but the text suggests it was written earlier.

25. Jacobs, oral history interview, 5.

26. Ibid., 12; "Performance in Black and White," 24.

27. Cary Reich, *Financier: The Biography of André Meyer* (New York: William Morrow, 1983), 275.

28. Jacobs, oral history interview, 8. Perhaps not coincidentally, although Kennedy had known of the FBI director's intentions for months, Hoover aired his side of the wiretapping story the same day the Bedford-Stuyvesant announcement was made. Fred P. Graham, "Hoover Asserts Robert Kennedy Aided Buggings," *New York Times*, December 11, 1966.

29. David E. Lilienthal to Robert F. Kennedy, October 24, 1966, Thomas Johnston Papers, box 1, Bedford-Stuyvesant, Correspondence, 10/17/66–12/19/66. Lilienthal had not previously known Kennedy, and his description of their meeting is similar to the accounts of others on meeting Kennedy for the first time: "I can't remember ever having my impression of a man change so much and so suddenly. . . . [C]ould this earnest young man possibly be the same fellow pictured by the press and TV as a cynical, ambitious ruthless trickster dealing only with political issues that would 'pay off'?" David E. Lilienthal, *The Journals of David E. Lilienthal*, vol. 6, *Creativity and Conflict* (New York: Harper & Row, 1976), 302.

30. "Performance in Black and White," 20.

31. Jacobs, oral history interview, 10; Newfield, *Robert Kennedy*, 104.

32. Jacobs, oral history interview, 25–26. Mayor John Lindsay also played a role in convincing Astor. See John V. Lindsay, oral history interview by Roberta Greene, April 21, 1970, transcript, 16, John F. Kennedy Library.

33. Jacobs, oral history interview, 29; "Performance in Black and White," 16–17.

34. Robert F. Kennedy to McGeorge Bundy, n.d., Adam Walinsky Papers, John F. Kennedy Library.

35. Jacobs, oral history interview, 29.

36. "Performance in Black and White," 18.

37. Jacobs, oral history interview, 9.

38. Benno Schmidt, oral history interview by Roberta Greene, July 17, 1969, transcript, 9, John F. Kennedy Library.

39. Ibid., 5.

40. Ibid., 6.

41. Edward J. Logue, oral history interview by Roberta Greene, January 23, 1976, transcript, 9, John F. Kennedy Library; Walinsky, oral history interview by Greene, 44–45.

42. Robert F. Kennedy to J. M. Kaplan, December 7, 1966, Thomas Johnston Papers, Bedford-Stuyvesant, box 1, Correspondence, 10/17/66–12/19/66.

43. J. M. Kaplan to Robert F. Kennedy, December 19, 1966; William S. Paley to Robert F. Kennedy, December 8, 1966; and James F. Oates Jr. to Robert F. Kennedy, December 8, 1966, Thomas Johnston Papers, Bedford-Stuyvesant, box 2, Planning/Structure, 9/28/66–2/22/67; Jones, oral history interview, 42.

44. David E. Lilienthal to Robert F. Kennedy, December 14, 1966, Thomas Johnston Papers, Bedford Stuyvesant, box 1, Correspondence, 10/17/66–12/19/66.

45. Jones, oral history interview, 12. Jones recalled later that Kennedy told him, "I have never been dealt with as rudely and as abruptly, by anybody—even my worst adversaries—than I have been dealt with by some of the women of Bedford-Stuyvesant." Ibid., 16.

46. "Performance in Black and White," 27.

47. Address, Senator Robert F. Kennedy, "Bedford-Stuyvesant Community Development Program Announcement," Robert F. Kennedy Senate Papers, Speeches and Press Releases, box 3, 9/11/66–9/10/67.

48. Memo, Adam to RFK, "Program for the Fall," n.d., Adam Walinsky Papers.

49. As cited in Jeff Shesol, *Mutual Contempt: Lyndon Johnson, Robert Kennedy, and the Feud That Defined a Decade* (New York: W. W. Norton, 1997), 249.

50. Newfield, *Robert Kennedy*, 105. See also Burke Marshall, oral history interview by Larry Hackman, January 20, 1970, transcript, 67, John F. Kennedy Library, on Kennedy's caution.

51. Daphne Sheppard, "New Look Coming to Bedford-Stuy.," *New York Amsterdam News*, December 17, 1966; "Hope in Brooklyn," *New York Amsterdam News*, December 17, 1966. Jackie Robinson also praised the project effusively. Jackie Robinson, "A Giant Step in the Right Direction," *New York Amsterdam News*, December 24, 1966.

52. Steven V. Roberts, "Redevelopment Plan Set for Bedford-Stuyvesant," *New York Times*, December 11, 1966.

53. Jones, oral history interview, 19.

54. Franklin Thomas, oral history interview by Roberta Greene, March 23, 1972, transcript, 2, John F. Kennedy Library.

55. Ibid., 4; Jones, oral history interview, 23.

56. Thomas, oral history interview, 5.

57. Ibid., 7. Jones, by contrast, did not have a problem with the two-board structure, finding it part of the reality of power relationships in the project. "I don't think this is a sociology class," Jones told Kennedy. "I'm interested in building and fashioning an instrument which will produce the change." Jones, oral history interview, 28, 56–57.

58. Jones also sought out representatives from the Puerto Rican community, labor unions, youth groups, and public officials. "New Blight Group Stirs Boro Fight," *New York Amsterdam News*, April 8, 1967.

59. Memo, Earl Graves to Eli and Tom, n.d. (text suggests mid-March 1967), Thomas Johnston Papers, Bedford-Stuyvesant, Community, 2/23/67–5/24/67.

60. Ibid.

61. Jones, oral history interview, 29, 32.

62. "Performance in Black and White," 33.

63. Newfield, *Robert Kennedy*, 113.

64. "Report of the Westinghouse Learning Corporation, 1969," Burke Marshall Papers, Bedford-Stuyvesant, Evaluations, box 1, folder 4.

65. "Performance in Black and White," 33.

66. "Brooklyn Groups Charge Meddling," *New York Times*, April 6, 1967.

67. Ibid.

68. Thomas Johnston to Lionel F. Payne, April 4, 1967, Thomas Johnston Papers, Bedford Stuyvesant, box 1, Correspondence, 1/10/67–4/4/67.

69. Kilvert Dun Gifford, "Neighborhood Development Corporations: The Bedford-Stuyvesant Experiment," in *Agenda for a City: Issues Confronting New York*, ed. Lyle C. Fitch and Annmarie Hauck Walsh (Beverly Hills, Calif.: Sage Publications), 429; Daphne Sheppard, "Bed-Stuy Blight Bedlam; Leaders Say More on Way," *New York Amsterdam News*, April 15, 1967. Sheppard also reported that Kennedy's poll numbers "took a deep dip" in the community. Daphne Sheppard, "King's Diary," *New York Amsterdam News*, April 15, 1967.

70. Thomas, oral history interview, 13, 23.

71. Tom Johnston described a later scene in which Kennedy (who was notoriously tight in paying employees), Meyer, Schmidt, and Dillon, all millionaires, were discussing Thomas's salary and complained when Johnston suggested paying him $40,000 a year instead of $35,000 to keep him from being tempted by other jobs. Eventually they came around to Johnston's way of thinking. Walinsky, oral history interview by Thomas Johnston, November 29, 1969, transcript, 86–87, John F. Kennedy Library. Staffer Carter Burden describes the somewhat absurd debate over the car for Thomas: "They were going to get him an Oldsmobile and he didn't feel that an Oldsmobile was suitable to his position. There was a big internal battle for about a month about whether he was going to get a Cadillac or an Oldsmobile." Burden, oral history interview, 23.

72. "Performance in Black and White," 39–40.

73. George Todd, "Mixed Boro Reaction Shown on Astor Foundation Grant," *New York Amsterdam News*, April 1, 1967.

74. "Performance in Black and White," 106. Pei argued that evidence of development would influence insurance companies to provide lower rates and help make mortgages more accessible.

75. Ibid.

76. Memo, Tom Johnston to Eli Jacobs and Edward Logue, "Areas of Specific Interest of Development & Services Corporation Board Members," February 13, 1967, Thomas Johnston Papers, Bedford-Stuyvesant, box 2, Memoranda, Miscellaneous, 8/27/65–4/10/67.

77. Jacobs, oral history interview, 18–19.

78. Memo, Judge Thomas Jones to Thomas Johnston, March 19, 1967, Thomas Johnston Papers, Bedford-Stuyvesant, box 2, Memoranda, Miscellaneous, 8/27/65–4/10/67.

79. Jones, oral history interview, 44.

80. "Performance in Black and White," 40.

81. Thomas, oral history interview, 18.

82. "Meeting of the Bedford-Stuyvesant Rehabilitation Committee," March 8, 1967, transcript, Thomas Johnston Papers, Bedford-Stuyvesant, box 1, Board of Directors Rehab Committee Meeting, 3/8/67.

83. Jacobs, oral history interview, 15.

84. Ibid., 16. In May 1967 Johnston implicitly blamed Logue and Jacobs for not grasping the role of D&S, writing Kennedy, "It is clear, however, both to members of the Board and the staff of the Development and Services Corporation and it has been frequently and explicitly stated to members of the community, that the Development & Services Corporation exists only to respond to the needs of the Bedford-Stuyvesant community as these needs are determined by the residents of Bedford-Stuyvesant themselves." Memo, Tom Johnston to Senator Kennedy, May 3, 1967, Thomas Johnston Papers, Bedford-Stuyvesant, box 1, Correspondence, 4/11/67–5/3/67.

85. "Performance in Black and White," 41.

86. Thomas, oral history interview, 9.

87. Jones, oral history interview, 47.

88. Jacobs, oral history interview, 33.

89. Ibid., 34. Jacobs's rationale seems to verify Thomas's suspicions about the sociocultural reasons for the two boards.

90. "Performance in Black and White," 28.

91. Jacobs, oral history interview, 36.

92. Ibid., 37.

93. Ibid., 36.

94. Ibid., 75.

95. Ibid., 73–74, 97–99. On Thomas's handling of the garbage problem, see Lilienthal, Journals, 6:497–98.

96. The SIP grant was nearly imperiled by the fact that members of the official community action agency in Bedford-Stuyvesant, Youth In Action, claimed that they were not consulted by Restoration. They believed that this was a legal necessity under the "maximum feasible participation" clause of Title II of the Economic Opportunity Act, but it was determined that the special impact funds through the Kennedy-Javits amendment were not subject to the same procedures as those earmarked for community action programs. See Gifford, "Neighborhood Development Corporations," 429–31.

97. Community Attitudes in Bedford Stuyvesant: An Area Study (New York: Center for Urban Education, 1967); Gifford, "Neighborhood Development Corporations," 431; "Performance in Black and White," 67.

98. Thomas, oral history interview, 19.

99. Another provision of the CHIP program was that participating residents had to maintain two garbage cans (provided by Restoration if homeowners were unable to afford them), sweep their sidewalk daily, and report any reduction in city services to both Restoration and city representatives. See Thomas, oral history interview, 21, and memo, Thomas Johnston to Robert Kennedy, "Bedford-Stuyvesant Development Project: Projects," September 1967, Thomas Johnston Papers, Bedford-Stuyvesant, box 3, Programs: Projects Report to Senator Robert F. Kennedy, September 1967.

100. Donald Webster, "The Web Must Be Grasped Whole: The Bedford-Stuyvesant Restoration Corporation, 1967–1988" (M.A. thesis, University of Virginia, 1991).

101. Thomas, oral history interview, 44–45.

102. Ibid., 8–9, on the "structural tension" between Thomas and Birenbaum.

103. Ibid. In a memo from Johnston to Kennedy outlining the progress of the project, an organizational flowchart actually showed D&S as only one unit among many over which Restoration had authority. Birenbaum's Educational Affiliate was presented as an offshoot of D&S. Memo, Tom Johnston to Senator Kennedy, May 3, 1967, Thomas Johnston Papers, Bedford-Stuyvesant, box 1, Correspondence, 4/11/67–5/3/67.

104. Memo, Tom Johnston to Senator Kennedy, May 3, 1967. For an assessment of Kennedy's plan, described by economists as "branch planting," as embodied here and as later proposed in his tax incentive bills, see Bennett Harrison, "Ghetto Economic Development: A Survey," *Journal of Economic Literature* 12, no. 1 (March 1974): 16–17.

105. Thomas, oral history interview, 57–58.

106. G. L. Phillippe to Robert F. Kennedy, July 28, 1967, Thomas Johnston Papers, Bedford-Stuyvesant, box 1, Correspondence, 6/20/67–8/14/67; Newfield, *Robert Kennedy*, 108.

107. Memo, Tom Johnston to André Meyer, "The Role of D&S Board Members," November 20, 1967, Thomas Johnston Papers, Bedford-Stuyvesant, box 1, Board of Directors, D&S Corporations, 10/2/67–12/7/67; memo, Tom Johnston to André Meyer, December 2, 1967, Thomas Johnston Papers, Bedford-Stuyvesant, box 2, Memoranda, Miscellaneous, 4/14/67—1/16/68.

108. Thomas J. Watson Jr., oral history interview by Roberta Greene, January 6, 1970, transcript, 15, John F. Kennedy Library; Thomas J. Watson Jr., *Father & Son Co.: My Life at IBM and Beyond* (New York: Bantam Books, 1990), 372–73; Thomas, oral history interview, 55; Burden, oral history interview, 29. Burden claimed that Kennedy, Schmidt, and Paley confronted Watson on the plant's location.

109. Burke Marshall, oral history interview by Larry Hackman, January 20, 1970, transcript, 67, John F. Kennedy Library.

110. Ibid., 67–68; Burden, oral history interview, 28.

111. Jacobs, oral history interview, 43–44.

112. The *Chicago Defender*, while declaring the merit of the initiative "incontestable," also editorialized that "much of the free enterprise money is concentrated in

the hands of men who want to preserve the status quo in any event and who, of course, have no interest in such social welfare programs as improvement of life in the black slums. In fact, they are the ones who keep the slums going by charging exorbitant rent and by refusing to improve or recondition their property." "Slums and Racism," *Chicago Defender*, September 23, 1967. See also the comments of Jack E. Wood in "Ghettos Boiling over Bad Housing," *New York Amsterdam News*, September 23, 1967. Investment in the inner city, said Wood, was "a 'finger in the dike' approach to the economics of job and industry migration to the suburbs."

113. "Sargent Shriver Gives Views on Poverty Program," *Chicago Daily Defender*, January 20, 1968; Richard Reeves, "Galbraith Doubts Urban Approach," *New York Times*, October 17, 1967.

114. Michael Harrington, "Can Private Industry Abolish Slums?" *Dissent*, January–February 1968, 4–6.

115. Renovation proved lengthy because of the use of less experienced local contractors. André Meyer said in 1969: "We could have finished the job months ago if we had brought in some big contractor from the outside. But the point was that we wanted to give an opportunity to local people, and so it is very slow." "Performance in Black and White," 64.

116. Ibid., 93–97. In 1970 Restoration organized a subsidiary to operate the mortgage pool, and this became an FHA-approved lender in 1971. Through 1976 over one thousand loans had been issued for a total of over $21 million with a foreclosure rate of under 1 percent. Ruth Bryant Mitchell, "Changes in Bedford-Stuyvesant," *The Crisis*, January 1977, 15–16.

117. Announcement of Bedford-Stuyvesant College, February 1, 1968, Robert F. Kennedy Papers, Senate File, Speeches and Press Releases, box 4, John F. Kennedy Library. See also the brief history of Medgar Evers College on the school's Web site, www.mec.cuny.edu/presidents_office/mec_history/mec_history_1.htm. Community suspicion of paternalism remained so strong that there was some organized resistance to the plan for a college. "Mixed Reaction to Pilot 2-Year College in Bed-Stuy," *New York Amsterdam News*, February 10, 1968.

118. A book-length scholarly history of Restoration still awaits, but a good overview of the development corporation from its founding through the Reagan years is Webster, "The Web Must Be Grasped Whole." See also Pratt Institute Center for Community and Environmental Development, "Community Development Corporation Oral History Project: Bedford Stuyvesant Restoration Corporation," prattcenter.net/cdc-bsrc.php.

119. Michael Harrington, "The South Bronx Shall Rise Again," *New York*, April 3, 1978, 38.

120. Michael Katz, *The Price of Citizenship* (New York: Henry Holt, 2001), 166. Katz estimated that there were closer to two thousand "fully established CDCs" at the time his book was published. Matthew Filner, "Community Development Corporations: An Historical Overview," University of Minnesota, Center for Democracy and Citizenship, Case Study, www.publicwork.org/3_2_casestudies.html; Neal

R. Peirce and Carol F. Steinbach, *Corrective Capitalism: The Rise of America's Community Development Corporations* (New York: Ford Foundation, 1987). A contemporary organization called the National Community Development Initiative proclaims that "today, 2,000 CDCs nationwide follow the historic example of BSRC." "Bedford Stuyvesant: Where It All Started," www.ncdi.org/2006 Files/2006_cities_new_york_success_bed-sty.htm.

121. Webster, "The Web Must Be Grasped Whole," 88.
122. Brian Dooley, *Robert Kennedy: The Final Years* (Staffordshire: Keele University Press, 1995), 38.
123. John Doar, oral history interview by Jean Stein, transcript, Jean Stein Papers, box 1, John F. Kennedy Library.
124. Robert F. Kennedy to McGeorge Bundy, n.d., Adam Walinsky Papers, John F. Kennedy Library.
125. Ford Foundation Proposal, March 9, 1967, ibid.
126. Bedford-Stuyvesant Development & Services Corporation Ford Foundation Proposal, ibid., quoted in "Performance in Black and White," 116.
127. Quoted in Thomas, *Robert Kennedy*, 341.
128. Schmidt, oral history interview, 52.
129. Jacobs, oral history interview, 101.
130. Thomas, oral history interview, 58.
131. Jones, oral history interview, 61.
132. Walinsky, oral history interview, 236.
133. Javits, oral history interview, 16.
134. Memo, Tom Johnston to RFK, "Bedford-Stuyvesant Program," n.d., Thomas Johnston Papers, Bedford-Stuyvesant, box 3, Programs—undated.
135. Robert F. Kennedy, *To Seek a Newer World* (Garden City, N.Y.: Doubleday, 1967), 61.

7. "IT BECAME HIS ISSUE"

1. "Harlem Went for Board, City Didn't," *New York Amsterdam News*, November 12, 1966.
2. "Meredith Blasts Integration," *Chicago Daily Defender*, October 13, 1966.
3. On the background of the testimony, see "SE Tenants Resume War over Heat," *Washington Post*, October 29, 1966; Carol Honsa, "White House Absolved in Slash of UPO Funds," *Washington Post*, December 13, 1966.
4. Kennedy demurred in his response, calling Johnson "a man of great compassion." U.S. Senate Subcommittee on Executive Reorganization of the Committee on Government Operations, *Hearings on Federal Role in Urban Affairs*, 89th Cong., 2d sess. (Washington, D.C.: U.S. Government Printing Office, 1966), December 12, 1966, 2624–31. Other local leaders expressed sentiments similar to those of Ridley. One youth worker who recalled Kennedy's efforts to reopen the Dunbar pool told him: "The young youths [*sic*] love you, they really do, and they think you can do miracles. They do. You may not be able to do miracles, but I really think, and the young youths really think that you can help this poverty program to be continuing" (2631).

5. Ibid., November 30, 1966, 1599.

6. Ibid., 1600–1601.

7. Ibid., 1517.

8. Ibid., 2002. Eisenhower had cautioned against the dangers of a growing "military-industrial complex."

9. U.S. Senate Subcommittee, *Hearings on Federal Role in Urban Affairs*, December 6, 1966, 2000. In an oral history interview Kennedy alluded to the gathering of black artists he had attended with James Baldwin as having first alerted him to the rising anger of young blacks. Robert Kennedy, oral history interview by Anthony Lewis, December 6, 1964, transcript, 538, John F. Kennedy Library; Kennedy believed that the problem of dashed hopes was the most dangerous one facing African Americans. He said: "We have given them rising expectations over the period of the last 6 years, particularly, about the great possibilities for their own future and for their own lives, and for them. And nothing has come of it. The voting rights bill made no difference to them. The civil rights bills of 1964 and 1965 made no difference to them, so they cannot see really any positive gains." U.S. Senate Subcommittee, *Hearings on Federal Role in Urban Affairs*, November 29, 1966, 1515.

10. Thomas J. Sugrue, *Sweet Land of Liberty* (New York: Random House, 2008), 339. Two studies that explore the varying manifestations of black power are Judson L. Jeffries, ed., *Black Power in the Belly of the Beast* (Urbana: University of Illinois Press, 2006); and Peniel E. Joseph, *Waiting 'til the Midnight Hour: A Narrative History of Black Power in America* (New York: Owl Books, 2007).

11. Sugrue, *Sweet Land of Liberty*, 338–40.

12. U.S. Senate Subcommittee, *Hearings on Federal Role in Urban Affairs*, December 8, 1966, 2312–25.

13. The metaphor—stemming from Bill Clinton's 1992 critique of a black rap artist—has entered the popular political lexicon as a liberal politician's attempt to chastise a perceived black radical to make himself or herself look more moderate to white voters or to play to white fears.

14. U.S. Senate Subcommittee, *Hearings on Federal Role in Urban Affairs*, December 8, 1966, 2319; Holmes Alexander, "Kennedy and McKissick Face Back-Turning Truth," *Danville Register*, December 15, 1966; Jack Newfield, *Robert Kennedy: A Memoir* (New York: E. P. Dutton, 1969), 82; Peter Edelman, oral history interview by Larry Hackman, August 4, 1969, transcript, 325, John F. Kennedy Library. Jack Newfield reported that Kennedy helped CORE raise funds at a critical period in 1967, and Edelman mistakenly thought that McKissick was likely to support Kennedy's presidential run. Instead he endorsed Richard Nixon.

15. Peter Edelman, oral history interview by Larry Hackman, February 21, 1970, transcript, 278–79, John F. Kennedy Library.

16. Ibid., 275.

17. U.S. Senate Subcommittee, *Hearings on Federal Role in Urban Affairs*, December 13, 1966, 2829; Edelman, oral history interview by Hackman, 275–76.

18. Helen O'Donnell, *A Common Good: The Friendship of Robert F. Kennedy and Kenneth P. O'Donnell* (New York: William Morrow, 1998), 322; Haynes Johnson, *The Bay of*

Pigs: The Leaders' Story of Brigade 2506 (New York: Norton, 1964); Lloyd Cutler, oral history interview by Francis DeRosa, June 22, 1964, transcript, 2, John F. Kennedy Library.

19. Newfield, *Robert Kennedy*, 114.

20. Memo, Peter Edelman to the Senator, January 25, 1967, Robert F. Kennedy Senate Papers, Legislative Subject File, 1965–1968, box 112, Urban Employment Opportunities Development Act, John F. Kennedy Library. On prevailing public sentiment supporting the closing of tax loopholes, see Benno Schmidt, oral history interview by Roberta Greene, July 17, 1969, transcript, 61, John F. Kennedy Library. Kennedy himself had entered into the Ribicoff hearings record a column by James Reston of the *New York Times* opposing "fat cat subsidies." U.S. Senate Subcommittee, *Hearings on Federal Role in Urban Affairs*, December 7, 1966, 2171.

21. Peter Edelman to John R. Newsom, January 16, 1967, Robert F. Kennedy Senate Papers, Legislative Subject File, 1965–1968, box 112, Urban Employment Opportunities Development Act. Sturz actually first shared information on the program when Kennedy began his Senate race in 1964 as a proposal to draw industry into Harlem.

22. For a good overview of the program, see J. L. Dietz, "Operation Bootstrap and Economic Change in Puerto Rico," in *Caribbean Freedom: Economy and Society from Emancipation to the Present*, ed. Hilary Beckles and Verene Shepherd (Princeton, N.J.: Markus Wiener Publishers, 1996), 421–35.

23. Adam Walinsky, oral history interview by Roberta Greene, October 5, 1973, transcript, 235, John F. Kennedy Library.

24. The allegations were unsubstantiated. Sam Washington, "Carmichael Ends Whirlwind Talking Tour," *Chicago Daily Defender*, May 16, 1967.

25. Robert Scheer, "A Political Portrait of Robert Kennedy," *Ramparts*, February 1967, 12.

26. Ibid., 12–13. At the time Reagan was governor of California.

27. Ibid., 14.

28. A prominent voice of the New Left, Newfield first began to reassess Kennedy after seeing his opposition to the Johnson administration's intervention in the Dominican Republic and his increasing concern, through 1965, about poverty. Victor Navasky, "Jack Newfield Talks about R.F.K.," *New Leader*, May 26, 1969, 24.

29. Newfield, *Robert Kennedy*, 147.

30. Ibid.

31. Tom Hayden, *Reunion: A Memoir* (New York: Random House, 1988), 166–67; Tom Hayden, *Irish on the Inside: In Search of the Soul of Irish America* (New York: Verso, 2001), 90–91.

32. Todd Gitlin, *The Sixties: Years of Hope, Days of Rage* (New York: Bantam, 1987), 310; Hayden, *Reunion*, 167.

33. Hayden, *Irish on the Inside*, 90–92. Both sides kept their communication quiet for fear of its being exploited by opponents. Newfield, *Robert Kennedy*, 147; Hayden, *Reunion*, 264.

34. For a good account of the CDGM affair, see John C. Donovan, *The Politics of Poverty*, 3d ed. (Washington, D.C.: University Press of America, 1980), 83–92.

35. Marjorie Hunter, "House G.O.P. Bloc Offers a Substitute Poverty Plan," *New York Times*, April 11, 1967. House Republicans had offered a similar proposal a year earlier, but it made little headway.

36. A sampling of stories in major periodicals includes Charles Mangel, "Warpaint for the Senator's Wife: LaDonna Harris of Oklahoma," *Look*, April 4, 1967, 24–29; "Where the Real Poverty Is: The Plight of American Indians," *U.S. News & World Report*, April 25, 1966, 104–8; "Forgotten American Is Aiding Himself: Anti-poverty Programs on the Rosebud Sioux Reservation," *U.S. News & World Report*, October 2, 1967, 66–67; Robin Richman, "Bright Vignettes of a Lost World," *Life*, December 1, 1967, 52–66. Noting the arrival of the hippies, Vine Deloria Jr. wrote in his "Indian Manifesto" that "strange beings began to appear on Indian land, proclaiming their kinship with the redskins in no uncertain terms." Vine Deloria Jr., *Custer Died for Your Sins: An Indian Manifesto* (New York: Avon, 1969), 228.

37. Fred R. Harris, oral history interview by Roberta Greene, July 29, 1970, transcript, 6, John F. Kennedy Library.

38. Lester David and Irene David, *Bobby Kennedy: The Making of a Folk Hero* (New York: PaperJacks, 1988), 277.

39. John P. Callahan, "Kennedy Visits Upstate Indians," *New York Times*, January 21, 1967.

40. Address by Senator Robert F. Kennedy, Oklahomans for Indian Opportunity, March 14, 1967, Robert F. Kennedy Senate Papers, Speeches and Press Releases, box 3.

41. Ibid.

42. Harris, oral history interview, 7.

43. Ramsey Clark, oral history interview by Larry Hackman, June 29, 1970, transcript, 16, John F. Kennedy Library.

44. Jean Stein and George Plimpton, eds., *American Journey: The Times of Robert Kennedy* (New York: Harcourt Brace Jovanovich, 1970), 285.

45. Ibid., 287.

46. Peter B. Edelman, *Searching for America's Heart: RFK and the Renewal of Hope* (Boston: Houghton Mifflin, 2001), 57; Frank Mankiewicz, oral history interview by Stephen Goodell, May 5, 1969, transcript, 2, Lyndon B. Johnson Library. Edelman contended that it was Robert Kennedy's suggestion that led to the 1968 CBS documentary *Hunger in America*, but both producer Don Hewitt and associate producer Philip Scheffler denied this convincingly to the author. Philip Scheffler, correspondence with author, January 19, 2001.

47. David and David, *Bobby Kennedy*, 4.

48. Edelman, oral history interview by Hackman, 10; Nick Kotz, *Let Them Eat Promises: The Politics of Hunger in America* (Englewood Cliffs, N.J.: Prentice-Hall, 1969), 6–7.

49. Kotz, *Let Them Eat Promises*, 15.

50. Edelman, oral history interview by Hackman, 16.

51. U.S. Senate Subcommittee on Employment, Manpower, and Poverty, *Hearings Examining the War on Poverty*, 90th Cong., 1st sess. (Washington, D.C.: U.S. Government Printing Office, 1967), April 10, 1967, 522, 537–38.

52. Ibid., 577.

53. Ibid., 548.

54. Ibid., 624–25.

55. Ibid., 593, 594, 655.

56. John Carr, "With RFK in the Delta," *American Heritage* 53, no. 2 (April–May 2002): 93.

57. Edelman, oral history interview by Hackman, 18.

58. Ibid.; Kotz, *Let Them Eat Promises*, 1–2.

59. Daniel Schorr, *Staying Tuned: A Life in Journalism* (New York: Pocket Books, 2001), 201.

60. Quoted in Evan Thomas, *Robert Kennedy: His Life* (New York: Simon & Schuster, 2000), 339.

61. *Assassinated: The Last Days of Kennedy and King*, exec. prod. Dan Halsted and Oliver Stone, videocassette (Turner Home Entertainment, 1998).

62. The classic account, which takes a very favorable view of Kennedy's role, is Kotz, *Let Them Eat Promises*.

63. Edelman, oral history interview by Hackman, 48.

64. Kotz, *Let Them Eat Promises*, 48.

65. Ibid., 66–67; Edelman, oral history interview by Hackman, 23–24. A letter from Freeman to Clark is reprinted in U.S. Senate Subcommittee on Employment, Manpower, and Poverty, *Hearings on Hunger and Malnutrition in America*, 90th Cong., 1st sess. (Washington, D.C.: U.S. Government Printing Office, 1967), July 12, 1967, 130–31.

66. Kotz, *Let Them Eat Promises*, 67; Joseph Califano, oral history interview by Jean Stein, transcript, Jean Stein Papers, box 1, John F. Kennedy Library.

67. Edelman, oral history interview by Hackman, March 13, 1974, 26; Kotz, *Let Them Eat Promises*, 67.

68. Kotz, *Let Them Eat Promises*, 47–48.

69. U.S. Senate Subcommittee of the Committee on Agriculture and Forestry, *Hearings on Food Stamp Appropriations Authorization*, 90th Cong., 1st sess. (Washington, D.C.: U.S. Government Printing Office, 1967), April 25, 1967, 10.

70. Robert Coles, *Lives of Moral Leadership* (New York: Random House, 2000), 3.

71. Ibid.

72. Ibid., 7.

73. Ibid., 20–21.

74. Ibid., 24.

75. Ibid., 33.

76. U.S. Senate Subcommittee, *Hearings on Hunger and Malnutrition in America*, 136. Analysis of the Javits-Freeman tussle received front-page coverage in the *New York Times*, while the testimony of the doctors was relegated to page twenty-two.

77. Ibid., 174.

78. Memo, Joe to the Senator, May 22, 1967, Joseph Dolan Papers, Memos to RFK, John F. Kennedy Library. Kennedy jotted on the memo, "We must work on this." On Kennedy's reliance on Dolan for political counsel, see Edelman, oral history interview by Hackman, 8.

79. Stein and Plimpton, *American Journey*, 124.

80. Edelman, *Searching for America's Heart*, 54; Marian Wright Edelman, oral history interview by Jean Stein, transcript, Jean Stein Papers, box 3.

81. Along with her private discussion of the story with Kennedy noted in chapter 2, Wright shared the Cinderlilly story with the audience at the tumultuous Citizens' Crusade Against Poverty conference in Washington, D.C., in April 1966. For the best examination of how King arrived at the idea of the Poor People's Campaign, see Thomas F. Jackson, *From Civil Rights to Human Rights: Martin Luther King, Jr., and the Struggle for Economic Justice* (Philadelphia: University of Pennsylvania Press, 2007), 202–3, 332–33. Welfare rights leader George Wiley and his Poverty Rights Action Center had already coordinated a march of two thousand poor people to the capital to support an expansion of the War on Poverty in September 1966. "Poor People to March on D.C.," *Washington Afro-American*, September 24, 1966; "The Poor Knew Why They Came," *Washington Afro-American*, October 1, 1966.

82. In preparation materials for the Ribicoff hearings Edelman urged Kennedy to ask Los Angeles mayor Sam Yorty if he knew who the emerging community leaders in Watts were, listing specifically the names of Watts Summer Festival organizers Tommy Jacquette and Booker Griffin, Ron Karenga of the black nationalist organization Us, and Westminster Neighborhood Association director Ocie Pastard. Yorty avoided another clash with Kennedy, posing for a smiling photograph with him before the hearings started and then jetting off to Philadelphia to examine a transportable airport lounge. "Questions for Mayor Yorty," Robert F. Kennedy Papers, Senate File, Cities: Ribicoff Hearings, Questions for Witnesses, Bundy-Wirtz; Andrew J. Glass, "Yorty, in Game of Hide-and-Seek, Avoids Meeting Arch Foe RFK," *Washington Post*, May 13, 1967.

83. Lawrence E. Davies, "3 Senators Tour Migrant Housing," *New York Times*, May 12, 1967.

84. Davies, "3 Senators"; Andrew J. Glass, "OEO Camps Stand Out in San Joaquin," *Washington Post*, May 12, 1967; Lee Fremstad, "San Joaquin Farm Camps Stun Senators," *Fresno Bee*, May 12, 1967, www.newspaperarchive.com.

85. "Blasts from 'Poor' Mark Senators' Poverty Probe," *Los Angeles Sentinel*, May 18, 1967.

86. Davies, "3 Senators"; "A Woman Who Stood Waiting," *Gallup Independent*, May 13, 1967, www.newspaperarchive.com.

87. Governor's Commission on the Los Angeles Riots, *Violence in the City: An End or a Beginning?* December 2, 1965, www.us.edu/libraries /archives/cityinstress/mccone/part7html.

88. Kenneth C. Burt, *The Search for a Civic Voice: California Latino Politics* (Claremont, Calif.: Regina Books, 2007), 238–39.

89. Kaye Briegel, "Chicano Student Militancy: The Los Angeles High School Strike of 1968," in *An Awakened Minority: The Mexican-Americans*, 2d ed., ed. Manuel P. Servín (New York: Macmillan, 1974), 215.

90. "Senator Kennedy Meets MASA," *La Raza*, November 15, 1967. The sympathetic story reported that Kennedy "listened attentively," prompting a letter to the

editor from angered Berkeley professor and Chicano leader Octavio Romano sneering: "You can readily see how uncontrollably overjoyed I was that at last we have found an 'attentive listener.' WE ARE SAVED!!" Octavio Romano, "To Kennedy with Love," *La Raza*, December 2, 1967. Ralph Guzmán, another important Mexican American scholar and leader, had helped organize the meeting and was more sympathetic to Kennedy.

91. Address by Senator Robert F. Kennedy, the Day Care Council of New York, May 8, 1967, Robert F. Kennedy Senate Papers, box 3.

92. Edelman, *Searching for America's Heart*, 69; Tom Wicker, "In the Nation: The Real Questions about Welfare," *New York Times*, May 11, 1967.

93. Edelman, *Searching for America's Heart*, 70; "Early Battle Fatigue," *New York Times*, May 10, 1967.

94. Edelman, oral history interview by Hackman, 72.

95. U.S. Senate Subcommittee, *Hearings Examining the War on Poverty*, April 10, 1967, 593; Remarks of Senator Robert F. Kennedy, Community Council of Greater New York, June 9, 1967, Robert F. Kennedy Senate Papers, Speeches and Press Releases, box 3. After reviewing a number of studies from the 1970s, historian James Patterson concluded that among welfare recipients, at most only 5 percent of marriages broke up as a direct result of the absent father rule and that instead the extreme stresses of living in poverty along with the typical problems that strained marriages at all economic levels—"alcoholism, drug abuse, infidelity, sexual and physical violence, simple incompatibility"—were the catalysts. James T. Patterson, *America's Struggle against Poverty in the Twentieth Century* (Cambridge: Harvard University Press, 2000), 169.

96. Remarks of Senator Robert F. Kennedy, Community Council of Greater New York, June 9, 1967, Robert F. Kennedy Senate Papers, Speeches and Press Releases, box 3.

97. "A Planner Talks of Role of Poor," *New York Times*, October 29, 1967. William Cannon of the Budget Bureau presented a contradictory portrait of Yarmolinsky's understanding of the aims of community action in an oral history interview for the Johnson Library. William Cannon, oral history interview by Michael Gillette, May 21, 1982, transcript, 9, 13, Lyndon B. Johnson Library, Austin, Tex.

98. U.S. Senate Subcommittee, *Hearings Examining the War on Poverty*, May 12, 1967 3921.

99. Ibid., 3491–92.

100. Daniel Patrick Moynihan, oral history interview by Jean Stein, transcript, Jean Stein Papers, box 5; Newfield, *Robert Kennedy*, 104. For his extended critique of community action, see Daniel Patrick Moynihan, *Maximum Feasible Misunderstanding* (Toronto: Free Press, 1969). On Moynihan's influence as a critical voice in the White House, see Cannon, oral history interview, 34. Moynihan had also counseled Kennedy against his Bedford-Stuyvesant initiative. Moynihan was a Keynesian aggregationist whose own prescription for poverty was a massive jobs program combined with floor-under income maintenance. Brian Dooley, *Robert Kennedy: The Final Years* (Staffordshire: Keele University Press, 1995), 24;

Robert Collins, *More: The Politics of Economic Growth in Postwar America* (London: Oxford University Press, 2000), 146–47. See also Daniel Knapp and Kenneth Polk, *Scouting the War on Poverty: Social Reform Politics in the Kennedy Administration* (Lexington, Mass.: D. C. Heath, 1971), 193–200; Daryl Michael Scott, "The Politics of Pathology: The Ideological Origins of the Moynihan Controversy," *Journal of Policy History* 8, no. 1 (1996): 96–97; U.S. Senate Subcommittee, *Hearings on Federal Role in Urban Affairs*, 2688–90.

101. The percentage was initially laid out as a nonbinding guideline by OEO in early 1965, meant to allow for some local flexibility. In late 1966 Republican congressman Albert Quie, concerned about both guaranteeing involvement of the poor on CAP boards and putting pressure on Democratic mayors, successfully proposed the Quie amendment, making the one-third figure a statutory requirement. Donovan, *Politics of Poverty*, 55; Scott Stossel, *Sarge: The Life and Times of Sargent Shriver* (Washington, D.C.: Smithsonian Books, 2004), 459.

102. Irwin Unger, *The Best of Intentions: The Triumphs and Failures of the Great Society under Kennedy, Johnson, and Nixon* (New York: Doubleday, 1996), 158–59.

103. U.S. Senate Subcommittee, *Hearings Examining the War on Poverty*, May 18, 1967, 4126–27, 4132–34, 4137. The Republican Party had been developing strategy memos for House members to counter the White House beginning in 1966. William C. Selover, "The View from Capitol Hill: Harassment and Survival," in *On Fighting Poverty: Perspectives from Experience*, ed. James L. Sundquist (New York: Basic Books, 1969), 170–71.

104. James A. Reichley, "He's Running Himself Out of the Race," *Fortune*, March 1968, 114.

105. U.S. Senate Subcommittee, *Hearings Examining the War on Poverty*, March 15, 1967, 212; James W. Hilty, *Robert Kennedy: Brother Protector* (Philadelphia: Temple University Press, 1997), 275.

106. Robert Kennedy, "Robert Kennedy on Government Injustice to Business," *Nation's Business*, June 1967, 70–76; Edelman, oral history interview by Hackman, 203.

107. E. Barrett Prettyman, oral history interview by Larry Hackman, June 5, 1969, transcript, 15–16, John F. Kennedy Library; E. Barrett Prettyman Jr., correspondence with author, June 11, 2001.

108. *Congressional Record*, July 12, 1967, 18444.

109. For a comparison of Kennedy's bill with another prominent housing initiative offered by Senator Charles Percy of Illinois see Robert B. Semple Jr., "The Slum Planners," *New Republic*, July 22, 1967, 8–10.

110. "500 Largest Corporations," August 4, 1967, Robert F. Kennedy Senate Papers, Correspondence: Robo Books, 1966–1968, box 2.

111. Frank Mankiewicz, oral history interview by Stephen Goodell, August 12, 1969, transcript, 87, John F. Kennedy Library. Johnson White House aide Harry McPherson also found the address too "legalistic." Arthur M. Schlesinger Jr., *Robert Kennedy and His Times* (Boston: Houghton Mifflin, 1978), 797. In the midst of rioting in Washington following Martin Luther King's death a year later, having

been politically battered by four years of rebellions and perhaps seeing things differently after dropping his reelection bid, Johnson confided to press aide George Christian: "I don't know why we're so surprised. When you put your foot on a man's neck and hold him down for three hundred years, and then you let him up, what's he going to do? He's going to knock your block off." Nick Kotz, *Judgment Days: Lyndon Baines Johnson, Martin Luther King, Jr., and the Laws That Changed America* (Boston: Houghton Mifflin, 2006), 426.

112. Newfield, *Robert Kennedy*, 115.

113. U.S. Senate Subcommittee, *Hearings Examining the War on Poverty*, July 18, 1967, 3283.

114. Ibid., 3282–84.

115. Ibid., 3276.

116. Bill Mullins to Frank Mankiewicz, n.d., R. Sargent Shriver Papers, box 40, John F. Kennedy Library.

117. Edelman suggested that Kennedy also stayed out of the CDGM fight because the alternative, more moderate Head Start program the OEO put together was to be headed by, among others, NAACP leader Aaron Henry and Kennedy friend Charles Evers. Peter Edelman, oral history interview by Jean Stein; and Charles Evers, oral history interview by Jean Stein, Jean Stein Papers, box 3.

118. Edelman, oral history interview by Hackman, 138.

119. Myron Curzan, oral history interview by author, December 5, 2002.

120. Newfield, *Robert Kennedy*, 115. See Weaver's arguments in U.S. Senate Subcommittee, *Hearings Examining the War on Poverty*, March 15, 1967, 116–40. Weaver later called it "a rich man's bill for a poor people's housing." Patrick J. Sloyan, "Kennedy Hits Johnson's Housing Program," *Atlanta Daily World*, March 21, 1968.

121. Kennedy included in the record dozens of positive responses to the letter sent to corporations across the country outlining the legislation.

122. U.S. Senate Committee on Finance, *Hearings on Tax Incentives to Encourage Housing in Urban Poverty Areas*, 90th Cong., 1st sess. (Washington, D.C.: Government Printing Office, 1967), September 14, 1967, 108.

123. Mankiewicz, oral history interview, 2; Edelman, oral history interview by Hackman, 78; Monroe W. Karmin, "'Follow the Leader' as Played by LBJ," *Wall Street Journal*, March 7, 1968.

124. "Stick-in-the-HUDs," *National Review*, October 3, 1967, 1056.

125. O'Donnell, *A Common Good*, 358–59.

126. Edelman, oral history interview by Hackman, 137–38.

127. Representative Albert Quie, who continued to urge the privatization and localization of the War on Poverty embodied in his Opportunity Crusade proposal, was upset with the survival of OEO but also with the threat the Green amendment posed to the principle of participation by the poor. Selover, "View from Capitol Hill," 178.

128. U.S. Senate Committee on Finance, *Hearings on the Social Security Amendments of 1967*, 90th Cong., 1st sess. (Washington, D.C.: Government Printing Office, 1967), August 29, 1967, 782, 776.

129. Ibid., 775–85; "Description of the Kennedy Bill to Amend the Social Security Amendments of 1967," December 14, 1967, Robert F. Kennedy Senate Papers, Speeches and Press Releases, box 4.

130. Edelman, *Searching for America's Heart*, 74–76; Harris, oral history interview, 11.

131. *Congressional Record*, Senate, December 14, 1967, 36783. Byrd lashed back: "I expect that more than any senator in this chamber I have this year sought to delay roll-calls for the junior senator from New York. I have sought to protect him on rollcalls time after time, and I would gladly do so again. But I cannot help but be resentful when it is implied that the leadership, and I included in that, has entered into any attempt to do something underhanded."

132. Ibid., 36783. Edelman related that Kennedy's comments were "sufficiently salty" that he felt compelled to edit them for the *Congressional Record*. Edelman, *Searching for America's Heart*, 77.

133. Address by Senator Robert F. Kennedy, Young Presidents' Organization Conference, Washington, D.C., October 20, 1967, Robert F. Kennedy Senate Papers, Speeches and Press Releases, box 4. In other speeches Kennedy contended that the unemployment rate in the inner cities of the nation was "far worse than the rest of the nation knew during the depths of the Great Depression." Testimony of Senator Robert F. Kennedy before the National Commission on Urban Problems, New York, September 6, 1967, Robert F. Kennedy Senate Papers, Speeches and Press Releases, box 3.

134. Remarks of Senator Robert F. Kennedy, Chamber of Commerce of the United States, Washington, D.C., October 3, 1967, Robert F. Kennedy Senate Papers, Speeches and Press Releases, box 4.

135. "A Marshall Plan for the Cities," *Wall Street Journal*, August 10, 1967.

136. The entire exchange is reminiscent of Kennedy's tactics as chief counsel during the McClellan hearings into labor racketeering. "The impression that you are giving me," Kennedy told Morris Atlas, attorney for La Casita Farms, "is that you are scared to have an election. You are frightened about an election, because you are concerned that [the workers] will vote for a union." U.S. Senate Subcommittee on Migratory Labor, *Hearings on Migratory Labor Legislation*, 90th Cong., 1st sess. (Washington, D.C.: Government Printing Office, 1967), August 2, 1967, 249–78.

137. Newfield, *Robert Kennedy*, 90–91; O'Donnell, *A Common Good*, 360–61; Carter Burden, oral history interview by Jean Stein, Jean Stein Papers, box 1; Peter Millones, "Kennedy and Javits Are Shocked by Housing of Migrants Upstate," *New York Times*, September 9, 1967.

138. Pierre Salinger, oral history interview by Larry Hackman, May 26, 1969, transcript, 30, John F. Kennedy Library.

139. "Kennedy Visits Navajos on Reservation," *New York Times*, July 5, 1967; U.S. Senate Subcommittee, *Hearings on Hunger and Malnutrition in America*, 174.

140. Pierre Salinger, *With Kennedy* (New York: Doubleday, 1966), 30; Nicole Salinger, oral history interview by Jean Stein, transcript, Jean Stein Papers, box 7; Thomas, *Robert Kennedy*, 352–53.

141. U.S. Senate Special Subcommittee on Indian Education, *Hearings on Indian Education*, 90th Cong., 1st sess. (Washington, D.C.: Government Printing Office, 1967), December 14, 1967, 56.

142. U.S. Senate Special Subcommittee on Indian Education, *Hearings on Indian Education*, 90th Cong., 2d sess. (Washington, D.C.: Government Printing Office, 1967), January 4, 1968, 246–47. Another example of Kennedy's outrage over the attitudes of local officials toward Native American children is telling. When, on a visit to an orphanage for Indian children in New Mexico, Ethel Kennedy commented to the director how cute one of the children was, he joked, "Would you like to buy one?" In the car as he was leaving, an angry Robert Kennedy snapped, "Remember who that guy is." Dick Tuck, oral history interview by Jean Stein, transcript, Jean Stein Papers, box 9.

143. Memo, Joe Dolan to Senator, November 1967, Joseph Dolan Papers, Memos to RFK, John F. Kennedy Library.

144. Thomas, *Robert Kennedy*, 320; Schlesinger, *Robert Kennedy*, 804.

145. Address of Senator Robert F. Kennedy, Citizens Union, December 14, 1967, Robert F. Kennedy Senate Papers, Speeches and Press Releases, box 4.

8. "YOU CAN'T DENY THESE PEOPLE THE PRESIDENCY"

1. Jack Newfield, *Somebody's Gotta Tell It: The Upbeat Memoir of a Working-Class Journalist* (New York: St. Martin's, 2002), 186; Arthur M. Schlesinger Jr., *Robert Kennedy and His Times* (Boston: Houghton Mifflin, 1978), 825.

2. C. Gerald Fraser, "Kennedy Makes Tour of Bronx, Disturbed by Filth and Conflicts," *New York Times*, January 26, 1968; U.S. Senate Special Subcommittee on Indian Education, *Hearings on Indian Education*, 90th Cong., 2d sess. (Washington, D.C.: U.S. Government Printing Office, 1968), January 4, 1968, 259. On Kennedy's plans for 1968, see Peter Edelman, oral history interview by Larry Hackman, July 29, 1969, transcript, 180–84, John F. Kennedy Library. He had hoped to give "concentrated time" in January to Bedford-Stuyvesant. Memo, Joe to the Senator, November 20, 1967, Joseph P. Dolan Papers, Memoranda, John F. Kennedy Library.

3. Edelman, oral history interview by Hackman, 184–85.

4. "Welcome, Senator Kennedy," *Lexington Herald*, February 13, 1968.

5. John Alexander Williams, *Appalachia: A History* (Chapel Hill: University of North Carolina Press, 2002), 318.

6. Ibid., 338.

7. Ibid., 342.

8. U.S. Senate Subcommittee on Employment, Manpower, and Poverty, *Hearings on Rural Poverty and Hunger*, 90th Cong., 2d sess. (Washington, D.C.: U.S. Government Printing Office, 1968), February 14, 1968, 21.

9. William Greider, "Kennedy Hears Stories of Grim Mountain Life," *Louisville Courier-Journal*, February 15, 1968; U.S. Senate Subcommittee, *Hearings on Rural Poverty and Hunger*, 65.

10. "Local Men Join March," *Mountain Eagle*, May 9, 1968; Mark Kurlansky, *1968: The Year That Rocked the World* (New York: Random House, 2005).

11. U.S. Senate Subcommittee, *Hearings on Rural Poverty and Hunger*, 29–32.

12. William Greider, "Despite Gimmicks Plight of Mountains Hit Kennedy," *Louisville Courier-Journal*, February 18, 1968; Fred W. Luigart Jr., "Senator Charges Kennedy Visit 'Blackened' State Image," *Louisville Courier-Journal*, February 16, 1968; "Criticizes Kennedy's Visit," *Louisville Courier-Journal*, February 16, 1968.

13. U.S. Senate Subcommittee, *Hearings on Rural Poverty and Hunger*, 16–17, 31, 54–55.

14. Willard Yarbrough, "RFK Takes on White Knight Image, Garners Potential Votes in Kentucky," *Knoxville News-Sentinel*, February 15, 1968.

15. Orville Rogers to Senator Robert F. Kennedy, February 21, 1968, Robert F. Kennedy Senate Papers, Legislative Subject File: Kentucky Trip, 2/68, box 7, John F. Kennedy Library.

16. Greider, "Despite Gimmicks Plight of Mountains Hit Kennedy."

17. Anne Caudill to Mr. and Mrs. James Stokely, February 21, 1968, Anne and Harry Caudill Collection, box 28, University of Kentucky Archives, Lexington.

18. "A New Ally for Eastern Kentucky," *Mountain Eagle*, February 22, 1968.

19. John Sherman Cooper, oral history interview by Jean Stein, transcript, Jean Stein Papers, box 2, John F. Kennedy Library.

20. U.S. Senate Special Subcommittee on Indian Education of the Committee on Labor and Public Welfare, *Hearings on Indian Education*, 90th Cong., 2d sess. (Washington, D.C.: U.S. Government Printing Office, 1968), February 19, 1968, 590.

21. Peter B. Edelman, *Searching for America's Heart: RFK and the Renewal of Hope* (Boston: Houghton Mifflin, 2001), 83.

22. Jean Stein and George Plimpton, eds., *American Journey: The Times of Robert Kennedy* (New York: Harcourt Brace Jovanovich, 1970), 282.

23. César Chávez, oral history interview by Dennis J. O'Brien, January 28, 1970, transcript, 17, John F. Kennedy Library.

24. Ibid., 16.

25. Ibid., 21.

26. On WLCAC, see Robert A. Bauman, "Race, Class, and Political Power: The Implementation of the War on Poverty in Los Angeles" (Ph.D. diss., University of California–Santa Barbara, 1998), 251.

27. Paul Schrade, *UAW Workplace and Community Action* (Los Angeles: Oral History Program, University of California, Los Angeles, 1996), 404.

28. Jules Witcover, *85 Days: The Last Campaign of Robert Kennedy* (New York: Quill, 1988), 52–53; Schlesinger, *Robert Kennedy*, 846.

29. Witcover, *85 Days*, 68.

30. Michael J. Aguirre, ed., *The Unfulfilled Promise: The Speeches and Notes from the Last Campaign of Robert F. Kennedy, 16 March 1968 to 5 June 1968* (San Diego: M. J. Aguirre, 1986), 2.

31. Schrade, *UAW Workplace and Community Action*, 407.

32. "Kennedy Enters Presidential Race," *Wisconsin State Journal*, March 17, 1968, www.newspaperarchive.com.

33. For example, former Justice Department official John Douglas, son of former Illinois senator Paul Douglas, advised Kennedy to "forget about civil rights: aid to

the poor. You just weaken yourself with the Indiana whites. 'Aid to the poor' is considered here to be a subsidy to Negroes paid by middle class whites. You and your speechwriters should get off this poverty kick. If it helps in California I'd be amazed." Memo, John W. Douglas to Senator Robert F. Kennedy, Re: Thoughts on the Indiana campaign as I go back to Washington, April 20, 1968, David Hackett Papers, box 7, RFK Campaign Materials, 1968, Douglas Memos, John F. Kennedy Library.

34. John Bartlow Martin, "RFK Notes," John Bartlow Martin Papers, Library of Congress, Washington, D.C.

35. Martin had been John Kennedy's ambassador to the Dominican Republic.

36. Martin, "RFK Notes." Martin called places such as Marion, Kokomo, and Muncie the "redneck backlash factory cities."

37. Ibid.

38. Ibid.

39. Witcover, *85 Days*, 107.

40. James E. Tolan, oral history interview by Roberta Greene, June 26, 1969, transcript, 12–13, John F. Kennedy Library.

41. Ibid., 12.

42. Aguirre, *Unfulfilled Promise*, 54.

43. U.S. Senate Subcommittee, *Hearings on Indian Education*, March 30, 1968, 990.

44. Ibid., 1021.

45. Judi Cornelius, oral history interview by Joseph H. Cash, n.d., transcript, 21, John F. Kennedy Library; "Kennedy Visits Destitute Sioux Indian Family," *Cumberland News*, April 17, 1968, www.newspaperarchive.com.

46. U.S. Senate Subcommittee, *Hearings on Indian Education*, April 16, 1968, 1232.

47. Quoted in Francis Paul Prucha, *The Great Father: The United States Government and the American Indians* (Lincoln: University of Nebraska Press, 1984), 1085–88.

48. U.S. Senate Subcommittee, *Hearings on Indian Education*, April 16, 1968, 1232.

49. Ibid., 1234.

50. Marie Ridder, "Many-Faceted Kennedy Wages Dynamic Campaign," *Independent Star-News*, April 21, 1968.

51. Stein and Plimpton, *American Journey*, 285.

52. Ibid., 286.

53. K. Dun Gifford, oral history interview by Larry Hackman, January 5, 1973, 24, John F. Kennedy Library; K. Dun Gifford, oral history interview by author, June 27, 2006.

54. Memo, Fraser Barron to Mr. Sorensen and Mr. Johnston, Re: Proposed operations of grassroots groups, April 9, 1968, K. Dun Gifford Papers, box 1, Correspondence, Fraser Barron, 4/1/68–4/15/68, John F. Kennedy Library.

55. Gifford, oral history interview by Hackman, 22.

56. Ibid., 23–24.

57. Ibid. Kennedy believed, however, and would stress to potential supporters, that there was no legal bar on individuals' participating of their own volition and on their own time. A year later the Hatch Act would face a legal challenge on those

grounds. Gifford, oral history interview by author. The campaign was nevertheless aware of the potential legal danger. Memo, Fraser Barron to Dave Hackett, "Ideas on Campaign Structures," May 13, 1968, K. Dun Gifford Papers, box 1, Correspondence, Fraser Barron. On a later legal challenge along these grounds, see "Doing Something Relevant," *Time*, May 9, 1969, 27.

58. Joseph A. Palermo, *In His Own Right: The Political Odyssey of Senator Robert F. Kennedy* (New York: Columbia University Press, 2001), 146; Gifford, oral history interview by Hackman, 27. The campaign referred to CCAP only cryptically in internal correspondence as "our friends across town" or "Mass Ave.," where its headquarters were located in the nation's capital, because its status as a tax-exempt organization would have been jeopardized by partisan political activity.

59. Richard Boone, correspondence with author, August 3, 2004; Gifford, oral history interview by author; Barron to Sorensen and Johnston, Re: Proposed operations of grassroots groups; Fraser Barron to Dave Hackett, April 2, 1968, K. Dun Gifford Papers, box 1, Correspondence, Fraser Barron, 4/1/68–4/15/68. About a dozen leaders attended the Hickory Hill gathering. One leader who attended the meeting— and whom the campaign courted with continuing difficulty—was New Jersey state assemblyman George Richardson. In mid-April, Barron wrote Hackett that losing Richardson's support meant "losing the key to New Jersey's 425,000 Negro–Puerto Rican community, and a potential registered vote, by November, of perhaps 200,000. . . . When we remember that JFK carried New Jersey by only 22,000 votes over Nixon, this matter assumes some importance." Memo, Fraser Barron to Dave Hackett, Re: Richardson Situation, April 12, 1968, K. Dun Gifford Papers, box 1, Correspondence, Fraser Barron, 4/1/68–4/15/68.

60. Peter Edelman, oral history interview by Roberta Greene, August 4, 1969, transcript, 329–30, John F. Kennedy Library.

61. Schrade, UAW Workplace and Community Action, 410–13; Kenneth C. Burt, *The Search for a Civic Voice: California Latino Politics* (Claremont, Calif.: Regina Books, 2007), 262; memo, Fraser Barron to Dave Hackett, April 15, 1968, K. Dun Gifford Papers, box 1, Correspondence, Fraser Barron, 4/1/68–4/15/68.

62. Mario T. García, *Memories of Chicano History: The Life and Narrative of Bert Corona* (Berkeley: University of California Press, 1994), 236–44; memo, Fraser Barron to Dave Hackett, Re: Daily Report on States, April 15, 1968, K. Dun Gifford Papers, box 1, Correspondence, Fraser Barron, 4/1/68–4/15/68.

63. Penn Kimball, *Bobby Kennedy and the New Politics* (Englewood Cliffs, N.J.: Prentice-Hall, 1968), 1. In an internal Kennedy campaign memo Arthur Schlesinger Jr. wrote: "We are witnessing the death of the old-fashioned political organization. . . . In the old days the political organization was the mediating institution between the candidate and the mass of voters. This role has now been taken over by television. The result will soon be to liquidate the traditional middlemen and mediatorial agencies of politics, leaving candidates with a diffused public opinion." Memo, "Confidential: The Old Politics and the New," April 9, 1968, John Bartlow Martin Papers.

64. Edith Green, oral history interview by Roberta Greene, February 27, 1974, transcript, 2, John F. Kennedy Library; memo, Peter Edelman to Senator Robert

F. Kennedy, Re: Upcoming Matters on Your Return, June 15, 1966, Robert F. Kennedy Senate Papers, Correspondence: Personal File, 1964–1968, box 3. On Green's antagonism toward the PCJD, see Wesley Barthelmes, oral history interview by Roberta Greene, June 5, 1969, transcript, 143–50, John F. Kennedy Library. Green told Barthelmes: "They cribbed that Community Action Program from the juvenile delinquency section. They put all the sociologists to work, and it's just causing trouble" (149).

65. Witcover, *85 Days*, 202. Hackett's grassroots initiative enlisted the Citizens' Crusade Against Poverty to look into potential contacts with an antipoverty program for Mexican American migrant workers, but nothing significant came of it. Memo, Fraser Barron to Dave Hackett, Re: Daily Report on Key States, K. Dun Gifford Papers, box 1, Correspondence, Fraser Barron.

66. Edelman, oral history interview by Greene, 9; Green, oral history interview by Greene, 3.

67. Kennedy aide Fraser Barron did worry that Green's authorship of the amendment routing OEO funding through mayors "is very unpopular with the black community in Portland" and advised that a "special effort" there was needed "to protect the senator's position." Memo, Fraser Barron to Dave Hackett, Re: Daily Report on Key States, K. Dun Gifford Papers, box 1, Correspondence, Fraser Barron.

68. Witcover, *85 Days*, 202. The campaign was not without levity. Kennedy campaign strategist and legendary political prankster Dick Tuck joked with the candidate about a plan to tranquillize rats and bring them to Portland along with 200,000 African American voters. "Bobby and I agreed that was the only answer to Oregon," Tuck said. Dick Tuck, oral history interview by Jean Stein, transcript, Jean Stein Papers, box 9.

69. Edwin O. Guthman and C. Richard Allen, eds., *RFK: Collected Speeches* (New York: Viking, 1993), 399.

70. Edelman, oral history interview by Hackman, 227–30, 127; Edelman, *Searching for America's Heart*, 89. Barron indicated that Kennedy's "flat rejection" of guaranteed income proposals was not helping grassroots efforts in the District of Columbia. Memo, Fraser Barron to Dave Hackett, Re: Daily Report on States, 5/1/1968, K. Dun Gifford Papers, box 1, Correspondence, Fraser Barron.

71. Joseph Kennedy had suffered a debilitating stroke in 1961.

72. Witcover, *85 Days*, 156.

73. Memo, John Bartlow Martin to Senator Robert F. Kennedy, Re: California, May 13, 1968, John Bartlow Martin Papers; Schrade, UAW Workplace and Community Action, 409–15.

74. Nick Kotz and Mary Lynn Kotz, *A Passion for Equality: George A. Wiley and the Movement* (New York: Norton, 1977), 255.

75. Elsie Carper, "Mother's Day Parade Opens Drive by Poor," *Washington Post*, May 13, 1968.

76. "RFK in Watts," *Los Angeles Sentinel*, March 28, 1968; "Kennedy Gets Hero's Welcome in Watts Tour," *Chicago Daily Defender*, March 26, 1968; Evan Thomas, *Robert*

Kennedy: His Life (New York: Simon & Schuster, 2000), 25; Gerald Horne, *The Fire This Time: The Watts Uprising and the 1960s* (Charlottesville: University Press of Virginia, 1995), 189; Elaine Woo, "Billy Tidwell: Aided Watts after '65 Riots," *Los Angeles Times*, June 29, 2001. The best overview of the Sons of Watts is Douglas G. Glasgow, "Sons of Watts," in *Black Power in the Belly of the Beast*, ed. Judson L. Jeffries (Urbana: University of Illinois Press, 2006), 116–34.

77. Sal Castro, oral history interview by author, June 15, 2009.
78. Ibid. Castro was aware of the political implications of involving a prospective presidential candidate. He would soon thereafter be arrested for inciting the protests, and both Kennedy and Democratic candidate Eugene McCarthy contributed bail money to free him from jail. "They were using us for the vote, and that's fine," Castro recalled. "Hell, I was a government teacher. I know American politics." Kennedy in fact invited Castro to be with him at the podium the night he won the California primary. Castro felt an obligation to visit McCarthy's campaign gala as well to express his thanks, and because of the delay he arrived too late.
79. Dolores Delgado Bernal, "Grassroots Leadership Reconceptualized: Chicana Oral Histories and the 1968 East Los Angeles School Blowouts," in *Women's Oral History: The Frontiers Reader*, ed. Susan Hodge Armitage et al. (Lincoln: University of Nebraska Press, 2002), 244; Paula Crisostomo, oral history interview by author, July 12, 2007; *Chicano! A History of the Mexican-American Civil Rights Movement*, prod. Hector Galán, videocassette (NLCC Educational Media, 1996). For an example of the embrace of Zapata—along with an advertisement for posters printed by the Farm Worker Press in Delano—see Gonzalo Molina, "Emiliano Zapata: Hombre de Revolucion," *La Raza*, December 25, 1967.
80. "Bobbie Joins the Blowout Committee," *Chicano Student News*, March 15, 1968.
81. *Chicano Student News*, April 25, 1968.
82. "Kennedy the Favorite among Minorities," *El Informador*, May 29, 1968.
83. "Bob Kennedy and the Hispanics," *El Informador*, March 27, 1968; editorial, *El Informador*, May 22, 1968.
84. In the same memo, however, Walinsky derided the commission's findings because it condemned the Black Power movement, which Walinsky called "the first real sign of self-respect, black consciousness, self-help, mutual aid." He derided the report as a "catalogue of things that nice people will do" for blacks and the "frontier" of liberal thought, which was "hopelessly blind and inadequate, well-meant but sentimental, soft-headed, and in the last analysis, cowardly." Memo, Adam to RFK, Re: Campaign themes, n.d. [1966], Adam Walinsky Papers, box 26, John F. Kennedy Library; memo, Adam to RFK, Re: Riot Commission, n.d., Adam Walinsky Papers, box 42, Urban Affairs: Riots.
85. Quayle Polls, 1968 Democratic Primaries, Rowland Evans Jr. and Robert D. Novak Papers, 1963–1973, box 3, State Historical Society of Wisconsin, Madison. Branigin was a conservative Democrat running in the primary as a favorite son. He was recognized as a stand-in for the administration and for the likely presidential candidacy of Vice President Hubert Humphrey.

86. Ibid.
87. Paul Cowan, "Wallace in Yankeeland: The Invisible Revolution," *Village Voice*, July 18, 1968, 19; Pete Hamill, "Wallace," *Ramparts*, October 26, 1968, 46.
88. Memo, J. Flug to EMK/G. Doherty/J. Douglas/R. Goodwin/R. Pritchard, Re: Canvassing Operations Survey—Indianapolis, Anderson, Muncie, Marion, Wabash, Kokomo, April 28, 1968, David Hackett Papers, box 7, Gerry Doherty (Memos for GFD), John F. Kennedy Library.
89. Stein and Plimpton, *American Journey*, 247–48.
90. Jack Newfield, *Robert Kennedy: A Memoir* (New York: E. P. Dutton, 1969), 286. For an interesting and skeptical analysis of Kennedy's ability to win the working-class white vote which has been accepted by many scholars until recently as conventional wisdom, see William vanden Heuvel and Milton Gwirtzman, *On His Own: Robert F. Kennedy, 1964–1968* (New York: Doubleday, 1970), 348–49. For recent arguments that Kennedy's performance in Indiana portended the real possibility of a coalition of minorities and working-class whites, see Ray E. Boomhower, *Robert F. Kennedy and the 1968 Indiana Primary* (Bloomington: Indiana University Press, 2008), 114–16; and Thurston Clarke, *The Last Campaign: Robert F. Kennedy and 82 Days That Inspired America* (New York: Macmillan, 2008), 220–22. For a contemporary argument that Kennedy was able to win in Indiana by welding together opposing forces because of his political persona and his economic message, see Joseph Kraft, "Appeal to Opposing Groups Was Key to RFK Victory," *Washington Post*, May 9, 1968.
91. Jules Witcover, "Bobby's Primary Path Rockier than John's," *Syracuse Herald American*, April 28, 1968, www.newspaperarchive.com; Pierre Salinger et al., eds., *"An Honorable Profession": A Tribute to Robert F. Kennedy* (Garden City, N.Y.: Doubleday, 1968), 99.
92. Salinger et al., *"An Honorable Profession,"* 143; Witcover, *85 Days*, 193.
93. Aguirre, *Unfulfilled Promise*, 273.
94. Witcover, *85 Days*, 165; Martin, "RFK Notes." Martin thought Kennedy's tone "angry and hard."
95. Willie Brown, oral history interview by Jean Stein, Jean Stein Papers, box 1.
96. Rafer Johnson, oral history interview by Greene, May 13, 1969, transcript, 7, John F. Kennedy Library; Witcover, *85 Days*, 237–38.
97. Tolan, oral history interview by Greene, 161.
98. Ibid.; Stein and Plimpton, *American Journey*, 306–8; vanden Heuvel and Gwirtzman, *On His Own*, 373–75.
99. Tolan, oral history interview by Greene, 163; Schlesinger, *Robert Kennedy*, 909; vanden Heuvel and Gwirtzman, *On His Own*, 373–75. On the same event, see the comments of John Seigenthaler, Fred Dutton, Curtis Lee Baker, and Hector Lopez in Stein and Plimpton, *American Journey*, 305–8.
100. Hector Lopez, oral history interview by Jean Stein, transcript, Jean Stein Papers, box 5.
101. Brian Dooley, *Robert Kennedy: The Final Years* (Staffordshire: Keele University Press, 1995), 41–42.

102. "Muhammad Ali at Fairleigh Dickinson," *New York Amsterdam News*, April 20, 1968.

103. Tolan, oral history interview by Greene, 43; Palermo, *In His Own Right*, 179.

104. Quoted in Witcover, *85 Days*, 140–41.

105. It is very difficult to assess the precise impact of Kennedy's presence and words in averting an urban uprising in Indianapolis, but popular memory has embraced the speech as heading off a violent rebellion in the city. The words of the speech are inscribed at Kennedy's gravesite, and a historical monument now stands at the site of the event. For an alternative explanation of the relative peace in Indianapolis after the King assassination, emphasizing the combined influence of the white power structure and the quiescent black middle class of the city, see Judson L. Jeffries, "An Unexamined Chapter of Black Panther History," in Jeffries, *Black Power in the Belly of the Beast*, 190.

106. "Assassin's Bullet May Have Killed McCarthy Negro Support," *Oakland Post*, April 24, 1968; J. F. Ter Horst, "King and Politics," *Independent Star-News*, April 9, 1968, www.newspaperarchive.com; vanden Heuvel and Gwirtzman, *On His Own*, 338–39; Donald Janson, "Rivals in Indiana Woo Negro Vote," *New York Times*, April 5, 1968; Boomhower, *Robert F. Kennedy and the 1968 Indiana Primary*, 69–70. Charles "Snooky" Hendricks, one of the leaders of the Radical Action Program, told a reporter, "The mere fact that Kennedy will come into the heart of the ghetto will pull the whole black vote." Janson, "Rivals in Indiana Woo Negro Vote."

107. Aguirre, *Unfulfilled Promise*, 771–72.

108. Ibid.

109. Stein and Plimpton, *American Journey*, 259.

110. Ibid., 260–61; Andrew Young, *An Easy Burden: The Civil Rights Movement and the Transformation of America* (New York: HarperCollins, 1996), 486; *Assassinated: The Last Days of Kennedy and King*, exec. prod. Dan Halsted, videocassette (Warner Home Video, 1998); *The Kennedys*, exec. prod. Elizabeth Deane, videocassette (PBS Video, 1992).

111. Edelman, oral history interview by Hackman, December 12, 1969, 18.

112. "Notes Made April 10, 1968," John Bartlow Martin Papers.

113. "RFK Tours Rubble, Calls Violence Tragic," *Pocono Record*, April 8, 1968, www.newspaperarchive.com; Bernadette Carey, "Sen. Kennedy Tours Areas Torn by Riots," *Washington Post*, April 8, 1968; Stein and Plimpton, *American Journey*, 261. See also Clay Risen, *A Nation on Fire: America in the Wake of the King Assassination* (Hoboken, N.J.: John Wiley & Sons, 2009), 184–86.

114. Johnson, oral history interview by Greene, 12.

115. Jack W. Germond, *Fat Man in a Middle Seat: Forty Years of Covering Politics* (New York: Random House, 1999), 80.

116. Tolan, oral history interview by Greene, 48–49.

117. Ibid., 167. According to Kennedy aide John Nolan, Unruh and his lieutenants believed that there weren't enough minority votes to make a significant difference, and that "the ones that there are, you can usually buy" through working

with local political bosses such as Mervyn Dymally in Los Angeles. John Nolan, oral history interview by Roberta Greene, July 24, 1970, transcript, 75, John F. Kennedy Library.

118. "Yorty Raps RFK Voter Procedures," *Los Angeles Sentinel*, May 30, 1968; Carl T. Rowan, "Says Kennedy Money Paves Way to Victory," *Waterloo Daily Courier*, May 22, 1968, www.newspaperarchive.com.

119. Memo, Jim Flug to Senator E. M. Kennedy, Ted Sorensen, Dave Hackett, Dun Gifford, Helen Keyes, Re: Paid-for registrations in California; possible violation of U.S. Code, May 27, 1968, Robert F. Kennedy Presidential Campaign Papers, Youth/Student File, box 5.

120. Joseph Dolan, correspondence with author, January 28, 2001; Martin, "RFK Notes."

121. John Seigenthaler, oral history interview by author, January 12, 2001.

122. Tolan, oral history interview by Greene, 182–83.

123. Quoted in George Rising, *Clean for Gene: Eugene McCarthy's 1968 Presidential Campaign* (Westport, Conn.: Praeger, 1997), 74. McCarthy later said that he had stayed away from the ghettos because he "didn't want to stir them up." Dooley, *Robert Kennedy*, 40.

124. Aguirre, *Unfulfilled Promise*, 620–21.

125. Adam Walinsky, oral history interview by Roberta Greene, transcript, 751, John F. Kennedy Library. Although Walinsky was kept out of debate preparations because his aggressive stances had begun to grate on Kennedy's older advisers, he claimed to be the author of the remark. William vanden Heuvel and Milton Gwirtzman (who was involved in the last-minute coaching of the candidate) claim that Jesse Unruh suggested the Orange County reference. Vanden Heuvel and Gwirtzman, *On His Own*, 377. While commentators did not generally view the debate as a dramatic victory for either candidate, a Quayle poll reported that 45 percent of California voters watched it and 58 percent saw Kennedy as the victor. Lawrence E. Davies, "Coast Tally Slow," *New York Times*, June 5, 1968.

126. Walinsky, oral history interview, 667; Dooley, *Robert Kennedy*, 38.

127. In later years an embittered McCarthy clung to the term. "He was really for apartheid; 'keep 'em in lots' was in effect what he was saying. I was saying that you had to have physical integration. . . . He was big on Bedford-Stuyvesant, which was segregated residential apartheid." Dooley, *Robert Kennedy*, 38–39. The phrase more commonly used by opponents of redevelopment strategies was "gilding the ghetto."

128. Davies, "Coast Tally Slow."

129. Ibid.; Chávez, oral history interview, 23–24.

130. Palermo, *In His Own Right*, 244; Edward W. Knappman, ed., *Presidential Election, 1968* (New York: Facts on File, 1970), 99.

131. John Lewis, oral history interview by Jean Stein, transcript, Jean Stein Papers, box 5.

132. Newfield, *Robert Kennedy*, 319.

133. Aguirre, *Unfulfilled Promise*, 151.

134. Witcover, *85 Days*, 263.

135. Ibid., 266; Charles Kuralt, *The Incredible Year*, LP recording (New York: CBS News, 1968).

136. Brandon Bailey, "Man Who Cradled Robert Kennedy's Head Recalls Assassination," *Roanoke Times and World News*, June 7, 1998, proquest.umi.com.

137. Stein and Plimpton, *American Journey*, 107.

138. SCLC president Ralph Abernathy, who was overseeing the Poor People's Campaign protest and was aboard the funeral train, later said, "The news media did not interpret it as a tribute to the poor—the brief stop there—but it was." Ralph Abernathy, oral history interview by Jean Stein, transcript, Jean Stein Papers, box 1. The stop was the result of planning between Abernathy, SCLC official Hosea Williams, and former attorney general Nicholas Katzenbach as to how the poor should be represented in the ceremony.

139. Stein and Plimpton, *American Journey*, 348; *Eyes on the Prize II: The Promised Land, 1967–1968*, prod. Paul Stekler, videocassette (PBS Video, 1990); Leo Rennert, "Poor Show Deepest Affection for RFK," *The Fresno Bee*, June 9, 1968, 4, www.newspaperarchive.com.

CONCLUSION

1. J. Anthony Lukas, "100,000 File Past Kennedy's Bier," *New York Times*, June 8, 1968.

2. David Ottaway, "Washington Negroes Take Death of Kennedy as Personal Loss," *Oneonta Star*, June 10, 1968, www.newspaperarchive.com; "Mourners Cite Kennedy's Deep Compassion for the Poor," *Washington Afro-American*, June 8, 1968; Jesse W. Lewis Jr., "Poor Voice Anger, Dismay over Kennedy Assassination," *Washington Post*, June 7, 1968.

3. "Last Pilgrimage to RFK's Grave," *Oakland Tribune*, June 10, 1968, www.newspaperarchive.com; "Kennedy Assassination Shocks Indian World," *Indian Truth* 45, no. 1–3 (1968): 5.

4. "Senator Kennedy Dies of Wounds," *Mountain Eagle*, June 6, 1968.

5. Thomas Knight, "Letter from Charleston," *Morgantown Dominion-Post*, June 9, 1968, www.newspaperarchive.com.

6. "WFMUs on the Download," www.wfmu.org/onthedownload.php/album/1978.

7. Ilya Adler, "Kennedy and the Death of Hope," *El Informador*, July 17, 1968.

8. Joseph A. Palermo, *In His Own Right: The Political Odyssey of Senator Robert F. Kennedy* (New York: Columbia University Press, 2001), 232; Almena Lomax, "Assassin's Bullet May Have Killed McCarthy Negro Support," *Oakland Post*, April 24, 1968.

9. Quoted in Jack Newfield, *Robert Kennedy: A Memoir* (New York: E. P. Dutton, 1969), 227. Karenga was the leader of Us, an African American cultural nationalist group that rejected the potential of integration and advocated increasingly militant tactics. For a sympathetic account, see Floyd W. Hayes III and Judson L. Jeffries, "*Us* Does Not Stand for United Slaves!" in *Black Power in the Belly of the Beast*, ed. Judson L. Jeffries (Urbana: University of Illinois Press, 2006),

67–92. To most whites across the political spectrum—and Hamill was a liberal journalist—Malcolm X and Karenga represented the threat of violence and separatism. For another example of John Kennedy's popular reach among racial minorities—and "pictures on those walls" elsewhere—see James B. Lane and Edward J. Escobar, *Forging a Community: The Latino Experience in Northwest Indiana, 1919–1975* (Bloomington: Indiana University Press, 1987), 244.

10. Robert Dallek, *An Unfinished Life: John F. Kennedy, 1917–1963* (Boston: Little, Brown, 2003), 702. Historian Ignacio M. García contends that this ethnic identification helped John Kennedy with Mexican Americans in 1960, but not as much as his Catholicism, which "represented a cultural bridge to the Mexican Americans." Ignacio García, *Viva Kennedy: Mexican Americans in Search of Camelot* (College Station: Texas A&M University Press, 2000), 58–59. For an interesting discussion of the Irish traits of the Kennedys, see Tom Hayden, *Irish on the Inside: In Search of the Soul of Irish America* (New York: Verso, 2001), 88–95.

11. "Yet Another Service," *Our Sunday Visitor*, December 1, 1963.

12. Dr. Leonard Duhl, oral history interview by Jean Stein, transcript, Jean Stein Papers, box 2, John F. Kennedy Library. Walinsky saw Kennedy's evolution similarly, later reflecting: "You know, if you had to put it on a scale, at the beginning the scale would have been weighted much more toward believing that you could work with an establishment to change conditions for those on the bottom. By 1968 . . . the scale had tipped much more toward believing that you had to work much more with the people at the bottom to change conditions in the society as a whole." Adam Walinsky, oral history interview by Roberta Greene, transcript, 157, John F. Kennedy Library.

13. Joseph Califano, oral history interview by Jean Stein, transcript, Jean Stein Papers, box 1.

14. Michael Harrington, *Fragments of the Century* (New York: Saturday Review Press, 1973), 130.

15. Alice O'Connor, "Swimming against the Tide: A Brief History of Federal Policy in Poor Communities," in *Urban Problems and Community Development*, ed. Ronald F. Ferguson and William T. Dickens (Washington, D.C.: Brookings Institution Press, 1999), 77–138. Also on the history of neighborhood and locally based efforts against poverty, see Robert Halpern, *Rebuilding the Inner City: A History of Neighborhood Initiatives to Address Poverty in the United States* (New York: Columbia University Press, 1995). For an interesting argument regarding the enduring value of local community economies which takes O'Connor's critiques into account, see Thad Williamson et al., *Making a Place for Community: Local Democracy in a Global Era* (New York: Routledge, 2002).

16. Bennett Harrison, "Ghetto Economic Development: A Survey," *Journal of Economic Literature* 12, no. 1 (March 1974): 16–17. Harrison focused on what he called "branch planting," the strategy of having larger corporations locate divisions, franchises, or branches in poor areas.

17. The Department of Housing and Urban Development released its first study of the program in 2002, finding that it yielded mixed results. See the full HUD

report at www.huduser.org/publications/econdev/ezec_rpt.html or a brief summary at www.americancityandcounty.com/mag/government_study_finds_ezec/index.html. A more extensive analysis of the program was still pending at this writing.

18. Holmes Alexander, "Kennedy and McKissick Face Back-Turning Truth," *Danville Register*, December 15, 1966, www.newspaperarchive.com.

19. For a powerful example of the costs of that exploitation in Appalachia, see *Stranger with a Camera*, Elizabeth Barret, videocassette (Appalshop, 2000).

20. Michael Harrington, oral history interview by Jean Stein, transcript, Jean Stein Papers, box 4. Richard Goodwin informed Kennedy when he introduced the two men that Harrington had publicly stated that New York governor Nelson Rockefeller was insincere when he said he would spend $50 million in New York City. Kennedy responded, "My God, you didn't say I would, did you?" (Harrington probably meant Mayor John Lindsay, who used that figure during Kennedy's questioning in the Ribicoff hearings.) In the same interview Harrington said that he envisioned a role for himself as a gadfly during a Robert Kennedy administration, an adviser who would work to convince him of the ultimate futility of trying to solve the problem of poverty through private initiatives.

21. Ibid.

22. Karl W. Deutsch et al., *Political Community and the North Atlantic Area* (Princeton, N.J.: Princeton University Press, 1957), 88; Dankwart A. Rustow, "The Study of Leadership," in *Philosophers and Kings: Studies in Leadership*, ed. Dankwart A. Rustow (New York: George Braziller, 1970), 21.

23. César Chávez, oral history interview by Dennis J. O'Brien, January 28, 1970, transcript, 16, John F. Kennedy Library. Edward Kennedy strove to continue his brother's politics, and while he compiled a lengthy and impressive legislative record on social welfare issues in the Senate, his ability to connect with this constituency was never quite the same as Robert Kennedy's. See *The Kennedys*, prod. Elizabeth Deane, videocassette (PBS Video, 1992); and Willie Brown, oral history interview by Jean Stein, transcript, Jean Stein Papers, box 1; César Chávez, oral history interview by Jean Stein, transcript, Jean Stein Papers, box 1.

24. Hayden, *Irish on the Inside*, 91. Karl Deutsch concluded that the most successful leaders of "amalgamation movements" emerged from established elites and had "in their backgrounds some evidence of partial alienation from their own elite or from the political community within which they were functioning." Deutsch wrote, "At the critical time such leaders perceived their own community of political allegiance, and their own membership role within it, as more problematical and as more open for reinterpretation and redefinition than did their more securely affiliated peers." Deutsch, *Political Community*, 88–89.

25. Jeff Greenfield, oral history interview by Roberta Greene, December 10, 1969, transcript, 67, John F. Kennedy Library.

26. Wesley Barthelmes, oral history interview by Roberta Greene, June 5, 1969, transcript, 147, John F. Kennedy Library.

27. Lester David and Irene David, *Bobby Kennedy: The Making of a Folk Hero* (New York: PaperJacks, 1988), 3–4.

28. Michael Beschloss, ed., *Taking Charge: The Johnson White House Tapes, 1963–1964* (New York: Simon & Schuster), 244; Robert Dallek, *Flawed Giant: Lyndon Johnson and His Times* (New York: Oxford University Press, 1998), 107. See also Adam Yarmolinsky, oral history interview by Michael L. Gillette, October 22, 1980, transcript, 35, Lyndon B. Johnson Library, Austin, Tex. Yarmolinsky called Johnson's trip to Appalachia "real gimmickry."

29. Newfield, *Robert Kennedy*, 98.

30. Simeon Booker, oral history interview by John Stewart, April 24, 1967, transcript, 30, John F. Kennedy Library. In contrast, when Daniel Patrick Moynihan arranged a meeting of civil rights leaders with President Nixon in 1969 that spiraled into an emotional attack similar to those Kennedy had faced, Nixon quickly left the meeting in the hands of Vice President Spiro Agnew and later repeatedly called the encounter the worst experience of his first term as president. Nicholas Lemann, *Promised Land: The Great Black Migration and How It Changed America* (New York: Vintage, 1992), 217.

31. James Baldwin, oral history interview by Jean Stein, transcript, Jean Stein Papers, box 1.

32. In May 2001 President George W. Bush attempted to cast the War on Poverty in a broader historical perspective, calling for a program of faith-based initiatives as the "third stage" of the struggle. Bush called the social programs of the 1960s the first stage and the welfare reform legislation of 1996 the second. In spite of this interpretation, the commitment to an "unconditional war" on the problem of the sort envisioned by Lyndon Johnson faded after 1968. Mike Allen, "President Urges War on Poverty," *Washington Post*, May 21, 2001.

33. Minnesota Democrat Paul Wellstone retraced Kennedy's poverty tours in 1997, as would presidential candidate John Edwards ten years later.

34. Robert F. Kennedy, *To Seek a Newer World* (Garden City, N.Y.: Doubleday, 1967), 12–13.

35. Edwin Guthman, *We Band of Brothers* (New York: Harper & Row, 1969), 230–31.

36. Brandon Bailey, "Man Who Cradled Robert Kennedy's Head Recalls Assassination," *Roanoke Times and World News*, June 7, 1998, proquest.umi.com.

INDEX

Blackwell, Unita, 178
Blaik, Earl "Red," 60
Booker, Simeon, 65, 228
Boone, Richard, 83, 90–92, 97–101, 123, 178, 206, 223, 264n17, 266n39, 273n21
Brademas, John, 117
Branigin, Roger, 210, 304n85
Brazier, Arthur, 206
Brown, Edmund "Pat," 142, 144
Brown, Willie, 212, 216
Brown Berets, 134
Brown v. Board of Education, 37–38, 65
Buchanan, James, 64
Buckley, William F., Jr., 75, 190
Bundy, McGeorge, 152–53, 167, 223
Burden, Amanda, 179
Burden, Carter, 164, 179, 285n71
Bureau of Indian Affairs, 83
bureaucracy, 71–73, 75, 97, 114–17, 143, 182, 185–86
Burnette, Robert, 81, 85
Burton, Phillip, 216
Bush, George W., 311n32
business community: Birmingham campaign and, 55; recruitment for Bedford-Stuyvesant, 151–53; RFK and, 127, 147, 172, 187, 191–92, 211, 214, 245n62, 281n9; tax incentive bills and, 173, 297n121
busing, 108–9, 269n83
Byrd, Robert, 191, 194, 298n131

Califano, Joseph, 120, 180, 223
California 1968 primary, 212, 216–18
California Eagle, 38, 49, 62, 246n67
Cannon, William, 260n113, 262n131, 262n139, 266n39
Carmichael, Stokely, 123, 173, 213
Carson, Sonny, 2, 157, 167
Castro, Fidel, 48
Castro, Sal, 209, 304n78
Catholicism, 10, 221–22; Catholic social teaching, 74–75, 105, 254n36, 254n40; communitarian tendency, 16–17,

275n36; John Kennedy's 1960 appeal to minorities and, 28–29, 238n90, 309n10; migrant workers, and, 277n55; poverty and, 253n34; Robert Kennedy and, 16, 211, 277n57
Caudill, Anne, 198
Caudill, Harry, 197–98
Cavanagh, Jerome, 139, 141
Celebrezze, Anthony, 83, 114, 185
Central Brooklyn Coordinating Council (CBCC), 129, 148–49, 154–58, 276n46
Chalk, O. Roy, 71, 107, 252n20
Charleston Gazette, 21
Chávez, César, 2, 28–29, 132–33, 199–200, 206, 209, 218, 221, 227, 238n92
Chicago Defender, 18–19, 23, 27, 30, 38, 51–53, 55, 61, 63, 66
Chicago School of sociology, 69, 83
Chicago Tribune, 85
Chicano Student News, 209
Chicanos, 209, 294n90
Child Development Group of Mississippi (CDGM), 134, 175, 177, 189, 297n117
Chisholm, Shirley, 149–50, 282n19
Cinderlilly story, 51, 183, 294n81
Citizens' Crusade Against Poverty (CCAP), 123, 134, 175, 178, 206, 294n81, 303n65
Civil Rights Act of 1957, 18, 24, 37–38
Civil Rights Act of 1964, 51, 290n9
civil rights bill, 61–62, 87–88, 103
civil rights movement: definitions, 5–6, 232n17, 232n20; RFK's understanding of, 88–89, 117, 248n93
civilian police review board (NYC), 169
Clark, Joseph, 143, 177–78, 180–85
Clark, Kenneth, 26, 56–57
Clark, Ramsey, 80–81, 85, 177
Clark hearings (War on Poverty programs), 178–88
Cleaver, Eldridge, 213
Clinton, Bill, 225, 290n13

Cloward, Richard, 69, 171, 261n124, 273n21
Cohen, Henry, 142
Cohn, Roy, 15
cold war, 5, 11, 14–15, 17, 49, 52
Cole, Nat King, 246n67
Coleman, J. P., 18
Coles, Robert, 170, 180–81
communitarianism, 5–7, 16–17, 69, 73–75, 124–27, 136, 138–39, 143, 167, 172, 185–86, 223–224, 275n36
community action: ambiguity of concept, 100–101, 124, 160, 266n35, 295n100; Community Action Program, 110, 175, 178, 185, 205, 273n12; criticisms and opposition to, 122, 186, 188, 224; debate over inclusion in War on Poverty, 97, 99–101, 262n131, 265n27, 266n39; genesis of, 90–91, 137, 223–24; Green amendment, 190, 205, 207, 297n127, 303n67; "maximum feasible participa-tion" and, 102, 185, 266n46; Quie amendment, 296n101; Republican "Opportunity Crusade" and, 175, 297n127; RFK defense of, 135–36, 185, 223; RFK failure to defend, 135–36, 223, 278n71
community control, 172, 203–4, 208
community development corporations, 137, 139–40, 143, 150–51, 166, 168, 208, 223–224, 288n120
Community Home Improvement Program (CHIP), 162, 287n99
community redevelopment (vs. dispersal or mobility strategies), 106, 125, 137, 190, 203, 217, 287n112, 307n127
Community Service Organization, 238n92
Congress of Racial Equality (CORE), 2, 43, 46–47, 58, 86–87, 111, 123, 156–57, 172, 290n14
Connally, John, 62

Connor, Eugene "Bull," 48, 55
consumerism, 14–15
Conway, Jack, 124, 129–30
Cooper, Gordon, 84
Cooper, John Sherman, 199
Corona, Bert, 206, 218
corporatism, 73, 138–39, 167, 223–25, 254n36, 275n36
Cosby, Bill, 56
Cottrell, Leonard, Jr., 69, 100, 251n6, 282n15
Craig, Lillian, 208
Crane, David, 154, 158
Crazy Horse, 2, 230
Criminal Justice Act of 1964, 78, 103
Cuban Missile Crisis, 52
Curzan, Myron, 173, 187

Daley, Richard, 103, 122, 136, 186, 205
Dawson, William, 23
debates: 1960, JFK vs. Nixon, 23–24, 33, 237n41; 1968, RFK vs. McCarthy, 217–18, 307n125
Delinquency and Opportunity (Ohlin), 69
Deloria, Sam, 203–4
Deloria, Vine, Jr., 2, 292n36
depressed areas legislation, 12, 22–23, 33, 82
Detroit rebellion, 188, 194
Deutsch, Karl, 226, 310n24
Development and Services Corporation (D & S), 153–55, 158–62, 164–65, 286n84, 287n103
Devine, Samuel, 85
Dillon, C. Douglas, 89, 152, 285n71
District of Columbia, 70–71, 93–94, 104–5, 138, 170, 215, 220, 278n80, 289n4f, 303n70
Divini Redemptoris (encyclical), 16
Dixiecrats, 22
Doar, John, 162, 166, 243n38
Dolan, Joseph, 182, 194–95, 201, 293n78
domestic Peace Corps: inclusion in War on Poverty as VISTA, 97, 205, 265n29;

Gibson, Althea, 25
Gideon v. Wainwright, 78–79
Gifford, K. Dun, 140–41, 205
Gilpatric, Roswell, 152
Gitlin, Todd, 174
Glenn, John, 58, 84
Goldwater, Barry, 105–6, 108, 110, 267n64
Goodell, Charles, 175, 264n19
Goodwin, Richard, 33, 113, 137–38, 273n21, 310n20
Graham, Billy, 119
Granger, Lester, 19, 30
Grant, Cary, 70
Graves, Earl, 148, 154, 157
Gray Areas project, 91, 152
Great Society, 8, 112–13, 145, 228
Green, Edith, 90, 103, 190, 207, 261n125, 303n64, 303n67
Green amendment, 205
Greenfield, Jeff, 227
Gregory, Dick, 50, 60, 87, 249n107, 263n14
Greider, William, 198
Griffin, Booker, 294n82
Gross, H. R., 85
guaranteed income proposals, 207–8, 224, 303n67
Guthman, Edwin, 58, 70, 278n71, 281n9
Guzmán, Ralph, 295n90

Hackett, David, 10, 21, 68–69, 72, 75, 77–78, 82–83, 91–94, 97, 98, 101, 121, 135, 204, 206–7, 223, 261nn124–25, 264n19, 265nn26–27, 266n39, 271n121, 303n65
Hamer, Fannie Lou, 177
Hamill, Pete, 221, 308n9
Hansberry, Lorraine, 56
Hansen, Carl F., 93, 263n141
Harlem Globetrotters, 18, 235n37
Harlem Youth Opportunities Unlimited, 121
Harriman, Averell, 55

Harrington, Michael, 4–5, 14, 82, 89, 104, 111, 130, 165–66, 224, 226, 273n21, 310n20
Harris, Fred, 176, 191
Harris, LaDonna, 176
Harris, Louis, 19
Harwood, Richard, 1
Hatch Act, 205, 310n57
Hatcher, Richard, 202, 211
Hayden, Tom, 123, 174–75, 227
Head Start, 134, 140, 180
Heller, Walter, 89–93, 96, 98–99, 261n124
Hendricks, Charles "Snooky," 306n106
Henry, Aaron, 297n117
Hicks, James, 24, 26, 44–46, 57–58, 109–10
Hill, Herbert, 87
Hoffa, Jimmy, 16–17, 31
Holmes, Hamilton, 42
Hoover, Herbert, 11, 72–73, 253n36
Hoover, J. Edgar, 16, 152, 281n9, 283n28
Hopkins, Harry, 67
Horne, Lena, 56
housing: Bedford-Stuyvesant and, 165–66, 288n116; JFK executive order and, 46, 49–50, 54; Johnson administration, 140; RFK Senate campaign proposal, 106; RFK lack of understanding of, 153–54; RFK tax incentive proposal, 188–90, 202–3, 297n120; Truman and, 11
Huerta, Dolores, 200, 218
Humphrey, Hubert, 2, 12, 19–22, 201, 216, 218, 227, 304n85
hunger issue, 1, 20, 33, 133, 178–83, 197, 199, 215, 292n46
Hunter, Charlayne, 42

IBM, 151, 163–64
Indian Claims Commission, 80, 256n71
Indian Truth, 220
Indiana 1968 primary, 210–11, 213–14, 305n90, 306nn105–6

Matthews, Ralph, 57

McCarthy, Eugene, 1, 8, 196, 201, 210, 214, 217–18, 221, 304n78, 307n127

McCarthy, Joseph, 15–16, 31

McCarthy hearings (communist subversion), 15, 18

McClellan, John, 39

McClellan Committee, 15–18, 31, 68, 70, 124, 298n136

McCone Commission report, 123–24, 184, 274n26

McCormick, Carlos, 28, 237n71

McGill, Ralph, 250n129

McGovern, George, 177, 204, 218, 228

McKissick, Floyd, 123, 171–72, 274n23, 290n14

McNamara, Robert, 189, 223

Medgar Evers College, 165

Meredith, James, 52, 55, 87, 133, 169

Mexican American Political Association (MAPA), 28, 206

Mexican American Student Association (MASA), 184

Mexican Americans, 24, 28–29, 79, 83, 183–84, 210, 217–18, 237n71; civil rights abuses against, 184; education and, 183–84, 209; walkout protests of east L.A. high schools, 209. *See also* Chicanos

Meyer, André, 151, 153, 159, 164, 285n71, 288n115

migrant workers, 2, 32, 34, 82, 84, 129–33, 142, 183, 192–93, 199–201, 207, 221, 276n49, 277n54, 298n136

Miller, Loren, 50, 242n33

Miller, Melody, 179

Milton Academy, 10, 68, 75

minimum wage proposals, 29, 32, 267n64

Mississippi: Clark Committee field hearings, 21, 177–82; Greenwood campaign, 50; violence in, 50, 133

Mississippi Freedom Democratic Party (MFDP), 177–78

Mitchell, Clarence, 109

Mitchell, Joseph, 110–11

Model Cities, 128, 137

Moore, Amzie, 178

Moore, George, 151–52, 159–60, 165

"The Moral Equivalent of War" (James), 84

Moraley, William, 3

Morton, Thruston, 27

Moses, Robert (SNCC), 47

Moses, Robert, 151, 160

Mountain Eagle, 199, 220

Moyers, Bill, 122

Moynihan, Daniel Patrick, 92, 95, 123, 186, 295n100, 311n30, 274n23, 295n100

Moynihan report (*The Negro Family*), 123–24

Mullins, Bill, 189

Mumford, Lewis, 5, 139, 279n84

Murphy, George, 132, 178–79

Murrow, Edward R., 34, 70

Nash, Philleo, 256n72

National Association for the Advancement of Colored People (NAACP), 23–24, 42, 47, 50, 63, 87, 109, 136

National Catholic Conference for Interracial Justice, 277n57

National Conference on Constitutional Rights, 24

National Congress of American Indians (NCAI), 29–39, 81, 86

National Defense Education Act, 114

National Newspaper Publishers Association, 241n16

National Resources Planning Board (NRPB), 13

National Review, 145, 190

National Service Corps. *See* domestic Peace Corps

National Welfare Rights Organization, 208

Native Americans, 2, 24, 29–30, 79–86, 176, 177, 193, 202, 204, 218, 220,

Shuttlesworth, Fred, 42, 54
sit-in movement, 36–37, 240n3, 242n33
Smith, Al, 253n36
Smith, Howard K., 90
Smith, Jerome, 56–58, 248n93
Smothers Brothers, 95
SNCC. *See* Student Nonviolent Coordi-
nating Committee
SNCC Freedom Singers, 36
social sciences, 12, 232n11
socialization, 75
Sons of Watts, 208
Sorensen, Theodore, 97, 201, 216, 231n10
South Dakota 1968 primary, 1968, 203
Southern Christian Leadership
Conference (SCLC), 25–26, 42, 47–48,
54–56, 197
Southern Manifesto, 37, 241n5
Southern Regional Council (SRC), 49
Sparkman, John, 12
Special Impact Program (SIP), 150, 188,
282n23, 286n96
Stafford, Thomas, 21
Stennis, John, 18, 175, 178, 182
Stevenson, Adlai, 2, 22, 202
Stone, Chuck, 49, 54
Stone, I. F., 106
Student Nonviolent Coordinating
Committee (SNCC), 46–47, 52, 60,
65, 241n13
Students for a Democratic Society (SDS),
174–75
Sturz, Herbert, 77–78, 173, 291n21
subsidiarity, 74–75, 254n36
surplus commodities. *See* hunger issue
Sviridoff, Mitchell, 157
Symington, Stuart, 22

taxation: JFK tax cut proposal, 90, 96,
127, 187; RFK tax incentive bills, 173,
182, 187, 189, 191–92, 202–3, 208,
224–25; popularity of closing tax
loopholes, 291n20
Teamsters, 16, 31

television, 15, 55, 144, 174–75, 177, 179,
225–26
Tennessee Valley Authority, 152
Tet Offensive, 196
Thomas, Franklin, 156, 158, 161–64, 167,
285n71
Till, Emmett, 17
Tillmon, Johnnie, 208
Time, 142
To Seek a Newer World (RFK), 229
Tolan, Jim, 202, 212, 216–17
Torres, José, 227
Truman, Harry, 11, 22
Tuchman, Barbara, 107
Tuck, Dick, 303n68
Tydings, Joseph, 138, 191

United Auto Workers, 125, 200, 208
United Mexican-American Student
Association, 184
University of Alabama, 58–59
University of Georgia, 41–42
University of Mississippi: James
Meredith and integration of, 52, 54,
87; RFK 1966 speech at, 133
Unruh, Jesse, 206, 216, 306n117, 307n125
urban crisis, 124; RFK urban addresses,
124–28. *See also* Ribicoff hearings
Urban League, 19, 47
urban renewal, 11–12
U.S. Gypsum, 165
U.S. News & World Report, 17
Us, 308n9

Valachi hearings (organized crime),
61, 108
Vann, Albert, 157
Vanocur, Sander, 8
Vera Foundation, 77–78
Vidal, Gore, 106
Vietnam War, 3, 7, 104, 122, 196, 211;
RFK and, 94, 117, 152, 210; impact on
War on Poverty, 134, 136, 176, 190,
203, 224